CHORAL TRAGEDY

Ever since Aristotle opened the discussion on the role of the chorus in Greek tragedy, theories of the chorus have continued to proliferate and provoke debate to this day. The tragic chorus had its own story to tell; it was a collective identity, speaking within and to a collective citizen body, acting as an instrument through which stories of other times and places were dramatized into resonant heroic narratives for contemporary Athens. By including detailed case studies of three different tragedies (one each by Aeschylus, Euripides and Sophocles), Claude Calame's seminal study not only re-examines the role of the chorus in Greek tragedy, but pushes beyond this to argue for the 'polyphony' of choral performance. Here, he explores the fundamentally choral nature of the genre, and its deep connection to the cultic and ritual contexts in which tragedy was performed.

CLAUDE CALAME is Director of Studies at the École des Hautes Études en Sciences Sociales, Paris (Centre AnHiMA: Anthropologie et Histoire des Mondes Antiques) and was previously Professor of Greek Language and Literature at the University of Lausanne. He has specialized in the study of Greek poetic texts from an ethnopoetic perspective, an approach relying on historical anthropology, the history of religions and discourse analysis. Many of his books have appeared in English translation: *The Craft of Poetic Speech in Ancient Greece* (1995), *The Poetics of Eros in Ancient Greece* (1999), *Choruses of Young Women in Ancient Greece* (2nd ed., 2001), *Myth and History in Ancient Greece: The Symbolic Creation of a Colony* (2003), *Masks of Authority: Fiction and Pragmatics in Ancient Greek Poetics* (2005), *Poetic and Performative Memory in Ancient Greece* (2009), *Greek Mythology: Poetics, Pragmatics and Fiction* (Cambridge, 2009) and *Humans and Their Environment: Beyond the Nature/Culture Opposition* (2023).

CLASSICAL SCHOLARSHIP IN TRANSLATION

Series editors
RENAUD GAGNÉ, UNIVERSITY OF CAMBRIDGE
JONAS GRETHLEIN, RUPRECHT-KARLS-UNIVERSITÄT HEIDELBERG

Classical Scholarship in Translation provides English translations of some particularly notable and significant scholarship on the ancient Greek and Roman worlds and their reception written in other languages in order to make it better known and appreciated. All areas of classical scholarship are considered.

Recent titles in the series:
The Names of the Gods in Ancient Mediterranean Religions
CORINNE BONNET

The Early Christians: From the Beginnings to Constantine
HARTMUT LEPPIN

Platonism: A Concise History from the Early Academy to Late Antiquity
MAURO BONAZZI

The Greeks and Their Histories: Myth, History and Society
HANS-JOACHIM GEHRKE

The Hera of Zeus: Intimate Enemy, Ultimate Spouse
VINCIANE PIRENNE-DELFORGE AND GABRIELLA PIRONTI

CHORAL TRAGEDY
Greek Poetics and Musical Ritual

CLAUDE CALAME
École des Hautes Études en Sciences Sociales, Paris

Translated by Vanessa Casato, Università Ca' Foscari, Venice

CAMBRIDGE
UNIVERSITY PRESS

Shaftesbury Road, Cambridge CB2 8EA, United Kingdom

One Liberty Plaza, 20th Floor, New York, NY 10006, USA

477 Williamstown Road, Port Melbourne, VIC 3207, Australia

314–321, 3rd Floor, Plot 3, Splendor Forum, Jasola District Centre, New Delhi – 110025, India

103 Penang Road, #05–06/07, Visioncrest Commercial, Singapore 238467

Cambridge University Press is part of Cambridge University Press & Assessment, a department of the University of Cambridge.

We share the University's mission to contribute to society through the pursuit of education, learning and research at the highest international levels of excellence.

www.cambridge.org
Information on this title: www.cambridge.org/9781009014427

© Cambridge University Press & Assessment 2024

First published in 2017 as *La Tragédie chorale*. Copyright © Société d'édition Les Belles Lettres 2017

This publication is in copyright. Subject to statutory exception and to the provisions of relevant collective licensing agreements, no reproduction of any part may take place without the written permission of Cambridge University Press & Assessment.

When citing this work, please include a reference to the DOI 10.1017/9781009029421

First published 2024
First paperback edition 2025

A catalogue record for this publication is available from the British Library

Library of Congress Cataloging-in-Publication data
NAMES: Calame, Claude, author. | Casato, Vanessa, translator.
TITLE: Choral tragedy : Greek poetics and musical ritual / Claude Calame, Ecole des Hautes Etudes en Sciences Sociales, Paris ; translated by Vanessa Casato, Universita Ca'Foscari, Venezia.
OTHER TITLES: Tragédie chorale. English
DESCRIPTION: Cambridge ; New York, NY : Cambridge University Press, 2024. | Series: Classical scholarship in translation | Includes bibliographical references and index.
IDENTIFIERS: LCCN 2023057354 | ISBN 9781316516256 (hardback) | ISBN 9781009014427 (paperback) | ISBN 9781009029421 (ebook)
SUBJECTS: LCSH: Drama – Chorus (Greek drama) | Greek drama (Tragedy) – History and criticism. | Music and literature – Greece. | Religion and literature – Greece. | Mythology, Greek, in literature. | LCGFT: Literary criticism.
CLASSIFICATION: LCC PA3136 .C3213 2024 | DDC 882.009–dc23/eng/20240304
LC record available at https://lccn.loc.gov/2023057354

ISBN 978-1-316-51625-6 Hardback
ISBN 978-1-009-01442-7 Paperback

Cambridge University Press & Assessment has no responsibility for the persistence or accuracy of URLs for external or third-party internet websites referred to in this publication and does not guarantee that any content on such websites is, or will remain, accurate or appropriate.

The theatre festival smells of the harvest season, parties,
and feasts of Dionysos,
of auloi, tragedies, Sophocles' songs, thrushes,
and the versicles of Euripides
                              Aristophanes, Peace *530–2*

Contents

Foreword by Simon Goldhill	*page* xi
Preface to the English Edition	xix
Note on the Translations	xxii
Methodological Prelude	xxiii

1 **The Essence of 'The Tragic'**   1
   1.1 Theory and Poetics of the Tragic   1
     1.1.1 The Tragic Hero and Choral Emotion   2
     1.1.2 Essentializing Excesses   5
   1.2 'Emic Categories': Lexical and Semantic Fields   8
     1.2.1 *Trugoidía*/*tragoidía*   9
     1.2.2 Tragic Composition and Training: *Poieîn* and *Didáskein*   10
     1.2.3 Melic Song and Choral Song   12
     1.2.4 Ritual and Sacrificial Origins?   14
   1.3 Towards a Choral Definition of Attic Tragedy   16
     1.3.1 Tragic Choruses Returned to Dionysos   17
     1.3.2 Choral Terminology   19

2 **Tragedy, Cult and Ritual**   21
   2.1 Contemporary Definitions: Anthropological Perspectives   21
     2.1.1 Aristotle's Inescapable Influence   22
     2.1.2 Approaches in the Humanities   25
   2.2 Attic Tragedy as Ritual   29
   2.3 Ritual Song in Attic Tragedy   31
     2.3.1 Hymnic Song and *Melos* in Euripides' *Ion*   32
     2.3.2 Choral Song and Hymn   34
     2.3.3 A Melic Lament   37
     2.3.4 A Hymnic Song and Its Pragmatics   38
   2.4 Attic Tragedy and the Cult of Dionysos   40
     2.4.1 Tragedy and Sacrificial Ritual   40
     2.4.2 Tragedy in Cultic Performance: The Great Dionysia   46
     2.4.3 Foundation Myths: The Arrival of Dionysos   51
     2.4.4 Dionysiac Rituality: Tragedy and the Mask   54

	2.5	Tragic Ritualities	57
		2.5.1 *Oudèn Pròs Tòn Diónuson?*	57
		2.5.2 Against Dionysiac Essentialism	59
	2.6	Cultic Dramatizations	61
3	Choral Polyphonies and Tragedy		64
	3.1	Tragic Choral Identities	66
		3.1.1 Political Identities, Dramatic Identities	66
		3.1.2 Fictional Identities and Gender Identities	69
	3.2	Semantic Polyphonies: The Functions of Tragic Song	72
	3.3	Enunciative Polyphonies: Between Poet and Audience	75
		3.3.1 Enunciative Stances	75
		3.3.2 Choral Performativity: The Melic 'I'/'We'	78
		3.3.3 Enunciative and Performative Self-Reference: The Case of Pindar	80
	3.4	A Case in Point: The Erinyes' 'Binding Song'	83
		3.4.1 Song Actions and Enunciative Self-Reference	83
		3.4.2 Double (Self-)Reference, Dramatic and Ritual	85
		3.4.3 Tragic Pragmatics and Its Twofold Reference: The Ending of the *Oresteia*	88
4	Aeschylus' *Persians*: Questioning Choral Identity		93
	4.1	A Contemporary Athenian Tragedy Set in a Barbarian Land	93
	4.2	A Song of Lamentation as Choral Ending	98
		4.2.1 Strophic Structure, Metre and Prelude	99
		4.2.2 Catalogue and Lamentation	100
		4.2.3 Amoebean Threnos and the Role of the Choregos	103
	4.3	Choral Identity, Cultural Identity	104
	4.4	Polyphonies of Identity and Emotions	107
5	Euripides' *Hippolytus*: Choral Song and Gender		112
	5.1	The Chorus of *Hippolytus*, between Feminine and Masculine	112
		5.1.1 The Final Choral Intervention: From Aphrodite to Artemis	113
		5.1.2 The First Choral Song: Sexual Ambiguity	115
		5.1.3 The Parodos and Its Consequences: Aphrodite versus Artemis	118
		5.1.4 First and Second Stasima: The Power of Eros and Aphrodite	122
		5.1.5 The Third Stasimon: 'Gendered' Enunciations	125
	5.2	Aetiological Closure	129
	5.3	Exodos: From Troezen to Athens	131
		5.3.1 Between Represented Space and Space of the Representation	131
		5.3.2 Ending in Choral Polyphony	133
6	Sophocles' *Oedipus Tyrannus*: 'Why Should I Dance (Chorally)?'		135
	6.1	A Malleable Heroic Plot	136
	6.2	The Hymnic Parodos	138
		6.2.1 Choral Opening and Cultic Appeal	139
		6.2.2 Hymnic Prayer and Dramatic Action	140
		6.2.3 Pragmatics of a Hymnic Song: Dionysos	142

	6.3 Choral Voices and Oracular Voices: The First Stasimon	144
	6.3.1 Parnassus' Oracular Utterance and the Heroic Destiny	145
	6.3.2 After the Choral Interventions, the Sung Exchange	146
	6.4 'Why Should I Sing Chorally?'	147
	6.4.1 The Power of Destiny and the Chorus's Doubts	147
	6.4.2 The Power of Zeus: From Dramatic Action to Representation	149
	6.5 Hymn to Cithaeron: The Third Stasimon and Tragic Anticipation	150
	6.6 Human Fate and Choral Identification: The Fourth Stasimon	153
	6.7 Choral Conclusions	154
	6.7.1 Affective Reactions in Song: The Second Kommos	155
	6.7.2 Human Destiny and Ritual Musical Action	157
7	Poets, Tragic Diction and Tragic Fiction	160
	7.1 From Diegesis to Mimesis: Bacchylides' Athenian Dithyramb	160
	7.2 Citharodic Nomos: Stesichorus	163
	7.2.1 Heroic Narratives and Poetic Creation	164
	7.2.2 Narrative Development and Dramatic Form	165
	7.2.3 Epic Diction and Metre	169
	7.2.4 The Citharodic Nomos: A Narrative Genre	171
	7.2.5 Towards Attic Tragedy?	175
	7.3 Poet/Chorus/Audience: A Return to Choral Polyphony	177
	7.3.1 The Audience: From the Second Person to the First	177
	7.3.2 The Tragic Poet as Author	179
	7.4 To Conclude: Musical 'Performances' and Oratorios	181

Bibliography 187
Index of Names 205
Subject Index 208

Foreword

At least since the moment when Aristotle (*Poetics* 1456a) wrote that the chorus of Greek tragedy should be 'like an actor, as in Sophocles' (though not in Euripides), theories of the chorus have continued to proliferate, and to provoke disagreement. The chorus is indeed a grounding *problem* both for antiquity and for today, and for performance as much as for literary criticism. The chorus is a problem on the one hand because it is a singing and dancing collective on stage in the midst of dramas which seem to be fascinated by the powers and dangers of decisions, actions and suffering of particular individuals. Aristotle indeed seems to want to make the chorus into another individual – 'like an actor' – rather than discuss its constitution as a group. The first problem thus is the chorus as *dramatic form*. What are we to make of this group on stage that refuses any simple claim of realism in its collective singing and dancing? In the history of modern performance, the chorus has consequently found many directorial responses, from, paradigmatically, Max Reinhardt's 'Theatre of Five Thousand', with its huge, mass chorus for *Oedipus Tyrannus*, to Rob Icke's *Oresteia*, where the chorus of Furies becomes a single, silent old woman. On the other hand, how the chorus's lyric songs relate to the action, or, more simply, what these dense poetic constructions mean, has provoked an equally intense history of debate, from the claim that Euripides' choral odes are detachable from the plays, that is, that they are no more than beautiful songs as a break from the action, to the insistence that tragedy's very core is in the choral performance, which could lead Nietzsche to insist that tragedy's birth was 'from the spirit of music'.[1] Is the chorus the heart of tragedy or a break in the action? The great strength of Claude Calame's book *Choral Tragedy* is not just his awareness of this long history of criticism of the chorus, but also, and most tellingly, his insistence

---

[1] On Nietzsche, see Silk and Stern 1981 and Porter 2000.

on what he calls the *polyphony* of the choral performance, both in terms of its formal structure and in terms of its semantic content.

The subtitle of Calame's volume, the latest in this excellent series bringing translations of exceptional classical scholarship from around the world to a wider anglophone audience, is *Greek Poetics and Musical Ritual*, and both parts of this phrase separately, and the connection between them, provide a guide through Calame's project. Let us begin with 'Musical Ritual'. Aristotle was the first scholar we know to have sought the origin of tragedy in ritual. Many thinkers since – anthropologists, literary historians, religious historians – have followed his lead. For this line of analysis, tragedy's chorality stems from its original form as a song in honour of Dionysos, which gradually became institutionalized into a festival with actors who responded to the choral narrative, gradually and experimentally transforming into the form of theatre we know from the later fifth century in Athens.[2] It is worth underlining that any evidence for such a teleological narrative is extremely hard to find beyond Aristotle and later speculation, often based on Aristotle, and it is far from clear that Aristotle had any better evidence than we do for such a prehistory. Calame, in contrast to this tradition of historical reconstruction, recognizes that the tradition of lyric poetry embodied most strikingly by Stesichorus, who wrote narratives of thousands of lines of mythic narrative for performance, offers a literary strand that fed into tragedy in a way that the narrative of Dionysiac ritual represses. More importantly, he also delineates the multiple layers of ritual within a play. First, the chorus itself remains a form of ritual performance. The group is constituted as a group within what we can call a religious framework (although the category of religion needs many qualifications when we are talking of the fifth-century city). To sing and dance as a collective is part of festival culture, a way to worship a god and to perform a sense of community before and for a community. Calame's own earlier work *Les Choeurs de jeunes filles en Grèce archaïque* (1977, Rome, 2 vols.) is one of the seminal discussions of this social function of chorality. In tragedy the chorus both performs such a role before the city and even discusses such a role; as the chorus of Sophocles' *Oedipus Tyrannus* famously sings, if the prophecies are not true, and the divine order is collapsing, 'Why should I be in a chorus?', *ti dei me choreuein?* – or 'Why should I dance?', as it is often translated. In a similar if more extended manner, the chorus of the *Bacchae* is a chorus of

---

[2] Lesky 1983 gives the standard view well; Burkert 1966 is more speculative; Sourvinou-Inwood 2003 discusses many aspects of tragedy as a religious event; Scullion 2005: 23–37 swims against the tide with customary robustness.

worshippers of Dionysos in the theatre of Dionysos in a festival of Dionysos. They honour Dionysos at these two interconnected levels, in the world of the festival and in the world of the play. The performance of the chorus of tragedy, what is more, is framed by a set of rituals on the days before the plays and the days of the plays themselves, which represent the city to itself through forms of collective procession, sacrifice and singing.[3] The chorus of tragedy is very much part of festival culture.

Second, however, the chorus also performs rituals within the play; it prays and sings what can be called hymns. The performance, which is in the festival of Dionysos, represents other forms of ritual and, in particular, plays often dramatize rituals of mourning, antiphonal song between an individual mourner, and a collective of consolatory mourners.[4] Sophocles' *Electra*, for example, in which the heroine refuses to cease mourning, repeatedly constructs the relation between the heroine and the women of the chorus as a scene of ritual lamentation. Third, the *language* of ritual becomes a way of understanding the action of the play, as mobilized by the chorus. Thus the sacrifice of Iphigeneia in the *Oresteia* opens a series of images of corrupt sacrifice through which the violence of the play is articulated – as eagles killing a hare can be called a sacrifice, and Clytemnestra, for example, is imagined to murder her husband, Agamemnon, in a parody of a libation and sacrifice. Most upsettingly, in Euripides' *Bacchae*, the young King Pentheus is ripped apart by his maddened mother and her sisters, in a form of *sparagmos* imaged as a corrupt religious ritual – overseen by the god Dionysos himself. A formative horror of the play is that the god smilingly instigates such a transgressive worship. Calame is particularly intent on showing how these different levels of ritualization interact to create the texture of tragedy. His iconic moment is Ion in Euripides' *Ion*, who begins the play on the steps of the temple of Apollo, singing in honour of the god Apollo, through addressing his broom – an individual taking on the lyric voice, honouring a god in an individual hymn – deliberately and, in dramatic terms, shockingly to celebrate the mundane act of sweeping the steps – in the festival but also in a play in which Apollo's role will be central and ironically questioned. As Calame argues, it is impossible to discuss the chorus adequately without taking account of this *polyphony of ritualization*.

Calame's phrasing is precise here: 'musical ritual'. What links Ion to the chorus in part is the fact that they both sing. For Calame, there is an

---

[3] See Goldhill 1987 and 2000.
[4] Foley 2001: 19–56; Loraux 1998; Holst-Warhaft 1992; Alexiou 2002; Swift 2010: 298–366; Weiss 2017; and more generally Andújar, Coward and Hadjimichael 2018.

integral link, when it comes to theatre, between the ritual and the music. Rituals are accompanied by music – the aulos at a sacrifice, the song at the festival, the singing choruses of initiation rites – and music always tends towards sacrality – the dithyrambic competitions for Dionysos, the song at the symposium, the hymn. Singing elevates speech into another register, as dance transforms movement. One of the essential dynamics of tragedy is the interplay between the chorus's collective singing and the actors whose iambic verse is, as Aristotle declared, the closest to usual human speech. But actors sing too, and the shared lyric voice, with its echoes of other lyric, ritual forms, is deeply embedded in the texture of tragic performance.[5]

'Greek poetics' may seem a provocative term; is there something specifically *Greek* about tragic aesthetics? Of course, what we call Greek tragedy is all from Athens and mainly from the last half of the fifth century, and it is all written in Greek. But there are deeper senses in which the word Greek is not merely descriptive of the provenance or context of the genre of tragedy. Tragedy cannot be fully appreciated without acknowledging that tragedy is repeatedly rewriting the inherited and authoritative narratives of Homer for the new social and political circumstances of the fifth-century city and its democracy – part of a Greek literary tradition. Many of the characters of tragedy and the plots of its plays find their source in Homer's epics and the epic cycle in particular. Tragedy is constitutionally an intertextual genre, a hybrid form. There are many ways in which this interaction with the literature of the past takes shape, but a foundational mode of transformation is turning the hexameter narrative poetry of Homer, which was publicly recited in Athens at the festival of the Great Panathenaia, into the dramatic, enacted stories of drama in iambic verse and sung lyrics, for performance at the Great Dionysia.[6] Where Homer's poetry was performed by a bard, a solo voice, drama brings together masked and costumed actors and chorus, talking, singing, interacting. The chorality of tragedy is one way that narratives of the past are made stories for the present, and become integrated into the ritual and political world of the contemporary city. The narrative of the origin of drama, familiar from Aristotle onwards, that sees tragedy as a development out of a ritual chorus into the theatre, where the chorus becomes less and less integral, does not acknowledge that the chorus is part of what actually made tragedy a modern and challenging rewriting of traditional stories, a new genre, with a new political purchase.

---

[5] Nooter 2012; Goldhill 2012: 81–108.   [6] Goldhill 1986: 138–67.

This challenging rewriting of tradition is most evident in the political force of the chorus as a dramatic form. The chorus is constitutionally a collective, a group that shares an identity, and sings and dances iconically as a group. Most commonly in Euripides, as Calame notes, it is a community of women, either married women as in *Hipppolytus* or *Medea* who speak from their experience as mothers, or, more contingently, in the *Phoenissae*, say, a group of pilgrims who have been stranded by war. For Aeschylus' *Oresteia*, it is a group of elders, political advisors to the king, as too in Sophocles' *Antigone*. It is very rare to have a chorus that simply reflects the audience as a group of citizens, adult males. The dynamic of every play, however, revolves around the interaction of an individual or set of individuals and this collective. Just as each individual in a tragedy has a narrative arc, so too does the chorus. The range of narrative arcs for the chorus is as varied and complex as it is for the individual actors. In Aeschylus' *Agamemnon*, the elders develop a contested and difficult relationship with Clytemnestra, as old men, persuaded gradually and unwillingly by a powerful woman, who express deep anxiety about the state of affairs in the city, an anxiety which is fulfilled with the murder of the returning king, Agamemnon, which prompts the chorus to break into fragmented individual voices in its confusion and inability to respond with any instrumental action to the violence. They signally fail to appreciate what Cassandra is trying to tell them. Yet when Aegisthus, Clytemnestra's lover, enters they articulate a more forceful opposition to their usurpation of rule, that prepares the way for the reversals of the following plays. Their long odes set the action in a deep contextual framework, repeatedly veined with their own miscomprehensions, fears and hopes. The chorus's story, both as participants in the narrative and as storytellers, is integral to the emotive and semantic polyphony of this richest of dramas. In Euripides' *Medea*, by contrast, the chorus of women of Corinth is persuaded easily by Medea in the first scene to help her. Like an archetypal hero, they declare 'I will act', *drasô*. Their support is based on their sympathy, as women, for the abused and suffering wife, Medea. But as the play unfolds through Medea's manipulation and then violent destruction of her enemies and finally her own children, their sympathy becomes an increasingly desperate complicity as they fail to stop Medea from infanticide. Their story, integral to the drama, is the gradually horrified recognition of the dangers of sympathy. Our understanding of the hero's narrative is formed in and through its dynamic interaction with the chorus's narrative and response.

This dramatized tension between collective and individual speaks with a particular force in the political frame of the democratic city. The constitution of democracy demands a commitment to the collective. Such a commitment is integral to the ideology of the city; taking part in the institutional collectives of the assembly, the law court, the army is a requirement of citizenship. Recognizing the claim of the city of an individual's efforts is a repeated tenet of democratic belonging. At the same time, the inherited values of individual glory and achievement forms a continuity from Homeric heroes' search for fame to the democratic politician's search for his place in history. How democracy as a principle deals with individual desire, will and achievement is a constant question of political theory. The chorality of Greek tragedy dramatizes before the city the very question of the dangers and lures of individual striving for exceptional excellence in and against the claims of a collective good. The fascination and horror of tragedy's heroes, for whom going too far is both excellence and transgression, is repeatedly expressed against the collective voice of the chorus. As such, the chorus is fully part of the modern politics of a democratic genre.

Yet, as we have already noted, the chorus of Greek tragedy is often made up of figures who do not simply represent the political collective of democracy or of a city. The chorus of plays like *Oedipus Tyrannus* or *Antigone* are men involved in the politics of city, for sure, and in Sophocles' *Philoctetes* the chorus of sailors may well have found echoes with an audience many of whom rowed in the Athenian navy. But far more commonly, choruses seem to be made up of more marginal characters – like the young slave women of Aeschylus' *Choephoroi*, or, even more alienatingly, the Furies of Aeschylus' *Eumenides*, or the wild eastern Bacchants of Euripides' *Bacchae*.[7] With what authority, then, can the chorus speak? Calame insists we explore with care the *status* of the voice of the chorus. He acknowledges how influential Schlegel has proved to be, thanks to his brief discussion of the chorus as an 'ideal spectator', and correctly points out both that the use of the word 'ideal', or, better, 'idealized', needs to be properly understood within the philosophy of (German) idealism, and that an oversimplified perspective on Schlegel has often led to oversimplified accounts of the chorus that treat its pronouncements as the voice of the author or the determinative account of the play's action. Schlegel's influence is evident, however, also in Vernant's influential description of the chorus as an 'anonymous and collective being whose role is to express through its fears, hopes and judgments, the feelings of the spectators who make up the civic community'.[8] Yet even Vernant's more nuanced description is inadequate in part because the chorus also

---

[7] See Gould 1996; Goldhill 1996. [8] Vernant and Vidal-Naquet 1981: 2.

repeatedly just gets things wrong – like the chorus of Sophocles' *Ajax*, which mistakenly celebrates the hero's salvation just as he is going to kill himself – and, in part, because, as we have just seen, the chorus does not merely mediate audience response but has its own story too. Consequently, Rehm argues, the chorus can 'support, ignore, question, or reject the actions of the central characters, reorienting our response to the rhetoric as they do. They compel us to experience the drama as an everchanging dynamic relationship' (1992, 61).[9] Yet, as Calame insists, the chorus is not simply an actor (whatever Aristotle may wish), because it is a collective, speaking within and to the collective of the citizen body. Hence the need to address the status of its voice with particular care.

The chorus makes a claim on the authoritative voice of the collective in democracy, on the one hand, and the authoritative voice of mythic tradition, on the other. It reaches towards a generalizing truth, based on the values of the community, embodied in traditional wisdom and myth, the embodiment of the community's self-understanding. Yet the chorus also speaks with all the contingency of an actor (as Aristotle would say), replete with partial understanding, complete misrecognition, hope, fear and desperation. The choral voice is constructed in the *tension between* these two trajectories – and the playwrights experiment with the potentiality of such a tension. The chorus of *Antigone* can sing with immense profundity of the very nature of humanity – but also respond to the argument of Creon and Haemon with a partial explanation of how sexual desire motivates young men, and, finally, to intervene – contingently and too late – in the particular events by suggesting to Creon that he has got things wrong and should listen to Teiresias' warning. The chorus of Euripides' *Bacchae* are wild women who shockingly celebrate the death of the king – but they insist that they sing what the common people believe. A chorus *mobilizes* the voice of authority – both in the form of myth, the will to see a story within the paradigms of the authority of tradition, and in the form of the generalizations of collective wisdom, the tradition of shared truths. And in this mobilization a chorus can both create profound reflections on the action, which transcend the contingencies of events, and yet offer clichés that fail to deal with complexities of the action before them (and many other positions between these extremes). The variety of choral engagement thus resists the sort of easy summary that phrases like 'ideal spectator' encourage, but rather requires a constant and attentive appreciation of the polyphony of the choral voice. It is thus precisely the multiple resources – the affordances – of the choral voice that Calame insists we pay attention to, and

[9] Rehm 1992: 61.

that he demonstrates in the close readings of the individual plays that follow his more general, theoretical explorations.

Choreuein – the verb that signifies participation in a chorus – is usually translated as 'dance', however, and it is in the performance of the dancing, singing chorus that Calame ends with a very stimulating reflection on how the chorus dances space into being. The chorus of Euripides' *Ion* enters and excitedly describes its experience of the temples at Delphi; its dance and song mark out the imaginative space of the drama, a space layered with the historical depth of the mythic images the chorus describes. The chorus's dance marks out the *orchestra* as an institutional space, and repeatedly choruses create an imaginative space, 'a cockpit [to] hold the vasty fields' of tragic action. It is always a space that the chorus's voice also deepens with a map of other stories, other landscapes of narrative. This cosmography is a definitional voice of tragic theatre. As Calame shows in his analysis of *Hippolytus*, such imaginative creation of space becomes part of the politicization of the narratives of the past as the scene of Troizen becomes closer and closer to the scene of Athens. The choral voice and the choral body – *choreuein* – is an instrument through which the stories of other times and other places become telling narrative for contemporary Athens.

'Greek poetics' and 'musical ritual' thus come together in the experience of tragedy. Chorality is constructed between such poetics and such ritualization. Claude Calame asks that the attention we pay to the chorus of drama keeps these different vectors in mind, together – the ritualization of the choral voice and dancing, the politics of theatre, the intertextuality of ancient poetics, the rich voicing of the past through song, the role of dynamic reflection and participation in narrative through storytelling, the dramatic mobilization of different forms of authoritative language, the dance of embodied space that becomes an imaginative landscape linking past and present – what, in short, he terms the polyphony of form and the polyphony of meaning. *Choral Tragedy* helps us see why the chorus has been such a problem over the centuries, thanks in part at least to the sheer complexity of its formal and semantic richness. It may help – we can hope – reduce the oversimplifications that plague discussions of the chorus in what Calame insists is the necessarily failing search for the Dionysiac essence of tragedy. *Choral Tragedy* is a book to engage with and find stimulation from – as the choral voice encourages.

Preface to the English Edition

The least one can say is that there persists a strong interest for the choral traditions – or 'song cultures' – of ancient Greek cities. One need only mention, where anglophone scholarship is concerned, the recent publication (2021) of Deborah Steiner's volume encompassing a range of 'choral constructions'; in preclassical Greece, 'chorality' underlies the making of tripods and cauldrons, but also representations of birds in flight or of the movements of animal herds, the choral aquatics of groups of nymphs and ships alike, the catalogues of young women associated with dance, the choral accompaniments to weaving and the manufacture of clothing, or again the sequence of the letters of the alphabet. Chorality thus denotes the work of craftsmen as well as the representations of groups of animals or men and women, as well as, of course, the ritual and religious practices distinguished by the musical performance of songs composed by poets.

This vein of scholarship is complemented in the francophone world by Vincent Azoulay's and Paulin Ismard's discussion of the political dimension of chorality (2020). Taking their cue from the political recompositions of the Athenian community following the Peloponnesian War, they have shown that the history of Athens can be explained as 'choral history'. This chorality finds expression in the debates, the rivalries, the oppositions and the reconstitutions of collective entities led by a coryphaeus, which expressed themselves as choral groups with polyphonic emotions in a divided city.

When it comes to the verbal manifestations of chorality, the field has been informed by the novel 'choreonarrative' approach, appropriately embodied polyphonically by the Europe-wide choral group led by Laura Gianvittorio-Ungar and Karin Schlapbach (2021). With choral dance as its point of departure, the red thread running through the choreonarrative approach enables the identification of the choreographic movement governing in turn the various narrative forms. Choreographic rhythm goes hand-in-hand with *shkḗmata*, gestures and figures, and, through these, the expression of emotions, whether this be in fifth-century Athenian comedy and tragedy or in the many modern and contemporary appropriations of these genres. Especially noteworthy are two choreonarrative studies of Iô's sung account of her wanderings as she is tormented by the spectre of Argus in Aeschylus' *Prometheus Bound* and, more still, of the messenger's account of Neoptolemus' death in Euripides' *Andromache*.

Tragedy is largely absent from the first two volumes mentioned above, yet chorality calls for interrogation more than ever in connection with these dramatized ritual representations of the great heroic sagas in so-called classical Athens. Should tragedy not be thought of as 'choral tragedy'?

The question impinges all the more insistently since the attempt by two Oxford scholars to reduce the manifestations of the 'Lyric of early Greece' to 'textual events'. Budelmann and Phillips (2018) claim that the anthropological approach sensitive to the different dimensions of the context of performance should be discarded because it ignores the aesthetic effects and emotions conjured up by these 'lyric' poems addressed by individual authors to an audience equally made up of individuals. To the anthropological approach one should prefer, according to Budelmann and Phillips, a literary approach that is sensitive to the aesthetic effects provoked in individual listeners by poems that they assimilate to the modern and fluid category of 'lyric'. On this view, every listener constructs for him- or herself the fictional world made available by the 'lyric' poem and by its poet as author of the text, thus turning it into a subjective aesthetic experience. Such an approach is leaving aside the fact that the musical performance of a melic poem, with its ritual gestuality and its equally ritual context, implies also a poetic semantics and, through this, an aesthetics. These poetic semantics and aesthetics cannot be reduced to those of a simple text.

The choral nature of melic song danced to a musical accompaniment on an instrument instigates a collective and practical engagement, of social, cultural and emotional order. In order to animate the poetic world created in the song and the relationship with the performers and the audience, this engagement is inscribed in the poem itself – for instance, in the alternation of the enunciative forms of the singular and plural first persons that render the poem a true act of song, or in the subtle enunciative and semantic polyphony that animates, as we will see, the choral songs of tragedy in particular. In this regard, the very notion of a 'textual event' is nothing more than a counterproductive oxymoron.

Be that as it may, this severe interpretative regression is an opportunity to reaffirm the various choral dimensions of the poetic recreation and ritual dramatization, in the sanctuary of Dionysos Eleuthereus, of the foundational heroic sagas of the Greek cities and their cultures.

Preface to the English Edition xxi

It follows that a further dimension must be added to the reflections here presented on choral tragedy: that of orchestics. Several recent works can come to our aid, first among these the sophisticated study by Matteo Capponi (2021) of the complementarity in Attic tragedy between the verbal gestures corresponding to speech acts and the terms that point to physical gestures. Capponi examines the protagonists' interactions with the chorus in Aeschylus', Sophocles' and Euripides' 'Electra' tragedies, and this approach would benefit from being extended beyond the *kómmos* to all the choral songs in these three plays. Promising too, for an approach that privileges the orchestic dimension, is the volume on antiquity in a series covering the cultural history of dance which is being edited by Michel Briand.[10] Mention must of course also be made of the various contributions edited by Laura Gianvittorio (2017) in the volume *Choreutika: Performing and Theorising Dance in Ancient Greece*. Her research group's studies on the choral songs of tragedy have been collected in this new edition.[11]

Finally, with specific reference tragic chorality, these last years have been marked, on the one hand, by Naomi Weiss' monograph on *The Music of Tragedy* (2018a), which focuses on the chorus's references to *choreia* in its musical and choreographic dimensions in Euripides' late tragedies. On the other hand, we have to consider the publication of the various contributions collected under the title *Paths of Song: The Lyric Dimension of Greek Tragedy* (Andújar, Coward and Hadjimichael, 2018). The most pertinent contributions for the purposes of our discussion have been flagged in the chapters that follow, not least in recognition of the ways in which they have enriched my thinking.

This English edition has benefitted not just from a bibliographical updating but also from the comments of its translator, Vanessa Casato, whose critical reading of the text has given me several opportunities to refine and on occasion even correct the text. Many thanks to her particularly for having eased in English my usual French abstract 'tournures'.

Finally, I wish to express my gratitude to Renaud Gagné and Jonas Grethlein for welcoming this translation of *La tragédie chorale* in their 'Classical Scholarship in Translation' series for Cambridge University Press.

---

[10] Briand (forthcoming).
[11] I deliberately sidestep the sophistic controversy initiated by Felix Budelmann 2013 with his study of the 'Greek Festival Choruses In and Out of Context', founded on a series of reflections arising from a literary reading of Alcman's First Partheneion and Pindar's Ninth Paean and involving also tragedy. In the play of binary oppositions, the distinction between 'in' and 'out of context' is as irrelevant as that between 'chorus-as-art' and 'chorus-as-ritual' is deceptive. See on this subject Naerebout's intelligent response (Naerebout 2017: 54–6), usefully included in the collected volume on *Choreutika*.

Note on the Translations

All translations are the translator's own, unless otherwise stated. Where Loeb Classical Library translations have been consulted, the following editions have been used.

Bury, R. G., *Plato: Laws, Volume II, Books 7–12*, Cambridge, MA (Harvard University Press) 1926

Campbell, D. A., *Greek Lyric, Volume II: Anacreon, Anacreontea, Choral Lyric from Olympus to Alcman*, Cambridge, MA (Harvard University Press) 1988

Campbell, D. A., *Greek Lyric, Volume IV: Bacchylides, Corinna, and Others*, Cambridge, MA (Harvard University Press) 1992

Henderson, J., *Aristophanes: Clouds, Wasps, Peace*, Cambridge, MA (Harvard University Press) 1992

Kovacs, D., *Euripides: Children of Heracles, Hippolytus, Andromache, Hecuba*, Cambridge, MA (Harvard University Press) 1995

Lloyd-Jones, H., *Sophocles: Ajax. Electra. Oedipus Tyrannus*, Cambridge, MA (Harvard University Press) 1994

Race, W. H., *Pindar: Nemean Odes. Isthmian Odes. Fragments*, Cambridge, MA (Harvard University Press) 1997

Sommerstein, A. H., *Aeschylus: Oresteia: Agamemnon. Libation-bearers. Eumenides*, Cambridge, MA (Harvard University Press) 2009

Sommerstein, A. H., *Aeschylus: Persians, Seven Against Thebes, Suppliants, Prometheus Bound*, Cambridge, MA (Harvard University Press) 2008

Methodological Prelude

> I believe I am not talking nonsense when I assert that this problem of origin has not yet even been posed seriously, far less solved, despite the many attempts to sew together and pull apart again the tattered shreds of ancient historical evidence in various combinations. This evidence tells us most decisively that tragedy arose from the tragic chorus and was originally chorus and nothing but chorus.
> Friedrich Nietzsche, *The Birth of Tragedy* (1872: §7), trans. Speirs (1999)

Bali, August 1976 – Bali, October 2014. Sukawati, Pura Puseh Batuan – Campuhan, Pura Gunung Lebah. Two village communities, two Hindu 'temples', two cultic spaces. At Sukawati, almost forty years ago, the Galungan festival is taking place to commemorate the triumph of the *dharma* on the *adharma*. It marks the beginning of the Balinese New Year and involves a long sequence of ceremonies punctuated by dances and dramatic performances. At Campuhan, a village close to Ubud now taken over by tourists with their shops and hotels and addiction to consumerism, a ritual ceremony is being carried out to purify the god's statues in the temple. The ceremony culminates with the *ngenteg linggih*, a sequence of sophisticated purification rituals, and the *padudusan agung*, which involves performances of music, dance and 'theatre'. At both events, the men and women of the village assemble in a large procession; they wear ritual costume and carry towards the 'sanctuary' statues of the gods symbolically seated on their golden thrones. Inside the sanctuary itself, perched on colourful and intricate structures, is a multitude of 'sacrificial' offerings. The officiating brahmins pronounce prayers for each of the participants while moving through a sequence of ritual gestures of 'blessing'. At the conclusion of the ceremony lasting several days, dramatic performances take place to the accompaniment of flutes and the *gamelan* percussions ensemble; there are dances by girls, dances by women and performances of *barong* featuring the demon Rangda before an informal audience. The performers wear elaborate ceremonial costumes in bright, vivid colours. The men, women and children who attend the purification rituals – the 'audience', so to speak – also wear ceremonial apparel, as do the few Westerners who watch the ceremony.

There is much here that is evocative for the anthropologically minded Hellenist, but while these festivals might suggest a point-for-point comparison with the Great Dionysia, the famous classical Athenian festival that included elaborate 'musical contests', any such comparison must ensure that key terms are firmly enclosed in inverted commas. The Athenian contests in the arts of the Muses featured dithyrambic performances by choruses of fifty boys and fifty men, and performances of comedies by masked actors and choruses in burlesque costumes; these were followed by the tragic competition, featuring sequences of three tragedies capped by a satyr play in which masked actors and choruses chanted dialogue dramatizing heroic stories drawn from the imposing heritage of Athenian and panhellenic narrative poetry. Part of this long ritual sequence of competitively performed song and drama accompanied by processions and sacrifices to the god forms the subject of this volume. The immediate comparison with my opening examples is rendered all the more compelling by the fact that, in the Balinese 'temples' of Sukawati and Campuhan just as in the Athenian sanctuary of Dionysos Eleuthereus, the ritualized song and dance performances occur inside the sacred enclosure reserved for the divinity's worship. In modern-day Bali, the space in the courtyard that is fitted out for these representations is called *jaba pura*; in fifth-century-BCE Athens, the space where the chorus performed was the formally demarcated *orchestra*, a dedicated space where the actors also moved.

The comparison will have to stop here. This brief comparative prelude was merely intended to open up a field of *Möglichkeiten* ('possibilities'), in Wittgenstein's sense:[12] possibilities of signification for dramatic and ritual performances whose ethnographical and anthropological contexts evidently lie beyond our knowledge, in both geographical and chronological terms as far as ancient Greece is concerned.

Let us then set aside this simple mode of comparison, which though evocative is also methodologically problematic; we will return to it briefly in our conclusions. Its main purpose here was to lend some ritual colour and some musical rhythm to an object of study that is known to us only from a few extant ancient texts. 'Temple, 'sanctuary', 'sacrifice', 'blessing'; all these words have been placed in inverted commas because their meaning

---

[12] See Borutti 2015: 15–18.

Methodological Prelude xxv

has been moulded by long use in the Judaeo-Christian tradition. It is important, on the other hand, to reach back to emic categories and practices, and to consider musical performances in the Greek sense of the term, that is to say, events involving poetic composition, singing, musical accompaniment and choreographed gesture. Our concern here is with poetical and vocal practices realized as ritualized musical performances of which the written texts that have come down to us are nothing more than distant traces. Far from any idea of 'literature', these vocal and ritual poetic practices, with their aesthetical effects, are to be grasped not as 'textual events' but as ritualized sung utterances in specific contexts of performance and specific institutional, political, religious and cultural settings.

Since Greek tragedies are manifestations of cultural poetics in action, their textual traces call for a combination of three approaches: an interpretation based on a semantics of utterances whose enunciative strategies often have a performative function; a pragmatic ethnopoetics aimed at reconstructing the semantic and aesthetical effects of these sung and ritualized utterances;[13] and, finally, a cultural and social anthropology allied to a history of religions, in order to explicate the extra-discursive reference of the dramatic 'here-and-now' of these ritual and musical performances.

The heroic action dramatized by Greek tragedy cannot fully be understood without accounting for the various ways in which it was situated in the specific political, religious and cultural contexts of fifth-century Athens. Through the mediation of some remarkable poets (in emic terms 'chorus teachers', *khorodidáskaloi*), these specific cultural realities gave shape to our tragedies; conversely, as poems in action, the tragedies referred within their fictional world to these realities and thereby imbued them with new meaning. From the point of view of ethnopoetic history, as we will see, Attic tragedy can be viewed as the sung and dramatic offspring of two forms of melic poetry: on the one hand, the citharodic nome – a narrative form with inserted dialogues composed in epic diction and sung by a citharode with the accompaniment of a dancing chorus; and, on the other hand, the various ritual and cultic forms of choral and musical *melos* (such as the pean for Apollo and the hymns to other deities), including song, instrumental accompaniment and dance.

Our effort, then, must be one of cross-cultural translation by means of discourse analysis aided by ethnopoetic history and cultural anthropology.

---

[13] The aims of this new ethnopoetics are outlined and illustrated in Calame et al. 2010. I am indebted to Kati Basset for valuable advice during my second stay in Bali.

Our engagement with another culture's expression in song will inevitably be asymmetrical, inasmuch as that culture is geographically and (especially) chronologically remote from ours. But it is precisely this disconnection from a culture that must be viewed as 'other' that compels us to adopt a critical stance towards our own operative concepts, however necessary these may be. A self-aware engagement with this other culture invites us in turn to look at ourselves from the outside, irrespective of any genealogical relationship between the Greek tragedy of classical Athens and the French tragedy of the seventeenth century or that of German Romanticism. Our mode of reappropriation must be at once anthropological and erudite.

In French scholarship, the standard approach to Attic tragedy is still heavily influenced – implicitly or explicitly – by Aristotle's *Poetics*. Through a genealogical or normative comparison with epic poetry, Aristotle presents tragedy as an essentially narrative form, one that is centred on *mûthos* (understood as 'plot') and its 'characters', that is, the protagonists of the dramatic action. We will turn to this issue at the beginning of Chapter 2. If Sophocles' and Euripides' tragedies are defined as 'the *mímēsis* of a noble action brought to completion, having a certain extension, expressed in rhythmical language', the last two of Aristotle's six constitutive elements of tragedy are explicitly discarded from the *Poetics*; there is no discussion of *ópsis*, 'vision', that is, the scenic aspects of tragedy, and, above all, none of *melopoiía*, that is, the poetics of (melic) song.[14] It follows that the focus is immediately narrowed to the tragic action and its protagonist, the tragic hero (who is often a woman), with no regard to the musical and ritual dimension of tragedy or the important role played by the chorus's sung interventions, with their melic diction and rhythm.

Since the developments that revolutionized the humanities in the 1970s, Greek tragedy has, of course, ceased to be considered solely as 'art' (or 'literature'); it is no longer understood merely as the dramatization of a hero's encounter with his or her destiny, as the Romantic definition of 'tragic' would have it. Instead, it is now viewed also as a social and cultural institution. Thus, if 'the city turns itself into theatre', this is not to say that tragedy reflects society straightforwardly, for according to this view the chorus, a 'collective and anonymous entity' engaging in contrastive dialogue with the actors, is held to express the affective and moral feelings of an audience that corresponds to the civic community.[15] In a further development in French scholarship, Attic tragedy is understood not so much as the city's own representation of itself, questioning the political through the

---

[14] Arist. *Poet.* 6.1449b 21–50a 14.   [15] Vernant and Vidal-Naquet 1972: 13–14 and 24–5.

intermediary of tragic fiction, but rather as an 'ineffable' lamentation and mourning acted out on the stage for a community of mortals rather than of citizens.[16]

Another recent view of Attic tragedy developed in France turns away from the perspectives opened up by the social sciences and humanities to conclude that 'through tragedy, theatre traces theory', that is to say, tragedy produces its own theory, for example, in the plays of Aeschylus. An essentialized notion of 'tragedy' appears to have replaced 'the tragic'. According to this view (Greek) tragedies rework the past, with all its uncertainties, reversals and discontinuities, to elaborate a set of theories regarding cultural and religious norms, and they do this through the intermediary of 'staged individuals' and by means of a 'theorizing chorus'. Thus 'tragedy analyzes and discerns' civic normativity.[17] Note how in all this not a word is said about the poetic and choral arts of the Muses as ritual and cultural practices. Does this not signal a return to a form of essentialism, if not with respect to 'the tragic', then at least with respect to 'tragedy'?

Hence – to anticipate the chapters that follow – my stark admonition. The fault lies with Aristotle, who established an approach at once descriptive, genealogical and normative towards Attic tragedy as a representational depiction of actions. This focus on dramatic action and its articulation into plot through the devices of reversal and recognition does away with all that belongs to the dimensions of musical 'performance' and pragmatics – even though in the end the author of the *Poetics* must recognize that music and spectacle give tragedy an advantage over epic by offering up something for the audience's gaze to fasten upon (*enargés*).[18] Nevertheless, this mistaken approach persists; Aristotle would establish for tragedy 'a literary reception rather than a ritual coenunciation'. But is it enough to 'understand the ritual and musical workings of tragedy by ceasing to view it merely as representation'? In wishing to rid oneself of *mûthos*, does one not then run the risk of 'tragic insignificance'?[19]

It is clear that the few tragedies that survive complete do not generally follow the German Romantic model of plot or the tragic principle calling for the fated expiation of a transgression. Does this mean that, if Greek tragedies are not tragic, 'they were something else and we will never know what'?[20] There is no doubt that there has been an effort to drain Greek tragedy of its poetic and musical reality. Ethnopoetics can now aid us in

---

[16] Loraux 1999: 45–66 and 120–37. [17] Judet de La Combe 2010: 295–332.
[18] Arist. *Poet.* 26.1462a 10–18. [19] As proposed by Dupont 2007: 50–61 and 294–5.
[20] Marx 2012: 54–60 and 67–83.

restoring this reality to Attic drama by contextualizing it within ritual performance and providing an anthropological perspective that brings back into focus, along with the poetic and aesthetical creation, the ritual, institutional, political and religious context of concrete tragic performances. This is achieved as much by pressing into use what contemporary evidence survives for the ritual execution of musical competitions marking the Great Dionysia and Lenaea as by examining the textual and enunciative traces of singing voices (both individual and collective) captured in their pragmatic function. But since what we have are texts (which refer back to musical enunciations), the anthropological and ethnopoetical approach becomes by necessity a hermeneutic one too; the results of our inquiry into the multifaceted poetic constructions of these polyphonic utterances will vary according to the point of view we adopt.

My ambition here is a modest one: to establish the choral dimension of the tragedies staged in Athens during the second half of the fifth century. I make no attempt at a general theory of (Greek) tragedy or at a comprehensive overview of this poetic, vocal and musical event taken in its totality. Instead, my aim is to cast new light on Greek tragedy through an anthropological inquiry animated by an interest in the enunciative strategies of song in action.[21] The path on which I invite the reader is admittedly a winding one. I begin (in Chapter 1) with a glance at some Romantic definitions of 'the tragic', before turning to what can be gleaned about the creation of tragedies and the tragic poets from the ways in which they are mocked in Attic comedy. Then (in Chapter 2) I move from the narrative conception of tragedy bequeathed by Aristotle and the contemporary debate prompted by his restrictive (to say the least) definition to an examination of all those aspects which, in performed tragedy, pertain to ritual practice: ritual in tragedy as well as tragedy as ritual, since tragedy itself belongs to a cultic celebration. In Chapter 3, I examine the effective ways in which tragic choral songs allude to other forms of ritual poetry, namely melic poetry, and discuss the dramatic and social identity of the chorus, whose voice is distinguished by a semantic and enunciative polyphony; ritualized poetic utterances have a double pragmatic significance crossing over from the internal world of the representation to the external world of the performance.

In the second half of the volume, I illustrate my argument by following the poetic and dramatic development of three tragedies with a focus on

---

[21] Some theoretical and practical consideration on this subject can be found, for example, in Calame 2006b.

Methodological Prelude xxix

their choral songs. In Chapter 4, I examine Aeschylus' *Persians*, which closes with a long threnodic song where the main character, the barbarian King Xerxes, takes on the role of a strikingly Greek choregos. Chapter 5 discusses Euripides' *Hippolytus*, in which the perfectly integrated chorus highlights the debate on the sexual ambiguity of the young hero while advising him to abandon Artemis in favour of Aphrodite. Finally, Chapter 6 turns to Sophocles' *Oedipus the King*, in which the chorus questions its own choral practice before appropriating the mortal hero's destiny to religious rituality and situating it within a real anthropological perspective.

In each of these cases, the chorus illuminates the collective dimension of the play's heroic plot, and its enunciative and pragmatic nature calls for the audience's participation in the here-and-now of the performance. By way of conclusion, Chapter 7 examines some forms of melic poetry that cast light on the development of the tragic form. It addresses anew two questions concerning the relationship between myth and ritual: on the one hand, the question of poetic creation by a playwright involved in a collective musical performance; and, on the other hand, the problem of fictions that are at once dramatized in poetry and, by reason of their enunciative and pragmatic modalities, strongly referential.[22]

This study on the choral nature of tragedy arises from my teaching and research activities at the École des Hautes Études en Sciences Sociales (EHESS) in Paris following my early retirement from the University of Lausanne at the turn of the millennium.

In the first instance, the ideas presented in this volume formed the basis of a research-based teaching module that I submitted for my election to the EHESS. Its abstract stated that 'the component that is not just "pragmatic" but above all "performative" of Greek melic poetry leads, by means of the rich evidence for the melic texts as poetic utterances in context, to a study of the social, ritual, and religious occasions of poetic practice'.[23]

Subsequently, the volume benefited greatly from collaborative interactions prompted by the Parisian seminar 'Antiquité au Présent' and by the Groupe de Recherche en Ethnopoétique; these two interdisciplinary seminars, jointly convened with Florence Dupont and others, bridged

---

[22] I have adumbrated some of the thoughts presented here in the following publications: Calame 1999a; 2006b; 2007; 2013a; 2014b; 2014c.
[23] In deference to our discipline's tradition, I have observed the usual technical conventions in matters of referencing. Primary sources are systematically cited in order to allow the reader the opportunity to judge my arguments on a case-by-case basis. Frequent reference is also made to relevant secondary literature in order to situate my arguments within the broader scholarly debate.

several institutions: the Center AnHiMA (Anthropologie et Histoire des Mondes Anciens), which is governed by the EHESS among other institutions, and the Institut des Humanités de Paris (IHP), which belongs to the Université Paris-Diderot, now Paris Cité. I cannot fail to mention two further constant sources of inspiration: the narratology seminar coordinated by John Pier, and the seminar on *l'objet littéraire* led by Annick Louis under the aegis of the Centre de Recherches sur les Arts et le Langage (CRAL, also under the umbrella of the EHESS), a hotspot for what one might dare term 'literary theory'.

Finally, the development and results of this study have benefited greatly from an unwritten rule guiding all teaching in the interdisciplinary graduate school that is the EHESS: that seminars should present research in progress. I would like to express my gratitude for the responses and suggestions of the students who participated in the original seminar on the anthropology of Greek poetics. The conviction that I have attempted to communicate revolves around a point of method. It is because the Greek texts are not in fact (merely) texts or even 'textual events' that they require that we approach them as anthropologists and practitioners of ethnopoetics, and this anthropological approach must warn against essentializing tragedy in any way. We must beware of turning (Greek) tragedy into an autonomous, natural entity, as is still sometimes done with (Greek) 'myth' when it is studied as a singular entity.

Harvard University has recently mourned the loss of Albert Henrichs; I dedicate this study to him and to his colleagues in the Department of Classics in gratitude for all they have done to establish a sensibility for 'Greek chorality'.

CHAPTER 1

The Essence of 'The Tragic'

'According to these principles, tragedy might be defined as the poetic imitation of a coherent series of particular events (forming a complete action): an imitation which shows us man in a state of suffering, and which has for its end to excite our pity (*Mitleid*)'; such is Friedrich Schiller's definition of tragedy at the end of the eighteenth century.[1] Schiller was influenced by Johann Joachim Winckelmann, and his model was inevitably Greek. With its notions of *Nachahmung* ('imitation'), *Handlung* ('action') and *Mitleid* ('pity'), his definition betrays once again the influence of Aristotle's *Poetics* on this distinctively Romantic quest: the quest for the ideal essence of tragedy.[2]

1.1 Theory and Poetics of the Tragic

Though he was both friend and collaborator of Johann Wolfgang Goethe in Weimar, Schiller was not significantly influenced by his fellow playwright. We find no allusion in his quasi-Aristotelian definition of 'Tragedy' to the famous triad canonized some thirty years later by the master of Weimar: *Epos, Lyrik, Drama*, the 'three natural and authentic forms of poetry'.[3] Admittedly, Goethe was at pains to nuance his thesis precisely in relation to 'das ältere griechische Trauerspiel' ('the ancient Greek tragedy'). He explained that in a first phase of development of the genre the three natural forms of poetry merged into one, inasmuch as the main character was still the chorus and the lyric mode was predominant. Later, the three

---

[1] Schiller 1792[1905] 159[356]: 'die Tragödie wäre demnach dichterische Nachahmung einer zusammenhängen Reihe von Begebenheiten (einer vollständingen Handlung), welche uns Menschen in einem Zustand des Leidens zeigt, und zur Absicht hat, unser Mitleid zu erregen'.
[2] In Aristotle's Greek we find (in this order) *mímēsis, he tôn pragmatôn sústasis, éleos (kaì phóbos)*; I will return to this (cf. Chapter 2.1.1, n. 3).
[3] Goethe 1819: 'Es gibt nur drey ächte Naturformen der Poesie; die klar erzählende, die enthusiastisch aufgeregte und die persönlisch handelnde: Epos, Lyrik und Drama.'

forms tended to diverge and to organize themselves in sequence within individual tragedies. Goethe therefore found within the genre of tragedy the clarity of narrative epic, the exaltation of lyric emotion and the personal action of drama.

To get to the root of the grave misunderstanding underlying modern notions of the lyric mode we must revisit this chapter in the history of criticism of tragedy.

1.1.1 *The Tragic Hero and Choral Emotion*

Let us begin by remarking that Romantic definitions link tragedy (understood in terms of dramatic action) to the choral expression of passionate emotion. It is with the aesthetics of Hegel that the matter takes a turn for the worse. In the evolutionary and teleological perspective implied by Hegelian dialectics, tragedy inevitably becomes the synthesis of epic and lyric poetry; moreover, this marks a shift in focus to the action and its protagonist, that is to say, to the hero as individual.

There are two consequences to this. On the one hand, drama, just like epic, becomes the presentation of a human action, but without this involving an unfolding of fate, for the action in tragedy is not directed by external circumstances but rather by the protagonists' 'inner will and character' ('aus dem inneren Wollen und Charakter'), the protagonist being considered as a 'self-conscious and active Individual' ('das selbstbewusste und thätige Individuum'). On the other hand, unlike lyric, drama enacts, according to Hegel, the human passions as they are played out in external circumstances; freed from the intimacy of lyric, the passions are objectified. This leads to the conclusion that in tragedy 'the happening . . . acquires dramatic significance only by its relation to an individual's aims and passions'.[4] Thus dramatic action appears as the real and passionate development of intentions and plans on the part of its characters; only they are responsible for the actions upon which, according to this understanding, they stake their entire existence. The drama is characterized by the three unities of time, place and action, and it is envisaged as the locus in which individual autonomous motives and passions are exteriorized and confronted, against the background of the subject's full freedom.

---

[4] Hegel 1842: II, 622–6; III, 480–6 for the original German [III1160 in the English translation]: 'Das Geschehen . . . erhält dramatische Bedeutung nur durch den Bezug auf die subjektiven Zwecke und Leidenschaft.'

The consequence of this for the understanding of Greek tragedy is explained in an introductory chapter of the *Aesthetics* devoted to the 'determination of the ideal' and, more specifically, to action. It is here that the chorus comes into play. In ancient tragedy the chorus appeared, according to Hegel, as a 'universal entity, devoid of individuality'; the chorus is deemed to be devoid of the feelings and thoughts that determine individual action, which is assumed instead by leaders, rulers or members of the royal families. This explanation pertains to the social status of the choral group; since the chorus portrays a socially inferior group, it suffers the weight of external necessity and of a dependence that hinders the development of individual freedom and 'internal subjectivity' ('eine innere Subjektivität'); the distinction, then, is between the actor as individual and the chorus as a collective.[5]

Hegel does not, of course, forget about the chorus in his chapter on drama. Together with the tragic hero, the chorus, too, is presented as constitutive of Greek tragedy. The choral songs are held as essential components of Greek drama on a par with the monologues and dialogues, and they express generic thoughts and sentiments encompassing epic pronouncements and lyric expression. The tragic chorus, then, 'is the actual substance of the moral life and action of the heroes themselves', in a reprisal of the Hegelian concept of the 'sittliche Substanz'; in contrast with the heroes striding across the stage, the chorus is held to represent the people. What appears to be anticipated here is the interpretative model of the three choral voices amounting to a collective polyphony that is as much semantic as it is enunciative. The notion of the polyphony of the choral songs of tragedy will be developed and illustrated in the following chapters. According to Hegel, the tragic chorus represents a moral conscience of sorts within the dramatic action, and this stands in explicit contrast to the characters' speeches, which reveal, by poetic means, their actions and passions.

But according to Hegel modern drama (including comedy as well as tragedy) differs from ancient drama precisely in that the part given to the classical chorus is now assigned to individual actors; these are the protagonists of the dramatic action who take upon themselves personally and subjectively all the suffering and passion, which is now individualized. In this way Romantic drama was able to free itself, according to Hegel, from

---

[5] Hegel 1842[1975]: I, 269–72; I, 262–4; the original German reads: 'So sehen wir den Chor ... als den individidualitätslosen allgemeinen Boden der Gesinnungen, Vorstellungen und Empfindungsweisen.'

music and dance; these are no longer obstacles to the full deployment of words, the 'true expression of the spiritual' ('echter Ausdruck des Geistigen'). For what counts in tragedy is the victory of the feeling of harmony that arises from the 'absolute domination' of eternal justice; in Hegel's view tragedy resolves into harmony the conflicts of individuals with their relative aims and exclusive passions.[6]

There is nothing surprising, then, in what Hegel makes of Aristotle's enigmatic dictum to the effect that tragedy arouses 'fear and pity' ('Furcht und Mitleid'), albeit for the purposes of catharsis.

> Above mere fear and tragic sympathy there therefore stands that sense of reconciliation which the tragedy affords by the glimpse of eternal justice. In its absolute sway this justice overrides the relative justification of one-sided aims and passions because it cannot suffer the conflict and contradiction of naturally harmonious ethical powers to be victorious and permanent in truth and actuality ... In tragedy the eternal substance of things emerges victorious in a reconciling way, because it strips away from the conflicting individuals only their false one-sidedness, while the positive elements in what they willed it displays at what is to be retained, without discord but affirmatively harmonized.[7]

We have here the triumph of the absolute, of the idea, of the spirit and of idealism.

In *The Birth of Tragedy*, Nietzsche added his own paradoxical twist to the reduction of 'the tragic' to heroic action. 'Tragic myth' ('der tragische Mythus'), he argues, was undoubtedly born of the Dionysiac and its discordance, just like music: 'The pleasure engendered by the tragic myth comes from the same homeland as our pleasurable sensation of dissonance in music' ('die Lust, die der tragische Mythus erzeugt, hat eine gleiche Heimat, wie die lustvolle Empfindung der Dissonanz in der Musik'). Moreover, 'music and tragic myth express to the same degree of the dionysiac aptitude of a people' ('Musik und tragischer Mythus sind in gleicher Weise Ausdruck der dionysischen Befähigung eines Volkes') and therefore they are inseparable from one another.[8]

But according to Nietzsche tragic myth and music must be subsumed into an Apollinian transfiguration to attain their full aesthetic effect; it is in

---

[6] Hegel 1842[1975]: II, 637–8; 679–81; 693–4; 654–5; and 665–7.
[7] Hegel 1842[1975]: II, 666[II 1198–9], picking up Arist. *Poet.* 6, 1449b 24–8; 'Furcht und Mitleid' translate *éleos kai phóbos*, which are better rendered as 'grief and fear', in this order in Aristotle; cf., for example, II, 1452b 1; see Calame 2009b: 31–3 and n. 12 in this chapter, and Chapter 7, n. 54.
[8] Nietzsche 1872: 152–4, in the conclusion of his essay. On the analogy with Wagnerian opera, see Marx 2012: 58–60.

Theory and Poetics of the Tragic 5

the collaboration between the impetuous power of Dionysos and the harmonious aesthetics of Apollo that the world of appearances, delivered from suffering, can be transcended and transformed into a universe of beauty through the metaphysical transfiguration of reality by means of art. For tragic myth centres on its protagonist, the tragic hero, and his or her ruin provokes pleasure in the spectator: 'tragic myth cannot be explained other than as the imagistic representation of Dionysiac wisdom through the means of Apollinian artistic processes' ('Der tragische Mythos ist nur zu verstehen als eine Verbildlichung dionysischer Weisheit durch apollinische Kunstmittel').[9]

What is the reason for this strange dissociation between tragic action and musical performance? It is clear that in the case of Greek tragedy the explanation is to be found in the dissociation of the chorus, which stands as the incarnation of the crowd at the mercy of Dionysiac emotion, from the (individual) protagonists of the dialogue, who speak with Apollinian clarity despite the grief that afflicts them. On the one hand, we have the chorus of satyrs, sympathetic attendants of Dionysos and dionysiac expression of nature, and, on the other, we have the eternal Sophoclean Oedipus, a noble soul who, despite errors and suffering, achieves a serenity that lies at the heart of tragedy and whose inspiration is doubtless Apollinian.[10] The keyword here is (Apollinian) individuation, which is allied to the tension between individual will and aesthetic representation.

1.1.2 Essentializing Excesses

Essentialized through individual heroic action, the idea of the tragic permeates German aesthetic thought throughout the twentieth century. As evidence of this – as late as the 1960s – we might cite the study *Versuch über das Tragische* by the idealist hermeneutist Peter Szondi.

The author of this *Essay on the Tragic* states that a tragic action is one that, while tending towards emancipation, turns back against its agent and dooms him: 'there is only one tragic downfall: the one that results from the unity of opposites, from the sudden change into one's opposite, from self-division'.[11] The focus is once again on the protagonist of the dramatic action, 'der tragische Held'. The model here is of course provided by Sophocles' Oedipus, the hero who is 'victim of his own myth' in *Oedipus Tyrannus* (no mention is made of *Oedipus at Colonus*). As an example of the hero cast down as he strives for emancipation and liberation, Sophocles'

---

[9] Nietzsche 1872: 141.   [10] Nietzsche 1872: 67–78.   [11] Szondi 1961[1978]: 60–73[55].

Oedipus assumes for Szondi the paradigmatic role that he had already occupied in Aristotle's *Poetics*. In his discussion of the reversal that characterizes the tragic plot (*muthos*), Aristotle cites the case of Oedipus to exemplify the passage from ignorance to (re)cognition through the dramatization of *peripeteia*. The story (*muthos*) of Oedipus recurs in the *Poetics* as the paradigm for the emotional effect provoked by simply hearing a tragedy and feeling grief and terror, independently of the visual effects of *mise en scène*.[12] We will return to the Sophoclean dramatization of this story in Chapter 6 when discussing the 'chorality' of *Oedipus Tyrannus*.

In basing his reflections on the notion of the tragic on *Oedipus Tyrannus*, Szondi was aligning himself to a long tradition. A key place in this tradition is occupied by Friedrich von Schelling, the disciple of Kant and Fichte, and fellow student and sometime friend of Hegel. Szondi's debt to Schelling is direct and explicit, since he begins his study with frequent citations of his work, in dialogue with Hegel. Here, too, *Oedipus Tyrannus* stands alone as the paradigm of Greek tragedy. In a reprisal of the Romantic triad, tragedy is held up by Shelling as a synthesis of epic and lyric.

> In the course of development (*Bildung*), this identity flared into a conflict within lyric poetry, and only the ripest fruits of later development provided the means by which unity itself became reconciled on a higher level with that conflict and both became one again within a more complete development. This higher identity is.[13]

In this struggle between the freedom that defines the essence of the self and the necessity attached to the object, in this trajectory of dialectical progress towards the fully fledged manifestation of (Greek) culture, the Romantic Idealist sacrament is celebrated.

Given these premises, it is not surprising that Szondi goes on to inscribe Aristotle's reversal within the dialectic of 'redemption' and 'destruction' (*Rettung* and *Vernichtung*); this is held to be the fundamental trait of 'the tragic' (*die Tragik*, later *das Tragische*). The tragic hero, on the example of Sophocles' *Oedipus* (*the King*), is punished for the contradiction which he harbours within himself: the will to freedom that constitutes the very essence of his self, coupled with the submission 'to the power of the objective'. The Tragic is here not so much an essentialized entity as

---

[12] Arist. *Poet*. 11, 1452a 22–33 and 14, 1453b 1–7 (cf. n. 7 in this chapter) as well as 29–31; see also 13, 1453a 7–12 (the hero whose fate takes a turn for the worse on account of a transgression) or 24, 1460a 26–30 (on the verisimilitude of plot, for which see also 15, 1454b 6–8).

[13] Schelling 1859[1989]: 687[247]; these lectures on aesthetics were given between 1802 and 1805. See on this matter the fine remarks in Marx 2012: 54–6.

a 'dialectical modality' (of dramatic action) that leads from Sophocles' *Oedipus Tyrannus* to Büchner's *Death of Danton* through, notably, Shakespeare's *Othello* and Racine's *Phèdre*.[14] And yet we find not a word on the subject of the chorus, if only as a dramatic character playing out this dialectic of redemption and destruction.

In francophone scholarship, the quest for the essence of tragedy has spanned the whole of the twentieth century and has gone hand-in-hand with a focus on the hero, inevitably conceived as ontologically tragic. This quest can be traced, for example, in the highly traditional vein of comparative literature defended by Pierre Brunel. This approach remains faithful to the Romantic triad, which is effectively canonized despite innumerable historical and critical warnings. Set within its untouchable aesthetical architecture, tragedy looms as the philosophical basis of human existence. Drama follows naturally from lyric, with its 'effusive expression', and epic, with its emphasis on the destiny of the primitive hero. With the help of Novalis we move quickly from tragic action, conceived as the dissolution of an organic form, to the terror provoked by the spectacle of a hero confronted and laid low by his destiny. Thence, with the help of Nietzsche, we can easily follow the transition towards a metaphysical 'Tragic', in which the unfolding of fate is marked by transcendence, necessity and freedom. The Tragic lies 'in the order of things', to expose 'the unconditional character of the consent to existence even in the greatest of griefs'. This development is inevitably philosophical, and it reaches its natural climax in Heidegger's 'grandiose' metaphysics.[15]

But the quest for the essence of the Tragic is in evidence also in the philological current that thinks of itself as 'critical'. It goes without saying that in order to avoid the pitfalls of reification, the Tragic is not reduced to a univocal conscience or concept; rather, it arises out of the dramatic characters as an interpretative hypothesis, and of course the Tragic allows for the polymorphism that comes with encompassing a multiplicity of characters. Nevertheless, not only is the Tragic assigned the status of a substance – by being substantivized as *the* Tragic – moreover, it achieves canonization through being capitalized as this essentialized Tragic; and

---

[14] Szondi 1961[2002]: 69/81 and 61/73–4; cf. Judet de la Combe 2010: 26–34. The significant absence of the chorus in Szondi's idealizing study did not escape Goldhill's attention; Goldhill 2012: 198–200.
[15] Brunel 2003: 225–54 (quotation on 254). Most 2000: 27 remarks pertinently that an idea of the Tragic was already presented by Theophrastus, who, according to Donatus (I, 487 Keil), drew a correspondence between tragedy and the 'circumstances of [heroic] fortune (*túkhē*)'.

once again the Tragic revolves entirely around the actions of its heroes.[16] We will return to this.

Definitions that are conceptual, philosophical and idealizing are presented as universals – as though modernity's only way of relating to classical Athens were through direct filiation. These approaches are in stark contrast to the critical perspectives advocating historical distantiation and cultural relativism that rose to dominance in the humanities in the 1960s; they show no awareness of linguistic discourse analysis or cultural and social anthropology. Not only do we not see any evidence of the 'linguistic turn', or of the 'pragmatic turn', but there is also no trace of any 'social sciences turn' in these attempts at an essentializing definition of the Tragic that focuses on the action of the lone (male) hero.

1.2 'Emic Categories': Lexical and Semantic Fields

Once again it is clear that there is a need for a sound methodology and proper critical distance. As scholars of antiquity, we must make use of the anthropological approaches (cultural and social) employed by historians, while also bringing to bear on our texts an ethnopoetical approach, for these texts demand to be considered as linguistic discourse. In the particular case of classical Greece, these forms of discourse correspond to various forms of poetic song whose oral, musical and ritualized performance argues against inscribing them in a 'literary history'. Instead, we must return to emic categories, despite the temporal distance that separates us from ancient Greece. We must remain keenly aware of the twofold challenge presented by translating from a different culture into the terms of our own culture; this challenge is twofold because of our intrinsically asymmetrical relation to a culture that is 'other' and because of the relative character of our own readings, which are necessarily filtered through our own cultural and intellectual paradigms and therefore in constant evolution.[17]

Let us therefore begin with an exercise in semantics, employing the now established notions of signifier, signified and reference. We will engage in a brief linguistic inquiry, spanning the lexical and the semantic fields, to investigate words that share a common root and terms that are employed in one domain: usages of Greek words in 'cotext' and context.

---

[16] Judet de La Combe 2000: 104–107, with the important development noted in Chapter 2.1. This focus on tragic action and on tragic heroes has led in practice to Jean Bollack's surprising and misguided separation between episodes and stasima in his extensive commentary on Aeschylus' *Agamemnon* (Lille: Presses universitaires du Septentrion, 1981–2001, in no fewer than five volumes).

[17] For 'intercultural translation' I limit myself here to a brief self-reference: Calame 2002a.

1.2.1 Trugoidía/tragoidía

In the second half of the fifth century, at the very moment when Attic tragedy reaches its fullest development, we see in use for the first time the term *tragoidía*. The term is put in the mouth of Euripides' slave, a character in Aristophanes' play *Acharnians*, and it is probably an allusion to Euripides' *Telephus* (which the comedy parodies). In this context, its use is connected to the poet's creative practice; Euripides is portrayed by Aristophanes as 'the mind that is not at home', who collects 'versicles' (*epúllia*) and composes (*poieî*) a tragedy. Though this is for us the first attestation of the word, it goes without saying that we are working with a tradition that is lacunose. Still, lexical field and semantic field converge here to direct us, in the first instance, to poetic activity. This activity is understood as *poieîn*, that is to say, as a 'craft'. In a fragment of Aristophanes' second comedy devoted to the women who celebrate the Thesmophoria festival, the comic poet's art becomes, on the other hand, a '*trugodico-poietico*-musical' technique.[18]

In *Acharnians*, a few lines later, just before the parabasis, Aristophanes speaking from behind the comic mask of the representative of the 'just city' addresses his Athenian audience; in a parody of Euripides' *Telephus*, he declares his initial intention to appeal to the city 'composing a *trugedy*' (*trugoidían poiôn*). The wordplay has been explained in various ways ever since antiquity, and it has been a privileged object of speculation by modern scholars in their quest for the cultic origins of tragedy. Whatever the ultimate explanation, it alludes to new wine (*trug*-), and it refers as much to the comedy's own performance as to the Dionysiac celebration that was the occasion of the *Acharnians*, that is, not the Great Dionysia but the Lenaea, the grape harvest festival which took place at the end of the month of January (of the year 425 BCE). The same wordplay recurs, later in the play, in Dicaeopolis' address to the eel as he prepares to cook it on the fire; here the eel is the object of desire (possibly erotic desire, *póthos*) on the part of the 'choruses of *trugoidía*'. A copyist introduced an error here by transcribing *tragoidikós* instead of *trugoidikós*, but, whatever the reasoning behind this naïve mistake, comedy and tragedy are here embodied in the chorus.[19]

---

[18] Ar. *Ach.* 397–401, cf. also 464 as well as fr. 347 K.-A. and *Vespae* 1511; for the joint use of *tragoidía* and *tragoidikós*, see, for example, *Ploutos* 423–4. On the Greek poet as creator, see Bouvier 2003: 96–102; for 'poetic fashioning', cf. Calame 2015: 78–86.

[19] Ar. *Ach.* 496–501 (parody of *Telephus*) and 885–7 (parody of another, lost tragedy by Aeschylus); see too fr. 156.8–10 K.-A. See Impero 2004: 117–19 for references to ancient interpretations of this famous etymologizing wordplay and for a modern bibliography.

As it turns out, while staging a chorus of charcoal burners from the Attic deme of Acharnae and critiquing the war, Aristophanes' play is also significantly punctuated by practical and critical reflections on the respective merits of tragedy and comedy. At the beginning of the play, Dicaeopolis is seized by a 'tragic pain' (*tragoidikón*) at the mere mention of Aeschylus' name. This leads to mention of another tragic poet, a certain Theognis, who is connected with the 'introduction (*eiságein*) of a chorus'. This is a technical term alluding to dramatic production (which centred on the training of a choral group) if not to the tragic performance itself.[20] It is once again the chorus that is at the forefront when the Acharnians citizens make their plea in defence of Aristophanes in the parabasis of the eponymous play. Chanted and danced to anapaestic rhythm, these verses betray the hand of the poet as chorus master (*didáskalos*) of the 'trugic' chorus. Before intoning a melic address to the Muse of Acharnae the chorus loops back in a ring composition to what might be termed the 'author function' of the comic poet (to adopt Foucault's terminology); the role of the comic poet, just like that of the tragic poet, is to defend justice by 'teaching the highest values' (*tà béltista didáskein*) to the city by means of dramatic performances. This is a function of moral and political pedagogy that the comic poet, like the tragic poet, appears to exercise essentially through the intermediary of the words and voices of the chorus.[21]

1.2.2 *Tragic Composition and Training:* Poieîn *and* Didáskein

This lexical field pertaining to poetic *didáskein* is activated at the beginning of the famous scene of the poetic contest between Aeschylus and Euripides. Both poets are staged in the *Frogs* with their 'author function' as tragic poets. Their long exchange under the arbitration of none other than Dionysos is marked from beginning to end by chorality. In order to stop the poets getting into a fight, a contest is set up in which they are to be judged not only on their verses (*tà épe*: referring here to the iambic trimeters spoken by the actors) but also on their melic songs (*tà méle*: the 'lyric' songs sung by the chorus and the actors). The melic songs are referred to remarkably as the 'sinews of tragedy'. It is at this point that the chorus of frogs, in a song (*mélos*) in 'lyric' dactyls, invokes the Muses; these nine respectable maidens are called to witness the two poets compete

---

[20] Ar. *Ach.* 9–12; cf. n. 45 in this chapter.
[21] Ar. *Ach.* 628–58; for the relevance of Foucault's notion of 'author function' in antiquity, see Calame 2004b: 11–17.

in vocal and verbal subtlety in this great contest (*agṓn*) of poetic composition. The Muses' patronage of this contest renders allusion to the *mousikòs agṓn* of the Great Dionysia highly likely. Aeschylus, on the invitation of Dionysos, addresses an opening prayer to Demeter of the Eleusinian Mysteries. Then Euripides imitates Socrates, as staged by Aristophanes himself in the *Clouds*, by petitioning for the help of Aether to refute his adversary. This double ritual prayer is followed by another choral song; composed in trochaics, this acts as a proem in praise of the two skilled (*sophoí*) poets, the one a master of the polished phrase, the other of convoluted verses. Both the term *lógoi* and the term *épē* feature in this section.[22] Consisting of both (sung) choral verses and (recited) iambic trimeters, this developed poetic prelude is reminiscent of the cultic proemial function fulfilled by the *Homeric Hymns* in the rhapsodic competitions.

From the beginning of this contest in *poíēsis*, references to the words of the heroic protagonists of tragedy alternate with references to the songs (*mélē*) sung by the chorus. To begin with, Euripides reproaches his senior rival for his allusions to hybrid beings, his involved expressions and his roughly hewn heroic figures. Against these he sets his own simple characters, his urbane heroes and the artfulness of his verses. The purpose of this subtly refined art is to 'produce (*poioûmen*) better citizens'. Aeschylus is outraged by this attack. The poet who occupies the tragic throne by virtue of the forcefulness of his art but who is now portrayed by the chorus as the founder of a turgid style of 'tragic wordiness' must stand in his own defence. He brings as evidence two tragedies to which choral song is central: the *Seven against Thebes*, a 'play full of Ares', and the *Persians*, a tragedy that praises excellence in action. These tragedies had been produced (literally 'taught', *didáxas*) recently, and Dionysos declares that he had enjoyed them (*ekhárēn*) and mentions in particular the chorus. This is reminiscent of Apollo in his eponymous *Homeric Hymn*, where he is said to enjoy hearing and seeing the choral songs and dances of the Ionians gathered in his honour on Delos for the great festival of the Delia.[23]

Aeschylus seizes this occasion to evoke the great founding figures of Greek poetry and consider their usefulness for the city: Orpheus for rites of initiation, Musaeus for oracles, Hesiod for the work of the farmer and finally the divine Homer for the values of war. All these poets were masters

---

[22] Ar. *Ran.* 851–74, 875–84, then 895–906 (for the use of the term *tragōidía* in this context, see also 802, 834, 1120 etc.); cf. *Nub.* 264–6 (Socrates invokes Air, Aether and the Clouds).

[23] Ar. *Ran.* 907–15, then 1004–12 and 1019–29 – Aesch. *Test.* 120 Radt (see also, for Aeschylus, 766–70); cf. *HHAp* 146–64, with my commentary, Calame 2011b: 354–7, for the invitation to the deity to enjoy (*khaírein*) the hymnic performance.

who taught (*edídaxen* is repeated several times) by means of their poetry. *Khrestà didáskein*, 'to teach useful things', is the phrase that dominates these alternating considerations and recommendations on a poetic tradition in which tragedy plays an integral part on account of its noble heroes, such as Aeschylus' valiant Patroclos or his Teucros – a far cry from the 'prostitutes' Phaedra and Sthenoboea 'fashioned' by Euripides through his brand of tragic *poieîn*.[24]

It is not a coincidence that Herodotus employs both the verbs 'to make' and 'to teach' (*poieîn* and *didáskein*) with reference to the staging of the *Sack of Miletus* by his contemporary, the tragic poet Phrynicus. The dramatic representation of this recent event that had taken place a few years before the Battle of Marathon is said to have caused its Athenian audience to break out into lamentation. Considered as craftsmen on a par with the Homeric singers, the poets of tragedies, 'tragic singers', assume within the city the 'author function' already taken on by the great choral poets such as Alcman and Pindar; both were *sophoí* and *didáskaloi*, wise poet-craftsmen and teachers of ritual practice and civic virtue.[25]

1.2.3 Melic Song and Choral Song

In the second round of this poetic contest, the object of debate are the tragedies' prologues, with their heroic protagonists such as Orestes in the *Choephoroi*. The metrical play on the iambic formula represented by the Greek for 'he lost his oil flask' ends with Euripides in disarray. This leads to a third round of confrontation focusing on *mél̄e*, that is to say, 'lyric' poems and songs, which are for the most part choral. As we will see, these are songs that correspond to ritual actions and that have nothing specifically 'lyric' about them, with the exception of a prominent poetic 'I' (often in its performative form: 'I sing') and the musical accompaniment of a lyre.[26] If Aeschylus set out to define the 'author function' of the tragedian

---

[24] Ar. *Ran.* 1030 = 1062; for these four founding poets, see Calame 2004b: 35–7.
[25] Herodot. 6.21.2 = Phryn. 3 test. 2 Snell. Bouvier 2004: 9–18 is a good account of what is at stake in the double meaning of *poieîn* as referring both to poetic fashioning and fashioning of men ('anthropopoetics'). For a collection of testimonies for what is here termed the 'author function' (cf. n. 21 in this chapter) of the tragic poets, see Saïd 2001: 74–81. For the melic and tragic poets as *didáskaloi*, see the passages collected and commented upon by Herington 1985: 24–5, 87–8, 184–4. The didactic function of Attic tragedy has been examined by ancient and modern readers; see the helpful survey of this issue in Croally 2005.
[26] At the risk of repeating myself, I take the liberty of reminding the reader that *mélos* is the emic term corresponding to the modern term 'lyric'; from the point of view of the signified, this term does not refer to a form of poetry that expresses the personal feeling of its author, but rather to a collection of

as that of teacher of the city, Euripides defines it as that of *melopoiós*, 'craftsman of ritual song', while boasting that he is going 'to demonstrate publicly' that Aeschylus is a poor and repetitive poet. Meanwhile the chorus of frogs is at pains to make explicit this new technical designation by wondering aloud (still singing in an Aeolian choral rhythm) about what critiques Euripides might address against his opponent, who 'has composed the most beautiful songs (*kállista mélē poḗsanti*) ever to have been composed to this day'.[27]

There follows a series of three parodies by Euripides of Aeschylus' melic strophes that display a redundant accumulation of emphatic and *recherché* expressions. These dactylic verses gather metaphorical phrases and grandiloquent qualifications drawn from different tragedies, and they evoke the citharodic nome, a poetic form to which we will return presently. They are, moreover, interspersed with onomatopoeic expressions reminiscent of the songs (*mélē*) of water carriers. Aeschylus wastes no time in counterattacking with a similar strategy, producing an accumulation of quotations parodying Euripides' contradictory descriptions and repetitions. These composite melic verses imitate not just the choriambic rhythms favoured by Euripides, but also the pompous style of vocalization characteristic of New Music, and they allude to various song forms, from *threnoi* to choral dances through sympotic song and prostitutes' songs.[28] In song-making (*melopoiôn*) Euripides' muse invites him to shift from choral songs to monody; this leads to a long composition about the obscurity of Night, Poseidon, Cretan archers, Artemis Dictynna and finally Hecate with her two torches – and all of this to recount nothing more than the disappearance of a humble cockerel.

But enough of this melic claptrap, 'enough of singing' (*paúsasthon tôn melôn*, l. 1364), declares the referee Dionysos. The moment has come to weigh the poets' craft (*tékhnē*). On the scales of justice, the verses (*épē*) of Aeschylus (once again iambic trimeters) are unmistakably heavier than those of Euripides, and still after all this Dionysos refuses to choose between his two friends. The intention had been to bring back from the underworld one of the poets to save the city, for the choruses dedicated to

---

self-referential and ritual poetic forms; see, for example, the references listed in Calame 2006a: 43–54 and Chapter 3.3.2.

[27] Ar. *Ran.* 1246–63 (lines 1255–6 for the quotation); cf. Dover 1993: 343–4. For these linguistic parodies, see the excellent study by Müller 2004.

[28] The rhythms of these different choral parodies (between lines 1265 and 1328) are the object of Dover's comparative metrical commentary: Dover 1993: 344–58; from the point of view of the musical and poetic forms involved, see most recently, see Di Marco 2011.

Dionysos are close to his heart. Since the question is ultimately framed in political terms, it is Aeschylus who comes out the winner.[29] The praise that ensues is, of course, entrusted to the chorus. The chorus sings of the winner's political intelligence, which is beneficial to the city, before denouncing Euripides' verbiage, which is of a piece with Socrates' since both act to the detriment of the art of the Muses, and especially of the tragic art (*he̲ trago̲idikè̲ tékhne̲*, 1495). The final word is given to Pluto, who steps in as a *deus ex machina* and proffers an affirmation of music; may Aeschylus exit the underworld by the light of the torches carried by the chorus of frogs – they will lead him in procession and celebrate him by their performance of his choral songs and danced melodies (*toîsin toútou toûton mélesin kaì molpaîsin keladoûntes*).[30]

In the comedy's ending, the tragic art is reduced to choral song and its musical performance, where 'musical' is understood in the Greek sense of poetic song allied to instrumental melody and choreography, in line with the definition given by Plato following the fifth-century musicologist Damon of Athens.[31] As early as Aristophanes, then, *tragoidía* is a poetic genre belonging to the larger generic category that is (in emic terms) *mélos*.

1.2.4 Ritual and Sacrificial Origins?

Let us now turn our attention from the semantic field of tragic practice (*poieîn*, *didáskein*, *mélos*) to the lexical field of *tragoidía*, a term whose etymology is hotly contested, despite the fact that it is made up of clearly identifiable etyma. At the level of etymology, the poetic genre of tragedy undoubtedly belongs to the field of song, since *aoidé̲* is the generic term designating sung poetry, however performed. For the moment, we will set aside the speculations assigning tragedy to a hypothetical ritual 'goat song'.

It is important (as we have insisted) to keep to emic terms, and to this end the terminology of the *Chronicle* inscribed on a marble stele dedicated on the island of Paros is a helpful guide. The *Chronicle* tells us that the first 'dramatic representation' (*drâma*) was staged in Athens sometime between 536 and 531 BCE (in our chronological system). The poet who 'taught' it (*edídaxe*) and who also took on the role of the actor responding to the chorus was Thespis; the prize was probably a goat (*trágos*). Diogenes Laertius informs us that tragedy was initially a purely choral dramatic

---

[29] Ar. *Ran.* 1364–9, 1411–13, 1417–21, 1471.
[30] Ar. *Ran.* 1382–99 and 1524–33 (the quotation is from 1526 to 1527).
[31] See Plato, *Resp.* 398cd, 400ac, 424bc, with reference in particular to Damon fr. 37 B 9 and 10 D.-K.

Lexical and Semantic Fields 15

performance, and that it was Thespis who introduced the element of the actor who responded to the singing chorus. Aristotle adds that Aeschylus then introduced a second protagonist.[32] There is also a late and contested testimony that ascribes to Solon the first extant use of the term *tragoidía*; the Athenian poet is said to have attributed to the dithyrambist Arion of Methymna the first 'action' (*drâma*), that is, the first tragic 'performance'. Already in the *Homeric Hymn to Demeter*, the mystery rites instituted by the goddess herself are defined in terms of 'accomplishment of ritual actions' (*dresmosúne hierôn*) and ritual practice (*órgia*, a term cognate with *érgon*, 'action').[33]

The modern and the ancient notions appear here to coincide to a degree, with regard to a singing contest for the prize of a goat, inasmuch as ancient *drâma* also implies a ritualized action. But what we do not find in these rare etymologizing testimonies is any explicit reference to a (tragic) goat sacrifice. There are, therefore, no grounds for mapping onto tragic ritual the many scenic allusions to human sacrifice, be that the sacrifice of Iphigenia in Aulis, or of Heracles on Oeta, or of Erechtheus' daughter in Athens itself. The tragic mask does not hide the tragic actor's guilt for the bloody deed. *Pace* Walter Burkert, the term *tragoidía* does not refer, by means of a hypothetical and original goat sacrifice, either to the prehistoric rituals of hunting and war or to the 'heart' of tragedy.[34] Etymologically speaking, tragedy is not an *Opferritual*; it is not a sacrificial ritual that elicits a primitive guilt; nor is tragedy a goat song by allusion to an original satyr drama; tragedy is simply, in the literal sense, a 'song for the prize of a goat'.

But the *tragoidikòs thrónos*, the 'throne of tragic song' occupied by Aeschylus in Pluto's Underworld, brings us back to the lexical field of *tragoidoí*, the tragic singers who are so prominent in Aristophanes' comedies, and specifically to four different shades of meaning of the term. The first of these shades of meaning is seen when one of the women at the Thesmophoria targets *tragoidoí* as tragic actors; she complains that they are

---

[32] *Marmor Parium FGrHist.* 239 A 43 = Thespis test. 2 Snell (with Herington's helpful warnings, 1985: 97–8, and Scullion 2005: 28–50 with regard to the etymology of the term *tragoidía*; see also Graf 2007: 105–7); Diog. Laert. 3.56 = Thespis test. 7 Snell; see the critical analysis in Else 1957: 17–19, and also below, nn. 55 and 56 in Chapter 2. On *aoidé* as the art of song, see already Hom. *Od.* 8, 498 (the inspired art of song is given by a benevolent god to the bard Demodocus at the Phaeacian court).

[33] Solon fr. 30a West = test. 714 Martina; cf. Stoessl 1987: 97–9, 139. For the meaning of *drâma*, see the use of the term at *HHDem.* 478, with the additional bibliography cited in Calame 1991: 60–2.

[34] Burkert 1990: 20–30, with the critique in Scullion 2002: 117–18; on tragedy as sacrificial ritual, see the references in Lesky 1971: 17–21 (in a critical vein) and 34–7 (in relation to satyrs), as well as Bierl 2007: 33–7; see also Chapter 2.4.1.

spokesmen of Euripides' insults against women, for he has 'taught' (*edídaxen*, once again) their husbands many wicked things.[35] The second shade of meaning is in evidence in an address to the audience by the coryphaeus of the *Birds*, who denounces the tedium engendered 'by the choral songs of tragedians' (*toîs khoroîsi tôn tragoidôn*). He is referring to the tragic poets, privileged target of comedy, such as Agathon, who in the *Thesmophoriazousae* is called both 'composer of tragedies' (*tragoidopoiós*) and 'teacher of tragic singers' (*tragoidodidáskalos*). The expression recurs in the humorous hymn to the Muse sung by the chorus of *Peace*; this playful exhortation to musical celebration (*thalía*) and choral dance directs its mockery against Aeschylus' grand-nephews, allegedly such bad poets that they had difficulty obtaining 'a tragic chorus'. But in a context such as this, *tragoidoí* can also designate the chorus members themselves, as is the case for the dancing tragedian who is the butt of Philocleon's humour in *Wasps*.[36] Finally, the term is used in a fourth sense in the plural to designate tragedy as dramatic representation and musical performance; this is the case in *Birds*, when Euelpides speaks of Priam appearing with a bird 'in the tragedies'. It is with this same meaning of tragic (and comic) celebration that Evegoros' law, cited by Demosthenes, employs the terms *tragoidoí* (and *komoidoí*).[37] Hence the use already in Aristophanes of the verb *tragoideîn* to designate tragic staging, whether in the context of Euripides staging women only to denigrate them or of poets who 'tragedize' and are despicably 'gaping-arsed' just like the lawyers, the orators and the audience itself.[38] Comedy is an inexhaustibly rich resource!

1.3 Towards a Choral Definition of Attic Tragedy

It will be clear that there is no trace in our sources of 'the Tragic'. *Tò tragikón* is entirely absent; the closest we get to it is in the first extant use of the adjective (unsubstantivized) by Herodotus to designate choruses, and specifically choral performances in honour of Dionysos. The story is well known since it is so often repeated and studied by those attempting to

---

[35] Ar. *Ran.* 768–9; *Thesm.* 390–400.
[36] Ar. *Av.* 786–7; *Thesm.* 29–30, 88; *Pax* 773–817 (805–6), *Vesp.* 1470, 1497–1505; cf. also Crates Com. fr. 28 K.-A. For the designation of tragic composition, cf. Herington 1985: 46–7 and 104–6.
[37] Ar. *Birds* 511–13; Dem. *Meid.* 10; see also *IG* II², 1214, which refers to the tragic contest as *tragoidôn ho agón*, and *IG* II², 3090, which mentions choregic victories on occasions when Aristophanes and Sophocles *edídasken* for *komoidoí* and *tragoidoí* respectively; cf. Pickard-Cambridge 1968: 127–32 and 47–8; and for the meaning of these two terms, see Graf 2007: 104–7, where both are strikingly related 'to a chorus performing a ritual'.
[38] Ar. *Thesm.* 85 and *Nub.* 1091–2.

reconstruct a ritual funerary origin for tragedy. A case in point is the Cambridge anthropological school, and in particular Jane E. Harrison, who argued that the original 'tragic choruses' dedicated to the Sicyonian hero Adrastus were transferred to Dionysos, so that the god became the incarnation of a *Daimon Hero* who acted as a tutelary figure in Greek religion. The death of Adrastus, Greek avatar of the *Eniautos-Daimon* and chief god of Frazer's calendar, was re-enacted every year in a cultic *drómenon* of ritual lamentation in anticipation of the god's rebirth and epiphany. This notion was too good to resist, and Gilbert Murray seized on it to attribute to Attic tragedy in all its manifestations a common underlying sequence: the suffering of the Year Daimon followed by his *threnos* or funerary song and finally his rebirth and theophany.[39]

1.3.1 Tragic Choruses Returned to Dionysos

What should we make of all this? According to Herodotus' *logos*, Clisthenes, tyrant of Sicyon, namesake and maternal uncle of the Athenian reformer, abolished the Homeric rhapsodic contests during the war with Argos because they contained too much praise of the Argive heroes. He also wished to banish from Sicyon the Argive hero Adrastus, who was the recipient of a hero cult there and the dedicatee of a *heroon* in the city's agora. For this purpose Clisthenes consulted the oracle of Delphi and was told that Adrastus had in fact been king of Sicyon. The tyrant reacted by bringing to the city the hero who according to epic tradition had been Adrastus' sworn enemy, Melanippus of Thebes. He ordered that a temple be constructed in the prytaneum for Melanippus and that a statue be erected; then he transferred Adrastus' sacrifices and rituals to Melanippus. The people of Sicyon had traditionally honoured Adrastus because their legendary King Polybus, unable to sire an heir, had bequeathed him his kingdom. In addition to the sacrifices and rituals already mentioned, we are told that there were also 'tragic choruses'; these celebrated the hero's trials, and they were therefore in honour of Adrastus and not of Dionysos. Clisthenes returned the choral performances to Dionysos and turned the other sacrificial honours to Melanippus.

In relation to the musical arts, Cleisthenes' reforms are reminiscent of the Spartan *katastáseis*: musical institutions featuring the singing of poetry

---

[39] Herodot. 5.67 1 and 4–5; Cf. Harrison 1927: 315–34 and (signed discreetly 'G.M.') 341–63 (Greek tragedy is a 'Sacer Ludus of Dionysus, as daimon of the Year Cycle of death and rebirth', 353); cf. Pickard-Cambridge 1962: 126–9. References to the many hypotheses on funerary origins of tragedy can be found in Stoessl 1987: 108 n. 105.

during the political and religious festivals that punctuated the civic calendar. The reforms were enacted in the second half of the sixth century, at a time of significant development in the musical arts in the various cities of preclassical Greece, from Mytilene to Sparta. The aim of the reforms was clearly political. Adrastus was an Aeolian hero who relocated from Argos to Sicyon to take up the throne of his uncle Polybus. In the *Iliad* he appears as the king of Sicyon and in Pindar he is the founder there of the equestrian games and their associated celebrations. By replacing him with Melanippus, Clisthenes is replacing an Aeolian and Argive hero with a Theban descendant of the Spartoi, the 'sown' men sprung up from the dragon's teeth. In several strands of epic tradition, the two heroes are indeed presented as sworn enemies; during the episode of the Seven against Thebes, Adrastus besieged the city on the side of Polynices while Melanippus defended the seven gates with Eteocles.[40]

By intervening in the heroic worship of one of the legendary kings of the city, and by rearranging the civic space accordingly, Clisthenes of Sicyon reoriented the community's political and symbolic memory and reordered its aesthetic and cultic space. Through its ritual nature, choral poetic performance played a key role in this re-institutionalization of collective memory. In this context where poetics is played out against a political background, Adrastus' *páthea* refer not to the hero's suffering but to his trials. His hero cult must have involved not *threnoi* – as historians would have it who are eager to derive classical tragedy from funerary cult – but the ritual performance of narrative choral poetry along the lines of the citharodic nomos or the dithyramb. We will return to this in our final chapter.[41]

Must we then follow Aristotle once again? Is it the case that, after the earliest improvised forms, tragedy arose from 'those who led the dithyramb' just as comedy originated in the choral phallic processions, according to the genealogical account presented in the famous fourth chapter of the *Poetics*? And does Herodotus' *logos* have an important role to play in this genealogy of poetic genres[42]? It is still early to draw conclusions. For the moment we must leave unanswered any questions about the content of the tragic choruses that Clisthenes of Sicyon returned to Dionysos.

---

[40] Hom. *Il.* 2.572 and 23.346–7; see also Pi. *Nem.* 9.9–14 and Aesch. *Sept.* 407–16.
[41] The *threnos* hypothesis is represented, for example, by Stoessl 1987: 106–8. Wellenbach 2016 rightly relates the designation of choral songs as 'tragic' to the singing of the *páthea* of Adrastus, and he lists all the interpretations recently given to this description. For the relationship between tragedy and dithyramb, cf. Chapter 7.1; between tragedy and citharody, cf. Chapter 7.2.
[42] Arist. *Poet.* 4, 1449a 9–15; on this difficult passage, cf. Chapter 2.5.1 with n. 83 and Chapter 7.1.

Towards a Choral Definition of Attic Tragedy

1.3.2 Choral Terminology

There is no tragic essence to be grasped by tracing the Greek term *tragikós*, and for all his emblematic status as the philosopher of ideal entities even Plato's etymological examination of the term in the *Cratylus* is diametrically opposed to any form of essentialization of the Tragic. According to Plato's Socrates, discourse (*lógos*) is of two kinds depending on whether it is true or false. The truth (*tò alēthés*) dwells on high, close to the gods, while falsehood (*tò pseûdos*) dwells below, among mankind. Plato illustrates this by appeal to the rough, false language 'of the goat' (*tragikón*), for it is there, in 'the tragic way of life', that 'myths' and falsehoods (*mûthoi kaì pseúde*) are at home.[43] This is, of course, reminiscent of the critical stance towards heroic stories we find in the *Republic*, especially when these stories are staged and dramatized through tragic performance, for then with the dramatization of the narrative there are three degrees of mimetic distancing. It is no surprise to find Plutarch wondering in very modern terms about the boundaries between myth and history when he writes at the beginning of his *Life* of the legendary hero Theseus that beyond that which is likely and founded on historiographical research there lies the realm of the prodigious and the tragic, which is best left to poets and mythographers.[44] We are faced with a paradoxical irony. If there existed a tragic essence from which Greek philosophers were likely to distance themselves in relation to their heroic past and its dramatic narration, then it lay on the side of prodigy and falsehood...

Be that as it may, in its emic definition Attic tragedy is fundamentally choral. Choral terminology runs like a red thread through the technical language relating to the organization of musical competitions at the Great Dionysia and the Lenaia. The poets who wish to take part in the *mousikòs agôn* must 'request a chorus' (*khoròn aiteîn*) from the eponymous archon; according to criteria that elude us, the magistrate then 'grants a chorus' (*khoròn didónai*) to three *khorodidáskaloi* of his choice. Hence a tragic poet is said to 'obtain (or have) a chorus' (*khoròn ékhein*), as we have seen in the hymn to the Muse sung by the chorus of *Peace*; he is therefore in a position to 'introduce the chorus' (*eiságein tòn khorón*), as indicated by Aristophanes at the beginning of *Acharnians*, in another passage already discussed.[45]

---

[43] Plato, *Crat.* 408c; for the use of *tragikós* to allude to a hero's fate, see Ar. *Pax* 135–6.
[44] Plut. *Thes.* 1.3 (cf. Calame 2011a: 74–6); for Plato and narrative *mimesis*, cf. Chapter 2.1.1 and Chapter 7.1.
[45] *Aiteîn*: Ar. *Eq.* 513–14 (for comedy) as well as Cratinus, *Boukoloi* fr. 17 K.-A. (for Sophocles; coupled with *didáskein*); *didónai*: Ar. fr. 590, 27–9 K.-A. (for the Lenaia) and Arist. *Poet.* 5, 1449b 1–2 (see also Plato, *Resp.* 383c and *Leg.* 817d); *ékhein*: Ar. *Pax* 801–7 (twice, of tragic poets) and similarly *lambánein*

The Essence of 'The Tragic'

Moreover, the ten judges, chosen by lot, one for each tribe, are called to 'judge the choruses' (*khoroùs krínein*), in a procedure which consists in taking only five votes out of the urn where each of the ten judges had deposited his voting tablet at the end of the contest. Not to speak of the name given to the public service (liturgy) of organizing the dramatic competitions: *choregía*. This name seems to ascribe to the citizen responsible for the liturgy the function of *choregós*, that is, teacher of the choral group in the traditional melic performances. Nominated by the eponymous archon, the Athenian *choregós* had to finance and organize the training of the chorus in collaboration with the poet and probably also the chorus leader; to this end he set up a dedicated space which was called – significantly – *khoregeîon* or *didaskaleîon*.[46]

In concluding this attempt at re-establishing emic categories by means of a dialectical investigation of lexical and semantic fields, we might remind ourselves of the threefold meaning of the term *khorós* in the classical period; it could refer to a choral group, a choral dance, but also a choral melody. Its etymology was as problematic in antiquity as it is for modern scholars, but Plato's etymological flight of fancy is illuminating; in a passage concerned with affirming the pleasure men feel in practising the rhythm and harmony given them by the gods he relates *khorós* to *khará*, 'delight'.[47]

---

in *Ran.* 94–5 (of tragedy); *eiságein*: Ar. *Ach.* 11 (of tragedy; cf. n. 20 in this chapter); other references in Pickard-Cambridge 1968: 84–7 and Wilson 2000: 6; on this subject, see the helpful discussion in Bacon 1994/1995: 6–7.

[46] For the procedure by which judges were chosen, see the texts commented upon by Pickard-Cambridge 1968: 95–9; the role of the *khoregós* is examined by Wilson 2000: 50–86, and 98–103 (on his relationship with the judges).

[47] Plato *Leg.* 654a; cf. Calame 2001: 19–20 on the meaning of *khorós*, with n. 3 on the controversial question of the term's etymology.

CHAPTER 2

Tragedy, Cult and Ritual

Are then Greek tragedies 'tragic'? And do they merely stage the drama of the tragic hero?

2.1 Contemporary Definitions: Anthropological Perspectives

In the wake of German Romantic aesthetic thought, Greek tragedy was appropriated by idealist philosophy as a basis for theories of the Tragic. This resulted on the one hand in a positive ontology that led, by way of tragic reversal, to man's absolute conscience and freedom, and on the other hand in a negative ontology in which human nature's fundamental indeterminateness eludes language. In this perspective, Greek drama acts as a salutary reminder that human reality eludes Enlightenment reason. A historicized version of these idealist theories of the Tragic, greatly influenced by Christian theology around divine Incarnation and Redemption, finds expression in recent work by various scholars; by staging divine men who suffer and gods who are all too human, Attic tragedy as a genre is held to refer to a 'minimal theology' based on the effects of time and animated by a 'theoretical need' that is instrumental rather than final; it presents on stage a series of paradoxical individualities. By relying on a template, it enables singular dramatic situations to 'make sense'.[1]

It is remarkable that in this new theory of the tragic the chorus features only in isolated remarks, usually prompted by Schelling's aesthetics of drama. In its Nietzschean role as representative of the 'traditional lyric experience', the chorus is set apart from the characters as they undergo their tragic crisis. Within such a perspective, tragedy is ultimately reduced to a dynamic construction of individualities in time. Illuminated by theories

---

[1] Judet de La Combe 2010: 34–45, 67–76, 324–9; on the role of the chorus, in an incidental fashion, see especially 74–5, 225–6, 245–8, 324.

of 'the' tragic, regarded as working on an ultimate reality by means of representations of a singular myth, and positioned in a varying relationship to 'the' truth, tragedy does not come out of this philosophical confrontation unscathed. It continues to be ontologized and essentialized, even though it is now viewed as traversed by time.[2] Such an approach to Greek tragedy obscures the fact that tragic heroes are not just fictional beings but also linguistic beings or, to use another term, *poietic* beings.

2.1.1 Aristotle's Inescapable Influence

Whether implicitly or explicitly, the influence of Aristotle in the modern quest for the Tragic is constant. It is therefore necessary to return briefly to the *Poetics*, if only in an effort to transition away from the philosophical focus that has been aimed at Greek tragedy ever since German Romanticism and towards other approaches recently advanced in the humanities. These approaches include first and foremost cultural and social anthropology, as well as linguistic discourse analysis.

Here is the definition of tragedy that Aristotle offers at the beginning of his short treatise on *tékhnē poietikḗ*, where tragedy features explicitly in its 'essence' (*ousía*). 'Tragedy, then is the representation (*mímēsis*) of an action that is noble and complete, having a certain extension, in rhythmical language (literally: 'seasoned') the varies according to the particular forms of its different parts, a *mímēsis* by actors rather than a narration (*apaggelía*).[3] As *drṓntes*, the protagonists of the action, the actors are they who 'act'. Aristotle is here briefly reprising implicitly the famous distinction established by Plato in his *Republic* between the narrative or diegetic mode and the dramatic mode.

We might remind ourselves that Plato's quarrel is with poets such as Homer, who tell inappropriate stories – 'myths' whose overall truthfulness is not contested, but whose moral value is questioned. He refers in particular to Achilles' impious actions in the *Iliad*; the hero is guilty at once of abusiveness and of arrogance, since according to the poet he did not hesitate to challenge Apollo, join battle with the river-god Scamander and slaughter Trojan captives on Patroclus' funerary pyre. When it comes to the form, as opposed to the content, of these *mûthoi* or poetic accounts it

---

[2] Judet de La Combe 2010: 310–15, 324–31.
[3] Arist. *Poet.* 6, 1449b 21–6. This definition leads to Aristotle's enigmatic pronouncement on the cathartic effect of tragedy: 'achieving by means of compassion and fear (*éleos kai phóbos*, in this order!) the purification (*kátharsis*) of such emotions'; for further references and comments on this controversial point, see Calame 2009b: 33–6.

Contemporary Definitions

is necessary to distinguish between simple *diegesis*, narration through *mimesis* and a mixture of the two modes. In simple narration the poet limits himself to recounting his heroes' actions in the third person and in the past tense, as is the case in some purely narrative forms of dithyramb. In the mimetic and dramatic modes the protagonists embody the action, as in the case of tragedy (*tragōdía*) and comedy. Finally, in the mixed mode exemplified by epic poetry narrative sections alternate with dialogue.[4]

Plato is not concerned with the poetic voice as such, and he makes no distinction between *récit* and *discours* (to use the terms of Benveniste's discourse analysis), between narrative and enunciation. But in relation to tragedy and comedy we do see the foreshadowing of a distinction between rhapsodes on the one hand, and actors of the récit in drama on the other; the former, just like the Homeric poets, are makers of 'representations' (*mimḗmata*); the latter accomplish actions that are copies (*aphomoiṓmata*) of imitations, separated by three degrees of *mimesis* from a reality which is itself merely appearance. Thus the *tragōidopoiós* can be compared in a way to the painter who reproduces an object fashioned by an artisan on the model of an original divine form.[5]

If in Plato's *Republic* poetic *mimesis* arouses the sort of distrust generally associated with the world of appearances, in Aristotle's *Poetics* on the other hand it is greatly valorized. For Aristotle, the capacity to represent (*mimeîsthai*) is what distinguishes man from animals, and it is an essential resource for learning.[6] Be that as it may, both in Plato and in Aristotle, poetic *mímēsis* is centred on narrative action. Its truth arises from the moral values of the civic community, and to this extent its function is a pedagogical one. In the *Poetics*, *mûthos* is conceived as 'arrangement of actions' (*hē tôn pragmátōn sústasis*). Equivalent to narrative plot, *mûthos* is at the heart of tragedy, which tends to represent man as better than he is. Tragedy inscribes within the order of the plausible or necessary (if not of the possible) the represented action: 'so that the actions and the plot are the goal of the tragedy, and the end is the most important of all'.[7]

---

[4] Plato, *Resp.* 392c–395d, with Gastaldi's commentary, 1998: 362–74; for a comparison with Émile Benveniste's operative distinction between *récit* and *discours*, see n. 28 in Chapter 3 in this book; for an example, see Chapter 7.1.

[5] Plato, *Resp.* 595c–7e; cf. also 602b on *hē tragikḕ poíēsis*; see Murray 1996: 3–6 and 189–98; cf. also n. 43 in Chapter 1.

[6] Arist. *Poet.* 4, 1448b 4–9; for a useful explanation of the differences between Plato and Aristotle from the perspective of their conception of *mímēsis*, see Lucas 1968: 258–72; see also Klimis 1997: 101–26 and Groneberg 2018: 147–61.

[7] See Arist. *Poet.* 6, 1450a 15–23 (a difficult passage: cf. Lucas 1968: 101–3 and also Dupont-Roc and Lallot 1980: 198–204), and 15, 1454b 27–32, to cite only the most significant passages; on tragic *mûthos* as plot, see also Ricœur 1983: 55–71, who points to the role played by this concept in modern structural narratology.

But if *mûthos* is tragedy's fundamental component, there are according to Aristotle a further five components: characters, diction, intention (or thought), staging (or spectacle) and composition – or, rather, the poetics of song (*melopoiía*). Now, just as the different forms of *mélos* are dismissed in the *Poetics* for not being part of the narrative arts, so too are tragedy's songs (and their poetics) relegated to mere instrumental status. Thus in Aristotle's conception of tragedy the chorus has no more than a subordinate role.

In the historical picture that complements Aristotle's simultaneously descriptive and normative approach the importance of the chorus started to wane from the moment Aeschylus introduced a second actor. After Thespis' single speaker, this innovation signifies the insertion of sections of dialogue and consequently the possibility of a distinction between *epeisódia* (literally, the sections of dialogue as insertions in the song) and *stásima* (etymologically, the sections during which the chorus stands still). Despite the bracketing of *mélos*, the episodes are conceived here in relation to choral song (*mélos khórou*), in keeping with their designation as being 'between songs'. These include, in particular, the parodos, which is the first expression of the chorus as collective entity, the stasima (in metres other than anapaests and trochaic metres) and finally the *kommós*, which is a *threnos*, that is to say, a song of funerary lamentation shared between chorus and actors, between orchestra and *skene* (whence apparently songs also come: *tà apò tês skenês*).[8]

When it comes to the role of the chorus, Aristotle's approach becomes decidedly normative: 'the chorus must be regarded as one of the actors; being part of the whole, it should take part in the action (*sunagonízesthai*), not as in Euripides, but as in Sophocles'.[9] In the other tragedians, the sung parts (*tà aidómena*) have become simple interludes (*embólima*: 'sections "thrown" in') in line with the practice introduced by the tragic poet Agathon at the end of the fifth century; Euripides does not seem to have

---

[8] I have paraphrased, in order, Arist. *Poet*. 4, 1449a 15–18 and 12, 1452b 14–25; on these different choral interventions, whose form is not always in keeping with the concrete examples we find in classical tragedy, see the fine commentary in Lucas 1968: 135–9; for the uncertain meaning of *tà apò tês skenês*, cf. Scattolin 2011: 161–7.

[9] Arist. *Poet*. 18, 1456a 25–32 (for the meaning of the term *sunagonízesthai*, cf. Ar. *Thesm*. 1059–60 and n. 1 in Chapter 5); on this further difficult passage, see the succinct commentary in Lucas 1968: 193–4 and the sophisticated remarks in Scattolin 2011: 176–99, whose translation of this passage lends the function of *sympatheia* to the chorus; cf. also n. 3 in Chapter 3. In her recent and relevant study on the chorus of drama in the fourth century, Jackson (2020, 3–4 and 147–65) has shown that the concept of *embolima* as choral interludes does not tally with what we know of the choral interventions from our (scarce) evidence of tragedy and comedy of this time. For late tragedies of Euripides, in relationship with the 'New Music', see, for instance, the case studied by Weiss 2018a.

followed this practice (which was doubtless linked to the introduction of New Music) except at the end of his career. We will return to this paradoxical statement by means of some examples, though the order of these examples does not follow' Aristotle's evolutionary arc from Aeschylus through Sophocles to Euripides.

But for now the point at issue is that, under the powerful influence of German Romantic aesthetics, philosophical conceptions of the tragic have ended up eliminating all the foundational traits of Attic tragedy as a form of choral song. Even though Aristotle cannot avoid recognizing the essential chorality of tragedy in the fifth century, modern scholarship has focused its attempts at definition on tragic action and on its (male) protagonists, the tragic heroes as victims of their destiny.

2.1.2 Approaches in the Humanities

As a result of the epistemological shifts that followed the civil unrest in France and Europe in May 1968 and the libertarian protest movements in California around the same time, the humanities directed a renewed attention to manifestations of Athenian Greek classical culture such as the tragic musical contests in honour of Dionysos Eleuthereus. ('the Liberator'). Despite all efforts by representatives of the reactionary currents of neoliberalism to nullify the political and social effects of these shifts, the disciplines of sociology, anthropology and linguistics played their part in questioning the direct genealogical relation with 'the Greeks' routinely traced by philosophers, whether implicitly or explicitly. For a sociology informed by Marxism and psychoanalysis it was, and still is, crucial to question the notion of the individual envisaged within the supposed freedom of an autonomous and intentional development. Cultural and social anthropologists adopted a critical distance towards alien cultures whose specific and autonomous developments they were trying to understand on their own terms. The discipline of linguistics, on the other hand, introduced a new sensibility towards the cultural and polysemic dimension of all forms of discourse, as well as towards the enunciative strategies underlying discourse in an aesthetical reality that, through pragmatics, has social and cultural repercussions.

Straddling the domains of historical psychology and structural anthropology, the essays on myth and tragedy originally published by Jean-Pierre Vernant and Pierre Vidal-Naquet in two jointly authored volumes offer testimony of this decisive turn.[10] These volumes lay claim to the traditions

---

[10] Published in English as a single volume, Vernant and Vidal-Naquet 1988.

of sociology of literature and historical anthropology. They present Attic tragedy as a phenomenon at once social, aesthetical and psychological; it is a social reality by virtue of the institution of tragic competitions, an aesthetic creation by virtue of its emergence as a literary genre and a psychological development by virtue of the rise 'of a tragic conscience and a tragic man'. It will be clear that the risk of essentialization is here still very much present. Be that as it may, through the institution of tragic competitions 'the city turns itself into theatre'. But two points need to be spelled out. On the one hand, if tragedy is a social institution, its manifestation in fifth-century Athens is also an art form; on the other hand, though tragedy depends institutionally on a social reality, this is not directly reflected in the tragedies themselves, which rather adopt a critical attitude towards the city, particularly in relation to its heroic past and foundational myths.[11]

This interpretative stance is reprised in Vernant's and Vidal-Naquet's second collection of essays, which is prefaced by a vigorous response to the attacks aimed at the first volume on the part of philologists still largely inspired by the Romantic hermeneutics as well as on the part of scholars loyal to Marxist orthodoxy. For the first cohort, the defenders of a science whose search is for a meaning encoded in a sacralized text, the practice of reading in a sociohistorical literary vein reduced Greek tragedy to a set of 'pre-established' codes mastered by the 'tragic author'. The Marxist voices, on the other hand, objected to the emphasis placed by such readings on tragic ambiguity and interference, the ambiguity inherent in tragic language and in the interplay between hero and chorus, between men and gods, but also between actors and audience. In addition to the philological critiques and the rebuttals of Marxist dogmatists, Vernant and Vidal-Naquet also addressed proponents of the 'scapegoat theory'. Finally, they reaffirmed their position by quoting from their earlier volume: 'But although tragedy, more than any other genre of literature, thus appears rooted in social reality, that does not mean that it is a reflection of it. It does not reflect that reality but calls it into question. By depicting it rent and divided against itself, it turns it into a problem.'[12] Tragedy can only offer a 'shattered glass' reflection (to quote the title of a later, especially lucid

---

[11] Vernant and Vidal-Naquet 1972: 25–6.
[12] Vernant and Vidal-Naquet 1986[1988]: 15[20–1]; this reiterated statement is aimed at the hermeneutic textualism of Jean Bollack, at the Marxist dogmatism of Vincenzo di Benedetto (who has revisited the issue in one of the best recent overviews of the problems posed by Greek tragedy as spectacle; Di Benedetto and Medda 1997: 327–42 and 365–7) and at the ritualist unilateralism of René Girard.

essay by Vidal-Naquet) of the political situation underlying the organization of the ritual of the Great Dionysia and the tragic staging of the heroic narratives that constituted the past of Athens and its neighbouring poleis. If the poetic play involves the metaphorical staging of a civic space, the metaphor itself implies a distancing; the same is true of the 'collective' principles of the citizen body confronted with the 'individual' values of the heroes' world.[13]

Is it then the case that tragedy opened up a new space in Greek culture, a space for what we conceive of as pure artifice? Tragedy as 'a fiction, an illusion, the imaginary'?[14]

A comparative analysis of the three extant versions of the tragedy of Electra and Orestes offers a good point of departure to tackle this question. The combination of the disrupting effect of the 'shattered mirror' with the fictional effect of dramatic representation results in a more radical hermeneutic stance towards Athenian tragedy. In these different dramatic versions Orestes' matricide is not the representation of the killing of a mother by her son such as might be committed in the city and be punished under its laws: 'it does not have any referent outside the theatre'. The matricide committed by Orestes belongs just as much to the domain of the *oikos* as to that of the *polis*, and it remains internal to the theatre. Thus, generally speaking, 'tragic events are cut off from any potential referent'. It follows that tragedy does not confront the civic community with real problems, but rather 'it plays at problematising reality by means of fiction'. Tragedy is neither 'civic preaching' nor a 'philosophy of the world'.[15] In this culture of immanence, Electra is in herself 'insignificant'. 'Tragic insignificance' is asserted through fiction.

According to this theory of *insignifiance tragique* it is about time that we abandon the notion of mimesis conceived, in the wake of Aristotle, as representation.

Doubtless this move away from referential explanations is influenced by radical postmodernist currents; it has nevertheless recently given rise to positive developments. Founded on the 'spectacle principle', the position in support of this rupture relies on a forceful critique of Aristotle's *Poetics*, and it concerns also modern theatre makers who lay claim to its heritage. If tragedy is

---

[13] Vidal-Naquet 2001: 77–87: 'In a sense, tragedy is the opposite of civic continuity. Tragedy is a crisis, negative or positive, following which no hero remains unchanged.'
[14] In the words of Vernant and Vidal-Naquet themselves (1986[1988]: 23[187]); on the question of 'dramatic illusion' by means of 'tragic acting', see Rehm 1992: 45–51. We will return to the issue of fictionality in the introduction to Chapter 7.3.
[15] Dupont 2001: 177 and 192.

the dramatic representation of an action, spectacle does not acquire meaning other than within, and by means of, the story. Such a perspective implies that in the history of modern theatre, three 'Aristotelian revolutions' have to be decried: the submission of actor to author; the reduction of play to text to the detriment of the various aspects of staging; and, last but not least, the new tyranny of the 'fabula' caused by the return of *mûthos* understood as plot. In its narrative manifestation, plot is therefore at the heart of theatre in general, and Paul Ricœur's contribution to this 'narrative imperialism' founded on Aristotle's notion of *mûthos* was to become crucial; beyond the poeticity of the (Greek) myths, it is a matter of affirming the equivalence of *mimesis* as representation and *mûthos* as arrangement of actions.[16] In fact, as we have seen, Aristotle's discussion of tragic poetic technique disregards entirely the aspects of staging and spectacle (*ópsis*) and poetics of song (*melopoiía*); from being an all-encompassing musical event, tragedy is reduced to a text. This is the reason why the stimulus for the distinctive tragic feelings is not so much the spectacle (*ópsis*) as the arrangement of actions; it is not the visual experience of the play but the hearing of the story (*mûthos*) of Oedipus that arouses 'pity and fear'.[17]

All this means that it is now necessary to rethink tragedy to take account of spectacle, poetic competition, the Great Dionysia. In short, we must regard tragedy essentially as musical performance; tragic fiction takes the form of a concatenation of musical sequences. The 'ludic principle' becomes a 'musical principle' or 'choral principle'. This principle finds its fullest expression in the sung exchange between chorus and protagonist that is termed *kommós*, the ritual song of lamentation in which the choreuts beat (*kóptein*, from the same root as *kommós*) their breasts.

The dramatic role of the sung lamentation that is central to many tragedies has recently been exploited to demonstrate that Attic tragedy is 'anti-political'; in declaring its 'ineffable grief', tragedy as 'oratorio' thus dismisses the unifying principles which stand at the heart of the city.[18] Such a conception of tragedy does not take into account either the ritual forms assumed by the chorus's songs or the semantic polyphony of the choral voice, which also takes on an interpretative role. We will return to this

---

[16] Dupont 2007: 84–188.
[17] Arist. *Poet*. 14, 1453n 1–14; cf. Dupont 2007: 25–61; for *mûthos* as plot cf. n. 7 in this chapter.
[18] Loraux 1999: 45–66 and 123–37; cf. Chapter 4 and Chapter 7.4. This song shared between chorus and actors, the *kommós* is defined by Aristotle (*Poet*. 12, 1452b 18–25) as a form of lament. The reflexive dimension of the *kommós* in relation to the emotion of the audience, in particular in Euripides' tragedies, was recently illuminated by Pucci 2016: 191–203. The technical designations 'parodos', 'stasimon', 'kommos', 'exodos' and so on, that is, all the various formal and functional components of vocal expression in Attic tragedy, are discussed succinctly by Battezzato 2005: 150–4.

Attic Tragedy as Ritual

matter when discussing the long choral ending of *Persians* lamenting the defeat of the barbarian army, and then again when discussing the amoebean song that provokes the hero of *Oedipus Tyrannus* to blind himself. For the moment let us remind ourselves that at the heart of this restoration of Attic tragedy as a sung ritual performance there stands the chorus with its songs and melic diction implying the participation, through 'co-enunciation', of the play's audience.[19]

So Athenian tragedy of the fifth century is not a genre founded on texts, and moreover it is a poetic form of a piece with *mélos*. As we will see, this sung poetry, wrongly labelled 'lyric', includes performative enunciations that correspond to ritual acts (e.g., Alcman's or Pindar's *partheneia*). The musical performance of tragedy, too, by virtue of being a ritual spectacle and a sung enunciation, is itself ultimately a cultic act. The ritual involvement of the protagonists of the staged action as also the involvement of the poet and audience play themselves out through the collective songs, the songs of the chorus. We will have to return to this, of course. 'Tragic insignificance' may be a relevant notion from the point of view of tragic action as it was conceived by Aristotle, but there is no doubt about the choral significance of Attic tragedy as a poetic form that is anchored in the musical, ritual and pragmatic poetic practice that is *mélos*.

The musical performance of Attic tragedy is not only a political act but also a religious act, in constant exchange between the heroic action ('myth') being represented and the ritual occasion inhabited by the poet and his public. Hence these sung poetic forms have a twofold pragmatic function: a mimetic ritual function through the dramatization of a heroic action represented chorally, and an indirect ritual function through the cultic celebration of the god Dionysos, in particular on the occasion of the Great Dionysia. We will return to all these ritual and cultic aspects of Athenian tragedy too.

2.2 Attic Tragedy as Ritual

Regardless of the influence of the Cambridge anthropological school, it is in the English-speaking world that a sensibility has developed towards all

---

[19] Dupont 2007: 242, 272 and 57 (see also 301). In focusing attention on the emotional aspects (collective expression of 'pity' and 'fear') of the tragic chorus, Visvardi 2015: 19–34 defends a similar hypothesis ('enacting choral emotions'). See also the new proposals by des Bouvrie 2018: 99–116 regarding the 'tragic process' creating 'tragic workings'; 'the tragic' is to be found in the abstract clash between the violations of the socio-cultural order and that 'socially unquestionable' order – that is, a relationship between the disruptive dramatic events and the cultural sensibility of the contemporary audience (115).

that tragedy as musical performance has in common with ritual. Adopting a wide anthropological perspective, ritual is here understood instrumentally as an individual or collective action that is culturally organized according to implicit rules and repeated according to stated rules. It is a practice that involves the body through gesture and voice, both of these being aesthetical and affective; ritual has a specific temporality, spatiality and logic. It unfolds in a dedicated space, which has a symbolic and pragmatic meaning whose scope is social, religious and cultural. Ritual is therefore a practice that is regulated, recurrent, social, institutional, conventional and symbolic of the body and the voice.

This is merely an operative definition; it refers to a conceptual instrument, and its function is on the one hand classificatory and on the other hand comparative, reflecting the two methodological pillars of classical cultural anthropology. Just like any operative definition, it is not meant to find an exact referent in the culture that is the object of anthropological study, and it is relative to an academic paradigm that is itself liable to changes and epistemological ruptures. As a result, this definition at once accommodates and pushes against some recent attempts at demarcating our subject matter. Ritual does not correspond to 'performative utterances', the definition proposed by philosophers of language, for this definition is too loose. Ritual is better thought of as a regulated performance at once vocal and gestural. Verbal performance implies not only the speaking 'I' who sometimes describes the vocal action that s/he is carrying out (*performative* in the technical linguistic sense of the term, as we will see), but also the voice in its rhythmical deployment as well as the body moving rhythmically and expressively, with all the cultural, aesthetical and pragmatic effects that ensue.[20]

From an anthropological point of view, verbal ritual will therefore be envisaged less as an act of communication than as a practical, often periodically repeated enactment of a regulated poetics of the body and the voice, dramatizing by means of interposed metaphors and metonymies a series of symbolic values, including values that we would consider religious. These symbolic moral utterances in the form of song are subject to a communal belief system and contribute to the formation of a dynamic cultural memory; this runs counter to any scenario inscribed in human

---

[20] I aim my critique at the arguments of Tambiah 1985: 128, who attempts to define ritual as 'a culturally constructed system of symbolic communication', according to the three parameters of (conventional) language acts, performance staged in different media; and indexical values attached to the actors of ritual performance; with reference to Greek poetry, see Kowalzig 2007: 32–41. For the technical linguistic meaning of 'performative', see n. 26 in Chapter 3.

ethological development or indeed belonging to the genetic or neural 'heritage' of man.[21]

Ritual in general will be subject to a very precise instrumental definition in relation to the criterion of regulated recurrence, whether individual or collective, in order to avoid such confusion as might arise, for instance, from the extension of 'ritualization' to include repeated everyday gestures, even though these be culturally marked, or various forms of representation, dramatization and spectacle of concern to the broadly inclusive discipline of 'performance studies'.[22] Rooted in an anthropological framework corresponding to the symbolic conception of man and his behaviour in a community with a shared belief system, ritual is a highly anthropopoietic practice, the collective and cultural construction of men and women.

In the particular case of the polytheistic cultures of the classical Greek cities, ritual action often assumes a cultic dimension and, through this, a direct symbolic and pragmatic function. It easily takes the form of a ritualized offering to a divinity: a sacrificial offering, but also a verbal offering such as a hymn or a paean or a dithyramb. The musical offering is the means by which the intervention of a divine or heroic figure is sought – here and now – in accordance with the requirements of a particular society and a civic culture at a particular historical conjunction, whether on an occasional or recurrent basis. In a sequence that easily links together procession, sacrificial offering and athletic contest, the ritualized poetic utterance in its choral dimension of song and dance occupies a central symbolic place and fulfils a key pragmatic function. It is particularly in choral performance as effective song that the founding heroic account that is 'myth' and the musical gestural expression that is 'ritual' come together; this is achieved through the 'poietic' work of a poet with a choral group.[23]

2.3 Ritual Song in Attic Tragedy

This instrumental definition of ritual not only enables us to identify the ritual sequences that punctuate the dramatic unfolding of individual tragedies, but it also makes us attentive to everything that renders the

---

[21] On this point I find myself in agreement with Rappaport 1999: 29–38: 'medium itself becomes a message'; but ritual must not be regarded solely as a system of (cultural and social?) communication. On the notion of 'cultural memory', reprised in a vein that is critical of Jan Assmann, see my 2014 essay.

[22] For the equivocal concept of 'ritualization', see Bell 1997: 164–9 and 262–7; 'in particular, ritual-like activities reveal an even more fundamental dimension of ritualization, the simple imperative to do something in such a way that the doing itself gives the acts a special or privileged status' (166).

[23] Cf. Calame 1991: 56–60 and Calame 2008, with references to other works.

musical performance of Attic tragedy a cultic ritual. So ritual in tragedy opens up tragedy as ritual as we shift from the intra-scenic to the extra-scenic.

It is once again essentially Anglo-American scholarship that has developed a sensibility towards the ritual sequences and gestures carried out either by the protagonists of the drama or by the chorus. Without a doubt, the absence of a definition of what counts as 'ritual' has led to a certain haziness in discussion of this controversial question. Key tragic scenes that have been held up as examples of 'ritual moments' include Oedipus' solemn imprecation against Laius' unknown murderer in Sophocles' *Oedipus Tyrannus*, the evocation of the procession and sacrifices of the Great Panathenaia at the end of Aeschylus' *Eumenides*, the appeal to Darius' apparition or the funerary lament at the end of the *Persians* and Creusa finding sanctuary at the altar of Apollo in Euripides' *Ion*.[24] This heterogeneous list includes individual and collective ritual gestures, both verbal and non-verbal, functional words and gestures enacted on the stage or simply related.

The situation is complex to say the least, both in relation to the forms of discourse at play and sequences of ritual acts carried out and in relation to the effects of ritual performance on the unfolding of the dramatic action. Let us then assess the pragmatic function of the choral verbal rituals within their context in the dramatic action.

2.3.1 *Hymnic Song and* Melos *in Euripides'* Ion

Let us take just one example from Euripides' *Ion*, and let us limit ourselves to the musical ritual form of the hymn, the cultic form of address and entreaty to a god with the aim of requesting or provoking an intervention. We find four kinds of hymn in the *Ion*.

After the prologue delivered by Hermes, Ion enters the scene. He is the son of Apollo and Creusa, and Creusa in turn is the daughter of Erechtheus (one of the great legendary kings of Athens) and the wife of the Achaean Xouthos.[25] At dawn, the 'guardian of the god's gold' arranges laurel branches at the entrance of the sanctuary in Delphi dedicated to his divine father. While he describes the cultic function assigned to him in Delphi

---

[24] See the illuminating study in Easterling 1988, as well as the list in Bierl 2007: 30–3; an overview of the question in Wiles 2000: 38–45. For the performative and ritual role of the choral sections in Attic drama, see the essential contribution by Bierl 2001: 30–64.

[25] Eur. *Ion* 112–43. For a similar identification of the hymnic elements integrated in Sophocles' choral songs, especially in the *Antigone*, see Rodighiero 2012: 139–65.

Ritual Song in Attic Tragedy 33

and the ritual gestures that he is in the process of carrying out, the young Ion addresses Apollo. His song, composed in Aeolian rhythms on a choliambic base, displays the tripartite structure that is, in modern academic perception, characteristic of ancient Greek hymns (ll. 112–43): invocation – praise – petition.

But in this first hymnic song of this tragedy the initial invocation is addressed not to Apollo but to the laurel branch with which the young singer is sweeping the god's altar. The praise section, introduced as is customary in hymns by a relative pronoun, does not include the usual narrative or descriptive section but rather is transformed into a celebration of the cultic service that the young man is offering up to the god Phoebus. This is achieved by means of the personification of the laurel branch, the 'young shoot' that alludes as much to Ion as it does to Apollo. It is only with the final refrain, which alludes to the generic marker of the paean song, that the god is revealed as the hymn's true addressee. The song then shifts to a different metrical pattern before it ends not with the expected petition but rather with the simple naming of the god, who is declared to be the speaker's father. The hymnic address includes a statement by the *persona cantans* of his cultic service towards Phoebus in Delphi and it concludes with the refrain 'O Paian, o Paian, be blessed, be blessed, be blessed, son of Leto' (ll. 141–3).[26]

Moreover, this hymnic song is preceded by Ion's twofold appeal in anapaests over roughly thirty lines (ll. 82–111): an invitation to the Delphians to purify themselves at the sacred spring Castalia in preparation for uttering well-omened oracles leads into a self-exhortation to protect the altar of Apollo from the birds threatening to defile the god's offerings. After the hymnic section with its paeanic refrains, Ion's song returns to anapaests (ll. 144–83). The wish to continue faithfully in Apollo's service is accompanied, on the performative level, by a libation with water drawn from Castalia's spring: 'I shall sprinkle (*rhípso*, l. 146) with golden vessels the water that wells up from the earth and is swept by the eddies of Castalia.' Then, still in the same anapaestic rhythm, the song continues with a new poetic evocation of the birds of Parnassos that threaten to defile the sanctuary: Zeus' eagle, then the swan of Delos, with a subtle allusion to Phoebus' musical associations.[27] This beautiful melic composition frames

---

[26] For a comparison of this 'para-hymnic' song with the standard hymns and the paeanic ritual refrain, see Furley and Bremer 2000: I, 320–4; II, 307–12, who include ll. 144–53 in the hymn despite the metrical change at l. 144 (see also Furley 1999/2000: 187–9). On the metaphorical meaning of the laurel branch as 'young shoot', see the excellent discussion in Noel 2014.

[27] For an analysis of the metrical structure of this melic song, see Owen 1939: 185–6.

the hymnic section and culminates with the reiteration of the speaker's wish to remain in the service of the god.

We have here, then, a hymn that is not a hymn, performed by a solo singer in a melic rhythm but without musical accompaniment and without audience and punctuated by a refrain that does not correspond exactly to the cultic refrain of the paean (for it is not choral). This tragic hymn turns out not to have any functional effect on the course of the dramatic action. In the event, the simple though repeated wish that takes the place of an explicit petition does not have any pragmatic value.[28]

2.3.2 Choral Song and Hymn

The chorus enters singing a fine Aeolian rhythm punctuated by a series of anapaests recited by Ion; the song describes the scenes depicted on the front of the Delphic temple of Apollo. Creusa then enters the scene that has been set before the temple; Xouthos enters the scene last. On the performative level, Xouthos indicates that he crosses the threshold of the temple as he affirms his will to consult the god's oracle on the matter of his wife's infertility. He asks Creusa meanwhile to take laurel branches and pray to the gods at each of their altars (ll. 417–24). This prayer will turn out to be a hymn sung by the chorus of Creusa's servants.

This choral song in Aeolian rhythm on a choriambic base (452–509) takes the form of a cultic hymn with its characteristic tripartite structure. The chorus begins with an invocation to Athena and a self-referential and performative (in the strict sense) supplication (*se hiketeúo*). There follows a brief section of praise that is reminiscent of the shorter Homeric hymns in which the chorus mentions the goddess' genealogy ('who was born of Zeus' head with the aid of the Titan Prometheus', l. 455). Finally, in the closing section, we find the petition to the goddess: Athena Nike the Athenian is summoned to Delphi to join Artemis, daughter of Leto, in the *hic et nunc*. That is to say that the choral group of heroic times invites the same Athena who is honoured by the spectators of the play in the sanctuary they have dedicated to her on the Acropolis to enter the space and time of the dramatic action. As is often the case in the choral passages of Attic tragedy, there is a striking permeability between the time and place in which the heroic dramatic action takes place and the here-and-now of the ritualized tragic performance.

---

[28] On this monodic, as opposed to choral, paean, see also Rutherford 1994/1995: 129–31.

But in this closing section of the prayer to the goddess the traditional form of the cletic hymn is modified. After the appeal to the goddess' presence in the here-and-now, the young chorus members delegate their supplication to the two divine young women (*parthénoi*) Athena and Artemis, who are both sisters of Apollo (all three being children of Zeus).

> Come as suppliants, young women (*korai*),
> so that the ancient line of Erechtheus
> might at long last win by pure oracles
> a fine progeny   (ll. 467–71)

The young women of the chorus appear to assimilate themselves to the two goddesses (who are also young women in the context of the ritual of supplication) at the same time as they adopt the spatio-temporal perspective of their Athenian audience inasmuch as they qualify the family of Erechtheus as 'ancient' (*palaión*); this *genos* belonged to Athens' heroic past. We see here a slippage with the time and space of the heroic action.

Unlike the monodic hymn sung by Ion, the hymnic supplication that is delegated to the two virgin goddesses will reveal itself to be effective as a ritual utterance within the dramatic action, for it achieves Xouthos' desired outcome. At the end of the play, it is in fact Pallas Athena, Athens' eponymous goddess, who intervenes *ex machina* to resolve the plot, marking yet another overlap between the time and space of the heroic action and the time and space of the dramatic representation. Not only will Ion, recognized as being the son of Apollo and the grandson of Erecteus on his mother's side, reign over his kingdom in Attica before colonizing the Cyclades and Ionia (a prefiguration of the Athenian 'empire' at the time of the play's performance), but furthermore Creusa and Xouthos will go on to have two sons, the future eponymous heroes of the Dorians and Achaeans.[29]

While this section of the choral song will fulfil its pragmatic hymnic function at the end of the play, at this point we see the song turn into something else, for what seemed at first a cletic hymn is in fact the first strophe of a triadic structure such as is characteristic of choral melic song. In the antistrophe (ll. 472–91), the women of the chorus offer some gnomic remarks on the blessings that come to mothers from having children. The epode consists of an address to Pan's cave on the side of the rock of the

---

[29] Eur. *Ion* 1553–1605; for the aetiological dimension of this outcome of the story, see Calame 2006c: 547–50.

Acropolis. This is the pretext to evoke the place where Ion, son of Apollo, was exposed as a newborn, as well as the dances of the daughters of Cecrops to whom Athena entrusted the upbringing of the young Erichthonios. By this 'choral projection', a frequent device in the choral songs of tragedy, the young women of the chorus once again bring together within their own spatio-temporal dimension the dramatic action and their own ritual action, here and now.[30]

This song sung by the chorus of women features the three semantic components that characterize all melic songs: the first-person ritual reference to the context of the enunciation (the here-and-now); the gnomic commentary on the present situation; and finally the reference to the heroic past, that is to say, to the plot and the paradigmatic protagonists of the corresponding 'myth' in relation to the pragmatics of the sung action in the present. While this cultic hymn to Athena and Artemis performs a pragmatic function and influences the outcome of the dramatic action, this ritual prayer is nevertheless enclosed within an extremely elegant melic choral song, with all its ritual effectiveness.

Ion is not the only main character to sing in this play. In a plot rich in the twists and turns that will later come to be associated with the novel, the first oracular response denies any descendance to Creusa while declaring the young Ion to be Xouthos' son. In a plaintive monody, Creusa sings of her despair in anapaests interspersed with paroemiacs (a metre corresponding to the second half of a hexameter, after the median caesura; ll. 859–922). Before that, the oracle's double pronouncement is communicated by the coryphaeus and elaborated upon by the old paedagogus, who sides with the house of Erechtheus; Creusa reacts with strong emotion. Technically, the dramatic exchange between the three protagonists is a *kommós* (ll. 752–803). It interlaces spoken lines in iambic trimeters (the old man and the coryphaeus) with Creusa's sung replies in emotionally heightened dochmiacs, and these dochmiacs are then echoed in the hymnic monody that follows.[31]

Thus tragedy's essential nature as musical performance is reinforced, and the boundary between the scenic space of the dramatic action and the orchestra occupied by the chorus turns out to be permeable. This interaction between the actors' space and the orchestra finds a dramatic counterpart in the interplay that we have identified between the space and time of the heroic action and the space and time of the dramatic performance.

---

[30] For 'choral projection', see Henrichs 1996; at least as far as the later tragedies of Euripides are concerned, Csapo 2017 prefers to speak of 'embedded choruses'; for the musical dimension of these choral projections, see Weiss 2018a: 23–57; see further Chapter 3.4.1.

[31] See the traditional metrical analysis in Owen 1939: 189–90. For the *kommós* cf. n. 18 in this chapter.

2.3.3   A Melic Lament

With the coryphaeus' indirect approval, the old paedagogus effectively calls for the boy's execution on the reasoning that his supposed illegitimacy will bring dishonour to the house of Erechtheus. He thus provokes the 'lyric' passage sung by Creusa, whom the oracle had condemned to sterility (859–922). This song, which has been identified as a hymn, is in fact preceded by a long melic address by Creusa to her own soul. The passage testifies to Creusa's full conscience of herself in a way that contradicts long-held views on tragic characters; these have often been regarded as merely an intermediate link in the evolutionary arc from a holistic conception of the social actor to the notion of individual personhood.[32] Creusa in effect declares, on a performative level, her intention to bring out into the open the union into which she was forced. By evoking Olympian Zeus and Pallas Athena, she will publicly denounce the mortals and immortals who have betrayed her pregnancy, namely Xouthos and Apollo.

The strictly 'hymnic' section of Creusa's song is marked by strong emotion; she begins in fact with an address to Apollo. In keeping with the conventions of cultic hymn, the god is invoked in the second person and his qualities and functions are listed (invocation and praise).

> You who cause the voice of the seven-toned
> lyre to ring out, when it accompanies
> with inanimate horns of untamed beasts
> the harmonius hymns of the Muses,
> you o son of Leto, by this light of day . . .   (ll. 881–6)

But this hymnic and musical praise of Apollo, leader of the Muses and player of an instrument made of animal parts, quickly turns into explicit reproach (*momphá*, l. 885). This occurs performatively (in the technical sense of the term): 'I will utter' (*audáso̱*, l. 886, a form of the 'performative future'). The act of singing is furthermore accompanied by verbal deixis; the reproach is uttered by the poetic 'I' in the here-and-now, 'by *this* ray of sunlight' (*tánde augáni*, l. 886).[33] At this point the narrative and praise section of the hymn, which is normally a narrative in the third person and the aorist past tense, becomes autobiographical. The characters in this narrative are the second person of the divine addressee and the first person

---

[32] Cf. Furley 1999/2000: 189–92, who provides a list (197) of hymnic songs in the Euripides' tragedies.
[33] On the 'performative future' and verbal deixis in melic poetry and Attic tragedy, see Calame 2004a: 423–37 and n. 30 in Chapter 3.

of the singer (still in the aorist), and they are identical to the characters of the dramatic action. The story pattern is that of the young woman snatched from a meadow (with its erotic associations) where she is picking flowers to make a garland; thus golden-haired Apollo seduces young Creusa. The girl's desperate calls to her mother and the assertion of Cypris' supreme power complete the scene. The infant born of this union was exposed and became prey for birds, 'while you' – Creusa adds, sliding surreptitiously from the time of the narrative to that of the present utterance – 'you play your kithara and sing your paeans' (ll. 905–6).

In the finale of Creusa's monody, the petition is more developed than generic convention would demand for cultic hymns. It begins with a performative appeal (*audô*, l. 907; *karúxo*, l. 911) to the god of oracles before culminating in a long imprecation of the god responsible for putting an unknown young man in the home of her husband after having left his own son begotten with her to die.[34]

> Delos hates you and the laurel
> branches hate you by the palms trees with their delicate foliage
> there where Leto in sacred childbirth
> bore you in Zeus' grove. (ll. 919–22; trans. Diggle 1981)

By morphing from a song of praise into a song of blame, this hymnic prayer becomes charged with irony; the god has condemned to death a child who was born in the same circumstances as him. What is at first sight a cultic hymn, with its tripartite structure, has become a song of reproach; this is for all intents and purposes an opera aria inserted into the dramatic action.

2.3.4 *A Hymnic Song and Its Pragmatics*

Creusa's long lament and accusation of Apollo leads to another exchange with the old paedagogus, the loyal servant of the house of Erechtheus. This takes the form of a stichomythia, a rapid-fire exchange of single iambic trimeters between Creusa and the old man. It is during this exchange that a plan is hatched in defiance of Apollo's unfair oracle. Ion will be killed as he pours a libation – not by the sword but by the poison of the Gorgon's

---

[34] Eur. *Ion* 859–80, then 881–922; according to Furley and Bremer 2000: I, 327–8 this is an 'anti-hymn' that recounts a 'perverted "epiphany"', in contrast with the monodic paean addressed to Apollo by Ion; see also II, 317–18 on Apollo, gold and eroticism. For the scenario of the erotic encounter in a meadow, see the parallels listed in Calame 2009a: 209–24.

serpents. Athena had gathered this poison when she had slayed the Gorgon and she had attached it to a golden chain that she then gifted to Erichthonios, her son born from the Earth, from whom Creusa had inherited it. It is not surprising, then, that in the ode that follows the chorus of Creusa's servants addresses itself to Einodia, daughter of Demeter. Often identified with Hecate, the goddess Einodia is the patron of magic potions and incantations and she is often associated with the liminality of crossroads.[35]

Comprising two strophic pairs in Aeolian rhythm, this third stasimon or 'standing song' (ll. 1048–1105) begins with a prayer that takes up the first strophe. Since it is sung, this prayer inevitably has the tripartite form of a hymn. Thus it opens, as we might expect, with a brief invocation to Einodia, presented here as daughter of Demeter. This is followed by the standard relative clause leading into a narrative descriptive section characterizing the goddess through one of her domains of competence: nighttime assaults. The chorus swiftly moves on to the petition enjoining Einodia to bring the wine-cup containing the drops of blood from the severed head of the Gorgon to the one who will enter the palace of Erechtheus' descendants (another shift from Delphi to Athens). The metaphor leads to an imprecation: 'May a foreigner from a foreign house never reign on the city if he is not a noble descendent of the Erechtheids' (ll. 1058–60).[36]

The hymn's brief petition turns into a formula of bewitchment. This is one more instance of the device by which the form of the hymn is adapted to insert the petition into the dramatic action in an attempt to influence it on a pragmatic level. The rest of the strophes sung by Creusa's servants only confirm this pragmatic articulation. The young women envisage the suicide that will be Creusa's fate should her plan not come to issue. Then they declare their shame before Dionysos, who during the Eleusinian mysteries causes the universe to dance, from the stars of the Aether to the Nereids in the depths of the sea. The young women's choral projection is followed by a discreet allusion to Athenian Dionysos; this is an allusion to the god being celebrated at the performance of Euripides' tragedy within the Dionysiac sanctuary at the foot of the Acropolis. It is, therefore, yet

---

[35] For the identification of Hecate Phôsphoros and Einodia, see, for example, Eur. *Hel.* 569–70 and Zografou 2010: 114–21; further references are in Zeitlin 1996: 310–11.
[36] On the tripartite structure of hymns and on the relation between hymn and prayer, see in particular Calame 2005: 47–67 (with n. 8); Furley and Bremer 2000: I, 329 are correct in remarking that this imprecation is a verbal form of *defixio* or, in Greek, *katádesmos*.

another convergence between the dramatic space of the heroic action and the space of the ritualized musical performance.[37]

The choral song ends with an imprecation that has the ring of modern-day feminism; the disrespectful songs of men who sing, inspired by a dissonant Muse, of the unholy unions and unlawful loves of women should rather direct themselves against the illegitimate unions of their sex; (just like Xouthos) men install in their home their bastard sons.[38] Here again the initial hymnic form, with its religious pragmatics, is turned in the service of choral song. This tends to comment on the dramatic action and enrich it emotionally at the same time as it seeks to influence its course by means of ritual formulas. In Chapter 3.2, we will go into further detail regarding these three voices of the tragic chorus: the performative, the hermeneutic and the affective.

2.4 Attic Tragedy and the Cult of Dionysos

There is no justification for claiming that Euripides' tragic choral songs are little more than musical intermezzos, or for being swayed by Aristotle into believing that only in Sophocles' tragedies, and not in those of Euripides too, the chorus has the significance of an actor.[39]

As a matter of fact, whether they are monodic or choral, Euripides' melic songs employ the conventions of traditional cultic poetry (hymn, paean, hymenaion). The tragic poets can be seen to reorient these forms on both a formal and a pragmatic level towards the heroic dramatic action. But tragedy can also on occasion use these poetic forms in the service of the cultic act that is the tragic performance itself. We turn, then, from ritual in tragedy to tragedy as ritual.

2.4.1 Tragedy and Sacrificial Ritual

But before moving on to this second issue, it will be necessary to sketch the question of the ritual gestures represented on the tragic stage, the ritual practices that are not acts of song. Among them, the sacrificial act occupies

---

[37] For this convergence in relation to the complex identity of the chorus of the *Ion*, see now the excellent discussion in Taddei 2016.
[38] Zeitlin 1996: 311–16 aptly points out the Eleusinian overtones of this choral song.
[39] See Arist. *Poet*. 18, 1456a 26–32 for the contrast between a chorus that takes part in the dramatic action (*sunagonizesthai*) and a chorus that is reduced to performing *embólima*, mere musical interludes having no relation to the plot (*mûthos*), for which the tragic poet Agathon is paradigmatic. This is a famous passage on which we will necessarily return in Chapter 5, devoted to Euripides' *Hippolytus* For the role of the chorus in Euripides' tragedies in general, see Calame 2020.

a special position. In modern anthropological interpretations of Attic tragedy, it is in fact sacrifice that has opened up the interpretation of tragedy as ritual as opposed to ritual in tragedy. From this point of view, tragedy is generally envisaged in the perspective championed by the philosopher René Girard, as an amateur anthropologist. These interpretations require therefore some remarks on what has come to be referred to as 'tragic sacrifice'. The peculiarity of tragic sacrifice is that it is always narrated, since bloodshed and violent death were not staged before the audience assembled in the theatre consecrated to Dionysos. Let us discuss here one example: the sacrifice of the young Iphigenia.

Since the 1960s, scenes of sacrifice staged in tragic plays have been interpreted as 'corruptions' of the norm. The key lies doubtless less in adopting a structuralist approach that privileges inversion and rupture than in paying attention to the language employed to describe the acts of violence that occur in tragic plots, for its use is very selective in relation to the different ritual moments of the blood sacrifice.[40] The most famous example, as well as that which has received the most commentary, is the human sacrifice of Iphigeneia at the hands of her father Agamemnon which is decreed by the goddess Artemis in retribution for a slight.

There is no doubt that in the opening song of Aeschylus' *Agamemnon* the chorus of old men of Argos portrays the killer of Iphigeneia as the 'sacrificer' (*thutḗr*, l. 227) of his own daughter. Agamemnon himself, in words that are repeated by the chorus, designates the killing of his daughter as a 'sacrifice of virginal blood'; the girl becomes a sacrificial victim whom the king prepares to 'apportion' (*daíxō*), taking the verb in its primary meaning. In this dramatized version of the myth Artemis does not demand the young woman's sacrifice in retribution for an animal hunted in her sanctuary. Rather, the sacrificial act arises from an omen: two eagles are seen to attack a pregnant hare and to feast on it (in a choral passage that is also shot through with sacrificial language); as a result, this *thusía* runs the risk of being a 'lawless' sacrifice, a sacrifice 'unshared' (referring to the meat; *ánomos*, *ádaitos*, l. 150). Initiated under 'the yoke of necessity' and by the effect of a divinely inflicted delusion, the sacrifice of the young woman is an impure and sacrilegious 'twist'.[41] Later on, in reply to the chorus's reproaches, Clytemnestra will explicitly accuse her husband of having sacrificed his own daughter, whom she compares to a ewe snatched from

[40] See the seminal study by Zeitlin (1965) dedicated to the 'corrupted sacrifice' in Aeschylus' *Oresteia*; for other examples of 'corrupted sacrifice', see especially Foley 1985: 155–67. On 'reciprocity' and the perversion of ritual in general in tragedy, see Seaford 1994: 364–405.
[41] Aesch. *Ag.* 206–36; see also 134–6 and 146–51; see Zeitlin 1965: 475–7 and 488–99.

its flock. Clytemnestra in turn strikes Agamemnon three times; she offers his body to Hades, 'Zeus, saviour of the dead, who reigns in the underworld' (l. 1386–7) in quasi-sacrificial terms. The chorus in the parados refers to Iphigeneia as a wild goat pinned to the altar; yet she is in human form when her saffron-coloured robe slips to the ground at the moment of the sacrifice; she becomes the figure of an image, voiceless but with a piercing gaze.[42]

It is essentially the act of slaying that is seized upon in terms of sacrifice; the many collective gestures which render blood sacrifice a long ritual sequence – from the procession leading the victim to the altar to the consumption of the meat in the ritual meal that concludes the sacrificial ceremony – are in themselves barely mentioned. Yet it has been demonstrated that these Aeschylean descriptions of sacrificial killings combine the vocabulary of ritual sacrifice with ideas drawn from the domain of hunting. The protagonists of these sacrificial scenes thus find a place between the relations that humans entertain with the gods through the intermediary of the domestic animal on the one hand, and the relations of mortals with the domain of the non-civilized through the intermediary of the wild animal on the other.[43] In connection with Iphigeneia's budding adolescence, it is relevant that the foundational stories behind the rituals of Artemis' cult place the goddess at the intersection of the complex metaphorical web relating the domain of the civilized to that of the wild. It is a matter of accounting, by the symbolic means of mythical narrative and ritual practice, for the moment of transition that is the first menstrual bleeding of adolescent girls and their entry into adulthood: a symbolic death, if that is what it is, through the shedding of blood, in the metaphorical transference from the biological sphere to the social and cultural sphere. For tragedy, these are 'sacrifices good to think with'.[44]

By contrast, in Euripides' *Iphigeneia at Aulis* the (human) sacrifice is not simply recounted as in Aeschylus' *Agamemnon* but rather it is enacted, at least as regards the first phase of the ritual. On her own invitation, the young woman is led (*pempéto*, l. 1462) towards the meadow where she has accepted that she will be killed (*sphagésomai*, l. 1463). There follows a sung exchange with the chorus, a *kómmos*. The chorus is made up of young women from Chalcis and the heroine addresses herself to them as being of

---

[42] Aesch. *Ag.* 1415–19, 1380–92 and 231–44; for a perceptive commentary of this latter scene, see Medda 2012; also Foley 1985: 39–43, who speaks of 'sacrificial metaphor'.
[43] Vernant and Vidal-Naquet 1972: 135–6 and 145–54.
[44] A phrase coined by Loraux 1985: 62–75, who examines some other tragic stagings of the death of a young woman and relates the sacrificial act to defloration and marriage.

the same age as her (*neánides*, ll. 1467 and 1491). Iphigenia asks to be treated as an animal victim, mentioning the customary elements of cultic sacrifice; she will be adorned with the sacrificial fillets and sprinkled with lustral water. The barley grains will be placed in ritual baskets to be consumed by fire while the heroine invites her own father to walk around the altar from the right. Above all, Iphigeneia enjoins the young women of the chorus to intone a 'paean' (l. 1469) to Artemis; Iphigeneia sings in a performative manner that 'with blood, with sacrifice' (*haímasi thúmasi te*, l. 1485) she will bring safety and victory to the Greeks while voiding the oracle's prediction. Iphigeneia thus becomes in some sense a leader of the chorus while the chorus in turn responds to the heroine in an *amoebaeon*, a 'lyric' exchange in iambic-trochaic rhythm. The young women promise glory (*kléos*, l. 1504) to Iphigeneia before effectively addressing their song to Artemis.[45]

Through this choral mediation the first phase of the cultic sacrifice is accomplished in practice between stage and orchestra. By intoning not a paean proper but a cultic song, the young women of the chorus describe the ritual gestures of the sacrifice as they are being carried out before addressing to Artemis the 'pean' Iphigeneia had requested. The first lines of the choral ritual song mention the young woman's progress towards the altar, her head decorated with fillets and sprinkled with the ritual purifying water, while the words addressed to the goddess in a performative mode (*kléisomen*, l. 1522) ask her to accept the sacrifice of a mortal (once again *thúmata*, l. 1524); the goddess is invited to rejoice in it and to accord *kléos* (l. 1531), 'everlasting fame', to Agamemnon and all the Greeks.[46] On the basis of the technical vocabulary of ritual sacrifice, the scene therefore takes on a choral twist according to the contract of *do ut des* specific to communication between men and gods. Is this, then, a ritual sacrifice not only reported and described on the tragic stage but rather effectively carried out in the orchestra? Not entirely.

On the one hand, as a consequence of Agamemnon's deception to bring Iphigeneia to Aulis under the pretext of marriage to Achilles, the description of the ritual scene is also marked by elements of the marriage ceremony. Not only does Clytemnestra interpret the sacrifice offered to Artemis as sacrifice in preparation for her daughter's marriage (*protéleia*, l. 718), but the procession, the garlands and the lustral water can also suggest the ritual of *numphagogía*; 'bridal procession' symbolizes ritually

---

[45] Eur. *Iph. Aul.* 1460–4 (the recited prelude in iambic trimeters), then 1475–99 (in a double song in iambic dimeters interspersed with cretics). The ritual reality of this human sacrifice has occasioned a rich bibliography, on which see Bremmer 2015.
[46] Eur. *Iph. Aul.* 1509–31; cf. also 883–5.

and materially the transition to the status of married woman through the crossing of the threshold of the conjugal home. Moreover, at the end of the choral scene, Iphigenia's final invocation to the light of day as 'torch-carrier' evokes the torch-bearer of marriage ritual.[47] Finally, when the chorus envisages, in the third stasimon, the marriage with Achilles which will turn into the sacrifice of the young woman, it is to mark the contrast with the evocation of the legendary nuptials of Thetis and Peleus amid the hymenaean songs intoned by the gods. As for Iphigeneia, her hair adorned with a garland like a betrothed, she is destined to be sacrificed, slaughtered like an unblemished mountain heifer, that is to say, a ritually pure animal, but still one that belongs to the wilderness. The comparison says as much about the ambiguous status of the young betrothed between wild animal and domestic animal as it does about the symbolic interplay between marriage (seen from the perspective of the young woman) and blood sacrifice.[48]

On the other hand the actual bloodshed can only be reported by a messenger, who quotes the words spoken by Iphigenia in the sanctuary of Artemis, with its sacred wood and its flowering meadow reminiscent of the locations of seductions and rapes by gods and heroes.

> I willingly grant that your men may bring me to the goddess' altar and sacrifice me (*thúsai*, l. 1555) if that is what the oracle requires. As far as depends on me may you all have good fortune, win victory in war, and return to your native land! In view of this, let no Greek take hold of me: I will bravely submit my neck to the knife.

After this, the gestures that are carried out are those of sacrificial ritual: ritual silence, the garlanding of the victim's head, the heroic sword (*phásganon*, l. 1566) that becomes sacrificial knife and is placed in the barley basket, the circumambulation while sprinkling lustral water and the ritual petition to Artemis to accept the sacrifice (*thûma*, l. 1572); the 'pure blood from her lovely neck' is offered in order to obtain – *do ut des* – a favourable crossing and assure the conquest of Troy.

It is at the very moment when the priest seizes the ritual knife to slaughter the victim that the miracle occurs: a doe drenches with its blood the goddess' altar, taking the place of the young woman who instead

---

[47] See Eur. *Iph. Aul.* 718–22 and 670–6, then 1505–9; cf. Seaford 1987: 108–10, with other examples of interactions between sacrificial death and marriage ritual, as well as Foley 1985: 84–92.

[48] Eur. *Iph. Aul.* 1074–88; Loraux 1985: 62–8 has written pertinently about this metaphorical 'animalization' of the young women sacrificed in Attic tragedy; on the poetic and tragic metaphors of ritual sacrifice see once again the seminal study by Henrichs 2000.

joins the company of the gods. The animal will be burnt as an offering to the goddess. The heroic narrative has returned to the ritual reality that which belongs to it (animal sacrifice) and has kept for itself the sacrificial (and matrimonial) metaphor. This accounts for the transformation of the young woman's killing into a virginal 'heroic death'.[49] The human sacrificial victim chooses death and offers her body to the fatherland. The blood sacrifice is therefore returned to ritual practice at the same time as the story of Iphigenia's apotheosis is explicitly given a founding account in the final exchange between Clytemnestra, Agamemnon and the chorus. At the end of the fifth century, even among Athens' sophists, the *mûthos* has not yet become 'myth'.

The killing of the young woman has therefore in a sense been simultaneously narrated and dramatized on the metaphorical plane. The sacrificial ritual is only partly staged in a sequence that is itself presented as a wedding ritual, while the actual bloodshed is confined to narration in accordance with dramatic convention. The metaphor of the sacrificed wild animal designates equally the killing inscribed in the heroic story and the initiatory and symbolic death of the adolescent destined for marriage.

There are no grounds for regarding Greek tragedy as an expression of the 'sacrificial crisis'. Undoubtedly *Iphigeneia in Aulis*, given that the plot turns on the young woman's killing, can be interpreted according to the schema of substitution of the ritual victim or that of the victim as scapegoat for the group. On this view, Iphigeneia's tragic sacrifice would illustrate the principle of double substitution outlined by Girard in relation to the origin and founding of ritual sacrifice.[50] By adopting the perspective of historical and contextual anthropology we will nevertheless be in a position to resist the unilateral application of a simplistic evolutionist psycho-anthropological schema concerning a 'sacrificial crisis' that is claimed to be universal. The hypothesis an original violent act and a scapegoat's sacrificial substitution engenders a constant confusion between what belongs to ritual practice and what belongs to ritual discourse (with its representation through interposed narratives) in a poetic play of metaphor. On the other hand such metaphorical play on a sacrifice that is narrated, and that is transferred into the fictional world of 'myth', forbids any direct mapping of the represented ritual sacrifice onto the rituality of tragedy itself. It is not legitimate to entertain by these means the speculations

---

[49] To cite once again the terminology of Loraux 1985: 79.
[50] Girard 1972: 152–5, with the caustic critique addressed by Marx 2012: 153–8 against a theory of tragedy vitiated by Christian notions.

offered up by many historians of religion on tragedy as a sacrificial act in general or as the sacrifice of a goat in particular.[51]

2.4.2 Tragedy in Cultic Performance: The Great Dionysia

So much for ritual in tragedy. But what about tragedy as ritual?

As indicated above, the context for the musical performance of tragedy was the tetralogy: three tragedies – often dramatizing in sequence a heroic story, as in the case of Aeschylus' *Oresteia* – combined with a satyr play sometimes thematically related to the *arkhaîon* staged in the tragic set. The trilogy devoted to Clytemnestra's killing by her son in vengeance for the killing of his father Agamemnon culminated in a satyr play entitled *Proteus*.[52] Let us remind ourselves that the sung performance of a tetralogy competed with two other tetralogies at the musical contest consecrated to Dionysos. From the fact that the contest was placed under the control of the eponymous archon we can deduce the political nature of the representation of tragedies. As we have seen, the archon 'granted' to three among the candidate poets their requested chorus, and he invited a 'choregos' to finance each of these. The tragic *mousikòs agṓn* thus belonged to a specific moment in time and space.

In terms of time, the competition between three tragic tetralogies belonged in Athens to the extended musical celebration of the Great Dionysia. It is worth reminding ourselves that the festival took place over nine days, from the eighth or ninth to the sixteenth of the month of Elaphebolion, a period that corresponds in the Julian calendar to the end of March. According to Thucydides, the celebration of these 'city Dionysia', *Dionúsia tà astiká*, took place at the end of the winter season to mark the arrival of spring. The festival opened with a preliminary contest in which the poets and actors were presented to the public and the programme of musical competitions was announced. The *musikoì agônes* properly speaking began with the dithyrambic competition: ten choruses of fifty adult singers whose members represented each of the ten tribes of democratic Attica, followed by ten choruses of fifty adolescents. Each of these choruses was financed by a single choregos. There followed the comic competition: five comedies, each involving a chorus of twenty-four singers. Finally, there were the three days dedicated to each of the tragic tetralogies, each involving a chorus of twelve or (later) fifteen singers. No complicated calculations are necessary to

---

[51] See n. 32 in Chapter 1.
[52] On the role of satyr drama within a tetralogy, see Voelke 2001: 18–20 and 389–403.

Attic Tragedy and the Cult of Dionysos 47

arrive at a total of 500 *paîdes* and 664 adult singers for a triple musical competition addressed to a citizen body estimated at 40,000 for the classical period, of whom 6,000 participated in the assembly. This means that, among the civic body of the citizens and their children, a significant proportion actively took part in the musical activities of the Great Dionysia.[53]

In the Athenian cultural calendar, the City Dionysia (*en ástei*) and the civic and religious festival of the Panathenaia in the summer were the most important celebrations marking the new political and religious year. The Panathenaia also included a musical component in the rhapsodic contest mentioned several times by Plato. The competitive element of the City Dionysia on the other hand was fundamentally choral. The audience of the musical contests of the Great Dionysia included not just citizens but also foreigners, among them the ambassadors and *proxenoi* of neighbouring or subject cities, as well as metics and probably slaves too. The presence or otherwise of women is still a matter of debate since the evidence is insufficient to adjudicate.

The spatial context of the City Dionysia was the theatre at the foot of the Acropolis. The remains of its fourth-century incarnation can still be visited today and feature stalls partly sculpted into the rock and divided into three sections (one of which was reserved for citizens representing the *boulê*), a stone stage raised on multiple occasions with architectural elements, a paved *orkhḗstra* (dance space), this too redesigned at various stages, and probably an altar, which would undoubtedly have been placed at the centre of the orchestra (*thumélē*). The classical theatre must have been built at the beginning of the fifth century; it featured stalls set into the slope of the Acropolis and perhaps lengthened with wooden benches, a round orchestra of compacted earth and a wooden stage on the same level as the chorus's orchestra. The *skḗnē* originally featured a simple tent but later a building was added to conceal the tragic action that could not be shown on stage. It was in front of this building that the actors moved and spoke their parts in dialogue with the singing chorus; it is essential to note that actors and chorus moved on the same level.[54] At the beginning of the fifth century, following Clisthenes' reforms, the musical performances of dithyrambs

---

[53] Thuc. 5.20.1; Dem. *Meid.* 10 (citing Euegoros' law, which may have dated back to the fifth century; cf. n. 69 in this chapter) and so on. For the composition of the audience at the Great Dionysia, see the re-examination of the evidence in Spineto 2005: 277–92; for the later participation of women, see 292–304, as well as the cautious remarks in Goldhill 1997: 57–66; see also Loscalzo 2008: 69–100 and n. 13 in Chapter 3. On the Athenian dithyrambic competition, see Kowalzig and Wilson 2013: 13–18.

[54] The early archaeological history of the theatre of Dionysos on the slope of the Acropolis is traced, in part conjecturally, by Wiles 1997: 41–67; see the summary in Rabinowitz 2008: 20–32; for the

48   Tragedy, Cult and Ritual

and tragedies were moved from the choral space or *orkhḗstra* north-east of the agora to the south of the Acropolis; the wooden platforms that surrounded the orchestra are said in an anecdote to have collapsed.[55]

The inclusion of performances by tragic choruses in the sanctuary of Dionysos is therefore likely to have been secondary. Let us re-read the entry in the famous chronicle of the Parian Marble (from the late third century) that mentions among other political and poetical events the intervention of the poet Thespis; the founding act of the first tragic poet is described here in the terms later made familiar by Aristophanes' comedies. As we have seen above, the Parian Marble presents Thespis as the first poet to have interacted (probably; there is a lacuna in the text here) with the chorus. He is also said to be the first poet to have 'taught' a play in the city; the Greek expression is *drama en ástei*, which is the same designation used by Thucydides for the Great Dionysia. It is striking, however, that there is no explicit mention of Dionysos himself. Thespis' intervention is mentioned in connection with a competition whose prize was the already-mentioned goat, and is dated by the context of the inscription to around 530 BCE (synchronous with Peisistratus' tyranny); this date is confirmed by a gloss qualifying Thespis (probably) as *tragoidopoiós*, that is, a poet of tragedies.[56]

Moreover, from Plato to the Byzantine *Suda* through Plutarch and Diogenes Laertius, none of the testimonies that mention Thespis as legendary inventor of tragedy attaches the shared performance of poet and chorus explicitly to Dionysos and his cult. The only exception is an epigram of Dioscorides that attributes to Thespis the creation of 'tragic song' for a chorus led by Bacchus for the prize of a goat (!) and a basket of Attic figs. The *Suda*'s biographical notice for Thespis indicates that he was the first to recite tragedies (facing the chorus) with his face painted with

---

organization of the scenic space, see Padel 1990: 341–54. According to Sourvinou-Inwood 2003: 160–1 and 142–5, the tent-scene was reprised in the ritual of the *xénismos* of Dionysos on the agora, in which the altar (whose controversial presence is attested by a mention in the *Etymologicum Magnum*, 743, 35 Gaisford) corresponded to an *eskhára* (clearly visible on the ritual scene depicted on the Pronomos vase).

[55] Cf. Photius *s.v. orkhḗstra* (O 544 Theodoridis) for the orchestra in the agora before it was located in the semi-circle of the theatre for the chorus's song and dance; see also *ibid. s.v. íkria* (I 96 Theodoridis) for the platforms in the agora for the Dionysiac competition before they were transferred to the theatre of Dionysos; for this transferal, see Kolb 1979: 507–15; for the shape of the orchestra, cf. Ley 2007: x–xv.

[56] *Marmor Parium FGrHist*. 239 A 43 = Thespis test. 2 Snell: DID D 3 = Thespis test. 3 Snell (cf. n. 32 in Chapter 1). In preference to Thespis, a legendary figure if ever there was one, Sourvinou-Inwood 2003: 168–70 attributes a greater role to Lasus of Hermione (see her references to n. 117). On Thespis, cf. n. 32 in Chapter 1, as well as Arist. *Rhet*. 3 1403b 21–4 for the first tragic poets in general.

Attic Tragedy and the Cult of Dionysos 49

white lead; no mention is made of the 'god-mask' that would represent to Dionysos. It is worth noting that the character of Socrates in Plato's *Minos* states that tragedy is an extremely ancient poetic form, and that it was invented neither by Thespis nor Phrynicus, but that rather by 'this city', that is, Athens.[57]

By contrast, all these biographical testimonies, as also the Hellenistic epigram, make regular mention of the chorus's songs and dances. And in this biographizing tradition we might cite a line that Aristophanes put in Aeschylus' mouth in which the poet boasted that he had created the dance figures for the chorus whose choreography he also took upon himself. The same tradition ascribes to the voice of the tragic poet and singer Phrynichus a choral line likening the production of rhythmical dance figures (*skhḗmata, órkhēsis*) to the rousing of waves by a night storm. As for Sophocles, he was still a boy when, having completed his musical education, he was selected to dance to the accompaniment of the lyre naked and anointed with oil for the ritual celebration of Athens' victory at Salamis.[58]

None of the above deducts from the ritual or cultic nature of tragic performance. In fact, the *mousikòs agṓn* comprising dithyrambs, tragedies and comedies was introduced by a large-scale procession as cultic in character as any other *pompḗ*. A recent reconstruction taking its moves from sources as heterogeneous as they are fragmentary allows us to imagine for the fifth century the following scenario, subdivided into three stages.

On the day preceding the first musical contest, the statue of the god was removed from the sanctuary of Dionysos Eleuthereus at the foot of the Acropolis. Pausanias states that the sanctuary's enclosure around the space of the theatre had two small temples: one consecrated to the statue of Dionysos Eleuthereus proper, the other sheltering the chryselephantine statue made by Alcamenes, who was both pupil and rival of Phidias. We have therefore on the one hand an archaic temple with the *xoanon* of the god and on the other a classical temple decorated with panels depicting various episodes from Dionysos' divine biography: the return of drunken Hephaestus; a representation of the heroes Pentheus and Lycurgus

---

[57] Plato, *Minos* 321a = Thespis test. 13 Snell, *Suda, sv.v. Théspis* (*Th* 282 Adler) = Thespis test. 1 Snell (on the question of the tragic mask, see n. 74 in this chapter), Plut. *Sol.* 29, 6 = Thespis test. 17 Snell, Diog. Laert. 3, 56 = Thespis test. 7 Snell; for dance, see also Athen. 1, 22a = Thespis test. 11 Snell; cf. *Anth. Pal.* 7, 410 = Thespis test. 8a Snell; commentary on these testimonies can be found in Pickard-Cambridge 1968: 130–2 and 250–1.

[58] Athen. 1, 21df = Cham. fr. 41 Wehrli = Ar. Fr. 696, 1 K.-A. = Aesch. test. 103 Radt (cf. n. 76 in this chapter); Plut. *Quest. Conv.* 732f = Phrynicus 3 test. 13 Snell; for Sophocles, cf. Athenaeus 1.20ef = Soph. test. 23 Radt. Other testimonies to the same effect can be found in Pickard-Cambridge 1968: 90–1, 291, 303–304.

pursuing the Maenads and thus resisting the introduction of the cult of the god at Thebes and in Thrace respectively; and the famous episode of Dionysos' rape of the sleeping Ariadne as Theseus sailed away from Naxos.[59] This collection of images illustrated equally well some founding myths of Dionysos' cult and the god's relation with Athens through Theseus, the founding hero of the democratic city; this iconography tended to place Dionysos at the heart of the city. The god's biography, then, has its place on the Acropolis in close proximity to the sanctuaries dedicated to Athens' two tutelary gods, Athena and Poseidon.

At this point the ancient statue of the god was transported to its little temple in the Academy, near Colonus, probably on the route leading from Eleutherae to Boeotia. Again in Pausanias we find mention of this sanctuary and the report that the statue of Dionysos Eleuthereus was led there each year at a fixed date, probably on the evening of the eighth or ninth of the month of Elaphebolion.[60] After the statue's removal and the sacrifice that followed, some late inscriptions dating from the second century BCE suggest that Dionysos was brought back 'from the hearth' (*eisḗgagon apò tês eskháras*) into the theatre by torchlight; they add that a bull was sacrificed in honour of the god. Does this mean that the hearth mentioned by the inscriptions was opposite the temple of Dionysos at the Academy? It might be preferable to identify this hearth with that located to the north-west of the Agora, by the Altar of the Twelve Gods. It was there that the goat sacrifice took place and above all the *xénismos*, that is to say, the ritual reception of Dionysos as he re-entered the city walls. As to the wine that Herodes Atticus is said to have served to the citizens and foreigners assembled in the Kerameikos, this was consumed on mats covered with ivy leaves at the moment when Dionysos' statue was carried to the Academy. It is not impossible that this report dating from Roman times referred to a later incarnation of the *theoxenia* organized to celebrate Dionysos' return to the city.[61]

Then the *pompḗ* mentioned by Euegoros' law (cited by Demosthenes) as well as many epigraphic documents led Dionysos' statue back to its sanctuary at the theatre so that the god might view the musical performances that

---

[59] Paus. 1, 20, 3; see the complex reconstruction of the procession's itinerary set out by Sourvinou-Inwood 2003: 67–99, with prudent remarks in Spineto 2005: 217–22, and the doubts expressed by the often-sceptical Parker 2005: 317–19; the evidence is carefully collected and analyzed in Pickard-Cambridge 1968: 59–64.

[60] Paus. 1, 19, 3; for the probable location of this *náos* of Dionysos Eleuthereus, see the discussion in Vanden Broeck-Parant 2015.

[61] This is the hypothesis developed by Sourvinou-Inwood 2003: 91–8, who posits that Pindar's dithyramb (fr. 75 Snell-Maehler) evoking Athens' Twelve Gods was composed for this ritual occasion; cf. Philostr. *VS* 549.

were to be offered to him. Taking part in the procession were metics carrying wine vessels, citizens carrying wineskins and metics and women carrying hydrias – that is, the necessary implements for the mixing of wine; at the tail end of the procession were the *choregoi* and the *canephoroi* ('basket bearers'). Second in importance only to the Panathenaic procession, this great procession culminated in a sacrifice in the sanctuary of Dionysos that must at one time have been performed by ephebes. Formally this *pompḗ* may have resembled the phallic processions of the Rural Dionysia mentioned by Dikaiopolis in Aristophanes' *Acharnians*;[62] in such case, it may have complemented the *kȏmos*, the procession of intoxicated banqueters as they made their way from the symposion in the throes of Dionysiac joy. The sacrifice itself took place inside the sanctuary, as we know from an inscription which adds that the victim was a bullock 'worthy of the god', echoing the anonymous cultic poem that addresses Dionysos as *áxie taûre*, 'worthy of a bullock'.[63]

2.4.3 Foundation Myths: The Arrival of Dionysos

Regardless of the details of this partly speculative reconstruction, there is little doubt that this ritual scenario reenacts Dionysos' original introduction to Athens. This ritual introduction coincides with the aetiological story recounted (once again) by Pausanias; on descending the Panathenaic Road, before reaching the agora, Pausanias pauses in front of the area occupied in the fifth century by the home of the rich citizen Poulytion; this wealthy home had been the setting in 415 BCE of the famous profanation of the Eleusinian Mysteries, in which the young Alcibiades had been implicated. After the probable expropriation of the house, the space was consecrated to Dionysos, specifically to an incarnation of Dionysos as patron of danced poetry, as indicated by the epiclesis Melpomenos given to him by analogy with Apollo Mousegetes. Flanking him were statues of Athena Paionia, of Dionysos' father Zeus, the Muses and their mother Mnemosyne, Apollo and a *daímōn* belonging to Dionysos' entourage whose face only was depicted; this divine figure, whose name was Acratos, may have represented unmixed wine. Close to this sanctuary associating Dionysos to the gods and goddesses of the musical arts stood a building decorated with terracotta statues depicting (among others) the

---

[62] Ar. *Ach.* 247–79; Dem. *Meid.* 9–10; cf. *Suda s.v. askophoreîn* (*a* 4177 Adler). The symbolic function of phallic processions is re-examined by Parker 2005: 317–23; see also Spineto 2005: 228–30. There is very little evidence on the early stages of development of the Great Dionysia, especially under Peisistratus and his sons: cf. also Spineto 2005: 209–17.
[63] *IG* II², 1006, 12; cf. also 1008, 14 and 1011, 11; *carm. pop.* fr. 871 Page (cf. Detienne 1986: 85–7).

legendary autochthonous king of Athens Amphictyon. According to the aetiological account, before the reign of Erichthonios-Erechtheus this autochthonous king was known to have hosted at his table in Athens various divinities including Dionysos; it is thought that it was from Dionysos that Amphictyon had learned the art of mixing wine in what must have been an original *theoxenia*.[64] The sharing of the Dionysos' gift becomes a means of civilized conviviality by enabling the consumption of wine without the extreme intoxication caused by its use unmixed.[65]

Also represented in this arrangement of terracotta statues was Pegasos of Eleutherae, to whom sources attribute the introduction of the god to the Athenians. In the usual aetiological perspective of Greek legendary biography, this Pegasus (as we learn from Pausanias) was aided in the introduction of the god by the Delphic oracle, which had evoked the god's Athenian 'sojourn' (*epidēmía*) in Icarios' day. A scholion on the phallophoria dramatized at the beginning of Aristophanes' *Acharnians* tells us that Pegasos of Eleutherae (a city in Boeotia) had seized the statue of Dionysos to take it to Attica. When the Athenians refused to pay him due honour, the wrathful god struck down their men with an illness affecting their genitals. The oracles proclaimed that the only thing that could return them their virility was to pay honour to Dionysos, and this was how the Athenian custom had started of offering phalluses to this god of reproductive generation. A different aetiological myth relates that Demeter and Dionysos visited Athens during the reign of Pandion, successor to Erichthonios-Erechtheus. While Demeter was received at Eleusis by Celeus, Dionysos was welcomed by Icarios; out of gratitude the god gifted the hero a vine branch and taught him how to produce wine. What happened next is well known; wishing to share the god's gifts, Icarios offered some wine to his shepherds, who drank it unmixed, became intoxicated and, believing themselves to have been poisoned, killed Icarios. On discovering her father's body, the young Erigone hanged herself and the god struck down the young women of the region with a plague of hanging that lasted until the institution of the Aiôra, the ritual of the 'swing'. This ritual was probably inserted into the celebration of the Anthesteria and involved the singing of melic songs by women.[66]

---

[64] Paus. 1, 2, 5; cf. Detienne 1986: 50–4; see also, for the role of Amphictyon in welcoming Dionysos, Athen. 2, 38cd, who cites the Atthidographer Philochorus, *FGrHist* 328 F 5b. The sacrilegious display of the mysteries that marked the beginning of the Sicilian expedition is duly mentioned by Thuc. 6, 28, 2.

[65] Dionysos' travels are discussed in a lively and pointed manner by Detienne 1986: 69–88; for the mixing of wine and its civilizing effects, see especially Lissarrague 1987: 7–22.

[66] *Sch. ad* Ar. *Ach.* 243 (Ib. pp. 42–3 Wilson) on the one count; Ps.-Apollod. *Bibl.* 3, 14, 7; Athen. 14, 618ef (referring to Arist. fr. 515 Rose) and so on, on the other count. For the Aiora and the

Attic Tragedy and the Cult of Dionysos 53

These two foundational myths converge into parallel scenarios: on the one hand the drama of the male adult citizens deprived of their descendance, and on the other that of the young women who do not reach marriage. Pausanias brings together the two protagonists of these stories, Pegasos and Icarios, in one place under the aegis of the god of arousal and intoxication, with their respective power of reproductive generation and social exchange when each of the states of ecstasy is mastered.

Even though the allusion is neither to Pegasos nor to Icarios, already in the fourth century when Demosthenes assumed a *choregía* he evoked the oracles enjoining the Erechtheids to pay attention to Bacchos and honour him in his guise as Bromios; next to Zeus, Heracles, Apollo, Artemis and Leto, he was the recipient of kraters of wine, garlands and choral dances. And Demosthenes added to the oracle's prescription the ritual rules of the Dionysia for choral performances and songs (*khoroí* and *húmnoi*) addressed to the god. The biographical tradition discussed above states that Thespis hailed from the Attic deme of Icaria or Icarion.[67] Though their content is not made explicit, song and music are key attributes of the Athenian Dionysos worshipped at the Great Dionysia. If in satyr play the chorus is always made up of satyrs whose masculinity is emphasized by the wearing of a prosthetic phallus, in tragedy the choral group is often made up of women who, as we will see, also intervene forcefully as protagonists of the action; they are close to the heroines who often react to their tragic aporia by committing suicide, sometimes by hanging (Jocasta, Phaedra, Antigone).[68] In observance of the gendered distribution of roles, masculine erection on the one hand and feminine hanging on the other evoke the two aetiological stories of the Great Dionysia.

Dionysos Eleuthereus, then, is the god who is reintroduced each year ritually and symbolically at the heart of the city from the place of liminality that is Eleutherae, on the mountainous border between Attica and Boeotia. But the epiclesis of the god honoured at his sanctuary during the Great Dionysia tells us also that he is the liberator, just as he is Lysios in other circumstances; and he is still, without doubt, the god who carries in his denomination the statute of freedom that applies pre-eminently to the Athenian citizen.[69]

Anthesteria, cf. Parker 2005: 301–2; the deme of Icarion certainly had a temple to Dionysos: cf. Parker 1996: 74.
[67] Dem. *Meid.* 21, 51–3; *Suda s.v. Thespis* (*Th* 282 Adler) = Thespis test. 1 Snell.
[68] The manner of suicide of tragic heroines is the subject of a fine study by Loraux 1985: 38–58.
[69] For the political aspects of the staging of tragedies at the Great Dionysia in an 'interplay between norm and transgression', cf. Goldhill 1990: 126–9; see also the relevant chapter in Saïd 1998 and the essay by Vidal-Naquet 2001.

2.4.4 Dionysiac Rituality: Tragedy and the Mask

We have seen that the spatio-temporal context of tragedy and the aetiological accounts of the celebration of the Great Dionysia place the musical competitions at the heart of the festival dedicated to Dionysos Eleuthereus. These musical events arise from religious practice, in particular the ritual practices connected with choral performance.

Let us remind ourselves once more that the final act of the Great Dionysia consisted in an assembly that – exceptionally – took place in the theatre of Dionysos. On the day following the celebration of Zeus known as the 'Pandia' on either the seventeenth or the twenty-first of Elaphebolion, the assembly was the occasion for reviewing the conduct of the Dionysiac festival (*heortḗ*) under the leadership of the chief archon (later termed 'eponymous archon') and for airing any complaints by wronged parties. One such wronged party was Demosthenes, who in his famous oration against Meidias (mentioned above) denounced the violence he had suffered at the hands of this citizen on the occasion of his *choregia* and then during the festival itself; he cites the law, probably dating from the end of the fifth century, prescribing that this assembly must take place *en Dionúsou*, in the 'home of Dionysos'.[70] The agenda for this special assembly highlights the religious character of the Great Dionysia and its poetical and musical contests. Public oversight was exercised in the first instance over the matter of the *hierá*, that is to say, the festival's ritual practices; following that, complaints were heard regarding any irregularities observed during the conduct of the Dionysia. The cultic celebration was considered to be the ensemble of musical contests together with the procession.[71]

On the other hand the political nature of this cultic celebration is evidenced by four elements highlighted in a seminal study by Simon Goldhill:[72] the jury, which from 468 onwards was made up of the ten *strategoi* and whose duties included the pouring of libations to the gods before the musical contests; the official presentation of the tributes paid by the cities under Athens' dominion; the public reading of the names of all the citizens who had earned an honour from the state together with the

---

[70] Dem. *Meid.* 8–9; see the commentary in Pickard-Cambridge 1968: 66, 68–70.
[71] The opening of the dramatic festival was marked, probably on the eighth day of Elaphebolion, by a preliminary ceremony in which the poets, actors and choreuts were presented; after its construction by Pericles in 444, the Odeon, which abutted onto the theatre, was the venue of this presentation; cf. Pickard-Cambridge 1968: 67–8.
[72] For the sources (chief among them Aristophanes' *Acharnians* 641–51) and a pertinent commentary, see Goldhill 1990: 100–106.

listing of these honours; finally, the presentation of the children of citizens and solders who had died in defence of Athens' interests. As usual in ancient Greece, the religious act is also a political act.

It is possible to argue that the ritual relation of the tragic competition to the cult of Dionysos Eleuthereus was in some sense secondary. Satyr plays, with their chorus of satyrs and their plots staging Dionysos as god of drunkenness and male sexuality, have only a loose relation to tragedy; and the comic competitions were probably introduced as late as 486, that is, fifty-odd years after the institution of the tragic competitions.[73] On the other hand, though this does not apply to the fifty-strong dithyrambic choruses, the wearing of masks has long been considered a fundamental marker of Dionysiac rituality in Attic tragedy and comedy. It is once again the testimonia for Thespis' life that transform the function of the tragic mask into a founding gesture. As we have seen, Thespis is said to have been the first to smear his face (*prósopon*) with white lead to 'sing tragedy'; after that he shaded his face with purslane, and eventually he introduced the use of masks (*prosopeîa*) made of linen fabric.[74]

If we leave aside the biographizing narrative that harks back to Aristotle' school, history indicates that the purpose of the tragic mask is not to represent (as current anthropological theory would have it) but rather to hide, to mask the civic identity of its wearer without representing a particular character, whether male or female. The tragic mask doubtless signals the ritual character of the play without pointing to the scenic identity of its wearer. Aristotle is the only ancient source to mention the comic mask (*prósopon*); he tells us that its origins are unknown, and that it is simply ugly and distorted but does not give an indication of emotion. According to Aristotle, just as the characters of comedy are base, so are its masks ugly, and the iconography confirms this. The purpose of the mask is therefore simply to indicate to the audience which kind of play they are watching, and its frontality belongs to ritualized representation. It signals the poetic genre to which the iambic trimeters and choral songs belong in their frontal performance. The tragic mask helps carry the actor's voice, amplifying its tone and volume (as stated by ancient theory) and doubtlessly highlighting the rituality of the singers' vocal scansion. From an enunciative perspective, the mask interposes a distance between the dramatic representation and the audience, which is confronted directly with the dramatic action. This

---

[73] For the history of the satyr play, see Voelke 2001: 16–21.
[74] *Suda s.v. Thespis* (*Th* 282) Adler = Thespis test. 1 Snell (cf. n. 54 in this chapter); see also Hor. *Ars P.* 275–7 = Thespis test. 14 Snell; on the iconography of the tragic mask, cf. Wiles 2007: 15–43. White lead was employed in classical Athens as a cosmetic: Ar. *Eccl.* 878, 929 and so on.

distance on the enunciative level allows the actors on the scene to speak without intermediary and the singers in the chorus to comment on the heroes' words, unlike in epic, where these are bracketed by narrative and ascribed to the Muse or assumed by the first-person voice of the poet.[75]

On the other hand it has been amply demonstrated that the ritual use of masks is not the prerogative of Dionysiac cultic activities. Dionysos Eleuthereus is not the god of the Other (in opposition to the Self) or of 'absolute alterity', as is too often stated in line with Structuralist paradigms. Nor is he the god of illusion and therefore of 'tragic fiction', since the heroic action being represented often has a ritual outcome *hic et nunc*. Dionysos is not the 'mask-god' whose representation some scholars have seen in the vases of the Lenaia; the effigy of the god represented by his face must not be confused with a mask, least of all with the 'non-representational' mask of tragedy.[76]

Whatever cultic function can be attributed to the mask or make-up worn by the actors and choreuts of classical tragedy, its function lies in the necessity to cover the actor's face and lend to his verbal expression a ritual dimension. The same principle applies to costume. Athenaeus attributes its invention to Aeschylus and declares that the costumes' elaboration and majesty evoked the dress of the hierophants and torch-bearers of the Eleusinian Mysteries. Citing Aristotle's pupil Chamaeleon, Athenaeus adds that Aeschylus also invented figures of dance (*skhḗmata orkhēstiká*) for the chorus. We might add to this catalogue of ritual dramatic accoutrements the wearing of buskins (*kóthornoi*).[77]

This aesthetical apparatus of mask, costume and rhythmical gestures corresponding to vocal and verbal tempo contributes to the ritualization of the drama; the same goes for the metrical diction – both in the spoken parts and the sung ones, the solo parts and the choral ones – and the use of poetic forms that are often ritual (paean, hymn, *threnos*, *humenaion* and so on).[78]

---

[75] Cf. Ar. *Poet.* 5, 1449a 35–7 and b 4–5; see also Gell. 5, 7: referred to as *persona*, the mask has the function of projecting the actor's voice; for the iconography, cf. Pickard-Cambridge 1968: 191–6. Defended in particular by Vernant (and Vidal-Naquet 1986: 22–43) in relation to Dionysiac possession, the theory according to which the tragic mask allows the actor to embody the character he is playing on the scene is contradicted by the testimonies on its use in tragedy and by enunciative approaches to tragic diction: cf. Calame 2000b: 151–63 (*contra*: Wiles 2007: 41–3 and 175–9).

[76] *Pace* Frontisi-Ducroux 1991: 203–30. On Dionysos as god of 'alterity' and tragic fiction, see Vernant and Vidal-Naquet 1986: 17–24 and 254–9.

[77] Athen. 1, 21 de = Aesch. test. 103 Radt (cf. Chamael. Fr. 4 Wehrli and n. 58 in this chapter); textual and iconographic attestations of the tragic actors' costumes can be found in Pickard-Cambridge 1968: 197–204, where they are the object of his customarily prudent commentary.

[78] It is once again to Pickard-Cambridge 1968: 156–76 that we owe the painstaking collection of testimonies on actors' and choreuts' diction and gesture.

Tragic Ritualities

It follows that Attic tragedy is much more than a 'performative art'. Attic tragedy is the poetic, vocal, musical and choreographic dramatization of episodes from the Panhellenic or Athenian heroic past.

2.5 Tragic Ritualities

Is tragedy ritual? By this stage the answer should come without the slightest hesitation. The development of tragedy as a poetic genre, the spatial context of its performance and indeed the various material and aesthetical dimensions dependent on holding a dramatic event as part of religious worship – all these elements point towards the ritual valence of tragedy.

2.5.1 Oudèn Pròs Tòn Diónuson?

What is less apparent is the tragic contests' connection to Dionysos and his worship as Liberator god at the sanctuary that also housed the theatre. *Oudèn pròs tòn Diónuson*; 'Nothing to do with Dionysos?' This question has become a *Leitmotiv* in anglophone scholarship.[79] 'What's in it for Dionysos?' or 'What does this have to do with Dionysos?' is in fact the double question that the ancients themselves asked about dithyramb even before tragedy.[80] The Late Antique commentator who picks up this proverbial expression explains it somewhat enigmatically as dithyramb's reorientation from a focus on subject matter relating to the divine figure of Dionysos to the heroic legend of the two Ajaxes and the Centaurs. The iambic poet Archilochus could boast of knowing how to intone the dithyramb, 'the lovely song of lord Dionysus, my mind thunderstruck by wine', but the extant dithyrambs have practically nothing to do with Dionysos either in terms of narrative content or of the ritual circumstance of their performance.[81]

---

[79] The expression was originally used as the title of a collected volume edited by Winkler and Zeitlin 1990; see, for example, the debate on the use of this expression between Friedrich 1996 and Seaford 1996; see also Bierl 1991: 4–13.

[80] If Plutarch, *Tabletalk* 1, 615a, and *Suda s.v. oudèn pros tòn Diónuson* (O 895 Adler) pose the question in relation to tragedy (notably Phyrinicus' and Aeschylus' tragedy), Zenobius 5, 40 (= *Dith*. test. 65 Ieranò) suggests that this rhetorical question was asked about the content of dithyramb; see Pickard-Cambridge 1962: 1–3 and 124–6; Kowalzig and Wilson 2013: 7–13; and my own contribution to the debate in Calame 2013c.

[81] Archil. Fr. 120 West; in a study of the generic norms and ritual contexts of Bacchylides' and Pindar's dithyrambs (Calame 2013c), I noted the variety of narrative subjects covered by the two poets' composition and the strong enunciative and cultic relation with Dionysos in the songs of Pindar alone. Cf. Chapter 7.1.

Take for instance Bacchylides' famous *Dithyramb* 17. This choral poem is entirely devoted to the narrative of the meeting between Theseus and Minos on the Cretan sea, the trial that the king of Cnossos assigns to the Athenian hero and the remarkable account of the hero's re-emergence from the depths of the sea. Its narrative style is 'mixed' in that, like epic, it includes both third-person narrative and dialogue. Above all, in the closing transition from 'narrative' to 'dialogue' it reveals itself as an explicit offering to Delian Apollo (Dionysos' great musical rival) for a choral performance that will certainly have taken place at the Delia festival.[82] Something similar can be said for the extant (complete) tragedies. Euripides' *Bacchae* is in this regard the great exception, and the many recent attempts to find in each tragedy a link to the figure of Dionysos and his cult, though not futile, are nevertheless problematic. Out of ninety tragedies attributed to Aeschylus by ancient tradition only roughly one tenth had a plot that related in some way to Dionysos.[83]

Relevant to this question is the origin that Aristotle assigns to tragedy in his *Poetics*, in a passage whose language is as obscure as that he uses to define the much-investigated subject of tragic *catharsis*. Beginning as improvisation, tragedy is said by Aristotle to have been born from 'those who initiate' (*exárkhontes*) the dithyramb, whereas comedy originated among those who initiated phallic songs. The technical term *exárkhein* is the same one we have seen employed precisely in relation to dithyramb in the verses of Archilochus just cited. It undoubtedly refers to the singer who gives the intonation at the beginning of a choral song. The expression 'to initiate (the song)' alludes therefore to the poet as he takes on the role of chorus leader.[84] The *Suda* uses similar terminology in attributing to the 'lyric' poet Arion of Methymna (*floruit* 627/4) the invention of the 'tragic mode' (*tragikòs trópos*). The Lesbian poet is said to have been the first to institute a chorus (*khoròn stêsai*) and sing a dithyramb while also giving a title to his choral song. He is also said to have been responsible for the introduction of satyrs who spoke lines. These biographical reports on

---

[82] For the contrast with the Apolline poetic form of the pean, see my analysis of Bacchylides' *Dithyramb* 17 in Calame 2009c (referring to an earlier study of this poem) and Fearn 2013: 135:52.
[83] For the links between the tragedies and satyr plays and the figure of Dionysos, see, for instance, the balanced contribution by Easterling 1997 (esp. 45–7); a good summary of the debate can be found in Bierl 1991: 5–17 (for the role of Dionysos in tragic performance, see 111–71); statistics can be found in Scullion 2002: 110–11.
[84] Arist. *Poet.* 4, 1449a 9–15; on the meaning of *exárkhein* in this much-discussed passage, see Stoessl 1987: 69–72, who refers the expression *hoi exárkhontes tòn dithúrambon* to an ancient form of song in which the chorus leader's singing was punctuated by interventions on the part of the chorus; for modern theories on the origin of Attic tragedy built on this statement of Aristotle's, see Lesky 1972: 21–7 and 38–40 as well as the sensible remarks in Rodighiero 2013: 89–92; see also Chapter 1.3.1 and Chapter 7.1.

Tragic Ritualities 59

a poet who was celebrated as a founding hero confirm dithyramb's nature as both narrative and choral, similarly to the 'tragic mode'; they also confirm that the first tragic poets took on the role of singers.[85]

The implicitly narrative dimension that Aristotle assigns to tragedy is evidenced also in the passage of the *Poetics* preceding the account of the origin of the genre. After the appearance of tragedy and comedy, some iambic poets became *komoidopoioí* while some epic poets became *tragoidodidáskaloi*; 'fashioning' (*poieîn*) and 'teaching' (*didáskein*) reflect the emic designations employed by Aristophanes. This does not mean, however, that tragedy derives directly form Homeric poetry. Aristotle recognizes that the rhythmic form of the trochaic tetrameter, which is found in some monologues, implies a comic diction that had (like comedy?) a 'satyric' origin; it was only with the introduction of the iambic trimeter, with its rhythm akin to that of spoken language, that tragedy acquired its serious tone.[86] In conclusion, while this passage of Aristotle does not seem entirely coherent and has given rise to a predictable amount of controversy, it suggests that tragedy arose at the confluence of three pre-existing genres; it owed to dithyramb its choral form, to Homeric poetry its narrative dimension and to satyr play a (Dionysiac) comic tone that gradually evolved towards a form of grandeur.

In none of these three passages, no more than in the biographical notices on Thespis, are Dionysos and his cult mentioned explicitly.

2.5.2 Against Dionysiac Essentialism

So there is not a Dionysiac essence of Attic tragedy.[87] It is time to abandon this controversy, in which too often three distinct problems have been conflated: the question of the connection between the known tragedies and Dionysos and his cult; the problem of the ritual aspects of tragedy, given that it was performed competitively in a theatre within a sanctuary consecrated to Dionysos; and the difficult question of the consonances between

---

[85] Cf. *Suda s.v. Aríon* (A 3886 Adler); *éxarchos* in the sense of chorus leader is found in Dem. 18, 260; cf. D'Alessio 2013: 113–18.
[86] Arist. *Poet.* 4, 1449a 2–8 and 15–28; the philological and hermeneutic controversies surrounding these two passages are summarized and discussed by Scullion 2002: 102–10, who rightly concludes that 'Dionysiac cult is relevant to tragedy merely as point of origin'; for the literal interpretation of the passage, see Dupont-Roc and Lallot 1980: 169–74; see also Chapter 7.1.
[87] This is the conclusion of the hypercritical examination of the question in Scullion 2002: 125. I hardly dare mention the essay by Bollack 2005: 102–10, who, in his quest for a Dionysiac essence, proposes a reading of Euripides' *Bacchae* that denies the 'alterity' of the god to affirm instead his creation by Zeus as an 'unsurpassable act of alterity and alteration'.

the tragic plays and particular political institutions, that is, those of Athenian democracy, with its distinct ideology.

Both from the point of view of its subject matter and from that of its ritual modes of performance, classical Attic tragedy has a merely incidental connection with the world of Dionysos. Ritual within tragedy and tragedy as ritual both present a certain autonomy vis-à-vis the cultic occasion in which the tragic performance takes place. It remains the case that this poetical and musical performance has a strong ritual and religious character, and for this reason it falls squarely within the scope of anthropological and ethnopoetical approaches.

Attic tragedy belongs to a ritual scenario that is shared with all cultic celebrations in Greek cities in general. There is a procession punctuated by songs, with the participation of various apparelled elements of the body politic. There is the elaborate sacrifice followed by a ritual meal involving male and female representative of these different groups. There are athletic competitions displaying the physical and moral qualities of the aristocratic citizens. There are musical contests with sung and danced performances that are offered to the deity as musical offerings.[88] In the Great Dionysia the musical function typical of all significant cultic celebrations seems to be become developed to an extreme, and this manifests not only in the tragic competitions but also in the dithyrambic and comic contests. The dithyrambic contest, with its organization according to the ten Cleisthenic tribes, is certainly related to the development of democratic structures and the corresponding increase in the number of citizens and their children. The comic contests should probably be related to the cult of Dionysos and the critical debate arising from the sharing of political power and the conduct of democracy. Doubtlessly the ironical mocking of Dionysos himself in Aristophanes' *Frogs* is only possible in a context in which it is ritualized and couched in the forms of blame poetry (in contrast with tragedy, which rather belongs to the forms of heroic praise poetry).

When we add the fact that the musical competitions themselves were introduced by a purificatory sacrifice of piglets and by libations carried out by the ten strategoi who in classical times judged the competitions as representatives of each of the ten Cleisthenic tribes, the scenario of the Great Dionysia begins to evoke also, in general terms, that of the ritual banquet such as it is described, for instance, by Xenophanes. Xenophanes' elegy details the purification of the banquet hall and the implements

---

[88] In my 1992 study I attempted to present the morphology of cultic celebration in Greece (Calame 1992, with bibliography).

utilized for the ritual consumption of wine, the ritual offering on an altar, libations, songs of praise and decorous stories of gods and men (celebrating the memory of the deeds of heroes and omitting to mention the transgressive battles of Giants and Centaurs); all this will have led to the *kômos* at the end of the *symposion*.[89]

2.6 Cultic Dramatizations

But the Great Dionysia are not the only festivals relevant to the question of tragic rituality. We must mention another cultic celebration dedicated to Dionysos in an Athenian sanctuary that has not yet been located but is thought to have been near the Agora. The Athenian Dionysia at the Lénaion consisted of a procession, a sacrifice and a musical contest mentioned in Aristophanes' *Acharnians* as *ho epì Lenaoíoi agón* (l. 504), 'the contest at the Lenaion'. We know from the law of Euagoros that *tragoidoí* and *komoidoí* competed; each poet presented only two tragedies, and there were no satyr plays.[90] This cult was organized by the Archon Basileus in the month of Gamelion, that is, in the depths of winter, and it must have related to the worship of Dionysos at Eleusis, for it featured the intervention of an Eleusinian priest. This priest invoked the god with his Eleusinian name of Iakkhos. The name of the festival and of the sanctuary must have derived from the epiclesis of the god who was worshipped there. Etymologically, the term must be connected rather to the Maenads, who are *lênai*, than to the wine press, *lenós*. The Lenai are represented in a rich series of images dating from the beginning of the fifth century depicting the ritual manipulation of wine around an effigy of Dionysos interpreted (wrongly) as a mask.[91]

The Rural Dionysia, too, deserve mention. This festival was celebrated in various Attic demes in midwinter; we find it attested at the Piraeus, at Eleusis and in the deme of Acharnae. Our main source for the Dionysia 'in the fields' (*kat'agroús*) is the phallic song that opens Aristophanes' *Acharnians*, a privileged source for Attic dramatic representations.[92] Here

---

[89] Cf. Pickard-Cambridge 1968: 67; Xenoph. fr. 1 Gentili-Prato.
[90] See especially Arist. *Ach.* 504–6 and 1154–5 (cf. l. 202), as well as Arist. [*Ath. Pol.*] 57, 1 and Euagoros' law cited by Dem. *Meid.* 10; other attestations are listed with commentary by Pickard-Cambridge 1968: 25–42 and 72–3; see also Parker 2005: 316–17 and 474 and Spineto 2005: 125–83. For dramatic representations outside Athens, particularly in the Attic demes and in the Sicilian cities, see the useful summary in Csapo and Wilson 2015.
[91] Cf. Frontisi-Ducroux 1991: 67–70, with the commentary by Parker 2005: 306–12.
[92] Ar. *Ach.* 242–79; further sources can be found once again in Pickard-Cambridge 1968: 42–54; see also Parker 2005: 316–17 and 467, as well as Spineto 2005: 327–50 (celebration of agricultural fertility and peace). The performative dimension of this phallic song is well discussed by Bierl 2001: 350–61.

wine and sex go together. In addition to the phallophoria procession and the obligatory sacrifices, tragic performances sponsored by choregoi are attested at Piraeus, where Socrates is said to have gone to view plays of Euripides;[93] tragic performances are also mentioned for the deme of Icarion, named after the hero who introduced Dionysos' wine to Attica according to the alternative foundation myth alluded to above; and the deme of Thoricos also had a theatre (whose steps are still visible) dating to the middle of the sixth century and abutting a small temple of Dionysos. All these are cultic celebrations of Dionysos that took place in the rural centres of Attica. Finally, mention must be made of the 116 sites spanning the whole of the Greek world from Magna Graecia to the Black Sea where we see traces of the performance of tragic plays in the fifth and fourth centuries. There is no reason to think that the ritualized performance of tragedies in all these sites was necessarily related to the cult of Dionysos. In Sicily, for instance, it was connected to Demeter, Aphrodite or Apollo, who were honoured with narrative and musical tragic dramas.[94]

On the other hand, in another famous passage of the *Poetics*, Aristotle himself compares Homer not just to Sophocles but also to Aristophanes. The three poets are said to be *mimetaí*, authors of representations inasmuch as they represent 'people who do and act' (*práttontas kaì drôntas*); hence tragedy and comedy's designation as *drámata*; hence also the requirement for the plots (*mûthoi*) of tragedy to have a 'dramatic' form.[95] This qualification brings up the question of tragic *mimesis* as we framed it at the beginning of the present chapter, with the distinction in narrative modes introduced by Plato precisely in relation to poetry and *mimesis*: the 'diegetic' mode when it is the poet who is speaking versus the 'mimetic' mode when it is the protagonists who are speaking (plus the 'mixed' mode when the narrative is interspersed with dialogue). Tragedy belongs completely to the 'mimetic' and consequently the 'dramatic' mode.[96] On the other hand, as we have already observed, not only is the tragic form introduced by Thespis presented as *drâma en ástei*, but already in the *Homeric Hymn to Demeter* various terms derived from the verb *drân* designate actions that we would qualify as ritual.[97] Not to mention the tragic question *par excellence*, uttered in the 'performative' form: *tí drô*; 'what am I to do?'.

---

[93] The relevant sources are collected by Parker 2005: 468.
[94] The repertoire is reconstructed in an excellent study by Csapo and Wilson 2015.
[95] Arist. *Poet.* 3, 1448a 19–29 (cf. also 4, 1448b 32–8); 23, 1459a 18.
[96] Plat. *Resp.* 392cd; cf. Section 2.1.1 with n. 4.
[97] Cf. nn. 32 and 33 in Chapter 1; see also Henrichs 2000.

Cultic Dramatizations

Whichever way we look at it, chorality is innate to tragedy as ritual. This is precisely what Xenophon is saying when he states that processions must please the gods as well as the spectators: 'The same goes for the Dionysia, where the chorus by their dances gratify the other gods and particularly the Twelve.'[98] Just like most melic songs, tragedies are offered, in their ritual performance, as musical offerings not only to Dionysos but also to other deities of the civic pantheon. And these musical offerings consist (in line with Plato's three defining features for *melos*) of choral or monodic song, instrumental melodic accompaniment and especially the choreographic figures corresponding to the metrical rhythms marked by the singers' voice.[99]

Provisional conclusions are that tragic performance in fifth-century Athens should be regarded as a strongly ritualized religious practice or even as a cultic act. Though the *mousikoì agônes* that constituted the ritual celebration of the Great Dionysia were highly developed and contributed to the creation of specific poetic genres, they must be considered as being of a piece with the other musical and/or athletic contests that marked many large-scale cultic occasion in Athens, such as the already-mentioned Panathenaia in honour of Athena Polias (which included Homeric rhapsodic contests), the Thargelia in honour of Apollo (with its dithyrambic contest), the Anthesteria in honour of Dionysos, patron of wine, the Eleusinia in honour of Demeter, the Theseia in honour of Athens' founding hero and so on and so forth. All these festivals are regarded uncontroversially as both religious and political festivals.[100]

As a sung and danced musical practice belonging to the cultic celebration of Dionysos Eleuthereus, tragedy in fifth-century Athens belongs fully to ritual as we have defined it: a practice that is regulated, recurrent, social, institutional and symbolic of body and voice, whose function is to serve the collective cultural and poetic memory of the city, with an anthropopoietic meaning.

---

[98] Xenoph. *Eq. mag.* 3, 2.
[99] Plat. *Resp.* 398b–d and 399c. Discussion of tragic song's musical accompaniment and choreography is problematic on account of the paucity of evidence; see respectively Ley 2007: 132–53 and 150–67; on metre and the corresponding choreography for choral songs in Attic tragedy, see once again Rhem 1992: 51–5.
[100] See Osborne 2003 for a list of all the relevant festivals.

CHAPTER 3

Choral Polyphonies and Tragedy

At the turn of the twenty-first century the chorus captured the attention of readers of Greek tragedy, especially anglophone scholars. In the field of cultural anthropology, the indirect influence of Victor Turner's work on 'theatrical performance' was particularly significant. Inspired by Wilhelm Dilthey's notion of experience as *Erlebnis*, and on the basis of ethnological field research on the initiation rites of male and female adolescents in the Ndembu tribe of present-day Zambia, Turner formulated a view of culture as a collection of individual experiences made available to society by means of expression (both verbal and physical). Theatrical performance is thus a 'structured unit of experience', a processual accomplishment or ritualized staging of the social drama.[1] Turner's work was a key influence on the Performance Group led by Richard Schechner, the founder of the Performing Garage in SoHo, New York and a seminal figure in the field of 'Performance Studies' that is still so prominent in the United States today.

Schechner's definition of performance ultimately came to include all public events by individuals or groups, a definition so capacious as to be meaningless: '"showing doing" is performing: pointing out, underlining, and displaying doing'.[2] Yet what remains relevant for our purposes is the idea that cultural events are ritualized, codified and dramatized; performance is a physical manifestation by means of its symbolic staging and gestures, but also by means of the power of the rhythmical spoken word and especially the verbal gesture of deixis (as we will see). Theatrical performance, then, has to be considered as poetical rhetoric, enunciated and acted out by means of ritualized dramatization. It is not a matter of 'From ritual to theatre', as the title of Turner's collection has it, but rather a matter of theatre *as* ritual.

When it comes to Attic tragedy, the role of the chorus has lately been approached in terms of its dramatic and political identity. From the point

[1] Turner 1982: 12–19.   [2] Schechner 2006: 28.

Choral Polyphonies and Tragedy 65

of view of its part in the heroic action of a given play as well as from the perspective of its ritual and social function, the tragic chorus plays a mediating role. On the one hand, as a character in the action, the chorus is invited to *sunagōnízesthai*, to 'take part in the contest' (this is the function assigned to it by Aristotle in the *Poetics*, as we have seen). The chorus is made to interact with the human and divine characters of the heroic action. It is thus integrated in the space and time of the plot, the *mûthos* (again, in the sense given to the term by Aristotle),[3] where it acts as a dramatic mediator both on the poetic and on the fictional plane. But the chorus is also made up of Athenian citizens, who are chorally educated in the arts of the Muses and gymnastic exercise, who sing in Greek, in fifth-century Athens, in the modalities of the ritual poetry that is *mélos* in its many forms. The spatial domain of the choreuts is the orchestra, whence they proffer their collective utterance arranged rhythmically along repetitive choreographic figures. This rhythmic utterance is addressed as much to the protagonists of the heroic action who speak or sing before the *skēnḗ* as it is addressed to the audience, which also takes part in the musical performance by assembling in the space of the sanctuary reserved for the 'spectacle', the *théatron*.[4] Thus dramatic and poetical mediation blends with political and social mediation.

The mask plays an essential role in this political and social mediation between the heroic time and space of the *palaiá* being dramatized before the *skēnḗ* and the historical, political, religious and social reality inhabited not only by the actors and choreuts but also by the poet and his audience.[5] Through their ritual definition and function the masks and costumes point to a third kind of mediation, that between humans and gods. Just as tragedy, considered as ritualized musical performance, is integrated in the musical *agṓn* offered to Dionysos, so also the space of the dramatic performance is integrated (as we have seen) in the sanctuary dedicated to Dionysos Eleuthereus.[6] While flagging this ritual and cultic insertion of the Dionysiac, the mask reinforces the distancing effect we have noted between the tragic action belonging to the heroic past and the present of the cultic celebration; it softens the audience's confrontation with the often destructive actions of their ancestors. It is particularly masked choral performance that, as a ritual and poetic offering, assures a religious

---

[3] 18, 1456a 25–9, with the commentary by Gentili 1984/1985: 33–5 and Bierl 2001: 37–41 (cf. n. 94 in Chapter 2); then 6, 1450a 7–23: cf. n. 7 in Chapter 2.
[4] For the choral education of the Athenian citizens, see Nagy 1990: 404–13 and Kowalzig 2007: 4–5, with the list of cultic occasions involving musical contests in Herington 1985: 161–6.
[5] Cf. Chapter 2.4.4 (with n. 72).   [6] Cf. Chapter 2.4.2 (with n. 53) and Chapter 2.5.2.

connection and mediation between the choreuts and the audience and between these and the god being worshipped in his sanctuary-theatre; this is achieved by means of a fluid dramatic and political identity that partakes of both masculine and feminine qualities.

3.1 Tragic Choral Identities

Tragedy, then, should be regarded mainly as ritual and musical performance, and tragic songs should be regarded as sung and danced poetic performances on the model of the melic poetry from which they derive. These songs are generally performed by the chorus, but they sometimes are performed by the actors, as we will see in the readings below. As ritual performances, these choral songs are dramatic mediations between the play's heroic action and the here-and-now of the musical performance in the political, religious and cultural context of fifth-century Athens. They achieve spatial mediations between the stage, the orchestra and the steps where the audience are seated; they are religious mediations between the melic performance and the cult rendered to Dionysos and other civic gods; they are enunciative mediations between the poet composing the song, the voice of the actors and (especially) the chorus performing the song, and the audience honouring the god. Between poet and audience, the choral voice is carried by dramatic identities and by enunciative procedures that are paradoxical to say the least. We will begin by interrogating the identity – dramatic, political and gendered – of the various choruses of Attic tragedy, before moving on to tackle the linguistic self-positioning of the male and female roles played by young, masked citizens in a choral polyphony that is both semantic and enunciative.

3.1.1 Political Identities, Dramatic Identities

Is it then the case that the tragic chorus can be regarded as the incarnation of the city, as suggested in Paris in the aftermath of 1968? Is the chorus 'the mouthpiece of the city which through its movements paid its respects to the altar of Dionysos, the god who of all the Olympians was the one most foreign to the city'? Does this mean that, ultimately, '(Attic) tragedy could be said to be a manifestation of the city turning itself into theatre, presenting itself on stage before its assembled citizens'?[7] In the context of a more

---

[7] I allude to the double definition offered by Vidal-Naquet on the one hand and Vernant on the other in their joint work: Vernant and Vidal-Naquet 1986[1988]: 159 and 22[311–12 and 185] respectively.

markedly Structuralist and Marxist interpretation, the chorus has been viewed as representative of the body politic in opposition to the action being played out on the scene and the heroic code representing 'alterity' and the 'other': a combination of social theory and structuralist duality.[8]

But we must remind ourselves that Vidal-Naquet, who formulated that first definition above, added on the same page that 'if the chorus is the organ of collective civic expression, it is absolutely the exception for it to be composed of average citizens, that is to say adult males of fighting age'. This is a way of drawing attention to the double identity of the chorus in Greek tragedy; as we have already noted, the chorus has both a dramatic, fictional identity and a political and civic identity. Independently of the political and ritual role played by the choreuts both as Athenian citizens and as singers honouring Dionysos Eleuthereus, the social and sexual identity that the poet assigns to the chorus as a character in a given tragedy is complex to say the least. This identity plays a decisive role with regards to the authority of the choral voice, in a semantic and enunciative polyphony whose parameters we will define below.

According to a statistical analysis by Donald Mastronarde, 67 per cent of extant complete tragedies attributed to Aeschylus have – somewhat surprisingly – a female chorus; the proportion of female choruses is 29 per cent in Sophocles' tragedies, and it rises to 82 per cent in those of Euripides.[9] Mastronarde interprets the prevalence of female choruses in Euripides' tragedies in terms of marginality and dependence. He views the marginality attributable to gender as a counterpart to the marginality attributable to age, for example, in the chorus of old men of Sophocles' *Oedipus the King*, and to foreignness, for example, in the chorus of Xerxes' advisors in Aeschylus' *Persians* (as we will see). Mainly on the basis of Euripides' *Medea*, whose chorus is made up of women of Corinth and whose protagonist is herself an exile, Mastronarde portrays the choral tragic voice as heterogeneous and the chorus as incapable of presenting coherent judgements. He explains this lack of coherence in the choral sections by reference to the world beyond the fictional world of the play, ascribing it to the social crisis in which Athens was mired at the end of the fifth century. We see here a clear shift of focus from the chorus's dramatic identity to its civic identity.

---

[8] See Longo 1990: 16–19.
[9] Mastronarde 1998: 61–6, who also includes statistics for the lost tragedies whose chorus can be identified; the proportions stand at 59 per cent, 38 per cent and 63 per cent respectively; see also Sourvinou-Inwood 2003: 265–75, as well as the morphology of female choruses in the extant tragedies outlined by Trieschnigg 2009: 313–29.

In actual fact, the apparent incoherence of the tragic voice in Attic tragedy points less to the external circumstances of a particularly unstable historical and political situation than to the internal structure of the tragedy. The performative, emotional and interpretative reactions of the chorus (to which we shall return presently) are shaped by the dramatic unfolding of the play. Their musical interventions bring together the different tensions and reversals that structure the plot and the dramatic action. The following observations on Aeschylus' predecessor Phrynichus pick up on the statistical approach mentioned above while focusing attention on the role of the chorus in the dramatic development of the tragedy. Out of nine tragedies by Phrynichus whose titles are known, discounting *Sack of Miletus*, five are named after the chorus (*Sons of Aegyptus, Daughters of Danaus, Persians, Women of Pleuron, Phoenicians*), three take their name from the protagonist (*Actaeon, Alcestis, Tantalus*), while just one has a double title (referring to the protagonist and the chorus: *Antaeus or Lybians*). The proportions for Aeschylus are similar. Out of six or seven extant tragedies, four have titles naming the chorus, generally a female chorus (*Suppliants, Libation Bearers, Eumenides, Persians*); in the first of these tragedies, the chorus of suppliants, the daughters of Danaus, is the play's main protagonist. Moreover, of all the Aeschylian tragic titles transmitted to us, around half name the chorus. On the other hand, out of seven extant Sophoclean tragedies, just one takes its name from the chorus (*Women of Trachis*), while only fifteen of some twenty-four transmitted titles refer to the chorus's identity.

When it comes to Euripides, out of fifteen extant tragedies, only four take their name from the (female) chorus (*Trojan Women, Suppliants, Phoenicians, Bacchae*).[10] These figures must be related to the increase in the number of actors from one to three and the growing emphasis on plot. As the fifth century progressed, Attic tragedy changed from being a melic performance to being a mostly epic dramatization, in line with the mimetic narrative mode alluded to in Plato's *Republic*.[11] But in Attic tragedy the dialogues which in Homeric poetry had been framed by the epic action are now ritually dramatized; they are taken on by masked actors who assume mimetically their enunciative stance, sometimes in song.

---

[10] See the detailed statistics presented in Sourvinou-Inwood 2003: 266–9.   [11] Cf. Chapter 2.1.1.

3.1.2 Fictional Identities and Gender Identities

Leaving aside these statistics, which are after all based on a highly fragmentary corpus, recent studies of the character and function of the tragic chorus have stemmed not just from the contemporary interest in performance but also from the recent debate surrounding fiction. As is often the case, Greek cultural phenomena are interrogated in relation to modern preoccupations. By the same token, the ancient world can in turn contribute to decentring our view of the concepts that underlie modern intellectual preoccupations. For instance, we are invited – once again by an anglophone scholar – to be attentive to 'the dramatic role of the (tragic) chorus within the fictional world created by the performances themselves and with our response to that world'.[12] Straightaway we must recognize that, inasmuch as it is a 'possible world' constructed and dramatized on the stage, this fictional world is 'interpenetrated' by the real-world musical and ritual performance. Thus, from an internal perspective, the identity of the chorus of tragedy participates of that of the protagonists of the dramatic action at the same time as it occupies towards them a position of 'social marginality'. The choruses of Attic tragedy are usually women, elderly men, slaves or foreigners; sometimes their identity is intersectional, for example, the Phoenicians in Euripides' eponymous tragedy are slaves and women.[13] Moreover, from the point of view of po(i)etic fiction, the chorus sings in the diction of high melic poetry. This means that on account of their metrical rhythm, dialectal colouring, lexical peculiarities and metaphorical language, the chorus's songs are removed from the more prosaic Attic language employed by the actors (though this too is marked, since it is metrical). The dramatic function of the chorus is therefore ritualized by means of the poetic language it employs in fulfilling its political and ritual function.

It has taken the intervention of a feminine scholarly voice receptive to the traces of gendered identities and social roles in Greek poetry to develop the notion of the tragic chorus's social marginality. The chorus does not represent the audience, and even less does it represent the political and religious community to whom, in one way or another, it belongs. It was another female scholar who demonstrated that the loyalty of Euripides' female choruses is often torn between their local community, be that

---

[12] Gould 1996: 218.
[13] Gould 1996: 218–22 and 233 for the citations. For Euripides' preference for female choruses, see Murnagham 2017.

Corinthian or Athenian, and their gender; choral identities, then, with their multiple affiliations, are often conflicted.[14]

Proper consideration of the different ways in which the chorus is implicated in the dramatic action produces a richer and more varied musical picture of the choral voices of the extant tragedies. On the one hand the profiles of the tragic choruses vary in the different authors and according to their gender; on the other hand the choruses of classical tragedy display moral and emotional attitudes that are essentially determined by their social status and their role in the dramatic action. The tragic choruses represent a sort of 'authoritative cultural memory' by reference to other examples drawn from the heroic world (which we call 'myths') and through their frequent gnomic statements based in traditional wisdom; they are, generally speaking, strongly implicated in the dramatic action with the other male and female characters. This is especially true of Euripides' female choruses, which display greater authority and express themselves in a more aggressive manner. It follows that '[e]stablishing links between separate worlds and mediating between male and female or Greek and foreign characters seems to be particularly, if not exclusively, common to female choruses'.[15] Finally, choruses of old men tend to be more concerned with political issues, while female choruses are more sensitive to domestic and religious matters.

Doubtless there is little that is surprising in this contrasted account of the gender differences in the dramatic and social roles of the chorus in Attic tragedy. The poetics of tragedy, just like that of *mélos*, enables the poet to imagine a gendered perspective that can correspond alternatively to the male or female identity of the chorus. A good example of this are the partheneia of Alcman and Pindar, melic and choral compositions sung by young women, to which we shall return presently.

In a work devoted to the relationship between Attic tragedy and religion and likewise animated by the key issue of gender, another female scholar, Christiane Sourvinou-Inwood, has focused not only on the stance adopted by the tragic chorus in relation to the dramatic action, but also on its identity as 'performer' on the occasion of a civic festival and as representative of the city in a ritual event. Rightly rejecting the notion of the 'otherness' of the tragic chorus, her study insists on the variability of the

---

[14] Foley 2003: 19–25; Swift 2013. The question of women's participation in the *mousikoì agônes* of the Great Dionysia is still controversial; in addition to the bibliographical references listed above (n. 53 in Chapter 2), see especially Henderson 1991 and Goldhill 1994, with my remarks in Calame 1997: 183 n. 4.
[15] Foley 2003: 23.

Tragic Choral Identities 71

chorus's identity and authority. Being mimetic and ritual, the 'persona' of the chorus is not static, but rather evolves as the performance progresses. Aristotle had in some sense already anticipated this when he stated that the aim of tragedy is an action (*praxis*) animated by a plot (*mûthos*), rather than a quality; thus the 'characters' (*ḗthē*) are created by and in the action. The tragic chorus is very close to the world of the audience, and it is for this reason that it plays a central role with regard to the function of tragedy by engaging in 'the exploration of problems that arose in the interstices of the religious discourse of the polis'. Regardless of a speculative reconstruction of tragedy's origins in a performance that first represented then problematized the Dionysiac myths, the suggestion is that the choreuts originally had a double identity that encompassed 're-enacting the past' of their 'persona' and their dominant 'persona' in the here-and-now of the ritual, in a performance that was not yet mimetic.[16]

On the basis of these observations, it is more appropriate when speaking of the 'persona' and role of the tragic chorus to acknowledge that the choral collective voice combines these two identities. On the one hand there is a complex heroic dramatic identity; existing on the fictional plane it enables the chorus's intervention in the dramatic staging of a different time and (usually) place from that of the performance, and it can evolve with the development of the action being represented. On the other hand the chorus also has a political and ritual identity related to the here-and-now of the poetic and cultic performance of tragedy.

With this polymorphic collective identity that is at once dramatic and political, in contrast with the singular identity of the protagonists, whose personal names situate them in the time and place of epic narrative tradition, the tragic chorus cannot be held to represent an 'assembly of citizens'. Neither in its dramatic heroic identity nor in its ritual and political identity does the collective voice of the tragic chorus have any of the communal authority characteristic of the democratic city. Then again, and with good reason, it has been argued that the tragic choral persona should not be defined by the label of 'otherness', even in its different modalities (female, foreigner, slave, elderly).[17] Marginality is not synonymous with absence of authority. We must not forget that the composition and performance of the choral songs of tragedy are a function of the

---

[16] Sourvinou-Inwood 2003: 275–84 (quotations from 283). Cf. Arist. *Poet.* 6, 1450a 15–23.
[17] Goldhill 1996: 252–5, in reply to Gould 1996 (cf. n. 12 in this chapter). On this view, the definition of the tragic chorus as a 'segment of a community' (Sourvinou-Inwood 2013: 265–6) is too restrictive. On the varied identities of the choruses of tragedy, see the survey of the *status quaestionis* in Battezzato 2005: 154–6 and in Visvardi 2015: 19–26.

musical education received by every Athenian citizen; they are dependent on a particularly developed culture of choral ritual song, for men as well as for women.

Despite the fictional and social marginality of the singers as character in the heroic action, the tragic choral voices, in their variety of identities and dramatic flexibility, draw their authority from a tradition of musical and ritual poetry; this tradition of *mélos* belongs to the political and religious culture of the city. It is in a sense by means of ritual and choral performance that the tragic chorus, drawing on the heritage of traditional wisdom and on the heroic stories that we call 'mythology', sings in the name of a very large audience. Is the chorus then a spokesperson for the audience? It is a question to which we will return when discussing the enunciative polyphony of the tragic choral voice. On the particular point of the relationship between the choral songs of tragedy and the shared culture of choral poetry and collective cultural memory we will limit ourselves here to quoting Simon Goldhill's cogent conclusion.

> The chorus requires the audience to engage in a constant renegotiation of where the authoritative voice lies. It sets in play an authoritative collective voice, but surrounds it with other dissenting voices. . . . The chorus thus is a key dramatic device for setting commentary, reflection, and an authoritative voice in play as part of tragic conflict. This mobilization and questioning of the authority of collective wisdom is one of the most important ways in which tragedy engaged with democracy.[18]

The question of the authority of the tragic choral voice leads us first to discuss its semantic polyphony, then its enunciative polyphony.

3.2 Semantic Polyphonies: The Functions of Tragic Song

Since the 1990s, scholarly approaches to the ancient world have been dominated by Poststructuralism, and anglophone scholarship has become receptive to the question of theatrical performance. Hence, for classical tragedy, the concentration on what has come to be referred to as 'chorality'; the first conference was organized at Harvard and Boston Universities with the title 'The Chorus in Greek Culture'. Thus the study of the tragic voice was reinvigorated by approaches that recognize its kinship to the voices of

---

[18] Goldhill 1996: 255. In Goldhill 2013: 102–9, the author revisits the role of the chorus to illuminate its contribution to the 'lyric voice' of Sophocles' tragedy, considering the polarities between individual and collective, spoken and recited poetry, and characters and audience; see also, along similar lines, Goldhill 2012: 81–90.

melic poetry. Let us begin by focusing on the semantic modalities of these choral utterances often spoken by women, before moving on to discuss their enunciative modalities.

But before setting tragic choral song against melic song we must make some preliminary remarks; in doing so, we will use as a term of comparison the only Pindaric partheneion of which substantial fragments survive. Composed by a male poet, this ritual poem was sung by a chorus of young women on the occasion of a daphnephoric procession to the temple of Apollo Ismenios. This sanctuary was located outside the walls of Pindar's home city of Thebes. The ceremonial bearing of an offering of laurel to the young god was probably, from a musical point of view, the climax of the ceremony. This ritual celebration of Apollo marked the adolescent girls' (and the doubtless boys', too) entry into adulthood on completion of a ritual cursus of initiation.[19] What remains of this unfortunately fragmentary melic poem begins with a long description, uttered by the young women in the first person, of the ritual action in which they are engaged; this is followed by praise of the aristocratic family of the young man who is leading the procession. As we will have reason to observe again below, this description of their ritual action unfolds in a performative mode; we find this mode of enunciation also in the choral songs of tragedy, particularly when the chorus is female. The difference between tragic and melic choral song is that in tragic representation the sung ritual action is in part elided from the cultic celebration (of which it is a central manifestation) in order to be inserted in the action that is being staged in the theatre's orchestra. The world of the play takes the place of the world of the ritual celebration and the former alludes to the latter only indirectly through the mediations that we have pointed out. This substitution involves a pragmatic slippage. It is for this reason that there is no point in attempting to interpret the apparent presence of forms of traditional *mélos* in the theatre's orchestra in terms of reference or 'allusion' (to autonomous 'lyric' genres).[20]

Through dramatization, the (female) choral voice achieves a particularly complex semantic depth. A comparison between the powerful parodos of Aeschylus' *Seven against Thebes* and the moving opening song of Euripides' *Phoenicians* had led me, since that first conference on tragic choralities at Harvard, to distinguish three dimensions in the choral voice brought into

---

[19] Pindar fr. 94b Maehler; the Theban daphnephoricon is described by Proclus *ap*. Phot. *Bibl.* 321a 34 32; cf. Section 3.3.
[20] As proposed by Swift 2010: 29–34 and 367–71.

the orchestra of theatre-cum-sanctuary of Dionysos. The different functions assumed by the choral group during the unfolding of the tragedy correspond to the following three different voices.

First of all, there is a 'performative' voice, insofar as the chorus adopts and adapts the traditional forms of melic poetry (hymn, paean, hymenaion, threnos etc.) in order to react ritually to the fictional action of the play and participate in it, while also trying to influence its unfolding. The tragic chorus then acts as a collective agent; it is implicated in the heroic action, engaging in dialogue and interaction with its protagonists. But, alongside its pragmatic role, the tragic choral voice also takes on an emotive turn that manifests particularly in the metrical cadence of its vocal expression, and consequently in the choreographic movements of the choreuts. This affective voice places the tragic chorus at the intersection between its position in relation to the dramatic action with which it interacts (*sunagonízetai*) as a collective character and its position in relation to the audience, which reacts emotionally to the play. Finally, the chorus's commentary on the dramatic action as it unfolds before it defines a 'hermeneutic' voice. Adopting an ethical tone, this interpretative voice draws on traditional wisdom and the heritage of heroic figures in order to draw examples and counterexamples. These are the two foundations of the political and religious culture of fifth-century Athens, and it is to this 'off-stage' dimension that the chorus often refers in order to make explicit the narrative and ethical challenges of the heroic action in which it is at the same time a participant; as we will see, from the enunciative perspective, this implicates the voice of the poet as well as that of the audience.[21] It goes without saying that this threefold distinction is purely instrumental, for the rhythmical flow of choral song fuses the three voices in a sophisticated poetics.

In his remarkable monograph on the plays of Sophocles, Charles Segal suggested that the songs of Attic tragedy offer some hypotheses by which to interpret the action that is played before the chorus and the audience: 'Unlike a choral song that is actually part of a performed ritual in non-mythic space, a tragic choral ode often constitutes a hypothesis about meaning at a particular stage of understanding rather than a final assertion

---

[21] See the conclusions of my brief comparative study, Calame 1997: 201–3, with further discussion in Trieschnigg 2009: 69–101. For the ritual form that emotions assume in Greek tragedy, see especially Di Benedetto and Medda 2002: 266–78, who discern, within the voice of the tragic chorus, emotive reactions to events that can prompt various forms of prayer, conceptual reflections and evocations of the narrative context of the mythical episode being represented (see also 249–53 and 260–3); for a *Rezeptionsästhetik* perspective, see Gruber 2008: 17–27 and 44–70.

of meaning.'²² I would add that these interpretative statements conveyed by the hermeneutic voice depend in the first instance on the ritual and sung verbal acts which we will discuss below; these acts of song involve the emotional dimension of the chorus's voice as well as its pragmatic dimension. The combination of the hermeneutic voice with the performative voice and the affective voice leads to a first form of polyphony that I shall call 'semantic polyphony', that is to say, a polyphony of content or of the utterance, that operates alongside the enunciative polyphony, which I shall outline below.

The complexity of the tragic choral voice in this vocal counterpoint of sorts corresponds as closely to the multiplicity of functions assumed by the words of the tragic chorus as it does to the chorus' multilayered social and gender identity. This polymorphic identity of the chorus of Attic tragedy is by now well acknowledged. Combined with its various mediating functions, it invites us to revisit the operative distinction between the interpretative voice, the affective voice and the performative voice of the chorus, and to examine instead their overlaps and their pragmatics at the semantic level, in the unfolding of the dramatic action according to its own syntax, which according to Aristotle is marked by reversal and recognition.[23]

3.3 Enunciative Polyphonies: Between Poet and Audience

But who assumes these three choral voices? Who stands behind the poetic 'I'/'we' speaking these vocal utterances? It is no doubt the chorus as a character in the play's action, but equally, as with melic poetry, it is the poet who composed the words to be sung by the chorus, or perhaps the audience, as the greatest voices of Romantic poetics have maintained in relation to classical tragedy.

3.3.1 Enunciative Stances

'Der Chor is mit einem Wort der idealisierte Zuschauer' ('the chorus is, in short, the ideal spectator'). Thus A. W. Schlegel concluded his introductory reflections on the chorus in classical tragedy in the fifth of his *Vorlesungen über dramatische Kunst und Literatur*, first published in

---

[22] Segal 1995: 196–8, who, in reference to the tragedies of Sophocles (see his 1981 study), speaks of the chorus as a 'participating character'. Nagy 1994/1995: 49–51 argues that the 'enactment' of the choreuts' marginal role as citizens in the making 'conforms to the ritual function of the chorus as an educational collectivization of experience'.

[23] Essentially Arist. *Poet.* 10, 1452a 12–18 and 11, 1452a 29–b 8; cf. Chapter 1 and Section 3.1.1.

1809.[24] But he immediately went on to explain that, through its identity as the ideal spectator, the chorus softens the profound impression provoked by a performance that is unsettling inasmuch as it communicates to the spectator, by means of music, its own transporting emotions. Moreover, the Greek tragic chorus must also be viewed as a representative of the poet; indeed, still according to the Romantic definition of its role, it is the incarnation of the poet's thought inasmuch as it is the 'spokesperson for the whole of humanity'. At once expression of the poet and ideal spectator, the chorus of classical tragedy, then, represents 'in general and before all else the collective national spirit, then common human participation' ('überhaupt und zuvördest den nationalen Gemeingeist, dann die allgemeine menschliche Teilnahme'). Beyond the spirit of classical Athens with its Bacchic festivals, it is the thought of the whole of humanity that the Greek tragic chorus, as a character, brings into play.

In the wake of Schlegel's formulation, too often abstracted from its context, contemporary interpreters of the tragic chorus and its functions have mainly seized on the notion of the 'ideal spectator'. This expression seems to anticipate the notion of the 'ideal reader' or *lettore modello*, an operative concept arising from an analysis of discourse that focuses on the reader's profile as it is constructed by and inscribed in the text. But he who says 'ideal reader' also says 'virtual author'. Beyond the figures of the plot's characters, the ideal or virtual reader emerges also in relation to the ideal or implicit author in the development of the text, or rather of the discourse. Each of these virtual figures acquires, in the enunciation, a particular ethos, an (enunciative) stance, that is to say, a 'mask of authority'.[25] Implicating medially both the poet and its public, this conjuncture of enunciative strategies inscribed in the text aims to orient its interpretation; it is all the more significant in classical Athenian tragedy, and in particular in the choral songs, for the fact that here the poetic enunciation is musical, and therefore ritualized.

In the tragic choral songs, the 'enunciated enunciation' – if I may be allowed to refer to a key notion of discourse analysis – has a direct pragmatic impact that is aesthetical and emotional before it is intellectual. This is especially the case since in Attic tragedy not only does plot ('récit')

---

[24] Schlegel 1846: 76–7. Schlegel's formulation is discussed especially in Kranz 1933: 219–25 and again in Hose 1990: I, 32–7; for a relevant historical and cultural *mise en perspective*, see Goldhill 2013b: 40–4. The complex relations between the chorus's identity and expression and the tragic audience are discussed by Loscalzo 2008: 133–56.
[25] The concept of the *lettore modello* was formulated in particular by Eco 1979: 50–66; for the authorial stance and the 'mask of authority' in the various forms of Greek poetry, see Calame 2005a: 13–40.

unfold *dià miméseos* as defined by Plato, but moreover this dramatic mode is also indebted to the enunciation at the level of 'discourse' (we will return to this key linguistic distinction). What remain to be investigated are the discursive forms and modalities of these enunciative strategies, all the more since there is a strong disparity, from the point of view of social identity, between the heterogeneous public that participates in the Great Dionysia and the polymorphous and generally marginal status of the chorus that is held to represent them.

If there were not a danger of this becoming an excessively abstract exercise, one might propose – in a paragraph that the reader unfamiliar with discourse analysis might wish to skip – a first attempt at integrating into a theoretical model of enunciative pragmatics, as a simple reading grid, the three voices of the chorus as well as the enunciative positions it takes up by means of choral performance. One might further propose that on the one hand in the represented actions (through its dramatic persona) and on the other hand in the extra-discursive reference (through its political status). At this intersection between semantic polyphony and enunciative polyphony there emerge no fewer than five roles. Three of these roles are internal to the discourse: the chorus as actor of the play, with its performative voice that implicates it in the dramatic action; the virtual author, with his enunciative stance, doubtless attached to the hermeneutic voice; the implicit spectator, who can take up the choral voice of emotion. On the other hand, from an extra-discursive point of view, these different enunciative postures and functions point to two empirical roles: the biographical author and his historical audience. Thus, were it not for the risk of conflating semantic polyphony with enunciative polyphony, we might wish to assimilate the ritual and performative voice of the tragic chorus to that of the plays' actors; the hermeneutic and evaluating voice would then become that of the poet by means of the stance of the ideal author with his knowledge of the unfolding of the action and its meaning, only partially known to the chorus in its capacity as one of the characters; and the emotive voice would correspond to that of the audience by the intermediary of its role as the ideal audience.

Just as these different voices intermingle in the tragic chorus' song without it ever being possible to distinguish them entirely, we will see that the enunciative polyphony, in combination with the semantic polyphony, tends in particular to confuse the implicit voice of the poet-choreographer with that of the public celebrating Dionysos. However that may be, the concrete analysis of the texts will demonstrate that the boundary between these two types of choral polyphony – the enunciative and the semantic – is in practice less than firm.

3.3.2 Choral Performativity: The Melic 'I'/'We'

In his fundamental work on the *Stasimon* in classical tragedy, already Walther Kranz proposed distinguishing several different trajectories in the words of the tragic chorus, in particular in relation to the action developing in front of its eyes, in the space before the *skēnē*.[26] According to Kranz, the tragic choreuts can add depth to the represented action by extending it towards a different domain, a different place or a different time; but they can also rise to more general considerations in order to draw from them a lesson, as is also the case in choral melic poetry. These two modes of commentary on the dramatic action correspond to the third voice that we have just identified, the hermeneutic voice. But, according to Kranz, the choral song of the stasimon represents essentially a 'lyric echo of the words by the actors' ('lyrischer Widerhall des Schauspielwortes'). An expression of the movements of the soul and the heart instigated by what goes on here and now in the theatre, this choral voice as carrier of emotions evidently corresponds to the second of the vocal functions that can be attributed to the tragic chorus. There remains the ritual and performative voice, to which Kranz makes only a fleeting reference when he argues that the expression of emotion often prompts the choreuts to turn to the gods for help.

Now, it is precisely on the chorus' performative voice that we must focus in a study that claims to be an investigation into Attic tragedy as ritual and cultural performance. A preliminary clarification is called for; the notion of 'performative' is here employed in the strict sense in which it is used by Émile Benveniste. We will therefore regard as 'performative' an utterance when 'it *denominates* the act performed because Ego pronounces a formula containing a verb in the first person of the present'.[27] This is a narrower definition than the one proposed by John L. Austin when he used the term 'performative' (of a sentence or utterance) to indicate that the 'the issuing of an utterance is the performing of an action'. Thus performative utterances are not only (by virtue of being spoken acts) 'illocutionary' utterances, though this notion is somewhat problematic, but they are also utterances that are linguistically marked by the use of the first person

[26] Kranz 1933: 214–25; see the complementary remarks in Segal 1995: 180–5.
[27] Benveniste 1971: 237.

(often positioned in relation to an agent in the second person), by the use of the present tense or forms expressing wish or intention, and by reliance on verbs that express vocal action: *I command, I vow, I invoke* and here *I sing/I dance* or *we sing/we dance*.[28]

Sung in the first person (singular or plural) and reprising the rhythms and dialects of traditional melic poetry, the choral songs of tragedy confront us, from the point of view of their performative dimension, with the controversial question of the nature of the 'lyric' 'I'/'we'. In the genres of paean, threnos or hymenaion, who is it that occupies the grammatical position of the first person? In largely ritualized sung performances, who is it who sings 'I' and who assumes the utterance of the melic poem or of the tragic choral song?

It is clear that the ritual component of choral melic poems and tragic choral songs alike inscribes them in the very large category of 'perlocutionary' utterances; by their specific verbal form and the very fact that they are sung, these *pragmatic* utterances aim to have an effect.[29] But melic compositions with pragmatic function involve utterances that are more specifically *performative*, in the sense of being spoken acts. Distinguished not only by the use of a verb expressing in the present tense the activity of singing and of choral performance, but also by the use of forms of the first-person singular or plural, these utterances can point as easily to those who are singing them as to the poet who composed them. From an enunciative perspective, the forms of 'I'/'we' that distinguish the poetry known as 'lyric' turn out to have a double reference. This poetry demands a further level of explanation in terms of discourse analysis (and this section, too, is not essential, so that the reader so inclined might choose to skip ahead).

On the one hand, on the verbal (intradiscursive) level, these forms of 'I'/'we' constitute the instance of enunciation and they point to the figure of the speaker as it is constructed in the poetic discourse. The speaker's identity and stance are conjured up in the discourse and by means of it, particularly by the markers of the enunciated enunciation such as are the first-person forms, the 'here' and the 'now' (with their respective referents). But they are also outlined through the enunciative and rhetorical modes applied to the discourse. A discursive figure, 'mask of authority', the speaker (or narrator) generally positions himself (or herself) in relation to an interlocutor (narratee) who emerges in the discourse through

---

[28] Benveniste 1963, discussing the concept developed by Austin 1975[1955]: 4–7 and 67–71.
[29] The subtle distinction between 'illocutionary' and 'perlocutionary' is intelligently discussed by Ducrot 1977.

the second-person forms. In the 'I'/'we' its stance also enters into relation with the 'he'/'she'/'they' of the protagonists of the 'plot', namely the 'mythical' plot that the melic poems often claim as their paradigmatic narrative subject.

Doubtless these various pronominal forms, with the profiles and verbal stances they imply, point us to the famous (operative) distinction proposed by Émile Benveniste between 'historical narration' ('histoire'/'récit') and 'discourse' ('discours'); the former is characterized by the third person, the aorist and a distinct space (namely that of the 'mythical' plot), while the latter is characterized by the first and second person, the 'here' and the 'now'.[30] But in tragedy, in the face of the 'I' and the 'we' assumed by the choral voice, the protagonists of the narrative action also express themselves in the first person; this is worth examining.

On the other hand these pronominal forms of the 'formal apparatus of enunciation' point to the reality of performance, with its own protagonists: poet, chorus, audience in the case of melic poetry. Thus as a complement to the useful instrumental distinction between 'story' and 'discourse', the forms of Greek melic poetry invite us to recognize also the equally instrumental distinction advanced by the linguist Karl Bühler between *Deixis am Phantasma* and *demonstratio ad oculos*. Indeed the demonstratives used in choral melic poetry offer the possibility, both from the point of view of 'story' and from the point of view of 'discourse', of appealing as much to the audience's imagination as to its faculty of sight in the here-and-now of the performance.[31]

3.3.3 Enunciative and Performative Self-Reference: The Case of Pindar

But let us try to illustrate these highly theoretical notions with a practical example.

> For Loxias has come
> gladly to shed immortal glory
> on Thebes.
> But quickly tying up my robe
> and carrying in my gentle hands a splendid branch
> of laurel, I shall hymn
> the all-glorious house of Aeoladas

---

[30] See Benveniste 1966: 237–50 and 258–66, as well as 1974: 79–88; for an illustration of the pertinence of this linguistic distinction for different forms of Greek poetry in relation to the poetic instance of enunciation, see Calame 2005: 17–26, with references to earlier works.
[31] Bühler 1934: 102–48; for melic poetry and Greek tragedy, see my study, Calame 2004a: 420–37.

and of his son Pagondas,
my maidenly head flourishing
with garlands,
and I shall imitate in my songs,
to the accompaniment of lotus pipes,
that siren's loud song
which silences the swift blasts
of Zephyr,
...
many are the former things . . .
as I adorn them in verses, while the others . . .
Zeus knows, but it is proper for me
to think maidenly thoughts
and to say them with my tongue.
Neither for a man nor woman, to whose offspring
I am devoted, must I forget a fitting song.
As a faithful witness for Agasicles
I have come to the dance
and for his noble parents   (Pind. *fr.* 94b, 3–17 31–40) (Loeb)

These lines are sung by the chorus of young women as they make their way in procession, as mentioned, to the sanctuary of Apollo Ismenios, outside the walls of the city of Thebes.[32] Though the poetic 'I' expresses itself in the feminine, these lines were composed by Pindar, himself a citizen of seven-gated Thebes; by the intermediary of the feminine choral and ritual performance, the poet offers up this partheneion as a musical contribution to the ritual of the daphnephoria. In an act of self-referential enunciation that is very common in melic poetry, the chorus describes in the first person the singing action in which it is engaged. The self-reference to the chorus' verbal and vocal expression is often couched in the 'performative future': in this instance, *humnḗso* (l. 11), 'I shall hymn' (and I am now hymning), and *mimḗsomai aoidaîs* (l. 15), 'I shall imitate in my song'. As we have already noted, the descriptions of the action in the first person turn these self-referential poetic utterances into verbal acts and consequently sung acts; we have here enunciative and performative self-reference. Through the sung words and the ritualized rhythm of the choreography imposed to the choral procession, these sung acts are inserted in the cultic celebration of Apollo Ismenios. Moreover, in declaring themselves faithful witnesses (*pistà mártus*, note the feminine) the young women of the chorus point to the poet's voice.

---

[32] Pi. fr. 94b, 3–17 and 31–40 Sn.-M., on this Pindaric partheneion and the circumstances of its enunciation, cf. Calame 2001: 59–62 and 101–4.

The disparity between the enunciative stances offered by the action poetry that is melic poetry in its various forms and the 'real' protagonists of the circumstance of enunciation is evident. It involves on the one hand, at the level of 'discourse', the phenomenon that I have referred to as 'choral delegation'. This enunciative procedure is particularly in evidence in Pindar's *Epinicians*, where the poet in a sense delegates his voice and his 'author function' to the chorus singing his poem. The melic poem is therefore carried, in its musical performance, by a veritable enunciative polyphony.[33] Furthermore, if it is indeed legitimate to speak of 'self-reference' when by means of the utterance of the enunciation through the use of performative forms the melic chorus describes the ritual act in which it is engaged, it is nevertheless necessary to specify the double dimension of this performative self-reference. The distinction must be made between on the one hand an internal (intra-discursive) reference to the choral activity that is constructed in the discourse at the same time as the enunciative posture pointing to the circumstance of enunciation (the young Theban women describe their choral activity while praising the family of their chorus leader in the first person on behalf of the poet), and on the other hand an external (extra-discursive) reference that designates the actual circumstances of the enunciation (the ritual of the daphnephoricon, with its protagonists, who are not all mentioned in the poem).

If the choral songs of tragedy present the same enunciative and performative procedures as the melic poems, these are now transferred to the orchestra, itself part of a cultic location; the sung action of the chorus is at once mimetic and ritual. To this extent, the internal self-reference of the choral songs of tragedy has as counterpart a double 'external' self-reference, mimetic and dramatic on the one hand and at the level of ritual performance on the other. The tragic chorus is simultaneously a mimetic and ritual actor in the play and in the musical celebration of Dionysos. The chorus acts as much in the time and space of the heroic action that is being represented mimetically as it does in the present of the ritual performance that is taking place in the choral space of the theatre, at the centre of the sanctuary consecrated to Dionysos Eleuthereus.[34]

---

[33] I have illustrated these two concepts by reference to *Olympian 6* in Calame 2009c; for an update on the question of the 'lyric I', see Calame 2010: 117–21 (with annotated bibliography).

[34] From this double point of the view the concept of self-referentiality (choral and tragic) introduced and illustrated by Henrichs 1994/1995 (cf. n. 40 in this chapter) requires clarification, for example, in the direction suggested by Kowalzig 2007b: 232–46, who demonstrates the role of the choral songs of tragedy for the ritual heroization of the dead hero; see also Visvardi 2015: 25–7 and, on 'choral enactment and anticipation' in the example of Euripides' *Electra*, Weiss 2018a: 75–90. The question

3.4 A Case in Point: The Erinyes' 'Binding Song'

But let us leave aside linguistic theory and try instead to illustrate this argument on performative self-reference, semantic and enunciative polyphony, and the choral delegation by means of a tragic song. The musical action to which this poetic song corresponds is carried by a chorus that is at once actor in the drama and protagonist of the tragic musical performance.

> Come, let us now join in dance (*khoròn hápsomen*),
> since we have resolved to display
> our horrifying artistry (*moûsan*)
> and to tell how our company (*stasis*)
> apportions the fortunes of men.   Aesch. *Eum.* 307–11

This is the beginning of the famous 'binding song' sung by the chorus of Erinyes in the first stasimon of Aeschylus' *Eumenides*.[35] This specific case is all the more interesting in relation to our argument for the fact that this song inscribes itself in the dramatic transformation of the identity of the chorus both from the point of view of the tragic action and from the point of view of cult; from avenging Erinyes they become benevolent Eumenides.

This choral song begins as a hymn, with the invocation of Night, mother of the Erinyes. It is announced by the chorus itself (or by its coryphaeus) in some spoken or chanted verses addressed to Orestes. Seeking to purifying himself of the killing of his mother Clytemnestra, the young hero has just invoked the aid of Athena (289–99) – the Athena of 'myth', protagonist of the battle with the Giants, but also the Athena worshipped by the spectators. This Athena with her double identity as a figure of heroic myth and of present-day cult will institute the Areopagus, which will absolve Agamemnon's son at the end of the trilogy. Designated as a 'binding song' (*désmios húmnos*, l. 306) with the deictic *hóde*, this song intended to restrain the young hero is addressed by the chorus as much to Orestes as to the audience.

3.4.1 Song Actions and Enunciative Self-Reference

Executed in a rhythm that combines iambic and dactylic metres, the hymn begins with the traditional opening *áge dé* ('come now'); this verbal expression includes the gesture of the presence implied by the particle *dé*, which refers to the time and space of the performance. Moreover, the

---

of the choral 'I' as subject of performative song acts has been illustrated by reference to the first stasimon of Sophocles' *Trachiniae* by Rodighiero 2012: 89–95.

[35] Aesch. *Eum.* 299–396 (307–11); translated in Sommerstein 2008.

exhortative subjunctive *hápsomen* in the first-person plural ('let us fasten', l. 307) evokes the forms of the performative future that often mark the beginning of melic choral songs. We might think of the performative forms which punctuate the beginning of Pindar's partheneion just mentioned above, or the first lines of Alcman's so-called *Second Partheneion*, to mention only songs performed by a female chorus. 'I shall ... shake (*tináxo*) my yellow hair',[36] declare the young Spartan singers as they begin their song and dance having placed themselves under the protection of the Muses. Just as young Theban women sing Pindar's poem, the young Spartan women sing the words composed by Alcman describing their choral movement towards the location of the musical performance (*mélos*).[37] These performative forms (in the technical sense of the term) generally turn choral melic song into a ritual act and consequently a cultic act that belongs to the sequence of the sacrificial offering to the deity in question.

The performative self-reference that marks the beginning of the song of the Erinyes therefore turns it into a cultic act. The rituality of their song is underlined by its complex metrical structures. After the introductory anapaestic verses there follow four strophic pairs in iambic and dactylic rhythms. The first three strophes are punctuated by an *ephúmnion* in a cretic metre distinguished by frequent resolutions. This hymnic and rhythmic procedure reinforces the incantatory function of the Erinyes' choral song.[38]

The hymnic song composed by Aeschylus and sung by the Erinyes, choral protagonists of the tragic action, is an incantation against Orestes. The goddesses condemn the young hero to pollution and derangement in the obscurity of Hades in retribution for the crime he committed. To the first deictic in the prelude (l. 306), the choral group adds a second deictic gesture. Describing in the first refrain (ll. 328–33) their own 'binding hymn' as a hymn 'without phorminx' (that is to say, without musical accompaniment),[39] the Erinyes designate this song of delirium as *tóde mélos* ('this song').

> And over the sacrificial victim
> this (*tóde*) is my song (*mélos*): insanity,
> derangement, the mind-destroying
> chant (*húmnos*) of the Furies

[36] For the question of the value of the "performative futures" in Pindar, see D'Alessio 2004: 284–294; see also Calame 2004a: 427–431 and above all Bierl 2009: 31-47.
[37] Alcm. fr. 3, 1–9 Page-Davies.
[38] For the complex metrical structure of this choral song, cf. Sommerstein 1989: 138 and 288–90.
[39] On this point, see the detailed commentary by Buè 2014, in contrast with the music of a 'solar' Apollo.

The Erinyes' 'Binding Song' 85

that binds (*désmios*) the mind, sung
to no lyre, a song to shrivel men up!

The effect is to enable this ritual melic song performed in the orchestra of the theatre of Dionysos to be identified as such by the choreuts who are singing it.

This self-referential deictic gesture is carried to its ultimate consequence when, in *Oedipus the King*, the chorus is led to ask itself: 'why should I dance?' (*tí deî me khoreúein*; a choral question to which we shall return in a later chapter). Identified in a seminal study by Henrichs, this kind of commentary by the chorus on its own choral activity and musical performance arises from the double authority discussed above.[40] Typical of dramatic chorality, this self-referential questioning is embedded in the dramatized heroic action; it therefore superimposes itself on the ritual self-reference, which is that of the various forms of melic poetry. Often (self-)critical in relation to the song that is being performed, these choral commentaries are common in Sophocles' tragedies, generally in relation to Dionysiac identity. Inasmuch as they point to the dramatic action being represented and at the same time to the ritual action taking place in the theatre-sanctuary, these self-referential gestures might be thought of as 'meta-theatrical self-reference'. This has been suggested in relation to the interventions of Dionysos himself in the various choral songs of Attic tragedy. But it is necessary to take into account also the evocations by the chorus of cultic celebrations involving choral songs and dance, such as the Spartan Hyacinthia in Euripides' *Helen* or the Delia and Panathenaia in his *Hecuba*; these often involve the sort of 'choral projection' we have identified in the first stasimon of Euripides' *Ion*.[41]

3.4.2 Double (Self-)Reference, Dramatic and Ritual

In the first section of their hymnic song, Aeschylus' Erinyes employ enunciative strategies that are very close to the most ritualized forms of enunciative rhetoric we find in melic poetry. These include the performative verb designating the choral activity in which the choreuts are engaged (*hápsomen*, l. 307), as we have seen; the indiscriminate use of the first-person singular and plural (*hápsomen*, 'let us fasten', but '*hamé*, 'my' – singular – in that same first

---

[40] Henrichs 1994/1995 (cf. n. 34 in this chapter, as well as Chapter 2.3.2), entitled after the self-referential dramatic question asked by the Sophocles' chorus at *OT* 896: cf. Chapter 6.4.1.
[41] See Bierl 1991: 111–72 on the idea of Dionysiac 'meta-theatricality'; for the musical festivals evoked by Euripides' choruses, see Panteli 2010.

strophe); reference to choral dance, with an allusion to the institution of the chorus itself (l. 307);[42] self-designation by the choreuts as witnesses (of the crimes committed) in the same way as Pindar's young chorus celebrating the Theban Daphnephoria declare that they have joined the choral performance (*ḗluthon es khorón*, 'I have joined the chorus') as faithful witnesses for Agasicles;[43] and finally, an invocation to Night, their own mother (ll. 321–2). It is only in the first refrain that the choral song is in a sense 'objectivized' by a sung deictic gesture: *tóde mélos* ('this song', l. 329 = 341).

In these lines just quoted we learn that this fateful song is to be sung without the accompaniment of the phorminx (*aphórminktos*, l. 332 = 344) and that it is performed by the Erinyes. Thus Orestes' pursuers designate themselves – in the third person – as authors of the song that they are performing (ll. 331–1 = 344–5). This gesture of authorial self-reference is reminiscent of the various instances of *sphragís*, authorial stamps familiar from Theognis' elegiacs or the proem of Herodotus' *Histories*.[44] Is it then the case that the voice of the choreuts points here to the voice of the poet? Are we assisting, in the context of the enunciative polyphony of choral melic songs, to an instance of choral delegation? Is Aeschylus expressing himself through the mouthpiece of the Erinyes whom he has conjured up in his play? Does he present himself here as implicit author?

Inasmuch as the tragic choral song is dramatized in the sanctuary-theatre consecrated to a god and is mimetically embedded in the heroic action, the answer is not straightforward. Let us return to the question of melic double self-reference and indulge in a little more theoretical reflection.

From the point of view of the semantic polyphony of the subject matter, it is not difficult to relate the enunciative self-reference of the tragic chorus on the one hand to the pragmatic voice engaged in the dramatic action and on the other hand to the interpretative voice of the choreuts singing in a mimetic mode in the theatre's orchestra. In the first, self-referential and performative stance the choreuts sing in character, with the often-marginal identity posited by their role in the tragic action. In the second, self-referential and hermeneutic stance the chorus intervenes as actor and ritual

---

[42] On this particular point, see the excellent commentary by Henrichs 1994/1995: 62–3 (with the bibliographical references in note 38) as well as, on the choral 'I'/'we', the commentary by Bierl 2001: 81–5; for the 'performative' aspects of this song, see Prins 1991. Cf. the conclusions drawn by Kaimio 1970: 150–7 and 177–9 on the collective meaning of the tragic first person and the 'I' of the coryphaeus, who generally sings as a member of the chorus.

[43] Pi. Fr. 94b, 39 Maehler.

[44] On the various forms of poetic signature, cf. Calame 2004a: 13–23, with extensive bibliographical references.

'performer' in the service of the poet (and his patrons) through the intermediary of the implicit author. In assuming these two voices – the performative and the interpretative – the emotional voice of the chorus takes on an intermediary function between these two roles (protagonist of the heroic action being dramatized and actor implied in the musical ritual of the Great Dionysia); this third voice points back to the virtual public implied by the discourse and, through this, to the real-life public of each tragic performance. They are therefore partners in this semantic and enunciative polyphony, while on the other hand the musical performance is what enables the poet and the spectators to pay honour to Dionysos. The emotive voice is the expression of the tensions provoked by the confrontation between the fictional heroic action being represented and the political, religious and cultural reality of the poet, the actors and chorus, and the audience.

'We believe we practise straight justice: against him who can display clean hands there comes no wrath from us' (*eph' hēmôn*, l. 314), say the Erinyes in the opening of their song, and their reassurance is doubtless aimed less at the protagonists of the tragic action than it is at the spectators. The choreuts are saying that their 'binding song' is not addressed only to Orestes, the main protagonist of the fictional dramatic action, but also to the audience. Thus their general statement, as well as their gnomic statements (which regularly punctuate melic poems just as much as the choral interventions of tragedy) can well be taken to represent an indirect address on the part of the poet to the spectators assembled in the theatre of Dionysos; it is a provisional address, always subject to the development of the dramatic action.

The double deictic gesture that marks the second strophic pair of the Erinyes' song equally indicates this double reference in the demonstrative suffixed in *-de*.

> From our birth we were ordained to have this lot (*táde*, l. 349),
> and to keep our hands off the immortals – there is not even
> anyone who feasts both with them and with us.

Twice in these lines the function of pursuing the killer that the gods have delegated to the Erinyes' is designated with the demonstrative *hóde* (see also l. 360). This double gesture of verbal deixis implies that the Erinyes' pursuit is both of Orestes (dramatic, mimetic reference) and of the spectators (external, cultic reference); the latter group is indirectly invited to revere the Erinyes. Moreover, in these verses not only the venerable goddesses are presented in the orchestra both as protagonists of the heroic action being dramatized and as goddesses who are worshipped by the Athenians. But from the point of view of choral self-reference we witness once more an alternation between the first-person singular (*etúkhthēn*, 'I was made', l. 352; *emaîs melétais*, 'by my efforts', l. 361) and the first-person plural (*eph' hamín*, 'onto us', l. 349). The same goes for the introductory strophe, as we have already remarked, as well as the second refrain (*heilóman*, 'I have chosen', in the singular, l. 354; *amauroûmen*, 'we enfeeble', in the plural, l. 359), and the beginning of the third strophe, where the alternation of 'I' and 'we' relates performatively to the Erinyes' choreographic movements. This is the enunciative stance characteristic of melic poetry.

Be that as it may with regard to enunciative strategies, which are those of choral melic poetry and imply that each chorus member takes individual responsibility for the words that are sung collectively, the song aimed at binding Orestes is a ritually effective song that has an immediate religious effect. It provokes Athena's epiphany to the young hero kneeling in supplication before the goddess's statue. At the end of the song Athena declares 'from far away I heard a cry summoning me' (l. 397; see l. 297 for Orestes' own appeal), and she explains that she is indeed the goddess Athena to whom Attica has been apportioned at the conclusion of the Trojan War, a gift to the sons of Theseus. Athena is thus not only present before the protagonists of the tragic action; she is equally addressing the spectators who worship her as tutelary deity of their city, thus linking the spatio-temporal domain of the dramatic action and the here-and-now of the tragic performance. We see here combined the semantic polyphony and the enunciative polyphony of the tragic chorus. This double polyphony presupposes that the chorus is both a protagonist of the action being dramatized and a 'performer' of a sung ritual declaring the power of the Erinyes and provoking the intervention of Athena (performative voice). It also presupposes the poet as implicit author of the warnings addressed to both the actors and the spectators (hermeneutic voice). And, finally, it presupposes the virtual audience, which through the appeal to Athena, tutelary deity of the city, points to the real-life audience (performative and affective voice).

3.4.3 *Tragic Pragmatics and Its Twofold Reference: The Ending of the* Oresteia

From the point of view of the sung words, the operative distinction between the mimetic (and dramatic) reference and the external reference of the tragic song is essential. The various gestures of verbal deixis play a strategic role in this respect; they punctuate choral songs and melic interventions in Attic tragedy and are often accompanied by a demonstrative in *-de*. The tragic poet exploits fully these demonstratives' capability for internal reference (anaphoric and cataphoric) and external reference: *Deixis am Phantasma* and *demonstration ad oculos*, to refer back to the terms set out by Bühler and already mentioned above. In the case of Attic tragedy, deixis to something that is visible can involve as much the protagonists of the dramatic and mimetic action as the audience viewing the performance.[45]

Thus at the end of the trilogy, in a long exchange between the chorus singing in 'lyric' iambics and Athena who recites in anapaestic dimeters, the goddess attributes to the Erinyes the *timaí* that transform them into Eumenides; they promote the soil's productivity, the prosperity of the flocks and the birth of future citizens, while assuring political concord and justice. Leaving aside the detail of this complex amoebean ('epirrhematic') scene, the choreuts reprise these different attributes in three successive strophic pairs. Here the Eumenides assume the functions that have been assigned to them verbally through promises phrased as intentional futures, that is, speech acts; their sung declarations are intercut with confirmations on the part of Athena (in anapaests).[46]

In particular, the goddess' interventions are punctuated by deictic gestures grounded in demonstrative forms in *-de*. When the Eumenides undertake to assure the resources necessary for the life of the city, which is described as the walls, the altar and the adornment of the gods of Greece, Athena reacts by affirming in a performative manner that she will accomplish (*prásso̱*, l. 928) that which the Eumenides have promised (*táde*, l. 927) to the benefit of 'these citizens' (*toîsde polítais*): the citizens of heroic Athens as well those assembled in the theatre of Dionysos. Then, after the Erinyes express their wish that the harvests, the livestock and the people of Attica be spared by the plague, the goddess addresses herself more specifically to the judges of the Areopagus in metaphorical terms: 'Bulwark of the city, do you hear what these words (*táde hoîa*) are accomplishing?' (ll. 949–50). The deictic *táde* designates the words just spoken by the chorus in the form of wishes concerning both the present of the heroic action and the historical present.

---

[45] Cf. n. 29 in this chapter; for tragedy in particular, cf. Calame 2004a: 420–3 with the various studies published in the relevant themed issue of *Arethusa* (37, 2004).
[46] The formal structure of this scene is laid bare by Fileni 2007: 151–5. For other examples of 'lyric-epirrhematic' scenes, cf. Di Benedetto and Medda 2002: 255–60 (and 265).

The same goes for the second strophic pair sung by the Eumenides. Their commitment to the good fortune of the city's youth and to justice is reprised by Athena's *táde* (l. 967). The goddess expresses her joy in observing the efficacity of the words that brought about the avenging Erinyes' permanent metamorphosis to the benefit of Attica; from the perspective of the tutelary deity, Attica is 'my land'. Athena's reply to Eumenides' appeal for the commonality of friendship to take the place of the law of vengeance in the city is saturated with gestures of deixis (990–5).

> From these (*tônde*) fearsome faces
> I see great benefit coming to these citizens (*toîsde polítais*);
> for by always kindly giving great honour
> to these kindly powers, you will keep your land and city
> on the straight road of justice

This projection into the near future is addressed (in the second-person plural) as much to the protagonists of the dramatic action as to the citizens who represent the audience.

The third strophic pair sings of salvation and rejoicing; this song is addressed alternately by the chorus and by Athena to the people of the city of Cranaus and its children. Once again these are both the Athenians of the heroic drama and those in the audience: residents of the city in which the Eumenides, in their final appeal, join together mortals and gods, under the aegis of Athena, daughter of Zeus.[47]

The songs of classical tragedy seem then to offer, through the example of dramatized heroic action, the pedagogic pragmatic value ascribed to tragedy by Aristophanes when he qualifies tragic poets as the *didáskaloi* of the people. Through dramatic reference and through external reference, the words of the Eumenides and Athena are addressed both to the citizens of the heroic past where the dramatic action is taking place and to their successors in the audience, in the here-and-now of the tragic performance. This dual reference is reinforced by the fact that in Athens in the fifth century the Eumenides were honoured as the Holy Goddesses (*Semnaì Theaí*) in a sanctuary near the Areopagus. As Eumenides, they were also worshipped in the cult of Colonus, duly mentioned by Sophocles, who stages there the death of Oedipus.[48] The aetiological overlap of the heroic past with the cultic and religious present of the audience is subsumed

---

[47] The structure and movement of this amoebean (ll. 916–1020) are well described by Sommerstein 1989: 260–2.
[48] Paus. 1, 28, 6 and Soph. *Oed. Col.* 40–3; on this Athenian double cult of the Eumenides, see Sommerstein 1989: 6–12, 281 and 284, as well as Parker 2009: 142–53 (with the obligatory references).

The Erinyes' 'Binding Song' 91

under the authority of the patron goddess of the city. Implicitly, virtually, the poet is addressing in this song the audience assembled in the theatre of the sanctuary of Dionysos Eleuthereus.

This convergence between 'myth' and 'cult' plays itself out dramatically and ritually at the end of the tragedy and therefore of the trilogy. At the conclusion of the epirrhematic song whose enunciative movement we have just traced, Athena herself introduces in a performative manner the procession that concludes the tragedy: *pémpsō* ('I will escort', l. 1022). By the light of torches, as leader of the chorus, the goddess leads the cortege formed by her priestess and her followers; she involves the Eumenides and the Areopagites (the text is uncertain here)[49] in a civic exodos. The chorus then intones the final processional song in 'lyric dactyls' (1032–47).

> Come on your way, you great, honour-loving,
> childless children of Night, with our friendly escort.
> . . .
> Favourably and righteously minded towards our land,
> come hither (*deûr' íte*), Awesome Goddesses, delighting
> in the fire that devours our torches on your way.
> Now (*nûn*) raise a cry (*ololúxate*) to crown our song (*molpaîs*)!
> May there be peace for the good fortune of whole people of Pallas
> and for their hearths. Zeus the all-seeing
> marches in step with Destiny.
> Now raise a cry to crown our song![50]   Aesch. *Eum.* 1032–47 (Loeb)

Included in this final song through the ritual cry of *ololugé*, the Eumenides are now called to sing here and now, as in all ritual melic song. Just as the use of *tóde* (*mélos*, l. 329 = 342) in the first refrain of the Erinyes' *désmios húmnos* played on the ambivalent reference of the deictic forms in -*de*, so too the call to utter the ritual cry characteristic of paean merges – chorally and ritually – the dramatic action at the conclusion of the trilogy with the tragic performance itself.[51] The dramatic staging of the heroic action represented by actors who speak and sing in the first person thus culminates in a processional song that brings together, on the performative level,

---

[49] For a tentative reconstruction of this passage despite the textual difficulties, see the commentary by Sommerstein 1989: 275–83, a precious aid in this as in many other matters. On the choral endings of Attic tragedy in general, see Rodighiero 2013: 171–4.
[50] Lines 1043–7 have been reconstructed by Casato. See fn. 49 in this chapter for difficulties of this corrupted text.
[51] Uttered by maidens or adult women, the ritual cry of the *ololygé* often punctuates the paean; see numerous references in Käppel 1992: 80–2. On the emotional and political charge of the songs in *Eumenides*, see Visvardi 2015: 94–120.

the voices involved in the dramatic action and those performing the tragedy.

In comparison with melic poetry, in tragedy reference and self-reference are therefore doubled; reference and self-reference (external, extra-discursive) are on the one hand to the mimetic action being played out in the first person in the spatio-temporal world of the heroes, and on the other hand to the ritual action being accomplished, also assumed in the first person, for the benefit of Dionysos Eleuthereus, here and now. And this ambiguity between dramatic action and musical and ritual action is even more marked when the heroic action takes place in Athens itself, as in the case of *Eumenides*. Its pragmatic import is split between two identities: the identity (or generic marginal status) of the chorus as protagonist of the action being represented and the identity of a heroic or divine figure belonging to the religious reality of the audience and of the Athenian community.

With its three dimensions, the semantic polyphony of the chorus of Attic tragedy relies on a strong enunciative polyphony. This vocal interweaving at the level of enunciation includes, in ways that we will illustrate presently, the poet and his public in the religious, political and cultural context of the tragic musical performance. QED? Our provisional conclusions must now be tested against three of the few Attic tragedies whose text has survived in good condition.

CHAPTER 4

Aeschylus' Persians
Questioning Choral Identity

Let us begin by looking at a tragedy that is largely choral. Aeschylus' *Persians* was staged at the Great Dionysia in 472, only one year after the Battle of Salamis, where the Athenian fleet had defeated Xerxes' armada. The Great King had invaded continental Greece, and on reaching Athens had set fire to the Acropolis and destroyed the temple of its tutelary deity Athena, the Old Parthenon. Aeschylus' *choregos* was none other than Pericles. Here we follow the dramatic – and choral – unfolding of this tragedy whose action takes place in Susa, the capital of Persia.

4.1 A Contemporary Athenian Tragedy Set in a Barbarian Land

It is significant that this tragedy too, like *Suppliants* (which was 'taught' by Aeschylus himself), opens with a choral song. At the outset the chorus of Persian elders of the Great King's council identifies itself self-referentially and deictically as Xerxes' faithful guard (*táde pistá*, ll. 1–2; see ll. 681–2). The chorus indicates its geographical position and the time of the dramatic action: Susa, 'city of the Persians', while awaiting the return of the Persian armada from its expedition to conquer Greece. In a technical and formal sense, then, *Persians* (just like *Suppliants*) blends the prologue with the parodos (the chorus's traditional entrance song), so that right from the beginning the chorus presents itself as one of the principal characters of the play. This prologue-parodos fulfils the conventional function of conveying the play's back story. Then, in a first catalogue, the chorus of Persians lists all those who have left Asia to impose on Greece 'the yoke of slavery' (l. 50); the perspective here is at once Persian and Greek, with a temporal movement that positions us at the beginning of the expedition against Hellas.

Now the chorus shifts its attention from the recent past towards the future, and it is here that the parodos proper – the chorus's entrance song – begins.[1] The prologue had been sung in 'marching' anapaests (ll. 1–64); the parodos comprises five strophic pairs sung and danced at first in minor ionics, then in 'lyric' iambics (ll. 65–139). Moving between the hermeneutic voice and the emotional voice, the chorus expresses its deep fear regarding the fate of the Persian army, which is condemned to wage conquest and thus blindly fulfil its divinely ordained destiny. The sentiment is Persian, but the interpretation is Athenian. The song ends with a return to anapaests, as the chorus of Xerxes' advisors prepares to sit in council. Then Queen Atossa, the protagonist, enters the scene; she is Darius' wife and Xerxes' mother. This 'mother of a god' (l. 157), who shares the bed of another god, engages the chorus in a sung exchange in trochaic tetrameters in which she seeks their advice. There follows Atossa's famous account (in iambic trimeters) of her dream involving a dispute between two flawlessly beautiful women, one an inhabitant of Greece and the other of a 'barbarian land' (l. 187). Xerxes' attempt to subjugate the two countries has failed, provoking the fall of the king and the despair of his father Darius. The chorus, reprising its song in trochaic tetrameters, advises the queen to address her supplications to Darius. Then, in a stichomythia in which Atossa and the chorus each alternate a trochaic verse, the chorus informs her regarding Athens and the status of its citizens: 'They are not called slaves or subjects to any man' (l. 242).

It is at this point that the chorus, or the chorus leader, announces the arrival of a man; the man's identity is stated explicitly, in line with the custom required by the wearing of masks. His appearance is Persian, though this does not stop him from speaking in impeccable Attic Greek. This messenger addresses himself first to Persia then to the chorus of Persians; he announces the total defeat of the 'barbarian' army. We will return to this double point of view that constantly blends the Greek (or even Athenian) voice and the Persian voice both enunciatively and in terms of content.

The messenger's initial reports are intercut by brief emotive interventions sung by the chorus in a 'lyric' iambic rhythm. From a metrical point of view, these choral interventions are structured as three strophic pairs sung in 'lyric' iambics (ll. 256–89, technically an *epírrhema*). These choral reactions turn to lamentation to denounce the part played by the gods and entertain resentment at the memory of Athens (ll. 284–7), echoing the messenger's own appeal. Later in the play, Darius will explain the meaning of the injunction to 'remember Athens and Greece' (824); here it is no

---

[1] On the singularity of the parodos of *Persians*, see Taplin 1977: 61–70.

longer an appeal to vengeance against the Greeks, who have twice defeated the Persian army (such as we hear from Darius in Herodotus' retelling of the story after the defeat at Marathon),[2] but rather an appeal to follow the example of the Athenians and Greeks, who, unlike Xerxes, know to avoid the trap of overweening pride (*húbris*, l. 821) and delusion that incur Zeus' punishment.

Encompassing song and rhythmical prose, this exchange between messenger and chorus effects the transition from the first part of the tragedy, which is dominated by the chorus and its songs, to the central part, which unfolds according to the epic modality of *dià miméseos*, in Plato's definition cited above, albeit a mimetic representation proper to tragic staging.

In response to the queen's questioning, the Persian messenger lists a second catalogue of the vassals of Xerxes who have died at the Battle of Salamis. Though Xerxes is safe and sound, the messenger discerns the will of a god (*daímon*, l. 345) in the routing of the barbarian fleet, which has fallen victim to its own size and disorder in the face of the paean of war sung by the Greeks, and whose soldiers are then butchered like a shoal of tunny. The second part of the messenger speech ends with the massacre of the infantry massed on the island of Psyttalia at the hands of the Greek soldiers, and the evocation of Xerxes' lament; his army has now been defeated on land and on sea. Making no mention of the Battle of Plataea, the third part of the messenger's speech narrates the dramatic retreat of the surviving Persian army, further reduced when a large number of soldiers is swallowed by the waters of the river Strymon, whose frozen surface gives way suddenly to the dawn's sunrays. The narrative perspective is Persian, but it is expressed in religious terms that are markedly Greek.

This long narrative section – in narratological terms it is an intradiegetic metalepsis – leads to the time and place of the dramatic action. The messenger's tripartite account provokes, on the queen's invitation, a choral song of lamentation; the coryphaeus recognizes the fateful power (again the divine *daímon*, l. 515) that affects the whole of the Persian *genos*. In an initial address to sovereign Zeus, once more sung in anapaestic metre (ll. 532–47), the chorus proclaims the grief afflicting the Persian cities and the wives of the soldiers whom Xerxes has led to their death. For this wounded people the contrast is now all the more striking between Persian submission to the power of the Great King and the Greeks' freedom of speech, which allowed them to vanquish their enemy.

---

[2] Herodot. 5, 105, 2: 'O Zeus, may I be allowed vengeance on the Athenians', and the Great King orders a servant to repeat to him three times before each meal: 'Lord, remember the Athenians.'

This first stasimon (ll. 548–97) is articulated into three strophic pairs sung first in iambic then in dactylic rhythm interspersed with aeolian metres and some rarer dochmiacs. It interlaces the three voices identified in the previous chapter; there is a performative voice, which by a sonorous initial *nûn dḗ* (l. 548) echoes here and now, in the moment of the performance, the wailing of the whole Asian land and punctuates its lamentations with ritual cries typical of funeral song; second, there is a voice that is at once descriptive and interpretative, which evokes the Persian soldiers who were massacred or drowned in the waters of Salamis, thus referring to the freedom of Athens, the city that the play's audience calls its own; and, last, there is a strong emotive voice singing of the grief arising from the recent destruction of the barbarian army.

Immediately after the mention of Salamis, the queen returns to the scene with the ritual offerings necessary to summon the ghost of her husband Darius. In order to be efficacious, the ritual gestures must be accompanied by sung formulas, and it is of course to the chorus that Xerxes' mother entrusts the singing of songs (*húmnoi*, l. 620) to petition for Darius' presence. It goes without saying that this third choral intervention unfolds entirely in a performative mode, in three strophic pairs sung in minor ionics preceded by a ritual prelude in anapaests (ll. 623–32, then 633–80 for the second stasimon). After an initial address to the relevant gods of the earth (*khthónioi daímones hagnoí*, l. 628, i.e., Ge, Hermes and Aidoneus), the chorus summons up the dead Darius. The singers list the qualities of the Great King as they would do for a Greek god. Even though they state that they are speaking their words of lamentation in the barbarian language, the terms in which the Great King's advisors invoke both the chthonian deities and King Darius belong to Greek religious practice: 'we in song will beseech those with power to send up the dead to be kind to us in their home beneath the earth' (ll. 625–7). We might note in passing the use of the 'performative future'. In fact, this necromantic ritual to bring about the dead king's epiphany is punctuated by cries that lend to this song of invocation also a veneer of Greek funerary lamentation, and it is as such that it is later recognized by Darius: 'sing songs of grief' (686) is the king's command to the chorus, and the song displays in equal measure the performative voice and the affective voice.

The chorus's performative voice is essentially semantic and enunciative, and it is thus, singing in poetic Greek language, that the Persian advisors succeed in summoning up Darius' presence. A figure may have risen into the audience's view above the tomb during the singing of the final strophic pair, which is punctuated with imperatives addressed to the Great King.

The king's long speech (in iambic trimeters) is initially interspersed with the chorus's sung remarks as it expresses its fear of approaching its erstwhile master (ll. 694–6 and 700–702 in minor ionics). Then the queen intervenes to inform her husband of the disaster that has struck down the army led by their son Xerxes. It is finally Darius' turn to make sense (in Greek terms) of the disaster inflicted on the Persian army. Xerxes, in his greed for power and wealth, did not recognize the limits that the gods had assigned to men. He thought that he could fetter the Bosphoros with a pontoon bridge in order to invade Greece, thus opposing the will of all the gods and in particular the will of Poseidon. After attacking the gods' altars, destroying their statues and burning their temples, those of Xerxes' soldiers who had escaped the massacre at Salamis are finally called to be defeated at Plataea. Uttered as an oracle, the lesson does not leave room for appeal (ll. 816–28).[3]

> so great will be the clotted libation of slain men's blood
> on the soil of the Plataeans, shed by the Dorian spear.
> The heaps of corpses will voicelessly proclaim
> to the eyes of men, even to the third generation,
> that one who is a mortal should not think arrogant thoughts:
> outrage (*húbris*) has blossomed, and has produced a crop
> of ruin (*átē*), from which it is reaping a harvest of universal sorrow.
> Look on the price that is being paid for these actions,
> and remember Athens and Greece: let no one
> despise the fortune (*daímōn*) he possesses
> and, through lust for more, let his great prosperity go to waste.
> Zeus, I tell you, stands over all as a chastiser of pride
> that boasts itself to excess, calling it to stern account.

The coryphaeus' brief response deplores the present and future suffering inflicted on the barbarians, while the queen addresses the *daímōn* to voice the dishonour brought on her son by the present disaster (*héde sumphorá*, l. 846). From here until its end, the tragedy resumes the entirely choral modality that characterized its opening. In a third stasimon, sung in 'lyric' dactyls articulated once again into three strophic pairs capped by an epode (ll. 852–907, without an anapaestic prelude), the chorus of Persian elders enumerates the catalogue of Darius' fortunate conquests. The emphasis is on the rich cities of Ionia and the large Aegean islands off the Asiatic coast. In his conquests Darius did not commit his son's error of transgressing the

---

[3] This and all subsequent translations of *Persians* are from A. H. Sommerstein, *Aeschylus: Persians, Seven Against Thebes, Suppliants, Prometheus Bound*, Cambridge MA and London (Publisher) 2008.

boundary between Asia and Europe; as in Herodotus, the boundaries assigned to the human condition correspond, in the exercise of political power, to territorial boundaries that must not be trespassed. By contrast, the reversal visited on Xerxes by the gods is all the more striking. The choral conclusion leaves no room for appeal (ll. 905–7).

> But now (*nûn dế*) we are experiencing the decisive reversal of all this by the gods in war,
> mightily smitten by blows struck at sea.

At this point Xerxes breaks onto the scene. From the outset, the king defeated by the Greeks presents himself as a true 'tragic hero', stricken by a terrible fate (ll. 908–17).

> Iố, iố!
> Hapless that I am, to have met
> this dreadful fate (*moîra*), so utterly unpredictable!
> How cruelly the god (*daímo̱n*) has trodden
> on the Persian race! What am I to do, wretched me?
> The strength is drained out of my limbs
> when I see these aged citizens.
> Would to Zeus that the fate (*moîra*) of death
> had covered me over too
> together with the men who are departed!

Once again sung in anapaests, this tragic poem introduces the long choral exchange whose performance stands, in the context of the tragedy as a whole, as a particularly developed exodos or 'exit' (ll. 918–30, then 931–1078); we will look at its chorality in detail.[4] A musical conclusion executed as we will see in different metrical rhythms, the alternating lamentation of the defeated Great King and his faithful elders transforms the play into an opera of sorts. In *Persians*, the number of sung verses exceeds that of the verses in spoken or chanted metres.

4.2 A Song of Lamentation as Choral Ending

What then of the semantic polyphony and enunciative polyphony of a Persian chorus that nevertheless sings in the diction of Greek melic poetry, with all its lexical, rhetorical, rhythmical, musical and ritual forms, and rooting itself in a characteristically Greek theology? What are

---

[4] For a good discussion of the role of the chorus in *Persians*, see the commentary by Broadhead 1960: xxiv–xxvi, referring to Kranz 1933: 171–2; according to Kranz the chorus lends to the dramatic action the meaning that the poet intends to present to his audience; see also Gruber 2008: 105–55.

A Song of Lamentation as Choral Ending 99

the modes of mediation of a tragic performance taking place in Athens but whose dramatic action is located in a barbarian land? The question is complicated by the fact that this spatial disjuncture is allied to a temporal paradox: instead of belonging to the heroic past, the dramatic action is situated in a time close to the 'now' of the performance. Named after its chorus, *Persians* was produced eight years after the Battle of Salamis, in which Xerxes had been defeated. If the location of the heroic action is a barbarian enemy city, its time is an all-too-recent past in whose events some of the audience will have been direct participants. The dramatic identity of the chorus of *Persians*, with its significant sung interventions, gives the lie to the notion of Greek tragedy as centred on the 'tragic hero'.

4.2.1 *Strophic Structure, Metre and Prelude*

In *Persians*, the chorus not only opens the play by blending together prologue and parados, but it also initiates the dramatic action, which begins with the dialogue with Atossa. Even before the queen, it is the chorus that reacts emphatically to the messenger's account of the Persian defeat; and it is the chorus that also provokes Darius' apparition. Finally, the chorus joins Xerxes in a sung dialogue that develops into the long threnos that concludes the play. The semantic and enunciative polyphony of this impressive final song of lamentation demands special attention. These melic verses turn out in fact to offer an enunciative poetics and a performative pragmatics of singular density, carried as they are by the voice of ritualized emotion.

The rhythmic structure of this song is particularly significant from the point of view of the aesthetics of poetry and ritualized utterance:

- prooimion (ll. 908–30): choral introduction (chorus and Xerxes) in anapaests;
- strophe/antistrophe 1 (ll. 931–47): introduction to the threnos, in the form of a kommos – anapaests + dochmiacs;
- strophe/antistrophe 2 and 3 (ll. 948–1002): sung catalogue of the heroes of the Persian army – anapaests + dochmiacs + paroemiacs;
- strophe/antistrophe 4, 5, 6 and 7 (ll. 1003–65): in some way a melic stichomythia (reciprocal lamentation) – iambs + cretics + choriambs;
- epode (ll. 1066–78): *exodos* proper – iambs + anapaests + dochmiacs.[5]

---

[5] See the discussion of rhythm in Belloni 1988: 259–62, and the detailed metrical study in Broadhead 1960: 294–7 (for the morphology of the *kommós*, see 310–17) with commentary from Webster 1970: 115–18; on the definition of *kommós* and its forms, see n. 18 in Chapter 2.

The defeated Xerxes' arrival in the *orchestra* arouses the grief of the chorus. From the outset this song, which is almost 200 lines in length and concludes *Persians*, is conceived as an exchange between the vanquished king and the chorus of advisors. This melic exchange directly follows the choral song constituting, as with the third stasimon, the chorus's interpretative response to Darius' long intervention; the exchange is in marked contrast with both the choral song and Darius' words. Xerxes begins his intervention with the ritual cry of mourning *ió* (l. 908) and goes to sing of the death wish mentioned above. The chorus replies to this opening song of despair with a further cry of mourning: *ototoî* (l. 918) with reference to the Persian soldiers descended to Hades, victims of the *daímon* (l. 921). The chorus's ritual lamentation (*aiaî, aiaî*, l. 928) echoes that of Asia (*aiázei*, l. 922), now on its knees, in the past giver of life to the youths destroyed by Xerxes.[6] Such is the melic proem, sung in an anapaestic rhythm, of the long concluding threnos taking the form of a kommos, the sung exchange between the Great King and the chorus.

4.2.2   Catalogue and Lamentation

It is Xerxes once again who initiates the song itself with an act of self-accusation and with a new wordplay on *aiaî*. His cry of despair – *oioî* – is reflected by his self-identification as a curse on his family and the land of his fathers, Xerxes worthy of lamentation: *hòd'egón, oioî, aiaktós* ('here I am, alas, one to grieve for', l. 931). In response, the Great King's counsellors sing of their wish to take part in ritual lament. There are frequent instances in Attic tragedy where the chorus gives a ritual expression to tragic sorrow through song. In the first part of this long lament sung by the Persian chorus, this manifests linguistically in the use of a series of verbs of speaking in the self-referential form of the 'performative future':

- 'I shall wail, honouring the suffering of the army stricken at sea' (*héso*, l. 944; there is a textual corruption in this line);
- 'I shall in turn cry out a tearful lament' (*klágxo*, l. 947);
- and especially, 'I shall escort your return with a woeful shout, a mournful lament worthy of the Maryandinoi's dirges, a song drowned with tears' (*pémpso polúdakrun iakhán*, l. 939).

---

[6] Cf. Sophocles' famous wordplay (*Aj*. 430–2 and 898–904) on the lament *aiaî* (*aiázein*) and the name of the hero *Aías*: Loraux 1999: 58–66.

A Song of Lamentation as Choral Ending 101

In this last verse the chorus employs the verb *pémpein* with reference to their song act; this verb is often used in a similar manner by Pindar in his epinicians. The verb refers metaphorically to the choral performance that escorts the athletic victory to the victor's *polis* while celebrating his achievement and his qualities. Pindar's victory songs – and melic poetry more generally – offer several instances of what I have already referred to as 'enunciative and performative self-referentiality'. For instance, inspired by the Charites whom he honours in their garden, the poetic 'I' expresses his intention to 'send' (*pémpsō*) a blazing song to the Olympic victor's *polis*; likened to a racing horse or a winged ship, this processional praise song corresponds to the song that is being sung in the young athlete's city.[7]

The analogy with Pindar's poetry is all the more striking when we consider that the choreuts of *Persians* assimilate their own voice to the mournful voice of the Thracian singers of dirges, who were reputed in Ionian musical tradition. The Maryandinoi of Anatolia were a Thracian people who were known for evoking in their funerary dirges the untimely death of the local hero Bormos. This figure finds a Greek counterpart in such characters as Linos or Hymenaeus; indirect founders of their eponymous melic genres, both these heroes met an accidental death while in the flower of youth.[8] Moreover, the Mariandynoi were said to have given their name to a flute that was specifically used in the musical accompaniment of threnodies. We find here, then, a very brief instance of 'choral projection' on the part of the chorus of Persian elders.

The evocation of the death of the Thracian hero Bormos provokes the performative utterances of the choreuts, who sing of their intention to engage in ritual lamentation; these self-referential exhortations to initiate a threnos that punctuate the first strophic pair are effectively followed by a choral song of mourning. The allusion to the sad disappearance of Bormos is followed by an evocation of the death of the Persian leaders who fell at the Battle of Salamis. This funerary catalogue contrasts markedly with the list that was sung in the *parodos* (ll. 21–57), before the messenger speech relayed the combat and death of the Persian leaders (ll. 302–28). Extending over two strophic pairs, this funerary catalogue is punctuated by the cries of despair of the chorus (*oioioî*, ll. 955 and 967) and Xerxes (*iò ió*, l. 974; *eè eé*, l. 977), who continue to share each strophe initiated by the king. This melic exchange between the

---

[7] Pi. *Ol.* 9, 21–8; see also *Nem.* 3, 76–9 (*pémpō*: sending a song sweet as honey mixed with milk, with a deictic gesture designating the present song) or *Ol.* 7, 7–10 (*pémpon hiláskomai*: sending and consecrating a gift of the Muses as poured nectar), as well as fr. 124a, 1–2 Sn.-M. (*pémpō*: a convivial song transmitted and executed as a dessert!); cf. Chapter 2.3.3.
[8] See Pindar's own poetry, fr. 128c Sn.-M., a fragment of a *threnos*.

chorus and Xerxes takes the form of a kommos in which the chorus and the protagonist of the dramatic action beat their chest as an expression of mourning; it therefore reprises the catalogues of Persian soldier at the beginning of the tragedy. The contrast between the poetic forms of praise and funerary lament turns this choral song into an expression of tragic reversal.[9] This fateful enumeration of names of illustrious and noble Persian warlords fallen in combat takes on the performative and emotional dimension implied by such speech acts and song acts as 'we miss' (*pothoûmen*, l. 992).

Just as in the play's opening praise song, the counterpart to this lament, the pragmatic effect of this list is emphasized by the particular sonorities of the barbarian names. In the parodos the chorus of elders speaks of the grievous longing (*póthos*, l. 62) provoked throughout Asia by the absence of the Persian soldiers (at l. 512 this affects more specifically Susa); this evokes the laments intoned by women at Susa and in other Persian towns when the army does not return.[10] Echoing this somber premonition, Xerxes can now sing of his grief.

> You do stir up in me
> a longing for my brave comrades,
> speaking of unforgettable, unforgettable things, hateful
> beyond hatefulness.
> My heart cries out, cries out, within my body![11] (ll. 987–91)

The chorus replies:

> And there are others too that we miss (*pothoûmen*),
> Xanthes the commander of ten thousand Mardians
> and Anchares of the Arians,
> and Diaïxis and Arsaces,
> lords of the cavalry,
> and Egdadates and Lythimnas
> and Tolmus, never surfeited with battle.
> I am amazed, amazed, that they are not following
> behind your wheeled tent. (ll. 992–1002)

---

[9] On this point, see Hopman 2009: 362–3. The names of the Persian captains in the three catalogues that punctuate the dramatic action are analyzed by Kranz 1933: 90–3; see also the commentary by Groeneboom 1960: 17–22, 76–88 and 188–91; for the relation of these names to Iranian onomastics, cf. Belloni 1988: 80–3. Said 1988: 328–33 has demonstrated the tragic reversal enacted by these catalogues between parados and exodos.

[10] See Hopman 2009: 362–4. Irigoin 1992/1993 draws attention to the sound play in the rhythmical catalogue of the parodos that acts as a verbal counterpart to the choreographic movements of the chorus; the names of the Persian captains exhibit an abundance of varied neologisms, as noted by Citti 1994: 21–37. If these soldiers' names sound Persian, their qualification as being in the flower of youth on the other hand sounds Iliadic: cf. Dué 2006: 57–60.

[11] The text is the beginning of the third antistrophe: cf. Groeneboom 1960: 190–1.

A Song of Lamentation as Choral Ending 103

4.2.3 Amoebean Threnos and the Role of the Choregos

This melic, threnodic and antiphonal catalogue of the fallen generals of the Battle of Salamis is followed by a long dialogue, also melic, between Xerxes and the chorus, still in the form of a kommos. This exchange in which each of the two protagonists speaks a verse in turn (stichomythia) takes up the four strophic pairs plus epode that conclude the tragedy (ll. 1003–77). It too is punctuated by cries of despair and lamentation, which mark its beginning and accumulate at its end (*oí, iè iè, iò iò* twice; ll. 1003–5; *papaî papaî*: l. 1031; *aiaî aiaî*: l. 1039; and an accumulation of *iò* and *eé* to introduce each of the short final lines of the exodos proper: ll. 1067–76).

In the prelude to their melic exchange with the vanquished Persian king, the Persian choreuts combine their ritual and performative voice with their hermeneutic voice. Accusing Xerxes of having caused the loss of so many young men and the defeat of their entire country, they refer once again to the power of the *daímon* (ll. 918–30). But in the song itself, the king immediately picks up the accusation of the chorus to declare that he too is a victim of the *daímon*. He joins the lamentation and takes its lead. Thus the king's invitation ('send forth [*híete*, l. 941] the lament of a plaintive voice') is answered by the chorus's performative expression noted above: 'I will send forth (*héso*, l. 944) lamentation'. Xerxes takes on the function of coryphaeus of the chorus of advisors, or rather the function of melic choregos of the group of choreuts. As choregos, Xerxes in a sense stands in for the coryphaeus. Hence, the catalogue of lost captains and heroes is also initiated by Xerxes, while the chorus prolongs it in each of its interventions, which are introduced by the cries of distress already mentioned (ll. 950–1001); the emotive voice punctuates the informative and interpretative voice, in a semantic polyphony that is redoubled on the enunciative plane by the amoebean exchange between choregos and choreuts.

As for the melic stichomythia, this is more and more characterized by emotion, whose plaintive expression is chiefly assigned to the chorus.

In the final two strophic pairs, the king-choregos invites the advisors-choreuts to continue the lamentation: 'cry out now in response to my cries', l. 1040; the exhortation is repeated at the beginning of the exodos proper (l. 1066); 'cry out a song (*mélos*) in tune with mine' (l. 1042); 'row, row and groan on my behalf' (l. 1046); and so on. First in this sixth strophic pair, the chorus laments the present grief with a gesture of verbal deixis and at greater length then refers to the ritual gesture of beating that accompanies lamentation. These two commentaries, the one interpretative, the other performative, are symmetrically preceded by the cry of grief *otototototoî* (ll. 1043–5 and 1051–3), doubtless intoned by Xerxes himself. And, finally, the seventh and last strophic pair describes, through the commands Xerxes directs at the chorus, the gestures of mourning that accompany funerary lamentation: fists striking breasts, the tearing of beards and hair, the rending of clothes, the shedding of tears – all gestures characteristic of mourning. This last strophic pair is introduced by an invitation on the part of Xerxes to sing a Mysian song (l. 1054) that the Greeks themselves traditionally associated with threnos.[12]

Xerxes' exhortation to the chorus to respond to his cries of lamentation is thus reprised at the beginning of the epode that concludes the sequence of seven strophic pairs, just as it had marked the melic stichomythia (ll. 1066 and 1040). Concluding the choral tragedy, this epode coincides so closely with the exodos that the ritual exit of the chorus is announced by one last performative enunciation: 'Yes, I will escort you, with loud wails of grief' (l. 1077). The future of performative value *pémpsō toí se* in this final line picks up *pémpsō*, also uttered by the chorus, at the beginning of this threnodic song (l. 940). From beginning to end, Xerxes is indeed the choregos who leads the chorus in the ritualized performance of the funeral song.

On the other hand, the choreuts respond to the repeated exhortations of the choregos with the requested lamentation, but also with the performative and deictic statement 'I shall do that too' (*kaì tóde érxō*, l. 1058). This statement underlines the performative dimension of the whole of this amoebean funerary song. Earlier in the play the chorus had already stated performatively then demonstrated the ritual efficacy of its songs in the hymnic invocation to the gods of the underworld and in the appeal for Darius' apparition. The final line sung by the chorus, by repeating the performative future *pémpsō*, not only confirms the transformation of the choral lamentation conducted by Xerxes into a ritual threnos, but it furthermore turns the whole of the tragedy into a funerary song, a dramatized and dramatic threnos, by means of melic, enunciative, and performative self-referentiality.

4.3 Choral Identity, Cultural Identity

How does this typically Greek melic and ritual self-referentiality affect the social identity and the enunciative position of this particularly active chorus? As we have already remarked, despite their barbarian dress and

---

[12] See the commentary by Belloni 1988: 250; for Xerxes as *éxarkhos* of the threnos, see Kaimio 1970: 121–4 and 219. By adopting the perspective of the choreuts, Xerxes is in a sense reintegrated within the community, as remarked by Hopman 2013: 72–4. For the correspondence between the words sung on the imperative mode (for instance, *e* at l. 1046) and the gestures of grief they refer to, see Gianvittorio 2017: 90–100.

the exotic setting of the action, the characters and chorus of Aeschylus' *Persians* speak and sing in Greek; they employ a language that, in formal and semantic terms, corresponds specifically to that of an Athenian poet of the fifth century. Moving on from enunciative self-referentiality to consider dramatic and mimetic self-referentiality, we must now interrogate the status and role of this chorus that is barbarian from the point of view of the location of the dramatic action (Susa) while being Athenian from the point of view of its temporal positioning. We will confine ourselves to the long threnodic song that concludes the tragedy and remark that from the outset Xerxes presents himself morally as a tragic hero in the Attic tradition; he is the victim of his destiny (*moîra*, l. 909; cf. l. 917 for the ring composition in this first section of the prelude) and he endures the most grievous suffering. Consequently, the defeated Great King addresses Zeus to demand death in response to the tragic question *par excellence*: *Tí pátho tlḗmon* ('What am I to do, wretched me?', l. 912).[13]

In the first stasimon, the chorus also address their first lamentation to Zeus; as we have seen, their song of mourning is provoked by the news of the destruction of the Persian army. The song itself is introduced by a prelude, which is sung and danced in an anapaestic rhythm (ll. 532–47). This first proem to a song that interweaves the three voices of the chorus – sung performance, interpretation and expression of emotion – includes initially a description of the grief that seizes the cities of Susa and Ecbatana, followed by the women's gestures of mourning, the rending of their garments and drenching of their chest with tears. The evocation of their longing (*pothéousai*, l. 542) following their recent marriage and of their insatiable affliction provokes the performative intervention of the chorus, which evokes the ritual expression of the young women's mourning. In the transition from the third person to the first person (*kagṓ*, l. 546), the chorus implicates itself in a speech act (*aíro*, 'I shoulder the burden', l. 547), and its voice becomes performative:

> O Zeus the King, now, now by destroying
> the army of the boastful
> and populous Persian nation
> you have covered the city of Susa and Agbatana
> with a dark cloud of mourning.
> Many <mothers in a piteous plight>

---

[13] Belloni 1988: 234–5 provides a dozen parallels for this tragic question about human destiny; he also remarks on the epic colouring of Xerxes' speech. For the Greekness of the key terms and notions in *Persians*, see also Broadhead 1960: xxx–xxxii; in contrast, Hall 1989: 69–100 is sensitive to the specifically barbarian traits of Aeschylus' *Persians*.

are rending their veils with their delicate hands
and wetting the folds of their garments till they are soaked through
with tears, as they take their share in the sorrow;
...
And I too shoulder the burden of the death of the departed,
truly a theme for mourning far and wide.   (ll. 532–40 and 546–7)

These words enact a 'choral projection' spanning both genders and leading to the present, as the chorus introduces its own song of lamentation in which men sing like women.

Some scholars have wished to see in this figure of a god with sovereign power an *interpretatio graeca* of Ahuramazda.[14] In fact, Zeus reigns over the Persians, often as sole divinity, in the same way as he reigns over Aeschylus' *Agamemenon*. The formulaic appeal addressed to the god by Xerxes' advisors (*O Zeû Basileû*, l. 532) corresponds exactly to that sung by the elders of Argos in that first tragedy of the *Oresteia* (l. 355).[15] Furthermore, this first stasimon concludes with a celebration of freedom of speech while relating it to liberation from the yoke of slavery that the Persians had attempted to lay on the Greeks: now 'the island of Ajax', that is, Salamis, is drenched with Persian blood (ll. 591–7). Here the descriptive and interpretative voice of the chorus manifestly adopts a completely Athenian perspective. Likewise, Darius' apparition denounces in entirely Greek terms the absence of moderation that has characterized Xerxes' actions. His son's *hubris* (l. 821) is the precursor to his delusion (*átē*, l. 822), which brings about the failure predicted by the oracles and sanctioned by Zeus.[16] The god punishes audacious and impious undertakings; he is the chastiser of intentions that trespass beyond the limits assigned to mortals by the gods. At the end of the third stasimon, which is sung in reaction to Darius' intervention, the chorus recognizes that the Persians's reversal of fortunes is doubtless the result of divine will in retribution for transgressing the limits assigned to mortals; as Persians, they must bear (*phéromen*, l. 904) the consequences.

The chorus's statement of Xerxes' complete reversal of fortune aligns with the tragic irony that is typical of Attic drama. In the parodos, the

---

[14] See the references in Hall 1996: 15; see also Garvie 2009: 232–5.
[15] On this point, see Bacon 1961: 15–63, with the references provided by Belloni 1988: xiv–xvii. The role attributed to Zeus by Darius, who is here a mouthpiece for the poet, in response to the chorus of Persians is illuminated by Winnington-Ingram 1973 and, more generally, by Lloyd-Jones 1971: 79–103.
[16] The logic of fault and retribution governs other tragedies, too; see the parallels flagged in the commentary by Groeneboom 1969: 170–4; in general, cf. Said 1978: 96–118 and 318–61.

Great King's advisors do not hesitate to say that Xerxes is a mortal who is equal to the gods (*isótheos phós*, l. 80); as a Persian, he descends from Zeus through Perseus, he is the 'descendent of the golden rain' (an allusion to the story of Zeus' metamorphosis to impregnate Danae). Moreover, the same chorus greets Queen Atossa's arrival on the scene by saluting her as both spouse and mother of a god. Here the perspective is Persian, but it immediately takes on a Greek shading: 'unless our old protecting power has now changed sides against our army' (l. 158).

In the exodos the chorus will state, in its interpretative voice, that the power of Xerxes embodied by the splendour of his army has been destroyed by a *daímon* (l. 921). The embodiment of a fate directed by the divinity, this power is also evoked by the chorus in the introduction of their first threnodic song, in the first stasimon: 'O you god who has caused such toil and grief (*o duspónete daímon*), how very heavily you have leaped and trampled on the entire Persian race!' (ll. 515–16); this echoes the messenger's allusion to the *daímon* (*theós*, l. 514) who has brought such evils to the Persians, and it also echoes the queen herself, who had referenced a 'cruel divinity' (*ô stugnè daímon*, l. 472) leading astray the Persians. Later in the play, Xerxes, while recognizing his own responsibility (*hód' egón*, l. 931), ascribes his reversal of fortune to the will of a *daimon* (*daímon hóde*, l. 942); the Persian messenger (l. 345), the coryphaeus (l. 515) and Darius (l. 825) had all spoken to the same effect. In addressing the Great King, as we have seen, the chorus adopts once again an Athenian point of view to evoke Asia brought to its knees.

In the same way as in Sophocles' *Oedipus the King*, the hero attributes his suffering not only to fate and the will of Apollo, but also to his unfortunate self (*egó tlámon*, ll. 1329–33). Likewise, Xerxes seizes in Greek tragic terms on the three causes at the root of his actions and his ruin: the *daímon*, Zeus and himself. From the first threnos at the beginning of the first stasimon to the long song of mourning at the end of the play, the chorus lament in Greek terms the fateful end of a hero of Greek tragedy.

4.4 Polyphonies of Identity and Emotions

Thus by poetic, dramatic and ritual means the musical performance of the threnos in the extended exodos of *Persians* turns Xerxes into the paradigmatic Greek tragic hero who suffers a reversal and loses his status and fortune. Herodotus remarked at the beginning of his 'inquiry' on the Persian Wars that reversal of fortune is the universal threat hanging over men and their cities; he made the Athenian lawgiver Solon the mouthpiece of this wisdom for the Lydian King Croesus: 'All of man is chance' (*pân esti ánthropos sumphoré*). And, as we have seen, Aristotle, in his prenarratological perspective on Greek poetics, placed reversal at the heart of proper tragic action.[17]

In this perspective, the debate on the 'moral' versus 'amoral' value of Greek tragedy becomes irrelevant. As a Greek hero, Xerxes is punished for his hybristic actions, and in his punishment he is the victim of his *daímon* by the will of Zeus.[18] For this reason and even though sometimes the conventions of Greek threnos are transgressed, the Persian king's lament in his role as choregos of the chorus of his advisors is expressed in a Greek voice; and, as we have seen, the chorus joins in with this voice in a performative vein. The semantic polyphony and the enunciative polyphony of Xerxes and his chorus, which at first had been redoubled, eventually come to coincide. Certainly the final song of lamentation and mourning that is shared between the choregos and the choreuts is characterized by the predominance of the emotive voice, which is accentuated by barbarian exaggeration, as well as by the pragmatic voice of ritual performance; thus it is suited to arousing in the audience the feelings of compassion and terror mentioned by Aristotle in his enigmatic dictum on the cathartic effects of Attic tragedy.[19]

This manner in which the voice of the chorus combines a semantic and dramatic polyphony with an enunciative and performative polyphony gives rise to a complex identity that, from a social and spatial perspective, is in some ways marginal. This double dislocation is especially apparent with regard to the chorus of Aeschylus' *Persians*. On the one hand the choreuts' dramatic identity as a character in the dramatic action lends them the status of guardians and elderly servants of the Great King. The king becomes in effect their choregos in the final song, where, in the enunciative and performative exchange he leads, the two voices end up coinciding. But the chorus's performative voice is essentially Greek, both on account of the poetic language it employs and on account of the ritual forms in which the long song of lamentation is couched. Though they are men, the chorus in a sense play the part ascribed by Thucydides to the wives of the Athenian

---

[17] Herod. 1, 5, 4 and 32, 4; Arist. *Poet.* 1451a 9–15 12–21; for the role of tragic reversal (*metabolé* ou *metástasis*) in *Persians*, see Said 1988; cf. Chapter 2.1.1.
[18] On the terms of the debate, see Garvie 2009: xxii–xxxii.
[19] For the probable effect on the audience of the ritual lamentation which closes the tragedy, see Swift 2010: 326–9; see also Pelling 1997: 13–19 on Aeschylus' presentation of the Persians as being at once close and alien, as well as Hopman 2013: 58–67 for the Athenian perspective adopted by the 'multireferential' chorus. For the controversial question of *kátharsis*, see n. 3 in Chapter 2.

Polyphonies of Identity and Emotions 109

war dead on the occasion of the annual funerary ceremony that was celebrated before the *demósion sêma* in the Kerameikos.[20] Any marginality that can be ascribed to the chorus of *Persians* doubtless has more to do with this blending of genders that with its barbarian identity.

On the other hand, with its essentially Greek interpretative voice, the chorus of Persians evaluates the dramatic action in which it participates in the terms proper to classical Athenian ethics; its interpretations are in line with essentially the male norms of Delphic wisdom and religious thought of the time. It follows that both from an ethical-theological perspective and from a linguistic perspective, the polymorphous dramatic identity of the chorus of *Persians* fundamentally belongs to Greek heroic world, just like the identity of the other dramatic characters. The chorus sings in a poetic language coloured with epic undertones like that of the chorus of the *Oresteia* or of *Suppliants*. But perhaps because the dramatic action belongs to the very recent past, the chorus lays claim, through its hermeneutic voice, to values and motivations of human action that are those of the present ideological conjuncture. From this point of view, in *Persians* the choreuts act rather like average Athenian citizens. Rather than insisting on the 'otherness' of the chorus of *Persians*, more recent scholarly interpretations have rightly shifted their focus to its 'Greekness', particularly in the threnos at the end of the play.[21]

Finally, between the performative dimension and the hermeneutic dimension of the chorus's song, the affective voice appears to assume the role of intermediary through a sort of universal emotional language that covers the Greek and the Persian identities, as well as the male and the female identities. This choral voice of emotion expresses a universal suffering in the face of the evils of war and the reversals of fortune to which all mortals are subject.[22] It stimulates the Athenian audience in a universal mode, here and now. Thus the social and ritual identity of the poetic 'I'/'we' of the chorus of *Persians* points to that of the members of its Athenian audience celebrating the festival of Dionysos.

---

[20] Thuc. 2, 34, 4. As Hopman remarks (2009: 373 n. 26) the feminine character of the kommos, considered as an 'un-Athenian, effeminizing song', is debatable, *pace* Hall 1996: 168–9; see also Gruber 2008: 145–55 and Swift 2010: 328–32, who describes the gendered and ethnic differentiations made by this kommos at the conclusion of the tragedy.

[21] The 'Greekness' of the chorus's song at the end of *Persians* has been well discussed by Hopman 2009: 272–6; she concludes that 'The Persian dirge spills over form the stage into the Athenian polis.' See also Alaux 2007: 119–23, who remarks on the wordplay in the interjections that punctuate this threnodic song.

[22] For the extension of tragic suffering to the audience in the civic theatre, cf. Nagy 1994/1995: 51–2 and Segal 1996: 157–68.

By way of conclusion to this discussion of the choral pragmatics of
Persians let us cite an anecdote from Herodotus' inquiry into the origin and
causes of the Persian Wars. These causes included the destruction of the
prosperous Ionian city of Miletus at the hands of the Great King Darius,
despite the aid lent by the Athenians to the Ionians in their revolt against
Persian domination. In 494, a few years before the Battle of Marathon,
Miletus had been annihilated by the Persian army, and its population
enslaved and deported to Persia. A few years after these events, in which the
Athenians had played a part and been closely affected, the tragic poet
Phrynichus had staged them in a play entitled *The Sack of Miletus*. The
Athenian audience burst out into wails at the spectacle of this tragic
dramatization of a heroic action belonging to the very recent past. The
committee charged with judging the correct conduct of the musical contest
condemned Phrynichus to pay a heavy fine.[23]

About fifteen years after Phrynichus staging of the Great King's first
attack against a Greek city, Aeschylus had certainly learnt the lesson.
Though his subject was a Greek victory rather than a defeat, it was
impossible for him to represent a recent heroic action without transforming it into a *palaión*. To temporal distance Aeschylus substituted, as
we have seen, geographical distance; seen from Susa, the victory at
Salamis becomes a tragic defeat whose meaning is yet exemplarily
Greek. If such spatial dislocations are common in tragedy, they are
nevertheless generally restricted to the Greek world, and they are combined with temporal dislocation, that is, the play is set in the heroic
past.[24] The Persian heroic and choral voices sing in Greek and turn the
outcome of the battle, as it would have been experienced in Susa, into an
exemplum for the disastrous consequences of a rupture in the order of
díkē through acts of *hubris* and sudden reversals of fortune; these are
cornerstones of the Athenian conception of the human condition. From
the point of view of emotion, the Persian choreuts, led by Xerxes as
choregos, intone the final threnos, which is punctuated by cries of grief
and lamentation. The Athenian public laments only indirectly, whereas
in the case of Phrynichus' *Sack of Miletus* the entire theatre had joined in
lamentation; *kátharsis* may have been facilitated by the geographical

---

[23] Herod. 6.21 = Phryn. Trag. test. 2 Snell (cf. Hopman 2009: 376 as well as Calame 1999b, in connection with Herodotus' account).

[24] These spatial dislocations are discussed by Froma Zeitlin, in particular Zeitlin 1993: 154–71; for *Persians*, in combination with the *mise en abyme* of Darius' speech in the perspective of the tragedy as an 'act of memory', see Grethlein 2007.

Polyphonies of Identity and Emotions

distance of the action, which will therefore have affected the spectator less as citizen than as mortal.[25]

The songs' semantic and enunciative polyphony, allied to the chorus's dislocated, polymorphous narrative and dramatic identity, enables the affective and hermeneutic mediation of the poetic dramatization; its objective is a collective action that belongs to the city's heroic past. Thus in the orations of Demosthenes and especially Isocrates, the *Persiká*, the Persian Wars, seen from a distance of a century and a half, belong to the city's *arkhaîa*, just like the *Tr̯oiká*, the deeds of the Trojan War.[26]

---

[25] For the probable purification of passions (cf. n. 3 in Chapter 2) operated in particular by the dirge that concludes *Persians*, see the fine reflections in Loraux 1999: 123–37.

[26] For the uses of the heroic past in fourth-century rhetoric, see Calame 1998.

CHAPTER 5

Euripides' Hippolytus
Choral Song and Gender

We have referred elsewhere to Aristotle's pronouncement in his *Poetics* on the role of the chorus in tragedy: 'the chorus must be regarded as one of the actors; being part of the whole, it should take part in the action (*sunagōnízesthai*), not as in Euripides, but as in Sophocles'.[1] In the wake of this famous normative statement it is often said that the chorus of Euripides' tragedies no longer played the central role it had played in those of Sophocles. According to Aristotle the tragic poet Agathon had been the first to turn the chorus's interventions into mere musical intermezzos or *embólima*, and many have ascribed the same tendency to Euripides. If there is one play of Euripides that does not justify this belief it is his second *Hippolytus*. This play shows the master tragedian at the apex of his poetic career.[2]

5.1 The Chorus of *Hippolytus*, between Feminine and Masculine

The main chorus of Euripides' *Hippolytus* is made up of women of Troezen, the city where the action takes place. The play's heroine, Phaedra, addresses the chorus as 'well-born daughters of Troezen' (*paîdes eugeneîs Troizēníai*, l. 710). From the point of view of the dramatic action, then, the choreuts are daughters of the aristocratic families of this small Peloponnesian city where Theseus was said to have been born.

At the time of the action Theseus, who is now king of Athens, has returned to the place of his birth to purify himself after killing the Pallantides. The young Hippolytus, son of Theseus and an Amazon, is

---

[1] Arist. *Poet.* 1456a.
[2] The question of Euripides' second *Hippolytus* as palinode is discussed exhaustively in the excellent commentary by Barrett 1964: 10–45. The tragedy was produced in 428 BCE. It is in this wider sense of participation in the dramatic action that I understand Aristotle's *sunagōnízesthai*, *Poet.* 18, 1456a 25–7; see on this matter the critique of Gentili 1984/1985: 33–5 in Di Benedetto and Medda 1997: 396–7 (cf. n. 9 in Chapter 2).

being educated in Troezen by his grandfather Pittheus, Theseus' mortal father. The plot of this second *Hippolytus* is well known. Aphrodite causes Phaedra, Theseus' wife, to fall in love with her son-in-law Hippolytus, who is exclusively and excessively devoted to the virgin goddess Artemis. Phaedra's nurse reveals to him his mother-in-law's passion, causing Phaedra to vow to bring about his ruin and commit suicide. On his arrival in Troezen, Theseus discovers in his dead wife's hand a note accusing Hippolytus of having raped her. The king curses his son, who is then fatally wounded in a chariot accident caused by Poseidon. Artemis intervenes *ex machina* to place the blame on Aphrodite; Hippolytus dies having received his father's forgiveness.

One thing is worth noting at the outset. In her various exchanges with the chorus, which is composed of women who share her same social status, Theseus' wife uses alternately the plural and the singular forms of the second-person address. This alternation shows that the coryphaeus' voice is conceived as collective, for he – or, better, 'she', in this instance – speaks and sings as representative of the chorus.[3] Above all, this grammatical oscillation is a sign of the integration of the chorus and its sung interventions in the action of the drama.

5.1.1 *The Final Choral Intervention: From Aphrodite to Artemis*

There are many functions to the songs of this group of fifth-century Athenian citizens who, by the interposition of mask and costume, play the role of heroic-age aristocratic women of Troezen. The best way to describe these functions is in the first instance to turn to the fourth stasimon. This is the chorus's last intervention before the brief final song of the exodos.

Returning from Athens, Theseus has learnt simultaneously of the suicide of his wife and her allegation justifying this act. Cursing his son Hippolytus to his divine father Poseidon, Theseus condemns the young man to exile and thus brings about his undoing, for as soon as Hippolytus has left Troezen, on the shore of the Saronic Gulf across the water from Athens, the horses pulling his chariot are startled by a bull emerging from the sea. Entangled in his reins and dragged behind his chariot, the young man is mangled by his own horses, the same horses he had boasted of

---

[3] The problem of the attribution of sung verses to coryphaeus or the chorus is approached with reference to the issue of the chorus's collective first person in Kaimio 1970: 31–5 and 207–8.

mastering during the hunt. He is carried on the scene drawing his last breaths.

Before Hippolytus' return to the scene, Theseus employs a performative future (*elégxō*, l. 1267) to indicate that he will refute his son. The king of Athens interprets Hippolytus' sudden change of fortune and his imminent death as a righteous punishment visited onto him by the deity; his words – 'with the misfortunes from the gods' (*daimónōn sumpohoraîs*, l. 1267) – echo the terms used a few lines earlier by the coryphaeus when he referred to a change of fortune and to destiny (*sumphorá* and *moîra*, ll. 1255–6). In reaction to this interpretative exchange, the women of Troezen address Aphrodite in a brief song.

> You lead captive the unyielding hearts of the gods,
> Cypris, and of men, and with you,
> surrounding you with his swift pinions,
> is he of the gleaming wings.
> Eros flies over the earth
> and over the loud-roaring salt sea,
> he bewitches the one upon whose love-maddened heart,
> winged and gold-gleaming, he flies;
> he bewitches the whelps of the mountain and those of the sea,
> what the earth brings forth
> and what the blazing sun looks down upon,
> and likewise mortal men. Over all these,
> Cypris, you alone hold royal sway. (ll. 1268–81) (Loeb)

Comprising just one strophe, this choral ode is sung and danced to a strongly emotive dochmiac rhythm. The form of this choral song has led to it being interpreted as a hymn addressed to Aphrodite and her attendant Eros.[4]

In actual fact, this song only includes the first part of a hymn or cultic prayer: the invocation, without either the narrative section or the request. The chorus of women of Troezen describe how the goddess of love exerts her power over her domain; she holds sway over animals, men and gods, on earth as well as in the sea, thanks to the spell cast by Eros that overcomes their hearts with madness. Beyond the emotion expressed in particular by the metre chosen for this ode, two instances of the second-person indicatives (*sù ágeis*, 'you lead', and *kratúneis*, 'you rule over', at ll. 1269 and 1281 in a framing structure) take the place of the imperative we would expect in

---

[4] Cf. Barnett 1964: 391–6. The functional character of this stasimon as reminder of Aphrodite's power is underscored by Hose 1990: II, 128–30.

a hymn; they transform the cultic petitions addressed to the divinity in a hymn into simple observations. These grammatical forms therefore transform the performative significance of this opening of a hymnic song into a choral commentary on the dramatic action.

And indeed, no sooner has this cultic song that blends performative voice and hermeneutic voice reached its completion than Artemis herself makes her epiphany. In an introductory song in anapaests the goddess declares her identity, as Aphrodite had done at the beginning of the play, and addresses herself to Theseus; she, the daughter of Leto, addresses the son of Aegeus. In her authoritative voice the goddess takes the place of the hero to present the meaning of the narrative action dramatized before the choreuts and the audience. Her focus is on the recent suicide of Phaedra and the imminent death of her son-in-law Hippolytus. Artemis' extended intervention at the conclusion of the tragedy is the counterpart to Aphrodite's long speech in the prologue of the play. The daughter of Leto does not hold back; Hippolytus and Phaedra, the young man and adult woman, the unmarried adolescent and the wedded wife, are both victims of the will and power of Cypris. Just before the final choral song of the tragedy the name of the goddess of erotic desire punctuates Artemis' lengthy revelations.

Carried by the emotive and performative voice, the hermeneutic voice of the chorus of young women of Troezen anticipates what Theseus himself will acknowledge in the last lines he speaks in the play: 'the woes you have brought to pass are many, Cypris, and I shall remember them' (l. 1461). The driving forces of the dramatic plot are connected, largely by the chorus and its songs understood as musical performances, to the power of the two female deities of adolescent and adult femininity: Artemis and Aphrodite. And this, at least apparently, with little regard to the difference of gender between Hippolytus and Phaedra.

5.1.2 The First Choral Song: Sexual Ambiguity

Certainly Aphrodite's prominence is unsurprising in a play dramatizing a heroic episode dominated by the power of eros and concerning a *númphe*, for Phaedra is a young bride who is not yet a mother. But in such a context, Artemis' crucial intervention can seem unexpected.

In order to make sense of it we must turn back from the final choral intervention to the beginning of the play. The prologue spoken by Aphrodite (ll. 1–57) is followed by a first choral song. Even before the parodos proper, this first choral intervention mixes the performative voice and the hermeneutic voice in order straightaway to relate the dramatic action to the divinities who direct it. But instead of being assigned to the young women of Troezen, as the parodos would lead us to expect, this short musical performance is assigned to a chorus of young men. Aphrodite herself introduces this chorus onto the scene at the end of her opening exposition. By a double gesture of verbal deixis the goddess refers to Hippolytus, the son of Theseus on his return from the hunt, then to his throng of servants, who enter the scene in procession (*kômos*, l. 55) to 'celebrate the goddess Artemis with hymns', as the goddess of love says. In place of the adult women of the main chorus, wives of prominent Troezenian families, these are young unmarried men, hunters and servants of Artemis, who distinguish themselves explicitly from the *néoi* or young adults (ll. 114–15).[5] The contrast between these two choral groups is significant; they differ in terms of sex, age and marriage status.

With a few performative words sung in a dactylic rhythm, Hippolytus enjoins the young men to follow him and sing heavenly Artemis (not Aphrodite) to honour her through a collective musical ritual (*melómestha*, l. 60). Hippolytus, then, presents himself in these lines not so much as a tragic coryphaeus but rather as a melic choregos of a chorus that is apparently secondary; in so doing, he introduces a processional hymn sung and danced in an Aeolian rhythm which takes the place of the initial parodos.[6] The young choreuts sing as follows during their choreographed procession.

> Mistress, mistress most revered,
> offspring of Zeus,
> rejoice, rejoice in my song, Artemis,
> daughter of Leto and Zeus,
> by far the most beautiful of young women,
> you who in the vast heaven
> dwell in the halls of a noble father,
> Zeus' golden palace.
> Rejoice in my song, o most beautiful,
> most beautiful of all goddesses of Olympus. (ll. 62–71)

Referred to by Aphrodite as a *húmnos*, this first song glorifies Artemis, goddess of erotic ambiguity and of adolescence. This song naturally

---

[5] The scholia refer to this group of choreuts an independent, complementary chorus of young hunters, companions of Hippolytus: cf. *ad* 58 (II, p. 12 Schwartz); see the commentary by Barrett 1964: 167–8 (with a good metrical analysis of this ritual song) and Section 5.1.5. A 'secondary chorus' or the division of the chorus into two semi-choruses is attested in many tragedies: cf. Di Benedetto and Medda 1997: 242–5.

[6] The role of 'leader' assumed by Hippolytus is recognized by Barrett 1964: 169.

anticipates the final stasimon, which, as we have seen, is addressed to Cypris, the goddess of adult love, whether harmonious or conflictual. Structural opposition is reinforced by chiasm; this first hymnic ode in honour of Artemis follows immediately after Aphrodite's prologue, while the final song addressed to Aphrodite by the chorus of women of Troezen comes immediately before Artemis' long concluding explanation.[7] This opposition is also underlined by the polarities of age and gender of the two choruses, the secondary chorus of unmarried youths and the main chorus of married women. We will return to this.

Though it glorifies Zeus' and Leto's daughter, most beautiful of maidens, this first choral song, too, is not a complete hymn. These lines appeal to the goddess to rejoice (in the present song), and thus essentially correspond to the concluding section of a prayer as it would be sung in its cultic form. In fact, this choral song plays a part in introducing the ritual offering that in the following lines Hippolytus himself will present to the goddess in a performative manner (*phérō*, 'I bear', l. 74): a garland that the young man designates with a deictic gesture that is frequent in ritual melic poetry (*tónde stéphanon*, 'this garland', l. 73); moreover this is a garland woven with flowers from a meadow whose ambiguity I have already remarked on elsewhere, though Hippolytus himself qualifies it as an 'undefiled meadow' (*akēratos leimṓn*, l. 74). Throughout the tragedy the hero in his devotion to Artemis behaves effectively like a virgin huntress, evoking for the spectators and for us the figure of Atalanta, who refused marriage. On the other hand the meadow is full of seductive flowers, like that where Pluto snatched Persephone as she was entranced by the fragrance of narcissus to take her to the depths of Hades and compel her to marriage. This meadow is ambiguous; Hippolytus regards it as being consecrated to the virgin Artemis, but in actual fact it evokes Aphrodite's erotic powers.[8]

From the perspective of the social role of the different genders, though Phaedra and Hippolytus are both victims of Aphrodite's discretionary power, this is in fact because Hippolytus behaves like a young woman who refuses marriage on account of his exclusive devotion to Artemis; in the execution of the ritual he confuses the domain of Aphrodite's seductive and erotic power with the virgin territory that he believes to be reserved for Artemis. Furthermore, in their closing song where they interpret the

---

[7] This structural parallelism in chiastic form is remarked upon by Barrett 1964: 392.
[8] The cultic characteristics of this first choral song are noted by Barrett 1964: 167: 70; on the ambiguity of this 'undefiled' meadow, see Segal 1965: 127–54; for meadows and gardens in connection with erotic seduction, see Calame 2009a: 209–37. Hippolytus' (not Euripides') contemptuous attitude towards (married) women is well commented by March 1990: 43–9.

dramatic action in the hermeneutic voice, the choreuts wearing the mask of women of Troezen express themselves just like Theseus in his concluding remarks; they denounce Aphrodite's power over mortals. By contrast, the chorus of Hippolytus' followers, expressing themselves in a cultic and performative mode, adopt an attitude that is determined by their gender; just like Hippolytus, these youths sing in the manner of young women who honour Artemis. They do not recognize Cypris' all-conquering power, leaving that duty to the Troezenian women instead.

If the tragic choral voice does not seem particularly gendered in its interpretative dimension, on the other hand in its ritual and performative function it is shaped by the gender of the speakers. It is determined by the gender and social status of the dramatic characters played by the choreuts in relation to the identity, the gender status and the field of action of the deity they invoke. In the dramatic world of the story of Hippolytus in Euripides' second retelling of it, both the hero and his followers tend towards the status of young women devoted to Artemis, in an ambiguity that is typically tragic; this *hubris* on the part of the young man attracts Aphrodite's wrath and her punishment.[9]

Both from the point of view of the main characters and from that of the two choruses, Hippolytus' and his companions' temporary transformation into quasi-young women, with their correspondingly gendered social role, is reinforced by an opposition between adolescent and adult. This opposition enables us to compare the two choruses, which appear to have femininity in common; on the one hand we have adult women and wives who recognize that power of Aphrodite holds equal sway over mortals; on the other hand we have young unmarried men who mistake themselves for young women devoted to Artemis. Social status, then, combines with dramatic and fictional status, and the whole of the tragic action plays on the dialectical tensions between the one and other, particularly through the medium of choral songs and ritual practices.

5.1.3 The Parodos and Its Consequences: Aphrodite versus Artemis

But let us return to the dramatic development of a tragedy whose choral songs play a decisive role. The processional song led by Hippolytus as choregos and the cultic gestures in honour of Artemis that accompany it provoke the intervention of a servant. In response to the gestures of ritual devotion to Artemis that Hippolytus describes at the same time as he is

[9] See the subtle analysis in Zeitlin 1985: 234–61.

executing them, the servant draws his attention to the presence of Aphrodite. He affirms the gratitude that is due to the goddess, and lends his words a performative value. What the servant says is in opposition to the youths (*néoi*, l. 114) and in contrast with Hippolytus, who has just been dismissing Aphrodite, 'your Cypris' (*tèn sèn dè Kúprin . . . egò khaírein légo*, l. 113; here *khaírein* probably alludes to the invitation to the divinity to rejoice in the verbal offering being paid or to the closing greeting of ritual songs). In fact, the servant employs the collective first-person plural and the performative future to address to 'lady Cypris' (*déspoina Kúpri*, l. 117) and her statue a brief ritual greeting: 'As for us, we shall pray to you' (*hemeîs dè . . . proeuxomestha . . .*, l. 116). After the prologue, in which the goddess herself had expressed her wrath against Hippolytus for disrespecting her, Aphrodite is now present in the scenic space and in the dramatic action thanks to the efficaciousness of the ritual utterances. Artemis' presence, too, is conjured up opposite that of the goddess of love by means of choral ritual utterances.

In this respect, the choral song of the parodos proper, sung and danced in a rhythm that is essentially Aeolian, marks a departure. As if to fan the dramatic tensions animating the plot, the young women of Troezen address themselves only to Phaedra, and in doing so refer to her as a 'maiden' (*ô koura*, l. 141). They inquire after the origin of the illness that is causing their queen to languish, and hypothesize the influence of some divinity: Pan, Hecate, the Corybantes, the mountain mother, Dictynna? These are all divinities of the outdoors who are liable to cause their followers to fall into a state of possession (*éntheos*, l. 141) and lose themselves.[10] Thus the chorus's hermeneutic voice employs interrogatives as a form of preteritio, while avoiding all mention of Aphrodite. When, in explaining the affliction that is eating away at Phaedra's heart, they suppose the influence of more natural causes, the women of Troezen advise her to call on Artemis rather than Cypris.

> Women's nature is an uneasy
> harmony, and with it is wont to dwell
> the painful unhappy helplessness
> of birth pangs and their delirium (*aphrosúne*, l. 164).
> Through my womb also has this breath

[10] The relationship between the various divinities mentioned by the chorus and wilderness and possession are noted by Barrett 1964: 189–90. Phaedra's and Hippolytus' relation to the domain of the outdoors (the sea) have been studied particularly by Segal 1965: 122–38. Hippolytus' relationship to Artemis and Aphrodite, with their ritual conclusion, are the subject of a fine study by Bruit Zaidman 2004.

> darted. But I called on the heavenly
> easer of travail, Artemis, mistress of arrows,
> and she is always – the gods be praised –
> my much-envied visitor.   (ll. 161–169)

It is remarkable that the women of Troezen refer to the pains of childbirth to explain Phaedra's abstractedness and seem to regard her as a young bride.[11]

This uncertainty regarding the origin of Phaedra's illness continues during the long dialogue – which is not spoken but rather sung in anapaests – between the heroine and the nurse, after the chorus has introduced them before the orchestra. In response to the grief shared by the old woman, the chorus (or its coryphaeus) presents itself as a collective entity: 'we see Phaedra's unhappy plight, yet it is unclear to us what is wrong with her. We want to ask you and hear your answer' (*horômen*, l. 268; *hemîn*, l. 269; *bouloímeth'án*, l. 270). The nurse herself, moreover, addresses this chorus in the plural, as a group of women (*gunaîkas*, l. 301).

But from the moment that Phaedra reveals her love for Hippolytus the mystery of the origin of her illness is resolved; it is the will of Cypris. The nurse recognizes Aphrodite from the beginning and attributes to the goddess of maddening love a power surpassing that of a deity (ll. 359–61). Advising Phaedra to give in to her passion and thus to the will of the goddess, the nurse will repeat this (ll. 443–50) in her long address to the heroine; this will anticipate what the chorus will sing on the kingdom of Aphrodite in the fourth and final stasimon (to which we have already alluded). Then it will be the turn of the chorus or of its coryphaeus to grasp that what had been unintelligible (*ásemos*, l. 371, looking back to the *ásema nósos* at l. 269) is so no longer; for Phaedra the destiny that is *túkhe* has merged with the will of Cypris. Finally, in her own reaction to the revelation, Phaedra does not hesitate to attribute her own madness to Cypris (ll. 397–402), whom she invokes finally in her sovereign power as *déspoina*, 'mistress' (l. 415).

This hermeneutic exchange carried out in iambic trimeters displays a deeply significant enunciative mechanism. At first the chorus, probably through the voice of its choregos – who has become coryphaeus in the tragedy – limits itself to questioning the nurse on the causes of Phaedra's 'illness'. It then remains silent until the moment at which the nurse

---

[11] The chorus is here doubtlessly referring to Artemis Lochia; it is worth reminding ourselves in this connection that Artemis Brauronia, who was worshipped by the Athenians on the Acropolis, was connected with menstruation and childbirth; see Calame 2002b.

The Chorus of Hippolytus

addresses it explicitly to express her wish to disappear at the news of Phaedra's love for her son-in-law by the will of Cypris. The nurse questions the chorus in their identity as a group of women (*gunaîkes*, l. 354; see already l. 301). At first the chorus (perhaps through its spokesperson, the choregos) reacts to the news with a sung strophe in dochmiacs in a strongly emotive voice combined with an interpretative voice that attempts to explain the action. This brief sung intervention begins with an apostrophe. Through a doubtlessly generic second-person singular, the chorus leader or each of the choreuts (*áies ó, éklues ó*, l. 362) addresses the other choreuts individually: 'Oh, did you catch, oh, did you hear the queen uttering woes past hearing?'. Then the choreuts turn to Phaedra to recognize that she is the victim of a fate brought about by Aphrodite; their address is introduced by cries of lamentation: *ió moi, peû pheû*.[12]

The frequency of self-referential apostrophes and questions that the choreuts address to themselves in the tragedies of Euripides suggests that, though this brief sung intervention should be assigned to the chorus leader rather than the chorus as a whole, the speaking 'I' (*égoge*, l. 364) stands to the chorus as a collective entity of women of Troezen, to which Phaedra will come to belong. Alluding to her fear of adultery provoked by the passion visited upon her by Aphrodite, she herself will say: 'it is precisely this, friends (*phílai*), that is bringing about our death' (l. 419). At the end of this sung, and most probably choral, intervention Phaedra in turn addresses the choreuts as a collective entity made up of women of Troezen (l. 373). There follows the long exchange of monologues in which Phaedra expresses her decision to die in order to save her honour and at the same time that of the free men of 'glorious Athens' (l. 423). Then the nurse promises to find a potion as remedy for her mistress' passion and thus give way to Cypris' will. The chorus or its leader approve Phaedra's virtuous restraint (ll. 431–2) and praise this attitude in the face of the nurse's misleading words (ll. 482–5).

Later in the play, Phaedra replies with a song of lamentation to Hippolytus' famous 'misogynous' monologue provoked by the nurse's revelations. This song is in metrical response to the chorus's intervention that marks the heart of the exchange between Phaedra and the nurse. Phaedra in turn laments in dochmiacs the fate inflicted on women and wonders which deity to turn to (ll. 668–79). Phaedra alternates between the

---

[12] The formal aspects of this choral passage are discussed by Barrett 1964: 224–6, who attributes the intervention to the chorus leader, as does (more hesitantly) Kaimio 1970: 140, citing multiple examples of consultations within the chorus (112–21).

first-person singular and a first-person plural that encompasses womankind in general; this, together with a renewed address to the chorus as *phílai*, confirms from an enunciative standpoint the identification between the heroine and the women of Troezen. Phaedra sings:

> How luckless, how ill-starred,
> is the fate of women!
> What craft do we have, what words,
> once we have faltered, that can undo the noose?
> I have received my just deserts! O earth, O sunlight!
> How shall I escape what has befallen,
> how hide the painful fact, my friends? (ll. 668–74)

The rhythm is associated with dance and strong emotion. Phaedra concludes, 'Unluckiest am I of women!' (l. 679).

In the play between semantic polyphony and enunciative polyphony, the play's chorality thus runs through the spoken dialogue in iambic trimeters. Performed by the choreuts or the actors, the melic songs are tightly woven into the play's dramatic unfolding.

5.1.4 First and Second Stasima: The Power of Eros and Aphrodite

To recognize a deity's absolute power is also to invoke it; it is to conjure up its presence in a ritual fashion. Thus the nurse's final call for help addressed to Cypris (ll. 522–3) in her attempts to bring to fruition Phaedra's love for her son-in-law is answered by the first stasimon (ll. 525–64). This choral song precedes the moment when Phaedra herself announces the disaster that has befallen her (l. 565). In two strophic pairs sung in Aeolian rhythm, the chorus of women of Troezen seek protection against the destructive powers of Eros and Aphrodite.

> Eros, Eros, distilling liquid desire (*póthos*)
> upon the eyes, bringing sweet
> pleasure (*kháris*) to the souls of those you make war against,
> never may you show yourself to me for my hurt
> nor ever come but in harmony.
> For neither the shafts of fire nor of stars are more powerful
> than that of Aphrodite, which Eros, Zeus's son,
> hurls from his hand. (ll. 525–34)

Eros is the 'sweet-bitter', the servant of Aphrodite, already in the poetic fragments of Sappho; Eros who uses the gaze to inspire a passionate desire that can turn out to be destructive. The extant fragments of erotic melic poetry have made us familiar with the relational physiology of erotic pulsion.[13] From the first strophe, this choral song moves from the performative stance of a cletic hymn, which invokes the deity by its name and enumerates its qualities, to an interpretative stance. Passing from its performative register to its hermeneutic function, the choral voice does not confine itself to observing the luminous force of Eros' power, 'mankind's despot' (l. 537), but it also invites the women to worship Eros through cultic devotion.

Then in the second strophic pair the Troezenian choreuts illustrate their statement by singing the twin examples of the heroic victims of Cypris: Iole, daughter of Eurytus, king of Oechalia, still inexperienced of the marriage bed, seized by Aphrodite and gifted to Heracles, who had slain her father and destroyed her city; and Semele, daughter of Cadmus of Thebes, who was loved by Zeus by Aphrodite's will and was consumed by the god's lightning when she was pregnant with Dionysos. Aphrodite, 'who flits like a bee' (ll. 563–4), is sweet as honey and bitter like the bee's sting, just as her servant Eros, who is 'sweet-pungent' throughout the tradition of erotic melic poetry. The performative voice, then, has given way to an interpretative voice that turns to religious wisdom as well as to examples drawn from the heroic past; that it is carried by a strongly emotive voice is suggested, from an enunciative perspective, by the interjections introduced by *ô* that intercut the evocation of the destructive marriage and fateful end of Iole and then Semele.

The chorus's performative utterance taking the form of a wish to their own advantage (*mé moí . . . phaneíēs*, l. 528) does not succeed in averting Phaedra's tragic death. Just before her suicide, the heroine ascribes to Cypris (l. 725) the final outcome willed and announced at the outset by the goddess (ll. 47–50). The choral address to Eros is followed by an exchange that is partly sung between Phaedra and the choreuts. In this kommos there is a return to the use of dochmiacs, so strong is the emotion aroused both in Phaedra and in her followers by the arrival on the scene of Hippolytus; this emotion leads finally to the heroine's demise. The chaste young hero's irruption onto the stage is preceded by his imprecations; the Amazon's son has heard the nurse's revelation of Phaedra's love for him. There is only one possible outcome now for Theseus' wife: death (l. 599).

---

[13] Sapph. Fr. 130, 1–2 and 159 Voigt. I have already given elsewhere a brief commentary on the dramatic function of this choral song: Calame 2009a: 12–19 (for the physiology of eros in melic poetry, cf. 23–42). On this choral song, see also Hose 1990: II, 156–9 and Crebo 1993; the staging of Eros' violence in hymnic poetry is ably analyzed by Pironti 2007: 122–6.

Phaedra reprises her decision after Hippolytus' monologue on his hatred for womankind. After obtaining the choreuts' sworn secrecy, she repeats her purpose; to die a death willed upon her by Cypris (l. 725) is the only means by which she can save her honour as a woman vanquished by passion. The mention of Phaedra's imminent suicide provokes the choral song of grief and lamentation that constitutes the second stasimon (ll. 732–75). After expressing her desire to flee to the ends of the earth, the grim shores of Eridanus (the River Po) where the Heliades weep for the death of their father Phaethon, or the furthest shores where the Hesperides sing as they drink ambrosia in the company of the gods, the choreuts return to Phaedra and Crete; hence they travel with their mistress towards the port of Munichion, where the young heroine had arrived to meet in illustrious Athens a fateful marriage.

> Therefore her mind is wrenched
> by a terrible malady of unholy passion
> sent from Aphrodite;
> and sinking under her cruel misfortune she will put about her
> as it hangs from the beams of her bridal chamber a noose,
> fitting it to her white neck,
> feeling shame at her bitter fate,
> choosing in its stead the glory
> of a good name, and putting
> from her heart her painful desire.   (ll. 764–75)

Such is the closing antistrophe of this song composed once again by two strophic pairs sung and danced in an Aeolian rhythm similar to that of the first stasimon. In an expression of solidarity between women of the same social status in the face of the onslaughts of passion willed by Aphrodite and carried out by Eros, the choreuts cannot but support and understand Phaedra's decision.[14] Linguistically, this validation is underlined by the repeated use of the intentional future, which in Greek expresses mood rather than tense. The choreuts' interpretative grief is in accord with the unfolding of the dramatic action, for the nurse brings immediate confirmation of the fateful outcome announced in the choral song. Phaedra has hung herself.

In a new form of dialogue with themselves, it is now the choreuts who pose the tragic (and performative) question *par excellence*: *tí drômen*: 'what shall we do?' (l. 782, in alternation with the first-person singular at l. 788).[15] Once again, both from a musical and from a dramatic point of view, the

---

[14] Loraux 1985: 31–60 offers a subtle analysis of female suicides in tragedy.
[15] The attribution of lines in this exchange in iambic trimeters following the second stasimon is highly uncertain: cf. Barrett 1964: 311–13. Kaimio 1970: 110–11 gives other examples of passages where the replies were doubtless spoken by different members of the chorus.

chorus shows itself to be entirely integrated in the heroic action being represented on stage.

The answer given to the ultimate tragic question when it is posed by the chorus rather than the hero is necessarily choral. On cue with Theseus' arrival as *theorós* and his remarks on the commotion outside the palace, the spectacle of the lifeless body of his wife elicits a brief song of mourning on the part of the choreuts, this too sung in dochmiacs.

> Alas, poor woman, how luckless you are!
> You have endured, you have done
> such things as to destroy this house!
> What hardihood was yours:
> you have died by a violent and unhallowed deed,
> given a wrestler's throw by your own unhappy hand.
> What was it, poor woman, that brought your life down to darkness?
> (ll. 811–16) (Loeb)

It is also in dochmiacs that Theseus in turn sings his wife's misfortune and his own at the same time as he inquires on their cause. The dochmiacs expressive of distress and intense grief intensify when the king of Athens discovers the message attached to his dead wife's hand revealing his son's alleged love for her. Theseus now reverts to speaking in iambic trimeters in order to cast on Hippolytus his curse; he invokes his divine father Poseidon, while the choreuts, in an outburst of intense grief, foresee the new misfortune that will add itself to Phaedra's death (*phrísso*, 'I shudder', l. 855).

5.1.5 The Third Stasimon: 'Gendered' Enunciations

The long exchange between the father and his illegitimate son, including the young man's decision to go into exile, leads into the third stasimon (ll. 1104–50). This long choral intervention was probably shared between the chorus of youths and the chorus of women; both animate the dramatic action with their ritual song at the same time as they react emotionally to its development and comment on its meaning. This song is also composed of two strophic pairs capped by an epode and sung in a rhythm mixing dactylic and iambic metres. The first section of the stasimon presents a complication around grammatical gender and it has been the object of philological controversy.[16]

---

[16] The issues relating to the establishment of a test of the third stasimon and the alternation between feminine and masculine forms are discussed by Barrett 1964: 365–70.

126   Euripides' *Hippolytus*

Whenever thoughts about the gods come into my mind,
they greatly relieve my pain. But anyone who hopes for understanding
fails to find it as he looks amid the fortunes (*túkhais*) and the deeds of mortals.
From one quarter comes one thing and from another another,
    and men's (*andrásin*) life is a shifting thing,
    ever unstable.
O that in answer to my prayer destiny (*moîra*) might give me this gift
    from the gods,
a fate that is blessed and a heart untouched by sorrow!
No mind unswervingly obdurate would I have, nor yet again one false-struck,
but changing my pliant character ever for the morrow may I share in happiness
my whole life through!   (ll. 1104–18) (Loeb)

In the transmitted text the chorus's reflections on the instability of the mortal condition on account of the gods' apportioning of *moîra* is spoken by a masculine speaker in the strophe (see the masculine participles *keúthon* and *leússon* at ll. 1105 and 1106 respectively) and by a feminine speaker in the antistrophe (*euxaména* and *metaballoména*, feminine participles, at ll. 1111 and 1117 respectively). The ancient commentaries ascribe the whole of this song to the chorus of women of Troezen, that is, the main, female chorus. But consideration of the play's gender issues and its choral pragmatics suggests a split attribution between the male and female choruses. The two strophes are doubtless sung by the male chorus of followers of Hippolytus, while the two antistrophes are sung by the female chorus of women of Troezen; at the same time all the stanzas are sung by the same group of choreuts, for all are male Athenian citizens. The masks they wear, which obscure their civic identity, enable the choreuts to assume alternately male and female roles, a masculine and a feminine voice.[17]

Let us devote an incidental paragraph to this philological question to try to unpack the grammatical sense of these verses. To those who have argued that Greek commonly employs masculine participles of female speakers we might answer that the distribution of masculines and feminines in our passage is too systematic not to be meaningful.[18] To those who demonstrate that in all known cases where a secondary chorus intervenes in

---

[17] For the hypotheses of the scholiasts cf. *ad* 1102 (II, 117 Schwartz); the possibility of an intervention by a complementary chorus is discussed by Barrett 1964: 368; see also Bond 1980: 59–60 and Swift 2010: 262–5, who draws a complex comparison with the exodos of Aeschylus' *Suppliants* and concludes in favour of a highly hypothetical mixed chorus (266–97).
[18] This problem had not escaped the scholiast (cf. n. 16 in this chapter), who improbably refers the use of masculine forms to the poet. See also Pollux 4, 111 (in connection with Euripides' *Danae*). Kühner and Gerth 1898: 83–4 provide some examples of the use of generalizing masculine forms to designate women and, in tragedy, of masculine participial forms referring to women speaking in the first-

alternation with the main chorus the former's song is announced explicitly, we will reply that said announcement is in fact made by Hippolytus in the lines that introduce the stasimon. The banished hero addresses his companion and asks them to follow him (*proeípath'hēmâs kaì propémpsate*, l. 1099), just like in the processional song at the beginning of the tragedy. Hippolytus moreover refers to them deictically (as we will see), by their identity as 'young men of like age' (*néoi ... homēlikes*, l. 1098); as such they have the same status as the women of Troezen themselves seem to allow them as 'young servants' (*próspoloi neaníiai*, l. 784) when they refer to the disarray provoked by Phaedra's suicide. As for the objection that *gár* (l. 1120) does not easily signify a relation of consequence between the first and second strophe, one might counter that the hope betrayed by the sight (*leússon* or *leússō* according to the manuscripts, l. 1121) of the exile inflicted on Hippolytus is but a particular instance of the vision (*leússon*, l. 1107) of the accidents of human fate; the two strophes are sung by Hippolytus' companions.[19]

We might remark at this point that, if the differentiated participial forms in this stanza invite us to attribute the first strophe to Hippolytus' young companions and the first antistrophe to Phaedra's adult female companions, in the second strophe the chorus insists rather on the masculine qualities of Hippolytus as hunter in the service of Artemis Dictynna. However, replicating the play of the first strophic pair, the second antistrophe leads us into the rather feminine world of poetry inspired by the Muse and the domain of young women competing in beauty to become the brides of young heroes under the aegis of Leto's daughter. Voiced in turn by the masculine then the feminine voice of the chorus, the two poles of this gendered contrast are suggestive of the sexual ambiguity of the hero; Euripides' Hippolytus is a young man who, as the son of a king and a hunter, behaves like a young girl who shrinks from Aphrodite and marriage.

As for the epode, this is marked by the feminine perspective implied by a direct address to Hippolytus' mother. The Amazon is called upon by the women of Troezen in her role as mother, in sympathy with the grief she is about to suffer on account of her son's death.

---

person plural; ll. 1103–10 (spoken by the chorus in the singular rather than by the chorus leader) therefore constitute an exception; see also Swift 2010: 327–8.

[19] The objections to the distribution of the stasimon's strophes between two choruses, against which we have attempted here a brief rebuttal, are set out in detail and with the necessary references by Barrett 1964: 365–9, to which add the remarks in Sommerstein 1988.

> But I for my part because of your misfortune
> shall live out in tears an unhappy fate.
> O unhappy mother,
> it was to no purpose that you bore him. Oh,
> I am angry with the gods!
> Ye Graces that dance your round, why do you
>   send the poor man, guilty of no mad deed,
> from his father's land
> and from this house?   (ll. 1142–50) (Loeb)

Thus in the final invocation to the chorus of Graces the choral song takes a performative turn that leads us back to a marriage in which the Charites are finally on the side of Aphrodite.[20] The final apostrophe to the Graces of the marriage yoke (*khárites suzúgiai*, l. 1147) has an invocatory ring more suited to the voice of married women, such as are the Troezenian choreuts, Phaedra's companions, rather than the young unmarried men who are Hippolytus' companions and followers. It seems, then, that the first and second antistrophes as well as the epode of the third stasimon are spoken in the feminine choral voice of the main chorus of Troezenian wives, while the first and second strophes are sung by the masculine voice of Hippolytus' young companions. Distributing the sung replies of the third stasimon between choreuts in character as young men and choreuts in character as wives according to the modern criterion of gender identity has a marked advantage from the point of view of the semantic polyphony that is characteristic of choral interventions in tragedy. In a song that is above all a gnomic commentary on the ephemerality of human happiness in the face of the all-powerful gods, and which therefore belongs to the interpretative voice, the proposed distribution reserves for the feminine voice the more performative interventions, which are accompanied by the expression of emotion. These are the wish for a response to the prayer addressed to the *moîra* (ll. 1111–13), the 'choral projection' in the feminine song and ritual worship of Artemis (ll. 1135–9) and the closing appeal to the Charites who, especially in marriage, cooperate with Aphrodite (ll. 1147–50).[21]

From the point of view of semantic modalities, this double choral voice combining a distinction of gender with the young/adult opposition draws our attention to two remarkable facts. When in the first strophic pair the

---

[20] On the relationship between the Charites and Aphrodite, see, for example, *Cypria* frr. 4–5 Bernabé. Pirenne-Delforge 1996: 201–3 has demonstrated the role played by the nuptial Charites next to Hera and Aphrodite in the Athenian prenuptial ritual of the Gamelia, apparently revolving more around the young women than the ephebes.

[21] The emotive aspect of the voice of the (female) chorus in these verses, in reaction to the dramatic action, is described by Kaimio 1979: 68–9.

Aetiological Closure 129

chorus adopts an interpretative mode to enlarge on the vagaries of human existence and invoke in general terms the gods' benevolence towards the vicissitudes of human life, the voice of youths and adult women blends into one voice. But when the protagonists of the dramatic action are implicated and the choreuts adopt, in the second strophic pair and especially in the epode, a more emotional tone and modalities of song that are more ritual or performative, Hippolytus receives a different attention from the point of view of gender relations; and the distress of a mother who is about to lose her son is only deplored by the choral voice of sympathetic adult women of Troezen, themselves mothers.[22] The concluding epode of this alternating choral song begins in the affective and performative mode of threnos by lamenting the destiny of a mother bereaved of her son and culminates in the invocation to the Charites of loving union, to whom the choreuts paradoxically attribute the exile of the young Hippolytus.

5.2 Aetiological Closure

This last paradox concerning relations between the sexes recurs in the play's ritual and aetiological conclusion. The dramatic action ends with Hippolytus' exile from Troezen in obeyance of his father's will. On the way to Argos and Epidaurus, travelling along the deserted shore of the Saronic Gulf, the young hero has a chariot accident; startled by the sight of a monstrous bull that rises bellowing from the sea, the young hero loses control of his horses and is dragged entangled in the reins by which he had tamed their savage force.[23] In the throes of death the young man is brought before the chorus, who sing the brief fourth stasimon (touched upon at the beginning of this chapter). The sung address to Cypris is immediately followed by Artemis' intervention explaining the meaning of the action just as it reaches its culmination and revealing Cypris' vengeful scheme. Then Artemis promises the dying young man that she will herself take her vengeance on Aphrodite, and moreover that she will accord to him, her devotee, heroic honours to be paid him in the city of Troezen.

> To you, unhappy man, I shall grant, in recompense for these sorrows, supreme honors in the land of Trozen.
> Unmarried girls before their marriage

---

[22] Except in connection with female crimes, the study that Loraux (1990: 88–91) devotes to grieving mothers does not discuss choruses of wives and mothers.
[23] The metaphorical reversal by which Hippolytus, male tamer of horses, if finally tamed by Aphrodite just as a young bride is tamed by marriage is elucidated particularly by Pironti 2007: 130–5.

>   will cut their hair for you, and over the length of ages
>   you will harvest the deep mourning of their tears.
>   The practiced skill of poetry sung by maidens
>   will for ever make you its theme, and Phaedra's love for you
>   shall not fall nameless and unsung.   (ll. 1423–30) (Loeb)

This aetiological ending connects the dramatic staging of the heroic and 'mythical' action to the institution of a ritual. Euripides' plays often culminate in an aetiological ending that consecrates the outcome of the tragic action through a cultic act that enshrines its memory.[24] 'The poetic memory of maidens inspired by the Muses will last eternally for you' (*aeì dè mousopoiòs es sè parthénon éstai mérimna*, ll. 1428–9), declares Artemis when she appears *ex machina*. Instituted as a prenuptial ritual carried out by young women, the process of heroic and musical immortalization ordained by the goddess definitively consecrates the gender inversion that had directed the young Hippolytus' actions throughout the tragedy. As we have said, the hero behaved less as an ephebe than as a young woman. The address to the Charites of the marriage yoke that paradoxically concludes the section of the third stasimon appears to anticipate this consecration in a female perspective, as it is sung by the women of Troezen.

On the affective level, the heroic cult instituted by Artemis reprises in a ritual repetition the choral lamentation of the women of Troezen for the tragic fate of the young hero; this choral dirge marks precisely the end of the third stasimon, which the mention of the Charites of marriage associates to the wedding ceremony. The correspondences are therefore significant between the ritual songs that, in the prenuptial offering on the part of the young women of the city, celebrate the heroization of Hippolytus, and the choral songs that, within the dramatic action itself, are addressed to Hippolytus and his mother. On the one hand, from a dramatic perspective, the tragedy weaves a complex relationship between Artemis' institution of this ritual of heroic celebration and the ritual gestures of lamentation and purification carried out by the actors and above all by the chorus before the skene and in the orchestra. On the other hand, with regard to actual religious practice, the prenuptial ritual instituted by the goddess to honour

---

[24] Cf. Barrett 1964: 3–4 and 412–13, who observes that besides the central heroic cult that was paid to him at Troezen (cf. esp. Paus. 2, 32, 4), Hippolytus had a heroic monument in Athens (Paus. 1, 22, 1); see the commentary by de Goff 1990: 105–17 on the 'structural irony' of this ritual compensation that balances violent deeds with commemorations. For the relationship between Euripidean aetiology and cultic practice, especially in *Hippolytus*, see the sceptical remarks of Scullion 1999/2000: 129, with the justified critique by Sourvinou-Inwood 2003: 326–32.

the memory of the young hero appears to take the place of the ritual of tragic representation for the benefit of the public, and consequently for the benefit of the civic community.[25]

5.3 Exodos: From Troezen to Athens

Time and space of the heroic action – time and space of the cultic action: from 'myth' to 'cult'. This is the issue we have attempted to tackle in connection with the complex relations between the ritual gestures carried out by the chorus in the dramatic action and the choral performance in which the choreuts are engaged as a group of citizens singing at the Great Dionysia.

5.3.1 Between Represented Space and Space of the Representation

The third stasimon of Euripides' *Hippolytus* poses a textual problem that touches precisely on the geographical and spatial reference of the choral song: is it Troezen or Athens? The philological answer to this question is crucial because it implies reference not only to the space of the dramatic action located in the heroic past but especially to the tragic performance itself, here and now.

The crux of the issue is as follows. At the beginning of the second strophe of the third stasimon the choreuts express their distress at the sight of Hippolytus' exile: 'We have seen Greece's brightest star, have seen him (*eídomen*, l. 1124) go forth sped by his father's wrath to another land.' This translation is certainly coherent, but this coherence comes at a price of a textual emendation that removes the manuscript's ungrammatical mention of Athena or Athens.[26] I mention here three key points from W. S. Barrett's long note on this textual problem: *athana* in its different forms cannot refer either to the goddess Athena or to the city of Athens; *Hellánios* is the cult-title of Zeus alone and only in the specific context of his Aeginetan festival, as attested in two poems by Pindar;[27] the plural form *Athḗnais* cannot be construed.[28] The only solution is to paraphrase one of the scholiasts and adopt the reading *astéra gaías*, 'star of the earth', supported by the occurrence

---

[25] According to the arguments in Segal 1996: 159–66 (see also 1988: 61–74) and Goff 1990: 119–29 respectively.
[26] The manuscripts at l. 1123 present the following readings: *asterathanas, asterathenas, asterathenes* or *asterathenais*. Among the scholiasts one identifies Attica after *aster'* and another paraphrases '(*Hellenikês*) *gês astéra*: cf. sch. *ad* 1123 and 1124 (II, 120 Schwartz).
[27] Pi. *N.* 5, 9–12 and *Paean* 6, 123–34; cf. Barrett 1964: 373–4.
[28] The emendation *Aphaías* can equally be excluded, since a reference to Artemis Dictynna is highly hypothetical and it implies and irrelevant connection with Aegina and its tutelary deity; the reading

of *Hellanía* twice elsewhere in Euripides to designate Greece.[29] The emendation is justified on palaeographical grounds since mention of Athena might have been occasioned by Hippolytus' naming of Athens in his address to Artemis in the lead-up to this choral song: 'Dearest of gods to me, daughter of Leto, you I have sat with, I shall leave glorious Athens as an exile' (v.1094):

With regard to the location of the dramatic action, Aphrodite says at the beginning of the play that Hippolytus is the son of Theseus and the Amazon and that he is a citizen of Troezen, which is referred to deictically as 'this land' (*têsde gês*, ll. 11–13). Later Phaedra specifies that the tragic action takes place in a territory situated on the edge of the land of Pelops (ll. 373–4); she also refers to the land of Troezen with the deictic *tóde*, and she adopts the point of view of an Athenian.[30] Now, in introducing the third stasimon with the line just cited, the exiled Hippolytus addresses Artemis, his hunting companion, in a double farewell; he must depart not only from the city and land of Athens where Erechtheus was born, but also from the plain of Troezen. With reference to his companions whom he invites to accompany him, the hero designates the latter with a gesture of verbal deixis, a demonstrative in *-de*, which points both to the location of the heroic action and to that of its staging (*têsde gês*, l. 1098).

After that, as we have just seen, the choreuts singing the third stasimon can broadcast the hero's shining light to the whole of the Greek word (ll. 11–21–5), but the starting point is the coastal and Artemisian landscape of Troezen (1126–34; cf. 148–50 and 228).[31] Then the messenger addresses his account of Hippolytus' agony not just to Theseus, but jointly and ambivalently to the 'citizens (*politai*) who dwell in Athens and in the land of Troezen' (ll. 1157–9). Furthermore, in his account he also refers deictically to this land, *hếde gế* (l. 1199). Finally, in the three final lines spoken by Theseus at the end of the tragedy, the Athenian king omits definitively Troezen to address his final words directly to the 'glorious territory of Athens and Pallas' (l. 1459); Theseus associates the city of Athens with its tutelary deity Athena and he deplores once more the woe brought about by Aphrodite.[32]

---

is suggested by J. W. Fitton (*Pegasus* 8, 1967: 33–4) and G. L. Huxley (*Greek, Roman, and Byzantine Studies* 12, 1971: 331–3) and is mentioned in apparatus by Diggle 1984: 256.

[29] Eur. *Her.* 411 and *Hel.* 1147 (*gế* understood).

[30] The question of the location of the action is cogently discussed by Barrett 1964: 9–10, 32–4 and 227. Chalkia 1986: 63–92 perceptively defines the scenic space of Troezen as a liminal space while insisting on the fact that Theseus leads his son Hippolytus into a nuptial, feminine space.

[31] See Barrett 1964: 109–10; according to Paus. 2, 30, 7, the sanctuary of Artemis Saronis dominated the marshy plain (cf. Calame 2015: 479–81).

[32] Here, too, the text is vexed: cf. Barrett 1964: 416–17.

5.3.2 Ending in Choral Polyphony

Thus by a series of subtle transitions we have moved from the peripheral space occupied by the small city of Troezen in the Peloponnese to the central space represented by glorious Athens. Through this complex referential process we are led from the scenic space conjured up by and in the heroic action towards the religious and political space of its dramatization; this is the space occupied by the audience assembled in the theatre of Dionysos to render ritual homage to the god of the boundary of Eleutherai, the Free god and the Liberator.

After this, the brief exodos is characterized by a polyphony that mingles the emotive voice and the hermeneutic voice and that is sung in anapaestic rhythm. With this brief conclusive song, the chorus of women of Troezen consecrates the transition from the space of the heroic action to that of the audience. The grief caused by the spectacle of the triple woes that have befallen the house of Theseus is now presented – once again deictically – as having come 'to all the citizens in common' (*koinon tód'ákhos pâsi polítais*, l. 1462). Whether they are authentic or not, the anapaests pronounced by the chorus at the conclusion of the play are a generalization of the lesson drawn in the third stasimon, as they bring together the community of citizens in the grief provoked by the action they have been spectating.[33]

> This grief has come unlooked for
> upon all the citizens in common.
> Floods of tears shall come over us again and again.
> For tales of grief about the great
> have greater power to move.   (ll. 1462–6)

Thus it is essentially in the orchestra, through the interpretative voice of the chorus and by the intermediary role played by the affective voice, that the narrative and dramatic space of 'myth' is related to the historical space of the ritual performance; this latter is enacted by the community consisting of the audience of classical Athens.[34] In the movement from

---

[33] For the issue of the authenticity of these anapaests, see Barrett 1964: 417–18. For a good discussion of the general problem posed by the final lines in classical tragedy, with their extra-discursive reference and doubtful authenticity, see Roberts 1987. For the relationship between the world of the play and the world of the theatre in *Hippolytus*, see Easterling 1991.

[34] On the undecidable question of the composition of the audience at the Great Dionysia, and especially on whether it included women, cf. Chapter 2.4.2, with n. 52. For the way in which the final scene of the tragedy transforms private grief into public spectacle, see Segal 1988: 127–32; see also the sound remarks by Nagy 1994/1995: 50–2, who interprets this ending in terms of 'intersubjectivity', in line with Zeitlin 1985: 94–6.

performative mode and emotional register to the interpretative processes that enable it to draw a universal lesson from the dramatic action, the semantic polyphony of the choral voice allied to a marginal dramatic identity combines with a collective enunciative polyphony. In this double polyphony tending towards the interpretative mode, the choral and dramatic identity appears to transcend any gender distinctions that might otherwise characterize the choral voice in its interventions in the heroic actions in the performative and affective modes. The chorus is fundamentally a character in the heroic fictional action being staged before the spectators, and it can therefore adopt both the position of the virtual author or implicit poet (which points to the author with his social and ritual identity) and the position of the ideal or virtual audience (which points to the audience that is engaged in a ritual and musical offering to Dionysos Eleuthereus).

It is in this choral dirge shared with the spectators in the here-and-now of the musical and ritual performance that the narrative tension engendered by the dramatic development of the heroic plot resolves itself.

CHAPTER 6

Sophocles' Oedipus Tyrannus
'Why Should I Dance (Chorally)?'

If there is a Greek tragedy that is not often associated with choral song, this must surely be Sophocles' *Oedipus Tyrannus*. The play has become synonymous with the story about the young Oedipus' fate made famous by Sigmund Freud, and as such it has been canonized as the founding myth of psychoanalysis. As Freud first put it, in the fourth of his *Five Lectures on Psychoanalysis*:

> The child takes both of its parents, and more particularly one of them, as the object of its erotic wishes ... the child reacts to this by wishing, if he is a son, to take his father's place, and, if she is a daughter, her mother's ... The myth of King Oedipus, who killed his father and took his mother to wife, reveals, with little modification, the infantile wish, which is later opposed and repudiated by the *barrier against incest*.[1]

Later, on rereading Sophocles' text, Freud formulated the 'Oedipal complex', the libidinal drive behind the unconscious desire of the young boy trapped in the family triad to kill his father in order to sleep with his mother, by reference to the ensemble of erotic and hostile wishes that the child feels towards his parents.[2]

But what was the significance of this story in ancient Greece? How should we interpret the play *Oedipus Tyrannus* that was staged as a musical ritual in the context of Athens' political, moral and intellectual crisis caused by the Peloponnesian War? As we have seen, already for Aristotle

---

[1] Freud 1910/1926 [2001]: vol. XI, 47; see already Freud's letter to Wilhelm Fliess dated 15 October 1897, translated in French and entitled 'L'abandon de la neurotica' in *Lettres à Wilhelm Fliess 1887–1904*, Paris (PUF) 2006.
[2] Freud 1917/1962: 168 and 192. See Lobo 2008 and the complex definition in Laplanche and Pontalis 1982: 79: 'Un ensemble organisé de désirs amoureux et hostiles que l'enfant éprouve à l'égard de ses parents. Sous sa forme dite positive, le complexe se présente comme dans l'histoire d'*Œdipe-Roi* : désir de la mort de ce rival qu'est le personnage du même sexe et désir sexuel pour le personnage de sexe opposé' ('A system of amorous and hostile desires which the boy feels towards his parents. In its so-called positive form, this complex presents as in the story of *Oedipus the King*: desire for the death of the rival, i.e., the same-sex parent, and sexual desire for the parent of the opposite sex').

136 Sophocles' *Oedipus Tyrannus*

Sophocles' Oedipus is the tragic figure par excellence. The young king of Thebes is the paradigmatic example of the hero who falls from the greatest good fortune to the greatest misery because of a transgression; he illustrates the reversal (*peripeteia*) at the heart of the tragic plot.[3] *Oedipus at Colonus*, Sophocles' tragedy staging Oedipus' disappearance and heroization in the eponymous deme outside Athens, receives no mention in the *Poetics*.

6.1 A Malleable Heroic Plot

And yet the plot conceived by Sophocles stages above all a hero 'without the complex'.[4] Sophocles' Oedipus is the hero of a tradition that featured different versions of the story, sometimes centring around the death of his mother and wife; in the *Iliad*, Oedipus is the recipient of a hero's funerary honours. On the other hand, Oedipus' parricide and incest replicates an archetype found in several traditional cultures. *Oedipus Tyrannus* is the dramatization of a somewhat arrogant young man's discovery of his true paternity. Setting out in search of the cause of the pollution that is plaguing the city after the king's murder, and realizing that he himself is the culprit he is searching for, Oedipus discovers the identity of his unknown biological parents, a father whom he has killed unknowingly and a mother whom he has married in all innocence. It is certainly not a complex, a universal predicament, that lies behind the 'myth' as it is reformulated by Sophocles; yet the young king's belated self-knowledge, the result of his inquiry on the Attic stage, is transformed into a psychoanalytic mechanism applied to all children regardless of their culture. Had it been possible for Oedipus to suffer from the complex that now bears his name, this would have expressed itself towards his adoptive parents, Polybus and Merope, the king and queen of Corinth who had taken him in shortly after he had been exposed. But the story staged by Sophocles in his *Oedipus Tyrannus* in fifth-century 'democratic' Athens has of course nothing to do with the historical and cultural environment of bourgeoise Vienna at the turn of the twentieth century.

Let us look at how the play unfolds and remind ourselves of the peculiar narrative orientation given to the plot by Sophocles the poet. In heroic times, the city of Thebes is afflicted by a plague (there may be some allusion

---

[3] Arist. *Poet.* 13, 1453a 7–22 and 11, 1452a 22–33; cf. also 8, 1451a 13–15; see Dupont-Roc and Lallot 1980: 215–16 and 238–49. Further refences in n. 12 in Chapter 1.

[4] '"Œdipe" sans complexe' is the title of a seminal study by Jean-Pierre Vernant; see Vernant and Vidal-Naquet 1972[1988]: 75–98[85–111]. Other Greek versions of the Oedipus story are mentioned, for example, by Bettini and Guidorizzi 2004: 64–82 (for the 'folkloric variants', see 130, with the references in n. 1); cf. also Chapter 7.2.2 with n. 15.

A Malleable Heroic Plot 137

here to the poet's and his audience's real-life experience of the epidemic that struck Athens at the beginning of the Peloponnesian War).[5] Flanked by young Thebans, the priest of Zeus addresses himself to Oedipus, who has unknowingly succeeded his father Laius to the throne; his accession was the reward for ridding the city of the Sphinx, with her beguiling rhapsode's voice, and the heavy tributes she demanded. The young king of Thebes has sent his brother-in-law Creon to Delphi to consult Apollo's oracle regarding the cause of the plague, and Creon has now returned announcing the oracle's instruction: Thebes must rid itself of its pollution by banishing the culprits of Laius' murder. To expose the transgressor, Oedipus summons the seer Tiresias, whose physical blindness is the counterpart of his god-given insight; Tiresias declares that the culprit is Oedipus himself. The young king reacts furiously, and in his limited human knowledge he accuses Creon of plotting against him. Jocasta attempts to mollify her husband by telling him that an oracle had predicted that Laius would be killed by his son, but that their only child had been exposed to prevent the oracle from coming to pass.

The account of the circumstances of Laius' killing nevertheless rouses Oedipus' suspicions. He remembers yet another Delphic oracle, which was given him after a guest at Corinth had cast doubt on his alleged identity as son of the king and queen of that city. The oracle had predicted that Oedipus was destined to lay with his mother and slay his father. Terrified by this prospect, Oedipus had resolved never again to set foot in Corinth; later he had killed an old man and his attendants after an altercation at a crossroads not far from Delphi. At this point a man from Corinth arrives on the scene to announce the death of Polybus, Oedipus' presumed father. The Corinthian goes on to tell Oedipus that Polybus was not his true father, for he himself had handed him to the king when he was a newborn, his ankles pierced and bound together, having received him from one of Laius' shepherds on Mount Cithaeron. Seized with anguish, Oedipus summons the shepherd, who is also the only man to have survived the attack at the fateful crossroads. The shepherd confirms Tiresias' statements: Oedipus is not the child of fortune he thinks he is but rather the son of Laius and Jocasta; the queen had handed him to the shepherd as a newborn with the command that he should expose him to thwart the oracle's prediction against her husband. Oedipus' identity is now beyond doubt, and he declares:

---

[5] The tragedy is traditionally dated to 429 BCE on account of the probable historical allusion.

Iou! Iou! All has become clear!
O light, may I now look on you for the last time.
I who am revealed as born of those from whom I should not have been born, married
to those whom I should not have married, and as having killed those I should not have killed. (ll. 1182–5)

Jocasta hangs herself in shame; Oedipus blinds himself in despair. Finally, he entrusts himself to Creon's two daughters and asks to be taken away from his land. The play ends with Creon leading him into the palace.

This simple mythographical summary displays the almost thriller-like tautness of the plot as it follows Oedipus' investigation to uncover his own culpability and with it his true identity. But this account of the drama's tight narrative logic, shaped by Sophocles' supreme dramatic artistry, tells us nothing about the emotions it may have provoked or about its sophisticated play on the visual component of human knowledge; nor does it tell us anything about the human being that it confronts with a fate announced by the oracles and enforced by the gods. Most of all, it effaces the poetic dimension of the play.

What is the role of the chorus in all of this? Does not the plot function without its interventions? This is what has been maintained implicitly ever since Aristotle. In actual fact, the dramatic poeticity of *Oedipus Tyrannus* relies not only on a rich and inventive metaphorical vein, but also on the musicality of its songs, which mark the rhythm of the unfolding action as it is narrated and represented on stage. The action that has prompted endless commentary is framed by choral interventions. The chorus plays a part throughout the dramatic action, and its songs not only contribute emotional expressiveness, but moreover they enrich the moral and theological significance of the play, lending it a strong ritual and religious dimension, sometimes in a critical vein.

6.2 The Hymnic Parodos

Right from the outset, the first choral song, the parodos, has ritual connotations. The chorus of Theban elders addresses a prayer of supplication to Zeus. This is an indirect prayer of a kind we find in Pindar, with the grammatical addressee being the 'word' (*pháti*, l. 151) of the king of the gods. This is then picked up in ring composition at the end of the first strophe when Zeus' voice is relayed by that of Apollo (*pháma*, l. 157).

In between, Apollo himself is invoked as Delian and Paian, in a ritual invocation that, however, does not make this long hymnic song a paean.[6]

6.2.1 Choral Opening and Cultic Appeal

Sweet-speaking message of Zeus, what are you that have come
from Pytho rich in gold to glorious
Thebes? I am prostrated, my mind is shaken by terror,
Delian healer invoked with cries,
in awe of you, wondering what thing you will accomplish, perhaps new,
perhaps coming again with the revolving seasons.
Tell me child of golden Hope, immortal oracle.   (ll. 151–8) (Loeb)

The choral voice's performative dimension in the opening of this collective song is evident in the double address to the divine word (which frames the strophe with two vocatives) as well as in the appeal to favour the speaking I (*eipé moi*, l. 157); its pragmatic significance in the execution of this verbal ritual finds expression in the ritual cry to Delian Paean (*iḗie Dálie Paián*, l. 154).[7] There is an extra-dramatic reference here to the political and religious authority that Athens attempted to maintain between the oracle of Apollo at Delphi and the sanctuary of the same god on the island of Delos. The Pythian oracle is said by Herodotus to have been the determining factor in Athens' reorientation of its defensive strategy towards the sea during the final phase of the Persian Wars, while the sanctuary of Apollo on Delos was the centre of the Delian League, credited by Thucydides with giving Athens its economic and religious hegemony in the Aegean.[8] So once again, the heroic fiction refers, by poetic interposition, to the political and religious context of the dramatic representation.

The ritual performance at the beginning of this first choral song echoes the prologue, which is also characterized by ritual and religious utterances. In fact, the voice of the chorus in the parodos follows seamlessly from the priest's appeals to Oedipus in the prologue. The priest of Zeus is accompanied by a group of Theban youths who kneel and hold boughs of supplications. Oedipus addresses the youths before he addresses the priest, declaring his identity and questioning them on the reason for their behaviour, the

---

[6] As proposed by Furley and Bremer 2001: 1, 306–7; the qualification as paean in l. 186 refers to the supplications sung by the women of the city, and it prompts an appeal not to Apollo but to Athena. See also Rutherford 1994/1995: 119, who speaks of simple allusions to paean.
[7] The many attestations of the paean's ritual refrain are listed by Käppel 1993: 65–71 (see also 31–42). On 'reshaping lyric genres' at the beginning of Sophocles's three tragedies, see Rodighiero 2018.
[8] See especially Herod. 7, 139–44 and Thuc. 3, 104.

burnt offerings and the paeans and lamentations that resound throughout the city. The suggestion is that the priest is regarded as their mouthpiece.

It is not surprising, then, that the priest's reply employs the first-person plural; this is a collective 'we' that explicitly includes the priest's 'I' (*egó*, at l. 18), the youths (who are designated by a gesture of verbal deixis, *hoíde*, in the same line) and ultimately the whole people of Thebes, young and old, gathered before the two temples of Athena and the prophetic sanctuary on the Ismenos. In other ways, too, everything suggests that the priest assumes the role of choregos of the adolescent suppliants. Thus he declares: 'we are seated at your altars' (ll. 15–16) and 'I and these youths (*hoíde paîdes*) sit as suppliants at your hearth' (ll. 31–2). Couched as a ritual supplication, this collective request to restore the city evokes the prayers addressed to gods, for the priest rests his choral supplication (*hiketeúomen*, 'we implore you', l. 41) on the mention of a past benefaction; just as in the past Oedipus delivered Thebes from the Sphinx, now again may he deliver the city from the plague that is afflicting it.

Oedipus responds to the priest's words by addressing himself to the youths as a choral group (*ô paîdes oiktroí*, 'Children, I pity you', ll. 58–9; see also ll. 78–9). He joins his grief to that of the priest and the youths, and he replies that he has dispatched Creon to consult the Delphic oracle and will act in accordance with the god's prophecy. At this point Creon returns with Phoebus' Apollo's oracular command 'to drive out from the land a pollution, one that has been nourished in this country'. Oedipus vows to throw light on the whole episode, on his own behalf as well as on behalf of the city, and the prologue closes with a final performative utterance: 'Children, let us stand up' (*ô paîdes, histómetha*, l. 147). The priest of Zeus and the Theban youths then rise and express the wish that Apollo become, like Oedipus in their first prayer (l. 51), the deliverer of the city by ending the plague. This evocation of the god as purifier and healer of the city polluted by Laius' killer leads into the cultic choral song of the parodos.

6.2.2 Hymnic Prayer and Dramatic Action

If the initial address to Zeus' oracular voice, then to that of Apollo, opens the strophe of this choral song, the antistrophe takes the form of a cultic prayer. In the three strophic pairs of this sung and danced choral poem we see a movement from a predominantly dactylic rhythm (particularly dactylic tetrameters) to one dominated by iambs interspersed with cretics.[9]

---

[9] See the metrical analysis in Giannachi 2009: 39–49, with the commentary of the sung parts of *Oedipus Tyrannus* in Webster 1970: 141–3.

The Hymnic Parodos

The first section of the parodos, then, is coherent with the traditional form of the ritual petition to a deity.

Just like the choral songs of Euripides' *Ion* discussed in an earlier chapter, this poetic prayer displays the tripartite structure of a cletic hymn. It opens with a standard direct address to three deities: Athena, carefully qualified by her filial relationship to Zeus (who dominates the whole of this choral song); Artemis, who is enthroned in the Theban agora; and, of course, the archer Apollo. Then the benefactions of these deities are mentioned in general terms; they have protected the city in the past. Finally, the three deities are invited to intervene once again in the present (dramatic) situation (*élthete kaì nûn*: 'come now too', l. 167).[10]

This is clearly a cultic prayer, with all the linguistic, enunciative and structural markers of a ritual verbal act; its cultic function is made explicit in the appeal to the gods to manifest themselves to the singers (*prophánete moi*, l. 163). This first hymnic prayer is closely related to the dramatic action inasmuch as the address to Pheme picks up on the mention of Apollos' oracle in response to Creon's Delphic consultation (ll. 86 and 95–7); moreover, Athena was indeed honoured at Thebes as protectress of one of the city's seven gates, and Artemis was worshipped there with the epiclesis Eucleia. At the same time, as we have seen, the chorus's cultic prayer can equally be related to the Athenian context beyond the dramatic representation, not only because Delian Apollo, apparently unknown at Thebes, points us to the sanctuary of the Delian League, but also because Athena, daughter of Zeus and patron goddess of the city, looms large in the first two-thirds of this choral prayer. She is invoked at its beginning (*prôta*, l. 159) and its end (ll. 187–8) in support of a polis that is never identified with a singular toponym; the reference, then, is no doubt to Thebes, but also to Athens, if not Delphi and Delos too.[11]

---

[10] For the structure of the cletic hymn (invocation, praise, petition) in relation to that of prayer, see the studies mentioned in Chapter 2.3.1, with n. 26. For a convincing discussion of Zeus' prominence in the choral songs of the *Oedipus Tyrannus* in general, see Segal 1995: 185–98.

[11] It is on account of her function as protectress of the city gates that the Theban cult of Athena Onca has been connected with the Athena invoked here by the chorus; it is worth noting, however, that there are difficulties in identifying the two temples of Athena mentioned by the priest of Zeus in lines 20–1; for a review of the evidence, see Schachter 1981: 130–2, with the complementary commentary in Zeitlin 1993: 160–1 on Athena's role in *Antigone*; Furley and Bremer 2001: I, 306 see here an allusion to Athena Pronaia at Delphi. As for Artemis, the identification with the Theban Artemis Eucleia (Paus. 9, 17, 2) is far from certain; cf. Schachter 1981: 104, as well as Bollack's turgid commentary, 1990: II, 98–100.

6.2.3 Pragmatics of a Hymnic Song: Dionysos

The parodos' second strophic pair is a description, in the form of a lament, of the evils afflicting Thebes and its inhabitants; the land is barren, births are thwarted, while deaths multiply – the city is perishing. This section of the song opens with a cry of lamentation by the defenceless choral 'I' and culminates with the evocation of the paean sung by the afflicted wives and mothers who throng the altars. The evocation of the Theban women's song provokes the appeal to Artemis (or Athena) that concludes this strophic pair: 'O shining daughter of Zeus, send clear aid against these things' (ll. 187–8).

On the other hand the third strophic pair, which concludes the parodos, is once again dominated by the authority of Zeus; in the third strophe the chorus prays to him urgently to cast down with his thunder and lightning Ares, destroyer of the city. Then in the repeated invocation of the protecting deities Athena is replaced by Dionysos, leading us back to Thebes, the location of the dramatic action.

> Lord of Lycia, I would
> gladly celebrate the invincible shafts
> coming from your golden bowstring as you stand
> by me bringing aid, and the fiery torches
> of Artemis, with which she darts
> through the Lycian mountains.
> And I call on him of the golden cap,
> him that gives his name to this land,
> ruddy-faced Bacchus, to whom they cry Euhoe,
> companion of the Maenads,
> to draw near with brightly blazing torch
> of pinewood against the god who lacks honour among the gods.
> (ll. 203–13) (Loeb)

At the conclusion of the chorus's entrance song, in this ritual invective against Ares, we see once again several defining traits of cultic prayer, especially in the new invocation of Dionysos: an explicit appeal to the god in a verbal act (*kiklḗskō*, l. 209); the use of a poetic epithet ('winefaced') combined with an epiclesis (Bacchus) and a cultic address (*eúios*, l. 211); the listing of these attributes in asyndeton; and the request to intervene in 'this land' (*tâsde gâs*, l. 210), in a gesture of verbal deixis such as we have already remarked upon elsewhere.

If this hymnic choral song closes with the expected ring composition, it nevertheless displays many traits that are not at home in a cletic hymn: the

The Hymnic Parodos

substitution of the narrative section (praise) with a descriptive section focusing on the state of the city and its female citizens (wives and mothers); the absence of the conclusive conceit of *do ut des*, with the final appeal expressed instead as a simple wish; the change in rhythm between the first and third strophic pairs; and above all the replacement of Zeus (who had been invoked at the beginning of the hymn) and Athena with Dionysos as the deity likely to assure the safety of the city.

Granted that Zeus played a part in the founding legend of Thebes and was associated with the cult of Apollo at Delphi, does this substitution nevertheless suggest that the hymn is here dissociated from its function within the dramatic action and reoriented instead towards the god who is the dedicatee of its musical performance? Is there a shift from the heroic time and place of the Oedipus saga to the space of the ritual performance in the sanctuary-theatre of Dionysos Eleuthereus in fifth-century Athens? It bears repeating that the question of the relation between the epic action dramatized in the tragedy and the cult paid to Dionysos through its representation in a ritualized performance is a controversial one.[12]

Be that as it may, the chorus's final invocation gestures point deictically to Bacchos as the eponymous god of 'this land' (as we have seen). Oedipus is not mistaken; the pragmatic effect of the choral song prevails. The hero immediately responds to the chorus's prayer; he responds to its questioning (l. 216: *aiteîs*, in the second-person singular) with the authority of the sovereign king of Thebes, but also in his capacity as an outsider, a 'stranger' (*xénos*, ll. 219 and 220 – so he regards himself) to the events in question, that is, the killing of Laius. He follows with a solemn appeal, a speech act (*prophonô*, l. 223), addressed to all the citizens of Cadmus' city. Combining the speaking 'I''s performative involvement with commands directed at the Cadmeans in the second-person plural, Oedipus issues an injunction to denounce the killer, even though he is likely to 'come from another land' (!). As the Delphic oracle has revealed, the killer must be driven out of the city like a pollution. This injunction then turns into an imprecation; it concerns 'this land', which has been abandoned by the gods.

After further imprecations against anyone who does not join in the inquiry that Oedipus has decided to undertake, the coryphaeus suggests that, given that Apollo has remained silent on the identity of the killer, it will be necessary to consult the seer Tiresias. From an enunciative

---

[12] Cf. Chapter 2.5.1. For this choral invocation of Dionysos Baccheios, see especially Bierl 1991: 59–62, and Kowalzig 2007b: 232–42, who notes the transformation of various Sophoclean chorus into Dionysiac choruses (in relation to the death of the hero: cf. l. 1105, Section 6.5).

standpoint this exchange between Oedipus and the coryphaeus is characterized by an alternation of second-person singulars and second-person plurals; hence the coryphaeus feels himself included in the imprecations aimed at all the inhabitants of Cadmus' city should they fail to comply with Oedipus' command. The demarcations between the community of citizens of Thebes, the chorus of elders of the city and the coryphaeus who leads their ritual song is fluid indeed. The enunciative inclusion of the civic community in the voice of the chorus, with its emotional and performative range, is all the more likely since their choral prayer echoes the paean of lamentation sung by the wives and mothers of the Thebans victims of the plague (ll. 182–6); this paean in turn echoes the paean and lamentations that Oedipus had remarked upon in the opening scene (l. 5). From the outset the dramatic action is firmly subsumed to cultic song.

6.3 Choral Voices and Oracular Voices: The First Stasimon

Stasimon after stasimon, the choral interventions of the Theban elders are almost obsessively influenced by the weight of Zeus' power and, above all, by echoes of the prophetic voice of Delphi, the voice of Apollo. The 'coryphaeus' himself does not escape this obsession. It is no accident that, in accordance with the rule requiring characters to be introduced when their mask does not allow them to be identified, it is he who announces Tiresias' entry onto the scene. It is he, too, who advises Oedipus to turn to Phoibos in his determination to hunt for the killer of Labdacus' son in the name of Justice. And it is again the choregos who plays a decisive role in the tragic action by directing Oedipus to Tiresias, who 'sees' like Apollo (l. 284). Inspired by the god, the divine seer is the only one 'in whom alone among mankind truth is implanted' (l. 299).[13]

The remarkable scene that follows revolves around the play between physical blindness and true insight: the dialogue between the blind man who reveals himself to be gifted with divine omniscience and the man who thinks he sees everything while denying a truth that will eventually blind him in the most literal sense. In barely veiled terms Tiresias points to the new king of Thebes as the killer of Laius: 'that man is here... blind instead of seeing... he shall be revealed as being to his children whom he lives with both a brother and a father, and to his mother both a son and a husband,

---

[13] The role of oracles and oracular voice in *Oedipus Tyrannus* has been well discussed by Segal 1981: 236–41, then Pucci 1992: 16–30. For the role of Tiresias in relation to knowledge based on sight, see the references in my study of 1996.

Choral Voices and Oracular Voices 145

and to his father a sharer in his wife and a killer' (ll. 454–60). Tiresias is safe from accusations of slander. In the face of Oedipus' denials, it will be up to the chorus to react to the seer's revelation.

6.3.1 Parnassus' Oracular Utterance and the Heroic Destiny

Doubtless shaken by Oedipus' provocative questioning, the chorus takes as the theme of its first stasimon (ll. 463–511) the oracular injunction pronounced by Apollo and conveyed by Creon. This choral song is composed of two strophic pairs, which are sung in a mixture of iambs and anapaests interspersed with choriambs.[14] After a first strophe dedicated to the evocation of the Kêres, the avenging goddesses who, like the Erinyes, pursue the guilty, and Apollo armed with his father Zeus' lightning in pursuit of the killer denounced at Delphi, the chorus focuses on the oracle.

Anticipated by Oedipus himself (at l. 86) and invoked by the chorus in the parodos (l. 158), Parnassus' oracular utterance (*pháma*, l. 475) in its radiance pursues implacably the man who would escape it. But against the uncontested intelligence and wisdom of Zeus and his son Apollo the chorus also casts doubt on the mortal words uttered by the wise seer. Its criticisms stem from the relative *sophía* (l. 502) of humans; the seer's words stand in opposition to the 'straight word' (l. 505) that shows itself through evidence. But by linking the truth of the seer's divinely inspired words to the relativeness of its human dimension, the chorus doubts its own, equally human, word. Because of its unwillingness to question Oedipus' established reputation, the chorus can no longer define its performative voice other than negatively: 'I do not know what to say' (*hó ti léxō d'aporô*, l. 486).

> For in sight of all
> the winged maiden came against him
> once, and he was seen to be wise
> and approved as dear to the city; thus shall he never
> be convicted of crime by my judgment   (ll. 507–11) (Loeb)

Playing an active part in the action in which Oedipus recognizes his true identity and therefore his double crime, the choreuts act as faithful citizens. It is in this capacity (*ándres polîtai*, l. 513) that Creon addresses them immediately after this song, which, by its self-referential self-questioning, seems to negate its own ritual effectiveness. By this stage the chorus/

---

[14] For a detailed colometry of this stasimon, see Giannachi 2009: 59–69.

choryphaeus can no longer defend Oedipus before either Creon, whom the king of Thebes accuses of plotting with Tiresias to overthrow him, or Jocasta. It will be down to his wife to draw attention to the power of the gods and the respect owed to Creon's word, for which the gods stand as guarantors.

6.3.2 After the Choral Interventions, the Sung Exchange

There is no doubt that it is Jocasta's affirmation of the gods' authority that prompts a double *kommós*. Defined by Aristotle as a song of lamentation shared by the chorus and the actors,[15] this melic exchange first between the chorus and Oedipus, then between the chorus and Jocasta, is composed in a mixture of iambs and dochmiacs aimed at conveying strong emotion. This melic amoebean is divided into two sections and acts as a prelude to the exchange between the king and his wife Jocasta. In these lines Oedipus recounts the fateful encounter at the crossroads with the man who will be revealed as his father, then the Delphic oracle foreseeing that he would marry his mother after killing his father; this rouses the chorus's anxiety in anticipation of the servant's testimony confirming the emerging truth.

The chorus's sung words are at first aimed at beseeching Oedipus to cease from his accusations against Creon, who is bound to him by ties of family as well as allegiance. The group of choreutai calls on the Sun as witness to its faithfulness towards Oedipus. Then, after Creon's departure, the chorus attempts to appease the quarrel by insisting to Jocasta on its confidence in Oedipus. The choral group thus enables the decisive exchange between the king and his wife leading to the recognition. In blending its 'performative' and its emotive voice, the chorus contributes to heightening the narrative and dramatic tension in anticipation of Oedipus' account of the fatal argument on the way back from Delphi, which is followed by Jocasta's intervention. At the end of the confrontation the chorus declares its anxiety while expressing its hope that the upcoming testimony will exonerate Oedipus (ll. 834–5).

One final linguistic observation can be made on the enunciative significance of the chorus's use of the first person. At the end of the first stasimon Creon addresses himself to the choreuts in the plural as to a collective of citizens (l. 513), but at the end of his speech he addresses the coryphaeus in second-person singular (*soû*, l. 522), and the latter seems to assume individually the ignorance professed by the choreuts (*ouk oîda* and *oukh*

---

[15] Arist. Poet. 12, 1452b 23–4; see the references in n. 18 in Chapter 2.

horô at l. 530). Then, during the double kommos, the choreuts regularly employ the first-person singular (*líssomai* at l. 650, *oîda* at l. 654 and so on), to which Oedipus replies with the second-person singular (though we would expect the plural after the choral song). But in a final intervention attributable to the coryphaeus on account of its iambic metre it is – surprisingly – the first-person plural that is employed (l. 834).

6.4 'Why Should I Sing Chorally?'

In response to Jocasta's theological doubts the chorus poses the basic question about the self-referential and performative value of its voice: 'why should I sing chorally?' (*tí deî me khoreúein?*, l. 896). Beyond the choral utterance, it is the action itself of the chorus as ritual actor that is brought into question in this dramatic inquiry. Endless commentary has been generated by this shocking formulation voiced precisely by those whose role it is to sing and dance in chorus. Some have remarked that the chorus's questioning of the legitimacy of its own performance arises from the doubts expressed by Jocasta in the previous scene with regard to the truth of prophets (especially at ll. 720–5 and 857–8). She cites the testimony of the old servant, the only surviving witness of the altercation at the crossroads, according to which Laius was set upon by several brigands, and she adduces the supposed death of the son born of her union with Laius. The oracle predicting that the king would die at the hands of his offspring cannot, she argues, have come to pass.

But what about the logic of the chorus's arguments? This second stasimon, too, is composed of two strophic pairs (ll. 863–910), but its rhythm is predominantly iambic, with the insertion of some cretics.

6.4.1 *The Power of Destiny and the Chorus's Doubts*

The first strophe consists of an evocation of the power of destiny, *moîra* (l. 863), in which abides a powerful god who never grows old; destiny obeys laws born of the celestial aether, and therefore it cannot be grasped by mortals. The mention of insolence (*húbris*, l. 873) that 'engenders a tyrant' prompts a performative intervention.

> ... I ask the god (*aitoûmai*)
> never to release the beautiful
> wrestling for the city.
> I will not cease (*ou léxō*) holding the god as my protector.
>
> (ll. 879–882)

Jocasta's doubts, then, provoke in the first part of the chorus's song a renewed affirmation of the lawful order assured by the god, probably Zeus, who is here singled out. In its performative voice the chorus commits to respecting the god so long as he strives for the benefit of the city against the tyrant's *hubris*. The two performative forms that enshrine this contract of reciprocity (*aitoûmai* and *ou léxo* at ll. 881–2) stand in opposition to the radical questioning of the chorus's activity at the end of the second strophe.

In the second strophic pair, the ceasing of song is envisaged only should the impious man triumph at the expense of justice.[16]

> But if a man goes proudly
> in deed or word,
> without fear of justice nor
> respect for the seats of the gods,
> an evil fate (*moîra*) will seize him
> on account of his wretched arrogance
> ...
> For if such behaviour is honoured
> why should we honour the gods with dances?   (ll. 883–96)

The second antistrophe situates the chorus's vocal action in the context of the cult of the gods. Specifically, the chorus will cease to pay honour to Apollo at Delphi (or at the Phocidian sanctuary at Abae) or to Zeus at Olympia, Zeus the master of all. Hence the spatial perspective adopted by the chorus in its theological inquiry is no longer a Theban one, nor an Athenian one, but rather it assumes a Panhellenic dimension. In this wider spatial perspective, the choral voice situates itself between the enunciative authority of the actor, who takes part in the dramatic and fictional action, and the social position of the empirical audience.

But the end of the chorus's song brings us back to Thebes, the location of the dramatic action; to cast doubt on the truth of Laius' oracular response means questioning both Zeus' supreme power and the honours due to Apollo. The threat to cease dancing and singing chorally is no more than a response to the erosion of the divine (*érrei dè tà theîa*, l. 910) adumbrated in Jocasta's sceptical remarks. The choral song has a direct impact on the action, for as soon as she has heard it Jocasta engages in a speech act (*hikétis aphîgmai*, 'I come a suppliant', l. 920) by addressing an urgent prayer to Apollo. She asks the god for a remedy against the pollution

---

[16] On this famous passage, see, in general, Burton 1980: 160–9, Segal 1981: 235–6 and of course Henrichs 1994/1995: 65–73 (cf. Chapter 3, with nn. 34 and 40). The equally controversial question of the relation between this stasimon and the action has been revisited by Sidwell 1992.

on behalf of the community (*hēmín*, 'for us', l. 921). The question arises again that was posed at the beginning of the tragedy: how is the city to be freed from the pollution afflicting it? It is once more from the deity that a response is sought.

6.4.2 The Power of Zeus: From Dramatic Action to Representation

There is nothing surprising in the fact that the chorus – self-referentially – makes sense of its songs and dances as cultic acts. We have only to remind ourselves that choral activity was in classical Greece one of four fundamental elements of all festivals for the gods.[17] Albert Henrichs, to whom this discussion is indebted, has shown clearly that interpretations of this second stasimon of *Oedipus Tyrannos* fall into two camps. On the one hand there are those who argue that only the chorus as character in the action can question its choral activity; in the other camp are those who would like to reach beyond the Theban choreuts to the Athenian citizens who have grown unwilling to serve in a chorus. Now, the performative function of the chorus's self-referential voice allows the statement that 'as a performer of ritual dance, the chorus exists simultaneously inside the dramatic realm of the play and outside of it in the political and cultic realm of the here and now'; this is all the more the case since the chorus, while it casts doubt on the legitimacy of its song in relation to the fictional action, effectively sings in the reality of the musical celebration of Dionysos (as Charles Segal, who was to join Albert Henrichs at Harvard on the shores of the Charles River, already pointed out).[18]

The chorus's crisis of confidence arises from the dramatic action taking place in Thebes insofar as it is provoked by Jocasta's doubts, but it also addresses the Athenian spectators who are in engaged in paying homage to the god of tragic music. The voice of the chorus of actors engaged in the fictional action played out between the *skene* and the orchestra therefore invites the spectators to occupy the choral first person corresponding to the mimetic actor in his performative dimension. The Dionysiac context evidently lends itself well to this kind of sceptical questioning of the relations between actors and gods as well as between spectators and gods by means of cultic activity.

This slippage of the dramatic, fictional action to the extra-discursive, referential situation is especially noticeable in the enunciative movement of

---

[17] I take the liberty of referring the reader to my 1992 study.
[18] Suffice it here to cite the position defended by Dodds 1966 (extra-discursive reference). For further details, see the exhaustive treatment of the question in Henrichs 1994/1995: 65–71, with the preliminary remarks by Segal 1981: 235–6; see also Bollack 1990: III, 581–4 and the important contribution by Hölscher 1975.

the second strophic pair of the second stasimon. Precisely on account of the invocation to Zeus that, in an echo of the allusion to 'father Olympos' (l. 867), closes the choral song to avert the threat weighing on the oracles given by Apollo to Laius, the deictics *toîsde, toiaíde* (*práxeis*) and *táde* (ll. 892, 895 and 900) appear to refer to the impious practices that are being presented to the audience's view. But with the generalizing forms *tis* ('someone', l. 882), *tís anḗr* ('what man?', l. 892) and *pâsi brótois* ('for all mortals', l. 901), the chorus's denunciation assumes on the other hand a gnomic function. The general validity of the chorus's utterance is underlined by the extra-textual reference to the Panhellenic sanctuaries of Delphi and Olympia. Through this slippage the choreuts' performative voice assumes the double reference outlined above, at the same time as it assumes an interpretative dimension.

The repeated use of the deictic *hóde*, with its dual capacity for intra- and extra-discursive reference, recurs in a similar manner in Hesiod's *Works and Days*. The difference, however, is that the choreuts of the *Oedipus Tyrannus* affect a move from the situation constructed by the text and dramatized on the stage to a general situation that finds its field of reference outside the play. In contrast, the speaker and narrator of the *Works and Days* refers to 'this' real-life situation, namely his quarrel with Perses, to imbue it through his discourse with a general applicability, so that it can be seen as comparable to other extra-discursive, concrete situations.[19] Thus the question of confidence arises from a fictional situation that, by the interposition of deictics, assumes a general validity and becomes applicable 'extra-discursively'. By this means, regardless of its affective voice, it is the performative voice of the chorus that ends up conjuring up an ideal spectator, a virtual audience with whom the real-life spectator can identify. As for the role of the author, which we have in principle associated with the chorus's hermeneutic voice, we will see this in action presently.

6.5 Hymn to Cithaeron: The Third Stasimon and Tragic Anticipation

We have remarked several times that the third choral song of *Oedipus Tyrannus* (ll. 1086–1109) is simultaneously in a relation of complementarity and contrast with the second stasimon – complementarity insofar as we

---

[19] I have discussed this play between the intra-discursive situation and the real-life communicative situation in Hesiod's *Works and Days* elsewhere: Calame 2005a: 73–106 (with references, notably to a parallel study by Pietro Pucci).

Hymn to Cithaeron 151

find there the same reference to Olympus and to the cultic honours paid to Apollo, and contrast because the chorus is gravely mistaken on the true identity of the king of Thebes. Though tentative, the chorus's initial self-referential identification with the figure of the seer puts it at odds with its earlier stance of attributing true knowledge to the gods alone (ll. 498–506, in the first stasimon). The tragic irony that permeates Oedipus' reassurances in the preceding lines is developed further in the chorus's song; mistaken in their faithfulness to Oedipus, the Theban elders replace their ignorance of the hero's true destiny with an escape into an idyllic landscape that will nevertheless turn out to be fatal.[20]

And so it is that at the end of the second stasimon, after Jocasta has made amends by ritually addressing Apollo, the Corinthian messenger steps in and announces the death of Polybus, Oedipus' father. Without the knowledge that Polybus was Oedipus' adoptive father, the oracle would seem to have been pre-empted; Oedipus can no longer kill his own father. But this reassurance is shattered by the messenger's second announcement, that the recently deceased king was merely Oedipus' adoptive father. The messenger is the same nomad shepherd who had received the newborn on Mount Cithaeron from the arms of a Theban shepherd; the wounds on Oedipus' feet act as recognition tokens. Jocasta understands and disappears distraught into the palace. The chorus also grasps the disaster, while Oedipus, determined to pursue his inquiry into his own identity to the bitter end, calls himself 'son of Tyche' (l. 1080): 'With such a parent, I could never turn out another kind of person, so as not to learn what was my birth' (ll. 1084–5).

At this point the chorus breaks out in a song composed of a simple strophic pair in dactylic rhythm (*kat'enóplion epítrita*, in the native nomenclature, the same metre as some of Pindar's epinicians).

> If I am a prophet
> and knowledgeable in my judgment,
> not unacquainted with Olympos,
> o, Cithaeron, tomorrow will not pass by
> without the full moon exalting you as the fellow-native of Oedipus,
> his nurse and mother,
> or without you being celebrated by us with
> dances for the benefits you bring

---

[20] See especially Sansone 1975 on the supposed tragic irony of this stasimon, with the commentaries by Bollack 1990: III, 698–723 and Henrichs 1994/1995: 71–3, as well as Segal 1995: 190–4. Pucci 1992:128–32, by contrast, insists on the chorus's recognition of Oedipus' semi-divine origin. For a metrical analysis, see Giannachi 2009: 89–93.

to my kings.
Iê, ié, Phoebus, may these songs
prove agreeable to you. (ll. 1086–97)

By invoking Cithaeron after Olympus, the chorus re-enters the perspective of the fictional action and its Theban location. It assumes once again its performative voice to promise a hymn to the Theban mountain. The promised song to Cithaeron, described in a series of future tenses as a choral dance performed by the first-person speaker (*khoreúesthai pròs hēmôn*, l. 1094), is postponed to the following day. This delay, whether or not it is touched with irony, proves premonitory, for after the revelation of his identity and his self-blinding Oedipus declares his intention to leave the city of his fathers to live on 'my Cithaeron, which my mother and father, when they lived still, appointed to be my tomb' (ll. 1452–3). These prophetic choral songs cannot fail to please Phoebus, who is invoked with the traditional ritual cry of the paean (l. 1096); the god will inevitably be charmed by the musical offering, just as he is in the Homeric hymn dedicated to him.[21] The echo is obvious between the future song addressed to Cithaeron and the song being executed in the orchestra for the musical and ritual performance of this stasimon.

Continuing with the 'isotopy' or semantic register of the mountainous space in the invocation of Cithaeron, the antistrophe of this third stasimon is dedicated to the choral evocation of Oedipus' putative parents. Pan, Loxias, Hermes and even Dionysos himself (ll. 1098–9; as also in the parodos) are associated with the Nymphs who frequent the valleys between Mount Cyllene and Helicon.

The third stasimon is characterized by the invocation of Apollo at its centre, and it effectively delivers to Oedipus, who has just referred to himself as 'child of Tyche' (l. 1080), the response of the farsighted seer. After the disastrous revelation of his true identity, under the seal of Apollo's knowledge, the hero will have no choice but to be the son of Cithaeron.[22] We must not forget that this brief third stasimon marks the transition towards the reversal brought about by the information given by Laius' old servant. In its hymn to Cithaeron, the chorus draws us by means of cultic speech acts into the domain that is the counterpart of 'ritual': that of 'myth'. Though it is fictional and centred on a space that is at a remove yet still closely related to the dramatic plot, this myth will soon reveal its cruel efficacy.

---

[21] On the *Homeric Hymn to Apollo* as a musical offering, cf. Calame 2011b: 350–7.
[22] The question of Oedipus' identity is reprised in Pucci 1992: 78–9; see also Ahl 1991: 145–52, and for this stasimon Bierl 2021: 35–8.

6.6 Human Fate and Choral Identification: The Fourth Stasimon

The first agent of the recognition will turn out to be the choregos himself, the mouthpiece of the chorus, which, through its performative voice, plays a crucial part in the plot. Immediately after the third stasimon, Laius' old shepherd appears. He is formally recognized by the choregos and then again by the Corinthian messenger, and he has a brief confrontation with Oedipus, who exhorts him to look him in the eye and speak (l. 1121). Under threat of torture, the old man quickly admits that it was he who took the newborn from Jocasta's arms, and he who failed to obey her order to expose him to avert the divine oracle that had predicted that he would kill his parent. At this point Oedipus speaks the lines cited above in which he identifies himself as the killer of his father and the husband of his mother (ll. 1183–5).
The chorus's reaction is immediate.

> Iò generations of mortals,
> how in my estimation you lead
> a life that is equal to nothingness!
> For who, who is that man who has
> more of prosperity
> than is enough to seem prosperous
> and then, after seeming prosperous, to decline?
> With your fate, yes, your fate as an example, o
> wretched Oedipus, I deem nothing
> blessed that pertains to mortals.   (ll. 1186–95)

This fourth stasimon (ll. 1186–1221) is composed of a strophic pair sung in an aeolian rhythm (essentially glyconics) followed by another strophic pair sung in a dochmiacs and choriambs. Uttered at the very moment when Oedipus becomes aware of his true identity and consequently of his double crime, this ode is essentially carried by the hermeneutic function of the choral voice, blended with a strongly emotional voice. These lines call for at least two kinds of remarks.

The choral song is framed by the double interjection *iò* expressing distress provoked by misfortune; the address to the generations of mortals at its beginning is echoed by the address to the children of Laius at its end (ll. 1186 and 1216; see also l. 1207). This double cry of distress underlines, in a manner that is at once emotional and performative, the applicability for all mortals of Oedipus' fate, which is held up as an example (*parádeigma*, l. 1193) by the interpretative voice of the chorus. The movement from a second-personal-plural address to mortals (*humâs*, l. 1187) to a second-person-singular address to 'wretched Oedipus' accentuates the performative dimension of the chorus's negative judgement (*oudèn makarízo* at l. 1195: 'I deem nothing blessed...'), then their lamentation (*odúromai* at l. 1218: 'how I lament you above all, cries of grief pouring from my mouth'). The intra-discursive reference to the fate of the man whom the chorus calls 'my king' (l. 1202–3) is also included in the extra-discursive reference to the sudden reversal of fortune that threatens all men. We have already remarked on this when introducing Sophocles' tragedy; such reversal was paradigmatic of a good tragic plot according to Aristotle, who illustrated his point precisely by reference to Oedipus. It is not just the characters of the play who are liable to encounter a *metabolē*, a reversal from good fortune to misfortune, but also the spectators. These latter are once again conjured up as an ideal audience to lead, by the intermediary of the chorus's voice, to the real-life public. This, no doubt, is the double reference of the pronoun *humâs*, 'you' (plural), in the opening address of the song.

On the other hand, in the ending of the last song the chorus demonstrates that it too follows the movement of this sudden reversal of fortune; through the phrasing it employs when referring to its own distress, the chorus not only associates itself to the ephemeral fate reserved for mortals, but it also anticipates in a sense Oedipus' self-blinding.

> ... To state the truth, from you I regained my breath
> and with you I close my eyes in sleep.   (ll. 1220–2)

In this context, the invocation to Zeus alone, the god who reigns over the destinies of men, becomes significant. After the reference to 'Time that sees all' (l. 1213), the appeal to Zeus in this stasimon reprises everything that the chorus had affirmed previously regarding the power of god as against the instability of the human condition.[23] Before Zeus, even he who was able to outwit the Sphinx must bow (ll. 1196–201). Once again, the chorus ultimately turns to the power of the gods.

6.7 Choral Conclusions

But the role of the chorus does not exhaust itself in this fourth stasimon. It is with the chorus that the messenger exchanges dialogue when, after the choral song, he announces Jocasta's suicide. The messenger's question about hearing and perceiving (*akoúsesthe, eisópsesthe*, in the second-

---

[23] As demonstrated by Segal 1995: 194–6. On the character of the speaking 'I' of this stasimon and its possible relation to the voice of the author, see Kaimio 1970: 95–6.

Choral Conclusions 155

person plural and the future tense, l. 1224) is addressed collectively to 'those of this land who are honoured'; in the long scene that concludes the tragedy it is the chorus that he speaks to (see the plural *eídemen*, 'we know', at l. 1232) rather than the coryphaeus alone.

The messenger relates not just to the death of Jocasta but also Oedipus' self-blinding. When he describes how he savaged his own eyes with brooches, the messenger quotes in indirect discourse the hero's own words: 'that they should not see the evils he suffered or those he accomplished' (ll. 1271–2). And it is to the chorus – in the singular – that the messenger directs the spectacle that Oedipus now intends all the Cadmeans to see, his father's killer and his mother's . . . – the messenger's speech trails into aposiopesis to avoid naming the dreaded deed (ll. 1287–9). If in terms of dramatic action the chorus represents the Cadmeans, in terms of the action being represented on stage the spectacle of the wounded hero is addressed to the audience. 'You will soon see such a sight as will stir pity even in one who hated him' (ll. 1295–6). Is this a poetic anticipation of Aristotle's remarks on *kátharsis*, with its probable dual effect on the play's actors as well as its spectators?

6.7.1 Affective Reactions in Song: The Second Kommos

However that may be, the chorus's response is sung in melic anapaests.

> O grief terrible for men to see.
> O grief most terrible of any I
> have yet encountered! What madness has come
> upon you, unhappy one? Who is the god that with a leap
> longer than the longest
> has sprung upon your miserable fate?
> Ah, ah, unhappy one, I cannot even bear to look
> on you, though I wish to ask you many questions
> and to learn many answers and perceive many things;
> such is the horror you inspire in me!   (ll. 1297–1306) (Loeb)

This choral intervention in the emotive voice and with a coda that once again brings to mind Aristotle' notion of *kátharsis* is followed by a kommos of sorts with Oedipus.[24] The hero joins the chorus in song to express his grief and look back on his childhood and destiny, and he employs in turn

---

[24] For a metrical analysis of this complex lyric exchange, see Dawe 1982: 229, 255 and Bollack 1990: I, 327–8; see also, for ll. 1297–1311, Giannachi 2009: 103–13. Nooter 2012: 89–94 traces the poetic and affective movement of the kommos and its refrains; her analysis is reprised and refined by Goldhill 2013: 120–33; see also Goldhilll 2012: 101–3 for the interferences between metre and narration.

a melic rhythm characterized by dochmiacs; the chorus's responses are occasionally in iambic trimeters. Distinguished by an intensely rhythmical lyric tension, this sung exchange stands as a veritable stasimon arranged in two strophic pairs (ll. 1313–68). The main division is enacted by Oedipus whose sung interventions, in the first strophic pair, are punctuated by cries of lamentation: *ió, oímoi, pheû pheû* after the twice repeated *aiaî* (l. 1307) that marks the reappearance of the now blind hero before the chorus and the audience. Oedipus addresses his laments at first to the 'coryphaeus' in the singular (*iò phílos*, followed by a series of second-person singulars at ll. 1321–6, in the first antistrophe), then to the chorus as a whole in the plural (*phíloi*, ll. 1339 and 1341; *apágete*, ll. 1340 and 1341; second strophe).

At first the choice of dochmiacs, the rhythm of strong emotion, enables Oedipus to express his painful dismay.

> Ah cloud
> of darkness abominable, coming over me unspeakably,
> irresistible, sped by an evil wind!
> Alas,
> alas once more! How the sting of these goads has sunk
> into me together with the remembrance of my troubles!
>
> (ll. 1313–18) (Loeb)

At the evocation of the self-blinding and its painful consequences the chorus cannot help but inquire after the motivation of such a shocking action. Oedipus' reply at the beginning of the second strophe is paradoxical to say the least.

> It was Apollo, yes, Apollo, my friends,
> who accomplished these evils, these cruel sufferings of mine.
> But no hand struck me save
> my own, wretch that I am.   (ll. 1329–32)

Then the stricken hero asks his friends, the choreutai to lead him away, a man accursed. Only the death which had been intended for him as a newborn could have prevented him from becoming, in the eyes of men, the killer of his father and the husband of his mother (ll. 1357–9). The chorus draws its interpretative conclusion: 'you would have been better off no longer alive than living as a dead man' (l. 1368). Despite the emotion of the scene, this is a perfectly lucid conclusion. Oedipus reprises in a sense the chorus's emotive voice and its hermeneutic voice to formulate his own affective and interpretative response.

Let us take another look at the anapaestic verses sung by the chorus to introduce the kommos proper. In response to Oedipus' first sung lament

Choral Conclusions 157

on his fate and the loss of control over his voice, the chorus/coryphaeus insists on the aural and visual aspects of the drama that is unfolding before its eyes (l. 1312, an echo of l. 1297; see also l. 1224). This horrific spectacle is addressed to the singing 'I' but also to man in general (*egṓ*, but also *anthrṓpois* at ll. 1297–8). This is one more reference to an ideal spectator, but it is formulated in the first person rather than in the second person as would be expected in accordance with the standard communicative schema. The upshot is that the public is assimilated, in terms of enunciation, to the singer(s).

6.7.2 Human Destiny and Ritual Musical Action

The kommos, with its emotive expressiveness, is followed by a long monologue directed at the chorus. In this monologue Oedipus reduces his identity to the pollution that dishonours the city through the gods' revelation, and he evokes the places in which key events of his story took place (Cithaeron, Corinth, the crossroads near Delphi, Thebes). In a final exchange with Creon, the wounded and polluted hero communicates his wish to be sent to Cithaeron to die: 'This Cithaeron, my Cithaeron, the tomb chosen for me by my mother and father' (ll. 1452–3). The mention of his impending withdrawal prompts Oedipus to reach out one last time to touch the hands of his two daughters, who are also his sisters, before entrusting them to Creon; Oedipus wishes for them a better life than that of their father.

Though Oedipus repeats his request to be banished (*ápoikos*, l. 519), Creon invites the deposed king to go back inside the palace, leaving the decision regarding his fate to the god. On his return to the scene, Creon had asked the chorus not to expose to the light of the sun 'such a pollution' (*toiónd' ágos* at l. 1426, with a deictic), but to take him back 'into the house' to the care of his kin. Now that Oedipus has recognized his guilt and been reabsorbed into the domain of the domestic, he is no longer a scapegoat.[25] Indeed the *Iliad* mentions the existence at Thebes of a tomb of Oedipus, which suggests that he was the recipient of a heroic cult. The Hesiodic *Catalogue of Women* mentions Oedipus' funeral, and Sophocles himself, in his final tragedy, stages Oedipus' death in the deme of Colonus, where King Theseus orders a 'sacred tomb' to be built.[26]

---

[25] *Pace* Vernant (and Vidal-Naquet) 1970: 117–23. Nooter 2012: 94–8 emphasizes the incantatory effect of the exclamations and apostrophes that punctuate these lines.
[26] Hom. *Il.* 23, 679–80, Hes. fr. 192 Merkelbach-West, Soph. *Oed. Col.* 1760–7; for modern speculation on this topic, see Marx 2012: 18–25.

158 Sophocles' *Oedipus Tyrannus*

In the final lines of the play, the spectacle of Oedipus' terrifying reversal, which had previously been narrated by the messenger to the chorus and then by the chorus and its leader in dialogue with the tragic hero, is now presented once again by the choreutai for the benefit of the Thebans. Sung in trochaic rhythm, these lines provide a controversial ending to the play.

> Inhabitants of Thebes our fatherland, behold, this is Oedipus,
> who knew the famous riddle and was the mightiest of men.
> None of the citizens could look upon his fate without envy.
> What billow of terrible misfortune has he encountered?
> For mortal man the only day to be considered in the last one:
> no one is blessed before he has reached
> the limit of his life without suffering anything painful.   (ll. 1524–30)

Though serious doubt has been cast on the authenticity of this brief song, these conclusive remarks align Oedipus' fate to the Delphic wisdom about the changeability of human fortune.[27] This wisdom had already been prominent in the first strophe of the fourth stasimon, the famous passage in which Oedipus' fate was held up as paradigmatic of the illusory nature of *eudamoinía* for mortals (ll. 1186–95). There, when invoking the unfortunate hero and then Zeus himself, the chorus addressed their Delphic commentary to the 'generations of mortals', whereas here, at the conclusion of the tragedy, they address it to the 'inhabitants of Thebes'.

The chorus's words construct, through the community in which the dramatic fiction is placed, the figure of an ideal spectator that can be inhabited by the tragedy's empirical audience. But from an enunciative standpoint this figure of the virtual spectator oscillates between the first person (singular or plural), where it is identified with the chorus/speaker, and the second person (singular or plural). In this partly extra-discursive broadening of its addresses, the choral first person is perfectly able to include, in the position of speaker, the ideal author, who corresponds to the ideal narrator. We will return to this in the conclusions. The performative voice, the affective voice and the hermeneutic voice here join in an instance of plural enunciation to create the enunciative polyphony that we have been at pains to outline.

The ritual and 'theological' unfolding of the narrative action reformulated by Sophocles effects itself through the chorus's singing. These songs communicate to the audience the knowledge of man's destiny revealed by Oedipus'

---

[27] The authenticity of the last lines of the tragedy is discussed in Dawe 1982: 247, and Bollack 1990: IV, 1038–54 (!). For the unusual change from singular to plural in Oedipus' address to the coryphaeus at l. 1321, cf. Kaimio 1970: 227–8 (see also 171–2 for the last lines of the tragedy).

Choral Conclusions 159

dramatic inquiry: a human identity founded on a divine destiny vouched by Zeus and revealed by Apollo. Through its religious rituality, the choral voice points to the audience's action of honouring Dionysos in his sanctuary-theatre on the slope of the Athenian Acropolis. In Sophocles' *Oedipus Tyrannus*, Oedipus is not the paradigm of the 'tragic hero' as this has been understood ever since Hegel and Nietzsche or even Aristotle. Through the poetic and dramatic fiction, altogether apart from the subject's exercise of his personal freedom, the Theban hero illustrates the divine dimension of the human condition such as it is conceived in the anthropological framework expressed in the chorus's songs. It is the function of the choral voice to assign to Oedipus' narrative and fictional destiny a significance in the conception of man that Sophocles offers to his audience of fifth-century Athenians.

CHAPTER 7

Poets, Tragic Diction and Tragic Fiction

Is tragedy choral? Let us return finally to the question of origins, but let us do so while keeping strictly to the poetical, narrative and ritual dimensions. We will now be able to draw some conclusions regarding the pragmatics of the tragic choral voice – both masculine and feminine – as it is orchestrated by the poets who stage, in the service of the city, an action belonging to its heroic past.

7.1 From Diegesis to Mimesis: Bacchylides' Athenian Dithyramb

Let us take one more look at Aristotle's definition of tragedy at the beginning of his *Poetics*, even though *melopoiía* (and consequently melic creation) is excluded from it at the outset: 'Tragedy, then, is the representation (*mímēsis*) of an action that is noble and complete, having a certain extension ... a mimesis by actors rather than a narration (*apaggelía*).'[1] As we have seen, Aristotle here applies to dramatic action Plato's famous distinction (in the *Republic*) between narration or diegesis on the one hand and the mimetic or dramatic mode on the other. In Plato as in Aristotle, poetic *mimesis* revolves around narrative action and its dramatization. With Attic tragedy, the narration of a heroic action moves in a sense from the diegetic mode to the mimetic mode.

Now, besides Attic tragedy, there is another form of choral melic poetry that (insofar as we can tell, given its fragmentary state of preservation) involves the developed narration of a 'myth' through the kind of dramatic *mimesis* envisaged by Plato and formulated by Aristotle: dithyramb. As discussed in Chapter 1, the musical event in honour of the Liberator god of the Great Dionysia included, in addition to the tragic and comic contests, a dithyrambic contest. Often narrative in form, dithyramb was sung – we must not forget this – by as many as fifty choreuts; ten 'circular choruses' of fifty young men and ten dithyrambic

---

[1] Arist. *Poet.* 6, 1449b 21–6; cf. Chapter 2.1.1 with n. 3.

From Diegesis to Mimesis   161

choruses of adult men took part in the competition, each of these choruses representing one of the ten tribes into which the citizen population of Athens and Attica was subdivided.[2]

If Pindar's dithyrambs display an enunciative turn that is closest to cultic songs such as paean, by contrast the few extant dithyrambs of Bacchylides display a marked narrative character. This is the case, for instance, of the dithyramb already touched on in Chapter 2, which alternates between the narrative mode and the 'mixed' mode to narrate Theseus' dive into the Aegean at Minos' command and his triumphant return from the home of Amphitrite and her father Poseidon. Paradoxically, from a narrative standpoint this long poem culminates with the performance of a paean by the young men and women who accompany Theseus on his expedition to Crete, while from an enunciative standpoint the poem ends, as we have seen, with a move to the mode of "discours" in a cultic address to Delian Apollo, to whom the song is dedicated.[3]

But from a mimetic and dramatic point of view the most remarkable composition is Bacchylides' other Athenian dithyramb (18), composed to recount and celebrate an earlier episode of Theseus' life, namely his heroic arrival in Athens and his recognition not as the son of his divine father Poseidon but as the son of his human father Aegeus. Composed in Aeolian rhythm (essentially in glyconics), this dramatic song is meant to be performed by a chorus in the mimetic mode and with melic diction; however, unlike the chorus of tragedy, the choreutai singing the poem did not wear masks. The chorus initiates a 'lyric exchange' in choriambic rhythm with the legendary king of Athens, the protagonist of the story that is being narrated and dramatized. In the voice of the speaking 'I' implied by its second-person addresses, and thus in the mode of 'discourse' (*discours*), the chorus sings as protagonist simultaneously of the heroic action being narrated and the musical event being performed.

> King of holy Athens,
> lord of the delicately living Ionians,
> why did the bronze-belled trumpet
> sound its war-song just now?
> Does some hostile army commander
> surround the borders
> of our land? . . .   (1–7) (Loeb)

---

[2] Cf. Chapter 2.4.2.
[3] Bacch. 17; for bibliographical references, see n. 82 in Chapter 2. On the dithyrambic contest, see Chapter 2.5.1 with nn. 80 and 81.

Aegeus replies singing in the same Aeolic rhythm, but in the narrative mode (*récit*), first in the present then in the past tense.

> A herald came just now, having completed
> on foot the long journey from the Isthmus,
> and he tells of indescribable deeds on the part
> of a strong man: he has slain the mighty
> Sinis, who was the foremost of mortals
> in strength ... (16–21) (Loeb)

There follows, still in the narrative mode, the sequence of three monstrous beings killed by Theseus on the road to Athens, which is both the location of the heroic action being narrated and the location of the dithyramb's performance.[4] This sequence of Theseus' deeds is comparable to Heracles' labours and, like it, is often depicted in Attic iconography of the period.

This surprising melic composition sung in a dramatic mode was undoubtedly intended for one of the large-scale civic and religious celebrations of the victorious city after the Persian Wars, whether the Great Panathenaia, the Theseia, the Thargelia or perhaps the Great Dionysia themselves. This choral song exemplifies one of the various possible ways in which melic poetry could narrate heroic episodes; here we have the choral dramatization of a foundational episode of Athens' heroic history. Through collective singing and dramatic performance, this song played a part in the musical legitimization and memorialization of Theseus, who was to become the tragic hero of classical democracy.

Admittedly, this composition is an exception; among the extant dithyrambs of Bacchylides and Pindar with demonstrable civic significance, this is the only one that is entirely dramatic.[5] The dithyrambs of Bacchylides in particular (which are more or less contemporary with Aeschylus' tragedies) display a striking prevalence of narrative compared to other melic poetry. Both Plato and Aristotle noticed this.

In his discussion of the three narrative modes prompted in the *Republic* by the debate on the moral value of mythology and poetry, Plato illustrates his argument precisely by reference to dithyramb. The fully mimetic mode

---

[4] Bacch. 18, 1–8 and 16–21; the possible context of performance of this dithyramb, as well as its form, are discussed in Maehler's commentary: Maehler 1997: 211–19. On the question of the 'dithyrambic' stasima once recognized by Kranz 1933: 228–65, in some of the choral songs by Euripides, see now the fine study by Fanfani 2018, who speaks of 'blending lyric genres' in the example of the first stasimon in *Trojan women*.

[5] Cf. Calame 2013b: 341–8. Wilson 2007: 169–82 has demonstrated the extent to which these different dithyrambs belong to a 'politics of dance'.

is represented by tragedy and comedy; the diegetic mode, in which the poet himself does the speaking (*apaggelía*), and thereby creates the narrative (*récit*), can be illustrated generally by dithyramb; finally, epic poetry is the result of mixing these two modes with the introduction of direct interventions by the protagonists of the the narrated action.[6] In this context, Bacchylides' dithyramb18, in which Aegeus sings before a chorus and dramatizes Theseus' arrival at Athens, stands as an exception; its use of the mimetic mode assimilates it to tragedy.

Aristotle on the other hand discusses dithyramb under the rubric of the genealogy of poetic genres, one of the structuring principles of the *Poetics* (together with the descriptive and the normative). Not only does Aristotle from the beginning of his treatise present 'dithyrambic poetics' (*hē dithurambopoietikḗ*) side by side with epic poetry, tragic and comic poetry, and the playing of the aulos and the cithara, as 'representations' (*mimḗseis*) and thus as narrative arts; moreover (as we have seen in Chapter 1) he focuses on an early, improvisational form of dithyramb, alongside epic, as the grounds out of which tragedy arose. Just as comedy replaced iambos, so did the *tragoidodidáskaloi* take the place of the epic poets; this process is ascribed to an initial improvisational stage in which tragedy was first composed by the poets who 'initiated' (*exárkhontes*) the dithyramb, while comedy arose from the poets who led the phallic songs.[7] The distinction here is probably between composition and poetic creation on the one hand and the musical function assumed by the poet in the ritual performance itself on the other.

Be that as it may, precisely on account of its narrative character allied with its melic diction, in its standard form the dithyramb offers a good example of the possible development of Attic tragedy from a form of choral and ritual poetic performance. But the development of choral dithyramb itself is certainly parallel to the development of the so-called 'song of the goat'.

7.2 Citharodic Nomos: Stesichorus

Is this a case of convergence between Homeric narrative tradition, as suggested by Aristotle, and the melic tradition of enacted poetry embodied in dithyramb? Are we making a return to the genealogical approach and the Romantic triad *Epos – Lyrik – Drama*?

---

[6] Plato, *Resp.* 394bc; see Murray 1996: 172–3 and the discussion in Peponi 2013: 355–60; cf. Chapter 2.1.1 with n. 4.
[7] Ar. *Poet.* 1, 1447a 13–17 and 4, 1449a 2–15; see already Chapter 1.3.1 as well as Chapter 2.5.1 with nn. 82 and 84. For the hypothetical genealogical relation with satyr play, see Scullion 2005: 25–6 and 27–8.

Thus far we have confined ourselves to fifth-century Athens, but what about Magna Graecia one century earlier, at the time of the flourishing of the remarkable Spartan 'song culture'?

If there is a poetic genre that, without giving rise to it, prefigures in terms of form and narrative Attic tragedy, then it is surely the citharodic nomos such as it was developed by Stesichorus of Himera. Stesichorus' origins are unknown; there is no agreement among ancient biographers. If he was not born in the small colonial Greek city of Himera in Sicily, he must in any case have spent part of his life there. His poetic activity is otherwise associated with Locri Epizephyrii and perhaps, in mainland Greece, with Sparta. He returned to Sicily and died in Catania, where an imposing monument was built in his honour and where he may have been the recipient of a hero cult.[8]

The poems of Stesichorus seem to have had a decisive influence on Attic tragedy and its poets, both for their subject matter (the choice of heroic episodes) and for their poetic form.

7.2.1 Heroic Narratives and Poetic Creation

The influence of Stesichorus' poems in Attic tragedy is perceptible in the first instance in relation to narrative development. According to a fragmentary papyrus commentary, Stesichorus drew his narrative subject matter from his predecessors, probably Homer and Hesiod (who are mentioned later in the text) – and later poets in turn drew on Stesichorus. Among the poets indebted to Stesichorus is Aeschylus, for the composition of his *Oresteia*. The poet of the *Choephoroi* is thought to have borrowed from Stesichorus the detail of Orestes' recognition by means of a lock of hair, whereas Euripides borrowed from him that of the bow gifted to Orestes by Apollo.[9] But this is not all. A scholiast indicates, still in connection with Aeschylus' *Choephoroi*, a variant for the name of the nurse: Cilissa in Aeschylus, Laodamia in Stesichorus; a different scholiast states that in the second 'book' of the *Oresteia* Stesichorus made Palamedes the inventor of the alphabet, 'agreeing on this matter with Euripides'. Moreover, several ancient critics have

---

[8] The entry in Stephanus of Byzantium's *Lexicon* (*s.v. Mátauros* = test. 9 Campbell – Ta 15 Ercoles) names Metauron as Stesichorus' birthplace; see also the Suda *s.v. Stesíkhoros* (S 1095 Adler = test. 1 Campbell = Ta 10 Ercoles).

[9] Stes. fr. 217 Page-Davies = 181a Davies-Finglass; cf. Aesch. *Choeph.* 168 and Eur. *Or.* 268–70; see also the scholion to Eur. *Or.* 268 (1, 126 Schwartz), which also attributes to Stesichorus the episode of Apollo's gifting of the bow.

remarked in Stesichorus' poems (whose text was available to them in its entirety) a dramatic manner and a pathos that would prefigure Attic tragedy.[10]

Finally, in Aristophanes' *Peace*, the chorus parodies some verses ascribed by ancient commentators to the same Stesichorean *Oresteia*. These are, in order, an invocation inviting the Muse to sing and dance (*khóreuson*) with the chorus to celebrate the weddings and feasts of the blessed gods as well as the banquets of men; the mention of the song (*humneîn*) of the 'wise poet' (*sophòs poietḗs*) inspired by the Charites of the beautiful hair; and finally the allusion to the resounding (*keladêi*) swallow song that announces the spring in this same choral hymn to the Muse that follows the parabasis.[11] These beautiful verses of melic and choral invocation of the Muse occur in the context of mockery of the sour voice of two mediocre tragic poets who struggle to 'obtain a chorus'.[12]

The great heroic saga of Agamemnon's return from Troy, his murder at the hands of Clytemnestra and Orestes' subsequent vengeance with the aid of Apollo was sung, then, in a narrative poem by Stesichorus, the poet of Magna Graecia. Composed and sung not in hexameters but in the dactylic stanzas (as we will see), this poem was roughly the length of two Aeschylean tragedies or two or three books of the *Iliad*. Hence the Alexandrian editors' need to divide Stesichorus' *Oresteia* into two rolls of papyrus. A stichometric mark on the margin of a papyrus fragment of the *Geryoneis* (a long poem in triads of anapaestic dimeters about Heracles' expedition to the Hesperides) indicates that it exceeded 1,300 lines;[13] a projection on this basis gives a length of approximately 2,500 lines for the *Oresteia*.

7.2.2 Narrative Development and Dramatic Form

The few lines of the *Oresteia* that survived in the indirect tradition have allowed us to reconstruct its melic rhythm and glean something of the opening, with its petition to the Muse for her cooperation. But they have not allowed us to identify the narrative mode. However, the discovery of the Lille Papyrus, which preserves a lengthy narrative fragment, has allowed

---

[10] Stes. fr. 218 and 213 Page-Davies = 179 and 175ab Davies-Finglass; for the different pre-tragic versions of the story of Orestes, see Neschke 1986, as well as the recent contribution by Pucci 2015. For ancient criticism, see the references in Ercoles 2012: 1–3.

[11] Stes. fr. 210, 212 and 211 Page-Davies = 172, 173 and 174 Davies-Finglass, corresponding respectively to Ar. *Pax* 773–9, 796–9 and 799–801.

[12] For the expression *khoròn ékhein* cf. n. 45 in Chapter 1.

[13] Stes. fr. S 27, 6 and 10 Page-Davies = 25 Davies-Finglass; cf. Gentili and Lomiento 2003: 112 *contra* Haslam 1974: 11.

substantial progress in this area. Let us sketch out the shape of this poem that belongs, despite appearances, to the large category of *mélos* (and not 'lyric'!).

The poem, whose title is unknown, narrated various episodes of the myth of Oedipus. From heroic narratives of the Trojan War we therefore move to the other great epic moment of heroic times according to Hesiod's *Works and Days*, the Theban saga.[14] The sixty or so legible lines of the papyrus give us the direct speech of a mother attempting to persuade her two sons to accept the apportioning by lot of Oedipus' goods proposed after his disappearance; to one son falls Oedipus' kingdom and to the other his possessions, his troops and his gold, but also exile. The sons accept and Tiresias assents; Tiresias is also an addressee of the 'divine woman' (*día guná*, l. 232). The mother's hope is that the gods, in their fickleness, have not established on earth once and for all either discord or friendly agreement; in direct discourse and in the mimetic mode, the woman therefore asks Apollo not to bring to pass all the grim oracles uttered by Tiresias.

> For the immortal gods have not ordained
> for all time alike that strife should be
> perpetual among men across the holy earth,
> no, nor friendship either; rather, the gods
> set men's [outlook for a day].
> May lord Apollo, who works from afar, not bring all your
> prophecies to fulfilment!   (204–10)

Nevertheless, if it is the fate of her two children to kill each other, or if the city must be besieged, then she would prefer to die before them. 'Jocasta' herself is not named in the extant lines, but the names of Eteocles and Polynices are preserved (ll. 281–3).

The verses that follow are more fragmentary, but they suggest that the actions anticipated in the woman's direct speech are then recounted in the diegetic epic mode; the lots are probably drawn, and the troops are assigned to Polynices. Then, after Polynices (?), Tiresias speaks with an allusion to the apportioning of fate (*[ka]t'aîsan*, l. 273) and to the house of Adrastus, who will receive Polynices in Argos and give him his daughter in marriage. Tiresias' lengthy direct speech also includes a warning to Eteocles not to aspire to Polynices' lot so that the hero may keep the city and his mother safe from grief. The remainder of the extant text describes in the narrative mode (in the third person and the past tense) the stages of Polynices' migration with his Theban companions to Argos via the Corinthian Isthmus. Nothing

---

[14] Stes. fr. 222 (b) Page-Davies = 97 Davies-Finglass, translation by M. Davies and P.J. Finglass, 2014, pp. 372–4. cf. Hes. *Op.* 156–73.

remains of Stesichorus' narrative after Oedipus' death or exile, the quarrel between his sons and Tiresias' intervention calling upon the authority of Apollo and his oracles regarding the fate of the Labdacids,

The episode of 'Jocasta's' attempt to reconcile her sons and avert the divine will illustrates perfectly the complex motivation – not merely double but triple – of the heroic narrative action: the will of the mortal hero or heroine resulting from a reasoned argumentation; the will of the gods, which mortals can bend by means of prayer and ritual offerings; and fate, *moîra* or that which is *mórsimon*, to which the gods themselves are bound. Just as in the *Iliad*, this triple motivation or determination of human action is staged in narrative form also in the actions of the protagonists of Attic tragedy such as Oedipus in Sophocles' *Oedipus Tyrannus*, Hippolytus in the eponymous play by Euripides or Xerxes in Aeschylus' *Persians*, as the chorus often makes clear. Furthermore, if the scene narrated by Stesichorus constitutes in our tradition the first (and no doubt only) attestation of Jocasta's attempt to arbitrate between her sons, this version of the story has not failed to influence Attic tragedy.

The few extant allusions and fragments of epic poetry that are earlier than Stesichorus' poem allow us to distinguish three versions. One of these, mentioned by Odysseus in the *Odyssey* in the account of his descent to the Underworld, centres on Epicaste; Oedipus' mother marries her own son who in turn has killed his own father; the double crime is revealed by the gods and causes the beautiful Epicaste to hang herself, while Oedipus continues to rule over Thebes by the fateful will of the gods and is nevertheless pursued by his mother and wife' Erinyes. No mention is made here of any sons. The second version is found in Hesiod's account of 'the five ages of man', in the section on the age of heroes; this version seems to focus on the war that was waged at the seven gates of Thebes over Oedipus' herds; here Oedipus probably found his death at last at the hands of the Mynians. Finally, according to Pausanias, the *Oedipodeia* (which focused on the episode of the Sphinx) recounted that Oedipus – probably after Jocasta's death – had married Euryganeia and had from her four descendants; the historian and genealogist Pherecydes of Athens adds that after he had fathered with Jocasta, his own mother, two sons who had died in the war against the Minyans, Oedipus had married Euryganeia and with her fathered Antigone and Ismene as well as Eteocles and Polynices.[15]

[15] Hom. *Od.* 11, 271–80; Hes. *Op.* 162–3; *Oedipodeia* fr. 2 Bernabé, cited by Pausanias 9, 5, 10, and whose plot is summarized by Pisander, *FGrHist* 16 F 10, 8, as well as Pherecydes, *FGrHist* 3 F 95. On these three versions of the story and their different attestations, see the commentaries by Bremer 1987: 164–6 and Davies and Finglass 2014: 258–67; see also the reinterpretation of Aluja 2014 arguing away a reading

Now, if Aeschylus' *Seven Against Thebes* barely mentions Oedipus' mother and wife (l. 927), Euripides' *Phoenicians* puts Jocasta on stage right from the prologue. In a famous scene, Jocasta confronts her two sons without the presence of Tiresias (who is here replaced by the chorus of captive Phoenicians) in an attempt to reconcile them. Compared to Stesichorus' plot, the timeline of this version is changed. To avoid the fulfilment of Oedipus' curses (which are not mentioned in the fragmentary text preserved by the papyrus) Polynices and Eteocles agree under oath that they will alternate in reigning over Thebes for one year at a time. Eteocles is first on the throne, but when his turn is over he refuses to step down and instead sends his brother away. Having sought refuge in Argos with Adrastus, Polynices returns to Thebes with an army of Argive allies; during a truce before the combat, Jocasta attempts to reconcile her two sons. Her argument is political and based on the principle of justice; the founding principle between friends, cities and allies is equality (*isótēs*, ll. 536 and 542; cf. l. 538). To break this principle is to fall into injustice, that is to say, tyranny in the case of Eteocles and violent aggression in the case of Polynices; the safety of the city depends on respect for equality.[16] What follows is well known. Eteocles refers Polynices to the etymology of his name; this will be the triumph of *neîkos* (l. 637). Jocasta will kill herself on learning of the death of her two sons and, as in the two later Sophoclean versions, Oedipus will be condemned to exile with Antigone.

If Euripides doubtless took inspiration from the plot of Stesichorus' narrative poem, he also clearly reoriented it and changed the ideological issues at stake; whether consciously or unconsciously, he adapted them to the historical conjuncture and political context of Athens at the end of the fifth century. This is a good example of the malleability of a Greek 'myth', which, being an *arkhaîon*, is a function of a constantly re-actualized representation of heroic history and the community's anthropology. With the help of a poet, this reshapes its cultural memory at each ritualized poetic and musical performance in line with the circumstances of the moment, while also modifying the conventions of the genre that delivers the dramatized heroic story to its public.

---

of Stesichorus as 'most Homeric' in favour of his innovativeness; on the different versions of Oedipus' death, see Cingano 1992. In the epic *Thebaid* the narrative is set in motion by Oedipus' curses against his sons: cf. fr. 2 and 3 Bernabé.

[16] Eur. *Phoen.* 55–87 and 446–593; see the remarks in Bremer 1987: 168–70, taking his moves from Arist. *Pol.* 4, 1298a 9–11. On Jocasta in *Phoenicians*, see Ercole and Fiorentini 2011: 24–32 and Swift 2015: 138–42 (also in Sophocles' *Oedipus Tyrannus*). Finglass 2018: 37 points out that 'Stesichorus was a crucial early antecedent for the representation of strong-minded women in Greek tragedy'.

From a formal point of view the narrative in Stesichorus' poem is in the 'mixed' mode associated by Plato (as we have seen) with the Homeric poems. It thus alternates between diegesis, corresponding to the level of the 'story' (*récit*, in the third person, in the past tense and taking place elsewhere from the location of the enunciation, to follow Benveniste's seminal definition) and direct speech by the protagonists (*discours*, in the first person, here and now). But the direct speech of the protagonists of the narrative is still subordinated to a diegesis in which the poetic 'I' is elided, with the exception of the opening invocation to the Muse. In tragedy there is no diegesis; the authorial first person gives way entirely to the voice of the individual protagonists of the action that is narrated and dramatized – they alone engage in direct discourse with the chorus. The (probably) choral voice that in Stesichorus' poem carries the narration in the mixed mode (narrative and dialogues) in Attic tragedy corresponds essentially to the voice of the chorus, which becomes a protagonist of the heroic action being staged here and now.[17]

7.2.3 Epic Diction and Metre

In short, from the perspective of poetic diction and enunciation, Stesichorus' lengthy fragmentary songs present the same paradoxical situation as the Homeric poems. Their enunciation alternates between the epic narrative mode and the dramatic narrative mode of tragedy. The technical qualities of their poetic diction, which point to a sung and ritualized execution, are here crucial, and they warrant further discussion.

On the one hand, in terms of lexical range, we find in the 'Jocasta' poem a vocabulary that is close to that of Homeric poetic tradition; this includes formulaic expressions that are often varied: *(ánax) hekáergos Apóllōn* ('lord Apollo who strikes from afar' at l. 209, just as in the *Iliad* and especially in the *Homeric Hymns*); but also *dîa gunấ* ('noble woman', l. 232); whereas we find *dîa gunaikỗn* in Homer and Hesiod, or (in the same line) *múthois aganoîs enépoisa* ('speaking with gentle words') to qualify the 'noble woman's' speech, whereas the *Iliad* has the formula *soîs d'aganoîs epéesin* (four times).[18] The transition from 'Jocasta's' direct speech to the diegetic passages follows the conventions of Homeric formularity, with some variations required by the metre and allowed by the plasticity of

---

[17] For the 'mixed' mode in Homeric diegesis according to Plato, cf. Chapter 2.1.1 with n. 4. Burnett 1988: 129–35 and 153–4 offers valid arguments for a choral performance of this poem.
[18] See, for example, respectively Hom. *Il.* 5, 439, *H.H.Ap.* 440, *Il.* 2, 164, 180, 189 and so on; for other formulaic expressions, see once again Bremer's commentary, 1987: 162.

Homeric language. The same goes for the poem's use of dialect; we find the same mixture of Ionian and Aeolian forms as in the Homeric poems, but with the addition of some 'Doric' forms that point not only to large-scale choral poetry, but also the choral parts of Attic tragedy.[19]

From the point of view of metre, as we have already noted, we move from the 'stichic' dactylic hexameter to a more complex articulation in melic *kôla* on a dactylic base; these 'limbs' are linked together in periods that are in turn organized into strophic structures. The metrical elements composing these melic periods are admittedly also the building blocks of dactylic hexameter, for they coincide with the metrical units defined by the hexameter's caesura and they correspond readily to formulaic expressions characteristic of Homeric diction: hemiepes (– uu – uu –) before the penthemimeral caesura, enoplion (x – uu – uu – x) before the more common feminine caesura, prosodiac (x – uu – uu –) and so on. This terminology keeps us close to that of the Greek metricians, for it is important to avoid the modern analytical attitude that introduces elements without a metrical and therefore musical or even choreographic rationale, such as D (– uu – uu –) or d^{I} (– uu –).[20] In Stesichorus' poems in particular, these brief metrical sequences are articulated in periods linking together into strophic units that are in turn organized into triads as in large-scale choral poetry: a succession of triadic sequences consisting of strophe, antistrophe and epode.

Thus in the recently discovered papyrus fragment of the *Thebaid* the strophe and antistrophe are entirely composed of cola that are found in dactylic hexameter; these metrical units are accompanied by the iambic structure that is anachronistically termed 'reizianum' (x u – u x; iambic penthemimera in the terms of ancient musicologists). These rhythmic sequences are graphically divided into seven lines or 'verses'. The epode has roughly the same length and repeats the same elements, but with a different organization that allows for the additional inclusion of a trochaic dimeter.[21] The few verses of the *Oresteia* that can be reconstructed on the basis of Aristophanes' parodies display an original combination of the same metrical cola, that is to say, hemiepes, prosodiac and 'reizianum', in a rhythm termed *kat' enóplion* (epitrite) by the grammarian Heliodorus.[22]

---

[19] On this point, see the helpful catalogue of dialectal forms compiled by Bremer 1987: 129–30.
[20] This analytic notation is connected with absurd (from the rhythmical point of view) introduction of the *anceps interpositum*, the long or short 'linking' syllable: cf. Gentili and Lomiento 2003: 29–30.
[21] See the analysis in Gentili and Giannini 1997: 8–12 (= 1995: 12–17) as well as the more analytical and less convincing analysis in Haslam 1979: 30–8; see also, in the same analytic vein, Davies and Finglass 2014: 47–52 and 370–1; for a comparison of these two interpretations of the metrical rhythm, see Ercoles 2013: 536–8.
[22] Gentili and Lomiento 2003: 201–2 (with n. 35); cf. the sch. *ad* Ar. *Pax* 797a (II.2, 125 Holwerda).

Citharodic Nomos: Stesichorus 171

As for the longer papyrus fragments of the *Sack of Troy*, they seem to display strophes articulated according to a similar combination, while the *Geryoneis* is composed of anapaestic dimeters also arranged in triadic strophes.[23]

It is possible that in antiquity Stesichorus was regarded as the inventor of the triadic form since the triad was called after him. An entry in the Byzantine *Suda* explains that the sequence strophe-antistrophe-epode is called *tría St*e*sikhórou* ('the three of Stesichorus') because the whole of his poetry is 'epodic', that is to say, arranged into triads; the entry adds that traditionally to be unaware of this expression is to be 'without culture or education', *ámousón te kaì apaídeuton*, a statement that is eerily reminiscent of Plato's *Laws*.[24] In his treaty *On the Arrangement of Words* Dionysus of Halicarnassus supports this; while *melopoioí* such as Alcaeus or Sappho composed in brief strophes, Stesichorus and Pindar expanded their periods by introducing a great variety of cola and arranging them into triadic stanzas by the addition of an epode.[25] Thus – in poems that are essentially narrative and epic – the melic cadence called *kat' enóplion* links into long rhythmic periods articulated into triads the basic metrical units that in the hexameter always appear in a fixed order on a stichic or 'homorhythmic' base.[26] In their metrical form Stesichorus' compositions are in a sense a symbol of Greek musical culture.

This is not to say that Stesichorus' metres derive from the Homeric dactylic hexameter, for all that this is implied by the histories of Greek 'literature' that place 'lyric' after 'Homer'. From a genealogical point of view the order is likely to be the reverse; the dactylic hexameter, composed of cola linked together with the familiar variations and simply repeated, is likely to have emerged from the varied periods whose tradition is attested in Stesichorus for narrative poetry.[27]

7.2.4 The Citharodic Nomos: A Narrative Genre

But what was the mode of musical execution and what was the poetic genre of these narrative compositions whose diction is epic but whose metre is melic and triadic? What is their relationship to choral performance?

---

[23] Stes. fr. S 88 and S 89 Page-Davies = 100 Davies-Finglass, cf. Gentili and Giannini 1977: 11; for the *Geryoneis*' particular metrical structure, cf. Davies and Finglass 2014: 249–51 and n. 35 in this chapter.
[24] *Suda s.v. tría St*e*sikhórou* (*T* 943 Adler) = test. 30 Campbell = Tb 9 (b) Ercoles; cf. Pl. *Leg.* 654a.
[25] Dion. Halic. *De comp. verb.* 6, 19, 7 = test. 28 Campbell – Tb 8 Ercoles; cf. Ercoles 2013: 531–6.
[26] Similar dactylic sequences are found in Pindar's and Bacchylides' epinicians: cf. Gentili and Lomiento 2003: 201–2.
[27] Cf. Gentili and Lomiento 2003: 279–83; Gentili and Giannini 1977: 28 (= 1995: 31) speak of an 'accostamento dei *cola* in funzione omoritmica' leading to the dactylic hexameter.

Nothing is known of the circumstances of performance of these long narrative melic poems such as the *Oresteia*, the *Thebaid* or the *Geryoneis*,[28] but some ancient testimonies appear to direct us to the genre of the citharodic nomos. This poetic genre has proved controversial when it comes to the manner of its musical execution. On the one hand the name itself *nómos* refers to a melody, and specifically a melody played on the lyre to a fixed tune. At first each *nomos* had its own 'tension' or tonality (*tásis*) referring to a particular harmony and an agreed rhythm.[29] Moreover, *nomoi* are connected with the sung poetic genre of citharody. Terpander of Lesbos, active at Sparta in the seventh century and, like his countryman Arion of Methymna, known as a 'citharode', was said among other musical innovations to have renewed the citharodic *nomos*.[30] Moreover, Terpander, who was attached to the first musical 'institution' at Sparta and winner of the first celebration of the Carneia in honour of Apollo, was also said to have 'clothed' his verses (*épē*) as well as those of Homer with melodies (*mélē*; this is the primary meaning of this technical term); this transformation of the Homeric poems into melic song according to different *nomoi* destined them to be sung in musical competitions. This action will define Terpander as 'poet of citharodic *nomoi*', a denomination that is supposed to be his. Finally, Terpander was the first to give his citharodic poems titles.[31]

In his brief history of citharody, Heraclides Ponticus (cited by ps.-Plutarch) displays the characteristic Greek concern with origins. He attributes to Amphion, son of Zeus and Antiope, the invention of citharodic poetry. It is in this time of heroic founders that Linos of Euboea is said to have composed his threnoi and Pieros, the eponymous king of Pieria, his poems on the Muses; Plutarch names as his successors the singers portrayed in the *Iliad* and *Odyssey*, that is, Thamyris of Thrace, Demodocos of Corcyra (identified with Phaeacia in antiquity) and Phemios of Ithaca. While Thamyris had composed a *Battle of the Titans and the Olympians*, Plutarch attributes to Phemios a *Return of Agamemnon from Troy*, and to Demodocos a *Fall of Troy* as well as, naturally, a *Marriage of Aphrodite and Hephaistos* (*sic*); thus the various bardic performances mentioned in the

---

[28] According to Cingano's hypothesis (1993: 356–8; see also Cingano 2003: 33–4), the *Oresteia* may have been sung during the cultic celebrations in honour of Apollo in one of the cities on the Straits of Messina.
[29] Cf. ps.-Plut., *De mus.* 6, 1133bc, *Suda s.v. nomos*.
[30] Strabo, 13, 2, 4 = Terp. test. 48 Gostoli; *Marm. Par. FGrHist* 239 A 34 = Terp. test. 5 Gostoli.
[31] See in particular Heracl. Pont. fr. 157 Wehrli (cited by Ps.-Plut., *De mus.* 3, 1132c) = Terp. test. 27 and 28 Gostoli. Ps.-Plut., *De mus.* 5, 1132 de (= Terp. test. 32 Gostoli) adds that Terpander also composed citharodic poems in epic verses (*épē*).

Citharodic Nomos: Stesichorus 173

Homeric poems are historicized and given a title, and they are inserted into the history of the citharodic *nomos*.³²

Though the setting is poetic and the musical performance is situated in the age of heroes, one of the songs performed by Demodocos at the Phaecian court seems to give a specific form to what Heraclides Ponticus regards as the citharodic nomos. The tale of the amorous entanglement between Aphrodite, Ares and Hephaistos is embedded in the narrative of the *Odyssey* and is therefore told in Homeric diction, but it is introduced and doubtless also accompanied by a choral dance executed by Phaeacian youths. The youths pound the choral dance floor (*khorós*, l. 264), which is also an *agṓn* (l. 260), and they surround the bard, who has been led into the middle by the herald. The bard accompanies himself on the phorminx to sing a poem announced as dealing with the 'the loves of Ares and Aphrodite of the beautiful garland'; this extended narrative (100 lines) has a title and sections of dialogue just like the poems of Stesichorus.³³ This being the case, we might agree with Quintilian's famous testimonium according to which Stesichorus sang the deeds of the epic heroes to the accompaniment of the lyre (*maxima bella et clarissimos canentem duces at epici carminis onera lyra sustinentem*). Above all, we should take seriously the biographical report in the Byzantine *Suda* stating that Stesichorus owed his name to the fact that he was the first to 'establish a chorus' (*khoròn éstēsen*) for citharodic performances.³⁴

Does this mean that Stesichorus also performed alone to his own accompaniment on the lyre a song synchronized with the choreographic movements of a chorus? Was his citharodic performance at once 'monodic' and accompanied by choral dance? This seems to be what Heraclides Ponticus (cited in Ps.-Plutarchus' *De musica*) suggests when, after mentioning Demodocos and Phemios, he compares the *lexis* of their citharodic poems to the diction of Stesichorus and 'the ancient melic poets' (*tôn arkhaíōn melopoiôn*).

Yet modern readers of the recently published papyrus fragments of Stesichorus' poems have tended to favour choral performance.³⁵ This view

---

³² See once again Herac. Pont. fr. 157 Wehrli, cited by Ps.-Plut., *De mus.* 3, 1132c; cf. Power 2010: 231–4 and 240–3.

³³ Hom. *Od.* 8, 256–369; cf. Burkert 1987 and Nagy 2010: 79–102. For other legendary choral performances that may be considered citharodic *nomoi*, see Calame 2001: 80–2, with the bibliographical references on p. 50 n. 126.

³⁴ Quint. *Inst.* 10, 1, 62 (= Stes. test. 41 Campbell = Tb 42 Ercoles), with the detailed commentary by Power 2010: 234–6; cf. *Suda s.v. Stesíkhoros* (S 1095 Adler = Stes. test. 1 Campbell = Ta 10 Ercoles); bibliography in n. 42 in this chapter.

³⁵ The bibliography is substantial; suffice it here to mention Cingano 1993: 347 n. 3 for a review of the various hypotheses (purely monodic execution, monodic execution accompanied by a silent chorus,

is based on the triadic structure of the poems, though these are certainly citharodic *nomoi* (even though in our tradition the generic term was not applied to this poetry before Plato).[36] As we have seen, the tradition ascribes the invention of the triad (strophe/antistrophe/epode) to Stesichorus. This metrical arrangement is thought to have facilitated the mimetic singing of *nomoi* by choruses of citizens rather than professional singers (as is the case in a later period); moreover, it will have aided in the performance of other choral songs, such as dithyramb in its classical form.[37] Once again the citharodic *nomos* and the dithyramb are brought together.

The argument in favour of the choral performance of *nomoi* is further supported by the recurrence of terms related to *molpḗ/mélpein* in three Stesichorean fragments relating to the song of the Muses or Apollo. These include the invocation to the Muse in the prelude to one of the two 'palinodes' of *Helen*: 'Come once again, song-loving goddess (*theà philómolpe*)'. Moreover, one of the fragments of the *Oresteia* that is reconstructed on the basis of Aristophanes' parody could be argued to have been performed chorally on a 'Phrygian melody (*mélos*)' on account of its enunciative modality.[38]

The unusual length of Stesichorus' poems is often used as an argument against the choral execution of citharodic songs, but it is not in fact an obstacle. Pindar's *Fourth Pythian* stands as an example of an extended choral narrative poem. This epinician narrates a version of Cyrene's foundation myth and, through this, an episode of the saga of the Argonauts. Metrically, it is composed of melic triads with some dactylic elements and some epitrites (*kat'énoplion epítrita*) that are strongly evocative of Stesichorus' rhythmical diction. Such a rhythmical structure doubtless points to a choral execution, as do the poem's various instances of 'choral delegation'.[39] Nevertheless, a 'monodic' performance accompanied by a choral choreography should not be excluded.

---

choral performance) and Power 2010: 234–43 (with numerous additional references); see also Ercoles 2012: 7–13, who speaks of a 'partecipazione del coro al canto', and Ercoles 2013: 561–75, Davies and Finglass 2014: 23–32, and West 2015, who revisits his 1971 study and once again declares himself in favour of solo song accompanied by dancers. For choral performance and the *Geryoneis*, see Curtis 2011: 23–6.

[36] Pl. *Leg.* 700b.
[37] Cf. *Suda s.v. tria Stēsikhórou* (*T* 943 Adler) = Stes. test. 30 Cambpell (cf. n. 24 in this chapter), then Ps.-Arist., *Probl.* 19, 918b 13–29, in a passage that implies the 'new' dithyramb in which, from the perspective of imitation, the *mélē* take precedence over the sung words.
[38] Stes. fr. 193, 9–10, 232 and 250, then 212 Page-Davies = 90, 8–9, 271 and 278, then 172 Davies-Finglass; see the exhaustive discussion on this matter in Cingano 1993: 349–56 (in French, 2003: 26–33).
[39] See Gentili et al. 1995: 103–15 ('un vero e proprio canto citarodico'!) and Calame 2011a: 96–103. On the various arguments against or on the contrary for a choral performance of Stesichorus' poems, see now the fine discussion in Finglass 2017.

Citharodic Nomos: Stesichorus 175

7.2.5 Towards Attic Tragedy?

In this quest for emic representations of tragedy and related poetic forms it is once again to Aristophanes, Euripides' contemporary, that we must turn, and specifically to the extended exchange in tragic *mélē* that concludes the poetic confrontation between Aeschylus and Euripides arbitrated by Dionysos in *Frogs*. After parodying Aeschylus' choral poems, Euripides adds one last song made up of Aeschylean quotations. For this 'establishment of songs' (*stásis mélōn*, a technical term we have already encountered), the tragic poet labels as citharodic *nomoi* the extracts that he parodies; this melic song in the manner of a citharodic *nomos* turns out to include three verses from the parodos of *Agamemnon*.[40]

One need only remember that Stesichorus was regarded in antiquity as a *melopoiós* just like Aeschylus in Aristophanes. This is indeed the term used by Aristophanes' Euripides to designate his rival in the lines of *Frogs* examined in Chapter 1. This is how the tragic poet begins his critique against the choral songs (*mélē*) that the chorus, in contrast, considers as the most beautiful of all; in their 'establishment', they are ultimately designated as citharodic *nomoi*.[41] Moreover, as we have seen, the bibliographical notice mentioned above accounts for the name *Stesí-khoros* with the etymologizing explanation that 'Stesichorus' was the first to have 'established' (*éstēsen*) a chorus for citharodes. We might remember that in ancient criticism the songs of tragedy were termed *stásima*.[42] Beginning as it does with citharodic song, Attic tragedy is a choral institution.

On a different note, it certainly cannot be an accident that, in the *Poetics*, which at the outset excludes melic poetry from the mimetic arts, Aristotle twice mentions dithyramb and nomos in the same breath. In the first section of the *Poetics*, dithyramb and *nomos* are mentioned with tragedy and comedy as the poetic forms that combine rhythm, metre and song (*mélos*); when discussing the essential *mimesis* that is the representation of individuals in action (as noble or base characters), Aristotle mentions the authors of *nomoi* and dithyrambs alongside Homer and the comic poets.[43] This is telling of

---

[40] Ar. *Ran.* 1272–7 and 1281–1300 (cf. Chapter 1.2.2 and 1.2.3); cf. Aesch. *Ag.* 104, 109 and 111; see Gostoli 1993: 176–8 and the detailed commentary by Power 2010: 236 n. 119 on the scholion to l. 1282a and b (III.1b, 213 Chantry) that attributes to Aeschylus the *órthios nómos*.
[41] Schol. *ad* Pi. *Ol.* 12, *inscr.* A (I, 349 Drachmann) = Stes. test. 8 Campbell = Ta14(I) Ercoles; cf. Ar. *Ran.* 1249–63; see the testimonia on *citharoidia* gathered by Herington 1985: 177–80.
[42] *Suda s.v. Stesíkhoros* (S 1095 Adler) = Stes. test. 1 Campbell (cf. n. 34 in this chapter), with Nagy 1990: 357:64, in connection to *citharoidia*, and Ercoles 2012: 4–5; cf. Arist. *Poet.* 12, 1452b 17 and 23–4.
[43] Arist. *Poet.* 1, 1447a 24–7 (cf. 6, 1449b 29) and 2, 1448a 12–18. See Scullion 2005: 26–7 and especially Power 2013: 239–47 on the relation between dithyramb and *citharoidia*.

the affinities sensed by Aristotle between these two poetic forms and the dramatic narrative genres. After all, in the biographizing tradition on the poet inventors of tragedy, Arion of Methymna, the first poet to have sung a dithyramb, is also held up as the inventor of the 'tragic mode'. And with regard to *citharoidia*, Thespis, the first poet to have 'taught' a tragedy, is perhaps also the one who involved the chorus in dialogue.[44]

Be that as it may, for Aristotle the third component of the rhetoric is a speech action which he describes in terms of 'response' or delivery (*hupókrisis*). The example chosen immediately after the introduction to the third book of the *Rhetoric* is *rhapsoidia* along with tragic diction: the use of the voice, with its intonations and rhythms, to express emotion. For before they were replaced by actors who were masters of imitations, it was the tragic poets themselves who 'answered' (to the chorus).[45] By means of the musical and mimetic effects of the human voice, it is then, 'at the beginning', the poet who plays the role of the protagonist of the tragic action. From this point of view, the scholiast's misunderstanding is significant when he comments on an oft-cited passage of Aristophanes' *Wasps*. In contrast with the modern tragedians, Thespis is cited as an example of the tragic poet who takes part in the ancient dance competitions; though the scholiast here designates Thespis not as a tragic poet but as a citharode, there is no doubt that he attributes to him the function of actor and speaker in relation to the chorus.[46]

On account of their titles, their heroic subject matter, their narrative quality, their melic diction, their 'mixed' mimetic mode (in Plato's sense of the term) and their ritualized choral performance, Stesichorus' citharodic nomes certainly offer us a partial response to the question of the poetic 'origins' of Attic tragedy. It is also worth noting, from a musical (in the Greeks sense of the term) point of view, that when the protagonists of the dramatic action are not singing, they do not express themselves in dactylic hexameters, nor in a melic dactylic rhythm, but in iambic trimeters, and moreover behind the cover of a mask.

The tradition of melic poetry as we have it today does not allow us to speculate any further back; outside of the poetic form, every answer to the question of origins cannot be other than pure speculation in a religious or philosophical vein.

---

[44] Cf. *Suda* s.v. *Aríon* (*A* 3886 Aldler) and Chapter 2.4.1 with n. 84; see also *Marmor Parium FgrHist* 239 A 43 = Tespis test. 2 Snell and Chapter Chapter 2.4.2 with nn. 55 and 56.
[45] Arist. *Rhet.* 3, 1403b 20–34.
[46] Ar. *Vesp.* 1476–81 with the double scholion to l. 1479 (II.1, 229 Koster-Howerda) = Thespis test. 5 Snell.

7.3 Poet/Chorus/Audience: A Return to Choral Polyphony

But what can be said about the pragmatics of songs that are no longer performed by the poet who composed them? What can the referential and pragmatic impact be of a fictional and dramatized action that is carried by the play's characters, including the chorus?

According to Jean-Pierre Vernant, 'A consciousness of the fiction is essential to the dramatic spectacle; it seems to be both its condition and its product.' Tragedy opens up in Greek culture a new space, that of 'fiction, pretence, *imaginaire*'.[47] On this view Dionysos blurs the distinction between illusion and reality, and this is to the benefit of 'Greek man', who, in late-fifth-century Athens, is in some measure 'tragic man' (always in the masculine), who finally gains consciousness of the fictional by means of a *mimésis* understood as simulation. It is Florence Dupont who extended this line of thought to tragic fiction by inscribing it in a 'culture of immanent meaning', in contrast with contemporary cultures of transcendence;[48] on Electra's example, the equality of women has also been reasserted in Attic tragedy, dominated as it so often is by female figures. Should we then, after all, settle for Dupont's 'tragic insignificance', or even go further and subscribe to Jean-Marie Schaeffer's 'shared playful feinting'?

7.3.1 The Audience: From the Second Person to the First

Surely such a conception of fiction cannot account for the pragmatic dimension of this dramatic poetry that was sung in a public ritual performance. This pragmatic finds its expression in particular in the songs of the chorus through enunciative processes that allow the audience to play an active part in the action that is being dramatized before it, heroic and fictional though this is.

Of course, the chorus never addresses the audience directly. From the perspective of linguistic enunciation, the second person addressed in song by the first person corresponding to the chorus and its coryphaeus can be occupied by various entities. As the songs follow one after the other, the second person refers variously to the protagonists, to whom the chorus directs its hermeneutic voice underscored with emotion, to the gods, who are ritually invoked by a performative voice, or to man in general – but never is the audience gathered in the theatre apostrophized directly.

---

[47] Vernant and Vidal-Naquet 1986[1988]: 86 and 23[187 and 244], underlining what had been said earlier.
[48] Dupont 2001: 192–8, in the conclusion of her essay on 'Tragic Insignificance'; cf. Chapter 2.1.2.

Rather, the audience is addressed only indirectly through exhortations aimed generally at citizens or mortals to see what the chorus sees and feel what if feels. The audience features as a collective of ideal spectators; they are the virtual addressees to whom the fictional characters of heroines and heroes are presented as matter for reflection and action.

But this discretion in the chorus's direct communication in no way prevents the audience from having an actual reaction in the here-and-now of the dramatic representation. Taking part in the various cultic honours being paid to Dionysos, the empirical Athenian spectator seems above all to be invited to assume the position of the choral first person; we see a process of 'choral identification' in which the audience is called to address the actor or the gods while identifying with the thoughts and feelings of the chorus. Such choral identification is rendered all the more likely by the fact that the audience of classical Athens had a physical and musical education essentially founded on epic recitation and choral practice; this consisted of reciting at school the Homeric poems and singing collectively ritual poetic forms such as the pean or dithyramb in various cultic occasions.[49]

By means of the different enunciative postures assumed by the choral first person, the audience honouring Dionysos delegates in some sense part of its ritual competence and authority to the chorus acting within the dramatic representation. Thanks to the performative dimension of the chorus's songs, and in combination with its emotive component and its hermeneutic reach, the audience is also doubtless invited to *sunagonízesthai*, to take part in the dramatic action; the terms of this participation are ritual, affective and intellectual. Absent as it is on the enunciative level as a second-person addressee and interlocutor, the real-life audience is called to place itself in the position of the choral first person that is that of the speaker and performer.

Indeed, in its performative enunciations the polyphonic voice of the tragic chorus lends a reality of sorts to the dramatic fiction. As ritual performances, the chorus's tragic songs inscribe the *mûthos* acted out in the theatre of Dionysos within the sphere of ritual as we have described it, with its pragmatic function, its ethical, social and religious import. The performative voice assures in a way the relation between the chorus's interventions in the dramatic action and the theatrical ritual offered to the gods in the public staging of the musical competition. This mediating function is reinforced by the affective voice and by the hermeneutic voice

---

[49] See the fundamental discussion in Marrou 1964: 69–81. In relation to tragedy, see Bacon 1994/1995, based on the notion of 'enactment'; see also, along the same lines, Nagy 1994/1995.

of a chorus that reacts emotively and that comments on the heroic dramatic action in a perspective that can be assumed by the audience. To this extent, the singing first person that intervenes functionally in the tragic action, with its ritual and collective component, embraces the audience also; this enables the inclusion into the text of the representations of the broader civic community gathered in the theatre-sanctuary to honour Dionysos.

Athenian tragic performance entails that the poet delegate in a sense to the chorus the ritual and musical role of the audience. Through the mediations of the masked play-acting, this overlap between the musical skill of the chorus (of citizens) and that of the audience doubtless involves a partial identification of the spectators with the sung reactions of the chorus and even with the reactions of some of the characters on the stage. Hence the many interferences that have been observed between the rituals within tragedy and tragedy as ritual performance.[50]

7.3.2 The Tragic Poet as Author

But does not the choral first person of tragedy essentially bring us back to the ideal author, the omniscient dramatic narrator? Is he not the mind behind the hermeneutic voice that describes and comments on the stage action and explains its invisible aspects? Leaving aside this discursive figure, does not the choral first person simply conceal the historical author whose name cannot appear in the dramatic text in the indirect form, of a 'signature' as was the case in preclassical poetry?

In discussing above the famous lines of Aristophanes concerning the fundamentally educational function assigned to tragedy in his time, we have mentioned the testimonia that attribute the function of (khoro) didáskalos[51] to the more ancient tragic poets, such as Phrynichus or Aeschylus. The production of a tragic performance seems, then, to centre on the training of the chorus of young citizens. Contemporary sources speak of the performance of tragedy as didáskein, that is to say, as a form of education. If the historical author is indeed addressing an audience, he is doing so – as Herodotus says in connection with Phrynichus – through poieîn (poetic creation) and didáskein (the training of the chorus).[52] But from the point of view of linguistic enunciation, it is perhaps to a certain extent inconsistent to state that both the poet and his audience can assume, through the figures of the virtual author and the virtual spectator, the enunciative and discursive position of the choral first person.

[50] Cf. Chapter 2.4.   [51] Cf. Chapter 2.2.2.   [52] Cf. n. 25 in Chapter 1.

At this point we must remember that in choral melic poetry the position of the speaker and narrator who speaks in the first person can be assumed both by the chorus that is actually singing the poem and by its 'author' and composer. We see here, then, a movement of 'choral delegation' expressing itself in the enunciative polyphony that we have outlined; the poet delegates his voice to that of chorus in the performance. This points in the final resort to a real poet who is exercising with respect to the chorus the same function of musical teacher (*khorodidáskalos*) as is the case for the poet of tragedy. The poet's authority, then, is poetic, choral and didactic. Thus the first person of the choral songs of classical tragedy, in its addresses to the protagonists, whether gods or mortals like the spectators themselves, adopts in the performance of the choral song in the here-and-now both the voice of the actual audience (with its musical competence and its ritual role) and that of the historical poet (with his educational 'author function'). Just as in melic poetry, the use of sung poetic diction, the recourse to a traditional poetic language and the appeal to a set of shared values allow a particular female chorus to express itself through a song composed by a male poet. It is thus that in the choral songs of tragedy, regardless of social and gender disparities, regardless of the dual identity of the choreuts as protagonists of the dramatic action as well as citizens taking part in the chorus, the audience can claim for itself not only the chorus's second person but also, and above all, its first person.[53]

The virtual spectator that is constructed within the text can blend, through the intermediary of the choral performer, with the figure of the ideal author. This overlap no doubt facilitates the adoption of the position of choral speaker by the historical audience. In particular, the enunciative polyphony of the choral voice, allied with the semantic polyphony of the three voices which we have described, explains how the chorus and the audience can react to dramatized heroic events that are removed from them in space and time. The masked production and, more generally, the cultic context in honour of Dionysos have the effect of reflecting back to the audience in its capacity as second-person spectator the drama in which it is invited to take part in its capacity as first-person choral actor, regardless of any social and gender distinctions.

From an emotive perspective this distancing procedure, especially owing to the fact that honour is being paid to Dionysos, can account for the much-debated phenomenon of *kátharsis*. We will not here revisit this

---

[53] For this reason the triangular relationship between author, narrator and character delineated by Genette (2004: 154–63) in relation to autobiography, historical narrative and fiction (homodiegetic and heterodiegetic) needs to be developed to account for the audience.

discussion except to remind ourselves of the affective component of the choral voice. No doubt the emotions expressed ritually in and by the rhythmical musical performance are shared by the chorus and the audience, which receives them and inhabits them by means of its own choral education, both individually and collectively.[54]

'Tragic fiction' is referential fiction: narrative action that corresponds to what we identify as 'myth', dramatized action that unfolds in heroic times, when heroes were still close to the gods. Beyond the words used by its protagonists and beyond the values they invoke to justify it, the heroic action dramatized in the theatre of Dionysos Eleuthereus refers, through the public musical performance, to the deities worshipped by the audience as well as to the ritual practices in which they engage in their honour. Moreover, by its choral ritualized form, Attic tragedy is more than the simple (critical) education of the Athenians citizens and inhabitants of the city; it is also, in its musical performance, a collective ritual action, if not a religious action, that through aesthetic experience animates a poetic culture of song and rhythm. Attic tragedy as 'shared ludic simulation'? Certainly, but always holding in mind the inescapable question of reference, 'if only because it is the basis of the ontological plurality that is the hallmark of fiction'.[55] The po(i)etic fiction that is Attic tragedy finds its reference as much in its anthropology (as a conception of human action) as in its emotional and aesthetic accomplishment as a ritualized action.

7.4 To Conclude: Musical 'Performances' and Oratorios

In the combination of enunciative polyphony and semantic polyphony that we have outlined when characterizing its voice, the tragic chorus partakes on the one hand of the generally marginal social identity of a 'character' involved in the dramatic action and on the other hand of the musical identity implied by its participation in the choral group. Whatever the dramatic character that they embody, as citizens the choreuts take part in the poetic and ritual performance that is (particularly) the

---

[54] The famous statement on *kátharsis* is in Arist. *Poet.* 5, 1449b 24–36; cf. also, more explicitly, *Pol.* 8, 7, 1341b 19–1342a 28 (in connection with the pragmatics of the musical arts) and n. 7 in Chapter 1 (on Hegel); see Calame 2009b: 33–8, with a rich bibliography, to which add Loraux 1999: 123–37 (whose conclusions are questionable).

[55] According to Lavocat 2016: 203–17 (quotation on 525), who is operating in a comparative perspective. In Calame 2009b, I developed the idea of 'referential fiction' on the example of Euripides' tragedy on Erechtheus, a founding king of Athens who received hero worship on the Acropolis next to Poseidon, patron god of the city; in addition to the studies on fiction there cited, see the terms of the debate between Heinich and Schaeffer 2004: 153–61, 171–85 and 190–6.

mousikòs agón offered to Dionysos Eleuthereus and celebrated at the Great Dionysia in his sanctuary-theatre. And by their songs, in dialogue with the protagonists of the heroic action, they invite the audience to do the same. Just like, for instance, the *Homeric Hymns* the tragedies are narrative and musical offerings to a god.

If we will willingly admit, with Charles Segal (specifically with reference to *Oedipus Tyrannus*), that the tragic chorus's songs are hypotheses aimed at illuminating the meaning of the dramatic action in which they participate, we must add that these hypotheses, which are carried by the chorus's hermeneutic voice and based on its affective reactions, correspond in general to ritual speech acts.[56] With its ambiguity modelled on the melic first person and reinforced by the occasional distinction between coryphaeus and choreuts, the position of the speaker of the choral songs of tragedy lends itself equally to being occupied by the master of the chorus in the figure of the poet as by the spectators who are participating in a ritual action in the theatre of Dionysos. Through the combination of semantic and enunciative polyphony that we have attempted to illustrate, both of these entities are called to cooperate in the collective mimetic and masked voice of the choral first person.

The chorus offers a ritualized and performative interpretation of the heroic action that is dramatized on the stage. Carried by the voices that are characterized in the drama as female or male, but which are – ritually speaking – always those of male citizens, this is a collective interpretation that has real-world social consequences. Thanks to the performative voice of the chorus in its capacity as virtual performer, and thanks to this performative dimension that orients the hermeneutic and affective dimension, the real-life audience is called not to rest in the attitude of a simple ideal spectator, as in the standard communicative schema, but rather to play an active part next to the virtual author.

By means of the ritual choral performance and the enunciative positions that it constructs, the tragic poet exercises the 'author function' attributed by Aristophanes to Aeschylus, Sophocles and Euripides. In the discursive and pragmatic field of tragedy, through the staging of heroic actions in *Persians*, *Oedipus Tyrannus* and *Hippolytus*, the poet can doubtless be considered as educator of the Athenian civic community. Nevertheless, not only is his voice collective and ritualized on account of

---

[56] Segal 1995: 196–8. Cf. the nuanced remarks in Kranz 1933: 220–3, which conclude thus: 'Also is (der Chor) alles andere als ein "Charakter"'. See also Kaimio 1970: 92–103, who develops Kranz's hypothesis according to which the voice of the poet transpires especially in the final strophe of stasima, in the judgements expressed in the first-person singular.

the chorus's mediation, but it is also poetical and critical vis-à-vis the heroic action whose controversial issues it brings into relief in the dramatization itself. Moreover, in contrast with the passive attention required by modern audiences, the Athenian audience too is involved in the musical and ritual performance, chiefly in the theatre-sanctuary of Dionysos Eleuthereus.

It is essentially in and through choral poetic performance, by means of collective and musical speech to the rhythm of choreographic movements, that Attic tragedy exercises its 'anthropopoetic' function of social and cultural construction of the human sphere. In these forms of creative cultural memory in action, the staged fiction cannot but be referential; between the performative voice of participation in the heroic dramatic action and the voice of the emotional and hermeneutic responses to this, the songs of the chorus play a large part in this referentiality. Whether we understand tragic *mimesis* in the Platonic or in the Aristotelian sense, it is always representation, it is always poietic. The ethnopoetic perspective enables us to return to tragic representation the aspect of 'performative' musicality and rituality.

Attic tragedy is undoubtedly fiction, as we have seen, but it is fiction in the literal sense of the term, which achieves its goal not by simple inference, but as a result of a collectively assumed poeticity in action. And this is all the more true for the fact that the ritualized and critical dramatization of an episode of a local or panhellenic heroic saga culminates less often with the lament of a 'bereaved voice' (as at the end of *Persians*, an atypical play) than with the institution of a cult through ritual song, as is the case, for instance, in the ending of the *Oresteia* (a trilogy, no less). Just as in the various forms of melic poetry, the dramatized narrative of tragedy implies a return, sometimes in an aetiological fashion and in general without recourse to Dionysos, to the here-and-now of the ritualized poetic performance and its context, which is at once civic, social and religious.[57] It is in particular the chorus that contributes to reconducing the heroic action to the here-and-now of the poet and audience.

Before ending our study of Greek tragedy, let us evoke once again Plato, and more specifically the character of the Athenian Stranger in the *Laws*. On the subject of dance and *khoreía* as education for beautiful bodies and noble souls, the question is once again posed about what role to attribute to the poets in the ideal city. The answer that must be given to these creators who are from the outset defined as poets of tragedy leaves no room for doubt.

---

[57] Dionysos should therefore not be considered as the 'god of tragic fiction': cf. Chapter 2.4.4 with n. 76; see Parker 2005: 138–47; on the aetiological vein of various poetic forms, see Calame 2006b.

What would be the right answer to make to these inspired persons regarding the matter? In my judgment, this should be the answer, – 'Most excellent of Strangers, we ourselves, to the best of our ability, are the authors of a tragedy at once superlatively fair and good; at least, all our polity is framed as a representation of the fairest and best life, which is in reality, as we assert, the truest tragedy. Thus we are composers of the same things as yourselves, rivals of yours as artists and actors of the fairest drama, which, as our hope is, true law, and it alone, is by nature competent to complete ... So now, ye children and offspring of Muses mild, do ye first display your chants side by side with ours before the rulers; and if your utterances seem to be the same as ours or better, then we will grant you a chorus (*dósomen khorón*), but if not, my friends, we can never do so.'[58] (817a–d) (*Loeb*)

We must conclude to that the same goes for the legal prescriptions concerning the choral art as a whole as well as its teaching. In the fourth century, Attic tragedy is still conceived in terms of choral poetry, but in the ideal city of the philosopher the place of theatre is taken up by the agora, and the best tragedy is the enacted constitution. Tragedy's political dimension has come to the fore.

Does this mean that Attic tragedy can be regarded as a sort of oratorio?[59] This suggestion invites us to revisit in conclusion the issue of the religious and political efficacy of a sung and ritualized collective utterance in musical performance by making a comparative pairing that offers a very different perspective from the comparison that opened this volume.

Having started this discussion with Balinese musical culture we will now conclude by following Nietzsche's invitation to look at modern German music. But we will not here evoke the metaphysical meaning that he attributes to contemporary music in *The Birth of Tragedy*. In the wake of Arthur Schopenhauer and Richard Wagner, Nietzsche says that music represents 'the metaphysical in relation to all that is physical in the world'. So music should be regarded as 'the thing-in-itself to every phenomenon', and to this extent Greek tragedy is held to correspond to the Dionysian art *par excellence*: '[tragedy] sits in the midst of this superabundance of life, suffering, and delight, in sublime ecstasy'. Thus *Tristan and Isolde* is held to illustrate, in the continuous musical phrasing of the third act, the Apolline force at work in the individual consciousness of desire in the face of death. But the point it is to shake us out of the Apolline illusion

---

[58] Pl. *Leg.* 817a–d (translation by Bury 1926), with Matthey 2014: 184–7; see also Peponi 2013: 17–24. For the technical sense of the phrase *khoròn didónai*, cf. Chapter 2.3.1.
[59] The suggestion is advanced in Loraux 1999: 9–27, without explanation of what precisely is meant by an 'oratorio'; see also Alaux 2007: 116–119.

into the aesthetic *jouissance* of the reality of Dionysiac music; this is 'the pure and unalloyed effect of a true musical tragedy'.[60]

In a perspective that is not that of inspired philosophy but that of ethnopoetics and historical anthropology, instead of the grand Wagnerian operas it is probably Johann Sebastian Bacg's Oratorios that provide the more fitting term of comparison to illustrate, in a densely musical performance, certain key issues of Greek choral tragedy: the Christmas Oratorio (BWV 248), the Easter Oratorio (BWV 249), the Ascension Oratorio (BWV 11). These three oratorios stage the cardinal episodes of the heroic founding myth of Christianity: the birth of Jesus of Nazareth, his death on the cross and resurrection, and his ascension.

Let us hear briefly at the Easter Oratorio. A highly elaborate orchestra partitura takes the place of subtle choreography and ritual gestuality, and the comparative approach must once again remain on a surface level. In the orsatorio Bach composed for Easter events are staged through the voices of some of their participants: Mary Jacobe, Mary Magdalene, Simon Peter and John the Apostle. These characters' parts are, respectively, soprano, alto (sung by a counter-tenor), tenor and bass. They are the emotional narrators of a story that, beginning with a sacrificial death and culminating in resurrection, is an evident *metábasis*, a clear reversal. The dramatization is polyphonic and it is entirely musical, with only brief spells of recitativo; the sung parts, often overlapping, alternate between narration of past events and description of present action, with an emotive commentary that moves from lamentation to joy.

The (mixed) chorus is tasked with introducing the oratorio with a sonorous appeal to protagonists and audience to come to Christ's tomb; the chorus announces Christ's resurrection. It is the chorus once more that concludes the sung dramatization of the Passion with a chorale to the ringing of wind instruments. This is a grateful song of praise, a musical offering to the Lord who has defeated the powers of death and evil for the sake of man; with respect to the audience gathered in a temple, its pragmatics is reminiscent of the sung endings of Attic tragedy. The hymn concludes thus:

> Jauchzet, ihr erlösten Zungen,
> Dass man es im Himmel hört.
> Eröffnet, ihr Himmel, die prächtigen Bogen,
> Der Löwe von Juda kommt siegend gezogen!

[60] Nietzsche 1872/1980 [trans. Speirs, 1999]: 80–7 and 107–11[77, 98 and 104]. See the pointed remarks in Goldhill 2012: 182–7.

> Shout and cheer, you loosened tongues,
> so that you are heard in heaven
> Open up, you heavens, your splendid arches,
> the lion of Judah comes victorious.

Is there any better way of singing and celebrating collectively and ritually, in a manner that includes the audience, the heroization and apotheosis of a founding hero? And above all, is it possible to appreciate any better the part played by music in performance and by poetic creativity in lending efficacy to a 'myth', which is ultimately a narrative fiction, a myth, finally, that is much less elaborate than the heroic sagas recreated and musically dramatized by the Greek tragic poets? The efficacy of these sacred words derives from the fact they are sung, and that they are sung chorally.

After all, the poet Aeschylus is 'chorus master' (*didáskalos*) at Athens, just like the composer Bach is 'chapel master' (*Kapellmeister*) at Köthen, then *Kantor* at the Thomasschule in Leipzig. We might add that our three Oratorios, just like the Cantatas and Passions, are generally sung in a holy place, especially among Protestants; they are total musical performances, with a strong pragmatic dimension both in a religious and in a political sense, and they are performed during the celebration of the three Christian Feasts that still dominate the calendar. This is the religious calendar that, year in, year out, still governs the life of women and men, despite the market and managerial culture emanating from North America the United States that would impose its notions of productivity and consumerism seven days a week, almost twenty-four hours a day, yearlong.

Beyond the obvious differences, beyond all tragic essence, does not the emotional and pragmatic force of Greek tragedy in its sung performance reside ultimately in musical poetics that aims at ritual efficacy? Whichever the religion, whichever the political and cultural community, the essential element is the rhythm of the poetic and musical song to which the narrative is dramatized, as well as its aesthetical, affective and symbolic pragmatics as it is borne out in the ritualized musical performance. In this way the sung performance inscribes the great actions of the civic community's heroic past into a cultural memory, a cultural memory that is active and dynamic, a cultural memory constantly being reoriented by the critical work of the great poets.

Bibliography

Ahl, F., *Sophocles' Oedipus: Evidence and Self-Conviction*, Ithaca, NY and London (Cornell University Press) 1991
Alaux, J., *Origine et horizon tragiques*, Saint-Denis (Presses universitaires de Vincennes) 2007
Alexiou, M., *The Ritual Lament in Greek Tradition*, 2nd ed., Lanham, MD (Rowman & Littlefield) 2002
Aluja, R., 'Reexamining the Lille Stesichorus: About the Theban Version of Stesich. PMGF 222b', in M. Reig and X. Riu (eds.), *Drama, Philosophy, Politics in Ancient Greece: Contexts and Receptions*, Barcelona (University of Barcelona Press) 2014: 15–37
Andújar, R., Coward, T. R. P. and Hadjimichael, T. A. (eds.), *Paths of Songs: The Lyric Dimension of Greek Tragedy*, Berlin and Boston, MA (de Gruyter) 2018
Austin, J. L., *How to Do Things with Words*, 2nd ed., Cambridge, MA (Harvard University Press) 1975
Azoulay, V. and Ismard, P., *Athènes 403. Une histoire chorale*, Paris (Flammarion) 2020
Bacon, H. H., *Barbarians in Greek Tragedy*, New Haven, CT (Yale University Press) 1961
'The Chorus in Greek Life and Drama', *Arion III* 3, 1994/1995: 6–24
Barrett, W. S., *Euripides: Hippolytos*, Oxford (Clarendon Press) 1964
Battezzato, L., 'Lyric', in J. Gregory (ed.), *A Companion to Greek Tragedy*, Oxford (Blackwell) 2005: 149–66
Bell, C., *Ritual: Perspectives and Dimensions*, New York and Oxford (Oxford University Press) 1997
Bellia, A., *Il canto delle vergini locresi. La musica a Locri Epizefirii nelle fonti scritte e nella documentazione archeologica (sec. VI-III a. C.)*, Rome (Fabrizio Serra) 2012
Belloni, L., *Eschilo. I*, Milan (Vita e Pensiero) 1988
Benveniste, E., 'La philosophie analytique et le langage', *Études philosophiques* 1, 1963: 3–12 (reprinted in 1966: 267–76)
Problèmes de linguistique générale, Paris (Gallimard) 1966
Problèmes de linguistique générale II, Paris (Gallimard) 1974
Bettini, M. and Guidorizzi, G., *Il mito di Edipo. Immagini e racconti dalla Grecia ad oggi*, Turin (Einaudi) 2004

Bibliography

Bierl, A. F., *Dionysos und die griechische Tragödie. Poetische und "metatheatralische" Aspekte im Text*, Tübingen (Gunter Narr) 1991

Der Chor in der alten Komödie. Ritual und Performativität, Munich and Leipzig (K. G. Saur) 2001 (trad. angl. revue par A. Hollmann, *Ritual and Performativity: The Chorus of Old Comedy*, Cambridge, MA and London (Harvard University Press) 2009)

'Literatur als Rito- und Mythopoetik. Überblicksartikel zu einem neuen Ansatz in der klassischen Philologie', in A. Bierl, R. Lämmle and K. Wesselmann (eds.), *Literatur und Religion I. Wege zu einer mythish-rituellen Poetik*, Berlin and New York (de Gruyter) 2007: 1–76

'Choral Dance at Play: *Paizein* in Greek Drama, or Body Movement as Sexual Attraction Between Gender and Genre', in V. Dasen and M. Vespa (Eds.), *Play and Games in Classical Antiquity: Definition, Transmission, Reception*, Liège (Presses Universitaires de Liège) 2021: 29–47

Bollack, J., *L'Œdipe roi de Sophocle. Le texte et ses interprétations*, 4 vols., Lille (Presses universitaires de Lille) 1990

Dionysos et la tragédie. Commentaire des Bacchantes d'Euripide, Paris (Bayard) 2005

Borutti, S., 'Wittgenstein et l'anthropologie', in D. Cerqui and I. Maffi (eds.), *Mélanges en l'honneur de Mondher Kilani*, Lausanne (A contrario) 2015: 9–21

Bouvier, D., 'Quand le poète était encore un charpentier ... Aux origines du concept de poésie', in U. Heidmann (ed.), *Poétiques comparées des mythes*, Lausanne (Payot) 2003: 85–105

'"Rendre l'homme meilleur!" ou quand la comédie interroge la tragédie sur sa finalité: à propos des *Grenouilles* d'Aristophane', in C. Calame (ed.), *Poétique d'Aristophane et langue d'Euripide en dialogue*, Lausanne (Études de Lettres) 2004: 9–26

Bowie, E., 'Stesichorus at Athens', in P. J. Finlass and A. Kelly (eds.), *Stesichorus in Context*, Cambridge (Cambridge University Press) 2015: 11–124

Bremer, J. M., 'Stesichorus: The Lille Papyrus', in J. M. Bremer, A. Maria van Erp Taalman Kip and S. R. Slings (eds.), *Some Recently Found Greek Poems*, Leiden, New York, Copenhagen and Cologne (E. J. Brill) 1987: 128–74

Bremmer, J. N., 'Body Politics: Imagining Human Sacrifice in Euripides' *Iphigeneia in Aulis*', in W. Staniewski and K. Bielawski (eds.), *Mantic Perspectives: Oracles, Prophecy and Performance*, Gardzienice, Lublin and Warsaw (Wydzial 'Artes Liberles' Uniwersytetu Warszawskiego) 2015: 35–56

Briand, M., Antiquity. *500 BCE - 350 BCE*, in A. Arcangeli & M. Kant, (eds), *A Cultural History of Dance*, vol. I, London (Bloomsbury) forthcoming.

Broadhead, H. D., *The Persae of Aeschylus*, Cambridge (Cambridge University Press) 1960

Bruit, L., 'Mythe et symbole religieux dans l'*Hippolyte* d'Euripide. Hippolyte entre Artémis et Aphordite', in S. des Bouvrie (ed.), *Myth and Symbol II: Symbolic Phenomena in Ancient Greek Culture*, Bergen (Papers of the Norwegian Institute at Athens) 2004: 333–51

Brunel, P., *Mythopoétique des genres*, Paris (Presses Universitaires de France) 2003

Budelmann, F., 'Greek Festival Choruses In and Out of Context', in J. Billings, F. Budelmann and F. MacIntosh (eds.), *Choruses, Ancient and Modern*, Oxford (Oxford University Press) 2013: 81–98

Budelmann F. and Phillips, T., 'Introduction: Performance and the Lyric in Early Greece', in F. Budelmann and T. Phillips (eds.), *Textual Events: Performance and the Lyric in Early Greece*, Oxford (Oxford University Press) 2018: 1–27

Buè, F., 'La vittoria di Apollo sulle Erinni nel contrasto musicale dell'*Orestea*', *Quaderni Urbinati di Cultura Classica* 135, 2014: 91–103

Bühler, K., *Sprachtheorie. Die Darstellungsfunktion der Sprache*, Jena (G. Fischer) 1934 (trans. from French: *Théorie du langage. La fonction représentationnelle du langage*, Paris (Agone) 2009)

Burkert, W., 'Greek Tragedy and Sacrifical Ritual', *Greek, Roman, and Byzantine Studies* 7, 1966a: 87–121 (trans. from German: 'Griechische Tragödie und Opferritual', in *Wilder Ursprung. Opferritual und Mythos bei den Griechen*, Berlin (Wagenbach) 1990: 13–39; reprinted in *Kleine Schriften VII, Tragica und Historica*, ed. W. Rösler, Göttingen (Vandenhoeck & Ruprecht) 2007: 1–36)

Burkert, W., *Greek Tragedy and Sacrificial Ritual*, Durham, NC (Duke University Press) 1966b

'The Making of Homer in the Sixth Century BC: Rhapsodes versus Stesichorus', in M. True (et al.) (eds.), *Papers on the Amasis Painter and his World*, Malibu, CA (The J. Paul Getty Museum) 1987: 43–62 (reprinted in *Kleine Schriften I, Homerica*, ed. Christoph Riedweg, Göttingen (Vandenhoeck & Ruprecht) 2002: 198–217)

Burnett, A. P., 'Jocasta in the West', *Classical Antiquity* 7, 1998: 107–54

Burton, R. W. B., *The Chorus in Sophocles' Tragedies*, Oxford (Clarendon Press) 1980

Calame, C., '"Mythe" et "rite" en Grèce: des catégories indigènes?', *Kernos* 5, 1991: 179–204 (reprinted in *Sentiers transversaux. Entre poétiques grecques et politiques contemporaines*, Grenoble (Jérôme Million) 2008: 43–62)

'La festa', in M. Vegetti (ed.), *Introduzione alle culture antiche III*, Turin (Bollati Boringhieri) 1992: 29–54

'Vision, Blindness and Mask: The Radicalization of the Emotions in Sophocles' *Oedipus Rex*', in M. S. Silk (ed.), *Tragedy and the Tragic: Greek Theatre and Beyond*, Oxford (Clarendon Press) 1996: 17–37

'De la poésie chorale au stasimon tragique. Pragmatique de voix féminines', *Mètis* 12, 1997: 181–203 (developed from 'From Choral Poetry to Tragic Stasimon: The Enactment of Women's Song', *Arion* 3(3), 1994/1995: 135–54)

'*Mûthos, lógos* et histoire. Usages du passé héroïque dans la rhétorique grecque', *L'Homme* 147, 1998: 127–49

'Performative Aspects of the Choral Voice in Greek Tragedy: Civic Identity in Performance', in S. Goldhill and R. Osborne (eds.), *Performance Culture and Athenian Democracy*, Cambridge (Cambridge University Press) 1999a: 125–53

'Tradition et mémorial. L'origine des guerres médiques entre tragédie et historiographie', in V. Mauron and C. de Ribaupierre (eds.), *Le corps évanoui. Les images subites*, Paris and Lausanne (Hazan) 1999b: 165–76

'La tragédie attique: le masque pour mettre en scène le récit héroïque', in *Le récit en Grèce ancienne. Énonciations et représentations de poètes*, 2nd ed., Paris (Belin) 2000: 139–63
Choruses of Young Women in Ancient Greece: Their Morphology, Religious Role, and Social Function, Lanham, MD, Boulder, CO, New York and Oxford (Rowman & Littlefield) 2001 (1st ed. 1997)
'Interprétation et traduction des cultures. Les catégories de la pensée et du discours anthropologique', *L'Homme* 163, 2002a: 51–78
'Offrandes à Artémis Braurônia sur l'Acropole: rites de puberté?', in B. Gentili and F. Perusino (eds.), *Le orse di Brauron. Un rituale di iniziazione femminile nel santuario di Artemide*, Pisa (Edizioni ETS) 2002b: 44–64
'Deictic Ambiguity and Auto-Referentiality: Some Examples from Greek Poetics', *Arethusa* 37, 2004a: 415–43 (in French as 'Pragmatique de la fiction: quelques procédures de deixis narrative et énonciative en comparaison (poétique grecque)', in J.-M. Adam and U. Heidmann (eds.), *Sciences du texte et analyse de discours. Enjeux d'une interdisciplinarité*, Geneva and Lausanne (Slatkine – Études de Lettres) 2005: 119–43)
'Identités d'auteur à l'exemple de la Grèce classique : signatures, énonciations, citations', in C. Calame and R. Chartier (eds.), *Identités d'auteur dans l'Antiquité et la tradition européenne*, Grenoble (Jérôme Millon) 2004b: 11–39
Masques d'autorité. Fiction et pragmatique dans la poétique grecque antique, Paris (Les Belles Lettres) 2005a
'The Tragic Choral Group: Dramatic Roles and Social Functions', in R. Buschnell (ed.), *A Companion to Tragedy*, Malden, MA and Oxford (Blackwell) 2005b: 215–33
'Identifications génériques entre marques discursives et pratiques énonciatives: pragmatique des genres "lyriques"', in R. Baroni and M. Macé (eds.), *Le savoir des genres*, Rennes (La Licorne) 2006a: 35–55
'Jeux de genre et performance musicale dans le chœur de la tragédie classique: espace dramatique, espace culturel, espace civique', in O. Mortier-Waldschmidt (ed.), *Musique et Antiquité. Actes du colloque d'Amiens*, Paris (Les Belles Lettres) 2006b: 63–90
'Récit héroïque et pratique religieuse: le passé poétique des cités grecques classiques', *Annales. Histoire, Sciences Sociales* 61, 2006c: 527–51
'Giochi di genere e *performance* musicale nel coro della tragedia classica: spazio drammatico, spazio cultuale, spazio civico', in F. Perusino and M. Colantonio (eds.), *Dalla lirica corale all poesia drammatica. Forme e funzioni del canto corale nella tragédia e nella commedia greca*, Pisa (Edizioni ETS) 2007: 49–73
'Entre récit héroïque et poésie rituelle: le sujet poétique qui chante le mythe', in S. Parizet (ed.), *Mythe et littérature (Poétiques comparatistes)*, Paris (SFLGC) 2008: 123–41
L'Éros dans la Grèce antique, 3rd ed., Paris (Belin) 2009a
'Émotions et performance poétique: la "katharsis" érotique dans la poésie mélique des cités grecques', in P. Borgeaud and A.-C. Rendu Loisel

(eds.), *Violentes émotions. Approches comparatistes*, Geneva (Droz) 2009b: 29–56
'Fra racconto eroico e poesia rituale: il soggetto poetico che canta il mito (Pindaro, *Olimpica* 6)', *Quaderni Urbinati di Cultura Classica* 121, 2009c: 11–26
'Apollo in Delphi and Delos: Poetic Performance between Paean and Dithyramb', in L. Athanassaki, R. P. Martin and J. F. Miller (eds.), *Apolline Politics and Poetics*, Athens (European Cultural Centre of Delphi) 2009d: 169–97
'Fiction énonciative et performance poétique. Voix chorales dans les *Épinicies* de Bacchylide', *Mètis N. S.* 8, 2010a: 117–42
'La pragmatique poétique des mythes grecs: fiction référentielle et performance rituelle', in F. Lavocat and A. Duprat (eds.), *Fiction et cultures*, Paris (SFLGC) 2010b: 33–56
Mythe et histoire dans l'Antiquité grecque. La création symbolique d'une colonie, 2nd ed., Paris (Les Belles Lettres) 2011a
'The *Homeric Hymns* as Poetic Offerings: Musical and Ritual Relationships with the Gods', in A. Faulkner (ed.), *The Homeric Hymns: Interpretative Essays*, Oxford (Oxford University Press) 2011b: 334–57
'Choral Polyphony and the Ritual Function of Tragic Songs', in R. Gagné and M. G. Hopman (eds.), *Choral Mediations in Greek Tragedy*, Cambridge (Cambridge University Press) 2013a: 35–57
'Soi-Même par les autres: pour une poétique des identités auctoriales, rythmées et genrées (Pindare, *Parthénée* 2)', in S. Boehringer and V. Sebillotte-Cuchet (eds.), *Des femmes en action. L'individu et la fonction en Grèce antique* (*Mètis*, Hors Série 1), Paris and Athens (Éditions de l'EHESS – Daedalus) 2013b: 21–38
'The Dithyramb, a Dionysiac Form? Genre Rules and Cultic Contexts', in B. Kowalzig and P. Wilson (eds.), *Dithyramb in Context*, Oxford (Oxford University Press) 2013c: 332–52
'From Cultural Memory to Poetic Memory: Ancient Greek Practices of History Beyond the "Great Divide"', *Fudan Journal of the Humanities and the Social Sciences* 7(4), 2014a: 639–52
'La tragédie et le nome citharodique; de la Grande Grèce à Athènes', in A. Bellia (ed.), *Musica, culti e riti nell'Occidente greco*, Pisa and Rome (Istituti Editoriali e Poligrafici Internazionali) 2014b: 49–66
'La tragédie grecque et le tragique: genre, génericité, pragmatique discursive', in M. Monte and G. Philippe (eds.), *Genres & textes. Déterminations, évolutions, confrontations*, Lyon (Presses universitaires de Lyon) 2014c: 135–49
Qu'est-ce que la mythologie grecque? Paris (Gallimard) 2015
'The Chorus in Euripides', in A. Markantonatos (ed.), *Brill's Companion to Euripides, Vol. II*, Leiden (E. J. Brill) 2020: 775–96
Calame, C., Dupont, F., Lortat-Jacob, B. and Manca, M. (eds.), *La Voix actée. Pour une nouvelle ethnopoétique*, Paris (Kimé) 2010
Capponi, M., *Parole et geste dans la tragédie grecque. À la lumière des trois 'Électre'*, Neuchâtel (Éditons Alphil – Presses universitaires suisses) 2021

Cerbo, E., 'Gli inni ad Eros in tragedia: struttura e funzione', in R. Pretagostini (ed.), *Tradizione e innovazione nella cultura greca da Omero all'età ellenistica. Scritti in onore di Bruno Gentili* II, Rome (GEI) 1993: 645–56

Cerri, G., *La poetica di Platone. Una teoria della comunicazione*, Lecce (Argo) 2007

Chalkia, I., *Lieux et espace dans la tragédie d'Euripide. Essai d'analyse socio-culturelle*, Thessaloniki (University of Thessaloniki) 1986

Cingano, E., 'The Death of Oedipus in the Epic Tradition', *Phoenix* 44, 1992: 1–11

'Indizi di esecuzione corale in Stesicoro', in R. Prestagostini (ed.), *Tradizione e innnovazione nella cultura greca da Omero all' età ellenistica*, Roma (Gruppo editoriale internazionale) 1993: I, 347–61

'Entre skolion et enkomion: réflexions sur le "genre" et la performance de la lyrique chorale grecque', in J. Jouanna and J. Leclant (eds.), *La poésie grecque antique*, Paris (de Boccard) 2003: 17–45

Citti, V., *Eschilo e la lexis tragica*, Amsterdam (Hakkert) 1994

Croally, N., 'Tragedy's Teaching', in J. Gregory (ed.), *A Companion to Greek Tragedy*, Oxford (Blackwell) 2005: 55–70

Csapo, E., 'Imagining the Shape of the Choral Dance and Inventing the Cultic in Euripides' Late Tragedies', in L. Gianvittorio (ed.), *Choreutika: Performing and Theorising Dance in Ancient Greece*, Pisa and Rome (Fabrizio Serra) 2017: 119–56

Csapo, E. and Slater, W. J., *The Context of Ancient Drama*, Ann Arbor, MI (University of Michigan Press) 1995

Csapo, E. and Wilson, P., 'Drama Outside Athens in the Fifth and the Fourth Centuries BC', *Trends in Classics* 7, 2015: 316–95

Curtis, P., *Stesichoros's Geryonis*, Leiden and Boston, MA (E. J. Brill) 2011

Battista D'Alessio, G., 'Past Future and Present Past: Temporal Deixis in Greek Archaic Lyric', *Arethusa* 37, 2004: 267–94

'"The Name of the Dithyramb": Diachronic and Diatopic Variations', in B. Kowalzig and P. Wilson (eds.), *Dithyramb in Context*, Oxford (Oxford University Press) 2013: 113–32

Davies, M. and Finglass, P. J., *Stesichorus: The Poems*, Cambridge (Cambridge University Press) 2014

Dawe, R. D., *Sophocles: Oedipus Rex*, Cambridge (Cambridge University Press) 1982

des Bouvrie, S., *Tragic Workings in Euripides' Drama: The Anthropology of the Genre*, Copenhagen (Museum Tusculanum Press) 2018

Detienne, M., *Dionysos à ciel ouvert*, Paris (Hachette) 1986

Di Benedetto, V. and Medda, E., *La tragedia sulla scena. La tragedia greca in quanto spettacolo teatrale*, Turin (Einaudi) 2002 (1st ed. 1997)

Diggle, J., *Euripidis: Fabulae, Vol. 2: Supplices; Electra; Hercules; Troades; Iphigenia in Tauris; Ion*, Oxford (Oxford University Press) 1981

Euripidis: Fabulae, Tomus I, Oxford (Clarendon Press) 1984

Di Marco, M., 'I *méle* di Eschilo e Frinico (Ar. *Ran.* 1264–1328)', in A. Rodighiero and P. Scattolin (eds.), '... *un enorme individuo, dotato di polmono sopranna-turali' Funzioni, interpretazioni e rinascite del coro drammatico greco*, Verona (Fiorini) 2011: 37–61

Bibliography 193

Dodds, E. R., 'On Misunderstanding the *Oedipus Rex*', *Greece & Rome* 13, 1966: 37–49 (reprinted in *The Ancient Concept of Progress and Other Essays on Greek Literature and Belief*, Oxford (Clarendon Press) 1973: 64–77)

Dover, K., *Aristophanes: Frogs*, Oxford (Clarendon Press) 1993

Ducrot, O., 'Illocutoire et performatif', *Linguistique et sémiologie* 4, 1977: 17–53 (reprinted in *Dire et ne pas dire. Principes de sémantique linguistique*, Paris (Minuit) 1980: 279–305)

Dué, C., *The Captive Woman's Lament in Greek Tragedy*, Austin (University of Texas Press) 2006

Dupont, F., *L'insignifiance tragique. Les Choéphores d'Eschyle, Électre de Sophocle, Électre d'Euripide*, Paris (Gallimard) 2001

Aristote ou le vampire du théâtre occidental, Paris (Aubier) 2007

Easterling, P. E., 'Tragedy and Ritual: "Cry 'Woe, Woe' But May the Good Prevail"', *Mètis* 3, 1988: 87–109

'Euripides in the Theatre', *Pallas* 37, 1991: 49–57

'A Show for Dionysos', in P. E. Easterling (ed.), *The Cambridge Companion to Greek Tragedy*, Cambridge (Cambridge University Press) 1997: 36–53 (trans. from French, 'Un spectacle pour Dionysos', *Europe* 837/838, 1999: 6–28)

Eco, U., *Lector in fabula. La cooperazione interpretativa nei testi narrativi*, Milan (Bompiani) 1979

Else, G. F., 'The Origin of *TRAGOIDIA*', *Hermes* 85, 1957: 17–46

Ercoles, M., 'Tra monodia e coralità: aspetti drammatici de la "performance" di Stesicoro', *Dionysus ex machina* 3, 2012: 1–22

Stesicoro: le testimonanze antiche, Bologna (Pàtron) 2013

Ercoles, M. and Fiorentini, L., 'Giocasta tra Stesicoro (*PMGF* 222 (b)) ed Euripide (*Fenicie*)', *Zeitschrift für Papyrologie und Epigraphik* 179, 2011: 21–34

Fanfani, G., 'What Melos for Troy? Blending of Lyric Genres in the First *Stasimon* of Euripides' *Trojan Women*', in R. Andújar, T. R. P. Coward and T. A. Hadjimichael (eds.), *Paths of Songs: The Lyric Dimension of Greek Tragedy*, Berlin and Boston, MA (de Gruyter) 2018: 239–63

Fearn, D., 'Athens and the Empire: The Contextual Flexibility of Dithyramb, and Its Imperialist Ramifications', in B. Kowalzig and P. Wilson (eds.), *Dithyramb in Context*, Oxford (Oxford University Press) 2013: 133–52

Fileni, M. G., 'L'amebeo lirico-epirrematico in docmi e giambi nella tragedia greca', in F. Perusino and M. Colantonio (eds.), *Dalla lirica corale alla poesia drammatica. Forme e funzioni del canto corale nella tragedia e nella commedia greca*, Pisa (Edizioni ETS) 2007: 129–57

Finglass, P. J., 'Dancing with Stesichorus', in L. Gianvittorio (ed.), *Choreutika: Performing and Theorising Dance in Ancient Greece*, Pisa and Rome (Fabrizio Serra) 2017: 67–89

'Stesichorus and Greek Tragedy', in R. Andújar, T. R. P. Coward and T. A. Hadjimichael (eds.), *Paths of Songs: The Lyric Dimension of Greek Tragedy*, Berlin and Boston, MA (de Gruyter) 2018: 19–37

Foley, H., *Ritual Irony: Poetry and Sacrifice in Euripides*, Ithaca, NY and London (Cornell University Press) 1985

Female Acts in Greek Tragedy, Princeton, NJ (Princeton University Press) 2001
'Choral Identity in Greek Tragedy', *Classical Philology* 98, 2003: 1–30
Freud, S., *Cinq leçons sur la psychanalyse*, Paris (Payot) 1926 (original ed. 1910; reprinted in Freud, S., Strachey, J. and Freud, A., *The Standard Edition of the Complete Psychological Works of Sigmund Freud*, London (Vintage) 2001)
Introduction à la psychanalyse, Paris (Payot) 1962 (original ed. 1917)
Friedrich, R., 'Everything to Do with Dionyso? Ritualism, the Dionysiac, and the Tragic', in M. S. Silk (ed.), *Tragedy and the Tragic: Greek Theatre and Beyond*, Oxford (Clarendon Press) 1996: 257–83
Frontisi-Ducroux, F., *Le dieu-masque. Une figure du Dionysos d'Athènes*, Paris and Rome (La Découverte – École française de Rome) 1991
Furley, W. D., 'Hymns in Euripidean Tragedy', in M. Cropp, K. Lee and D. Sansone (eds.), *Euripides and Tragic Theatre in the Late Fifth Century*, Urbana, IL (*Illinois Classical Studies* 24–25) 1999/2000: 183–97
Furley, W. D. and Bremer, J. M., *Greek Hymns*, 2 vols., Tübingen (Mohr Siebeck) 2001
Garvie, A. F., *Aeschylus: Persae*, Oxford (Oxford University Press) 2009
Gastaldi, S., 'Paideia/muthologia', in M. Vegetti (ed.), *Platone. La Repubblica II. Libri II e III*, Naples (Bibliopolis) 1998: 333–92
Genette, G., *Fiction et diction précédé de Introduction à l'architexte*, Paris (Seuil) 2004 (original eds. 1979 and 1991)
Gentili, B., *Poesia e pubblico nella Grecia antica. Da Omero al V secolo*, Rome and Bari (Laterza) 1984 (4th ed. Milan (Feltrinelli) 2006, mise à jour)
'Il coro tragico nella teoria degli antichi', *Dioniso* 55, 1984/1985: 17–35
Gentili, B. (et al.), *Pindaro. Le Pitiche*, Milan (Mondadori) 1995
Gentili, B. and Giannini, P., 'Preistoria e formazione dell'esametro', *Quaderni Urbinati di Cultura Classica* 26, 1977: 7–51 (reprinted in M. Fantuzzi and R. Pretagostini (eds.), *Struttura e storia dell'esametro greco*, Rome (Gruppo Editoriale Internazionale) 1995/1996: II, 11–62)
Gentili, B. and Lomiento, L., *Metrica e ritmica. Storia delle forme poetiche nella Grecia antica*, Milan (Mondadori) 2003
Giannachi, F. G., *Edipo Re. I Canti. Sofocle*, Pisa and Rome (Fabrizio Serra) 2009
Gianvittorio, L., 'A Dance of Death: Evidence about the Tragic Dance of Mourning', in L. Gianvittorio (ed.), *Choreutika: Performing and Theorising Dance in Ancient Greece*, Pisa and Rome (Fabrizio Serra) 2017: 90–118
Gianvittorio, L. (ed.), *Choreutika: Performing and Theorising Dance in Ancient Greece*, Pisa and Rome (Fabrizio Serra) 2017
Gianvittorio-Ungar, L. and Schlapbach, K. (eds.), *Choreonarratives: Dancing Stories in Greek and Roman Antiquity and Beyond*, Leiden and Boston, MA (E. J. Brill) 2021
Girard, R., *La Violence et le Sacré*, Paris (Grasset) 1972 (éd. poche 1980)
Goethe, J. W., *Noten und Abhandlungen zum besseren Verständnis des west-östlichen Divans*, Stuttgart (Cottaische Buchhandlung) 1819 (reprinted in *Goethes Werke II, Gedichte und Epen II*, ed. Erich Trunz, Hamburg (Wegner) 1949)

Goff, B. E., *The Noose of Words: Readings of Desire, Violence, and Language in Euripides' Hippolytos*, Cambridge (Cambridge University Press) 1990
Goldhill, S., *Reading Greek Tragedy*, Cambridge (Cambridge University Press) 1986
'The Great Dionysia and Civic Ideology', *The Journal of Hellenic Studies* 107: 58–76, 1987
'The Great Dionysia and Civic Ideology', in J. J. Winkler and F. I. Zeitlin (eds.), *Nothing to Do with Dionysos? Athenian Drama in Its Social Context*, Princeton, NJ (Princeton University Press) 1990: 97–129
'Representing Democracy: Women at the Great Dionysia', in R. Osborne and S. Hornblower (eds.), *Ritual, Finance, Politics: Athenian Democratic Accounts Presented to David Lewis*, Oxford (Clarendon Press) 1994: 347–69
'Collectivity and Otherness: The Authority of the Tragic Chorus, Response to Gould', in M. S. Silk (ed.), *Tragedy and the Tragic: Greek Theatre and Beyond*, Oxford (Clarendon Press) 1996: 244–56
'The Audience of Athenian Tragedy', in P. E. Easterling (ed.), *A Cambridge Companion to Greek Tragedy*, Cambridge (Cambridge University Press) 1997: 54–68
'Civic Ideology and the Problem of Difference: The Politics of Aeschylean Tragedy, Once Again', *The Journal of Hellenic Studies* 120, 2000: 34–56
Sophocles and the Language of Tragedy, Oxford (Oxford University Press) 2012
'Choreography: The Lyric Voice of Sophoclean Tragedy', in R. Gagné and M. G. Hopman (eds.), *Choral Mediations in Greek Tragedy*, Cambridge (Cambridge University Press) 2013a: 100–29
'The Greek Chorus: Our German Eyes', in J. Billings, F. Budelmann and F. Macintosh (eds.), *Choruses, Ancient and Modern*, Oxford (Oxford University Press) 2013b: 35–51
Goldhill, S. and Osborne, R. (eds.), *Performance Culture and Athenian Democracy*, Cambridge (Cambridge University Press) 1999: 125–53
Gostoli, A., 'Il nomos citarodico nella culture greca arcaica', in R. Prestagostini (ed.), *Tradizione e innnovazione nella cultura greca da Omero all' età ellenistica*, Rome (Gruppo editoriale internazionale) 1993: I, 167–78
Gould, J., 'Tragedy and Collective Experience', in M. S. Silk (ed.), *Tragedy and the Tragic: Greek Theatre and Beyond*, Oxford (Clarendon Press) 1996: 217–43 (reprinted in *Myth, Ritual Memory, and Exchange*, Oxford (Oxford University Press) 2001: 378–404)
Graf, F., 'Drama and Ritual: Evolution and Convergences', in E. Medda, M. P. Pattoni and M. S. Mirto (eds.), *Komoidotragoidia. Intersezioni del tragico e del comico nel teatro del V secolo a. C.*, Pisa (Edizioni della Normale) 2007: 103–18
Grethlein, J., 'The Hermeneutics and Poetics of Memory in Aeschylus' *Persae*', *Arethusa* 40, 2007: 363–96
Groeneboom, P., *Aischylos' Perser II. Kommentar*, Göttingen (Vandenhoeck & Ruprecht) 1960

Groneberg, M., 'La mimésis: aspects ludiques et poétiques', *Études de Lettres* 306, 2018: 145–67
Gruber, M. A., *Der Chor in den Tragödien des Aischylos. Affekt und Reaktion*, Tübingen (Gunter Narr) 2008
Hall, E., *Inventing the Barbarian: Greek Self-Definition through Tragedy*, Oxford (Oxford University Press) 1989
Aeschylus: Persians, Warminster (Aris and Phillips) 1996
Harrison, J. E., *Themis: A Study in the Social Origins of Greek Religion*, 2nd ed., Cambridge (Cambridge University Press) 1927
Haslam, M. W., 'Stesichorean Metre', *Quaderni Urbinati di Cultura Classica* 17, 1974: 7–57
'The Versification of the New Stesichorus', *Greek, Roman and Byzantine Studies* 19, 1979: 29–57
Hegel, G. W. F., *Vorlesungen über die Ästhetik*, 2nd ed., ed. H. G. Hotho, Berlin (Verlag von Duncker und Humbolt) 1842 (trad. fr. par Charles Bénard, Paris (Librairie générale française) 1997)
Heinich, N. and Schaeffer, J., *Art, création, fiction. Entre sociologie et philosophie*, Nîmes (Jacqueline Chambon) 2004
Henderson, J., 'Women and the Athenian Dramatic Festivals', *Transactions of the American Philological Association* 121, 1991: 133–48
Henrichs, A., 'Why Should I Dance?: Choral Self-Referentiality in Greek Tragedy', *Arion III* 3, 1994/1995: 56–111
'Dancing in Athens, Dancing on Delos: Some Patterns of Choral Projection in Euripides', *Philologus* 140, 1996: 48–62
'Drama and *Dromena*: Bloodshed, Violence, and Sacrificial Metaphor in Euripides', *Harvard Studies in Classical Philology* 100, 2000: 173–88
Herington, J., *Poetry into Drama: Early Tragedy and the Greek Poetic Tradition*, Berkeley and Los Angeles, CA and London (University of California Press) 1985
Holst-Warhaft, G., *Dangerous Voices: Women's Laments and Greek Literature*, London (Routledge) 1992
Hopman, G. M., 'Layered Stories in Aeschylus' *Persians*', in J. Grethlein and A. Rengakos (eds.), *Narratology and Interpretation: The Content of Narrative Form in Ancient Literature*, Berlin and New York (de Gruyter) 2009: 357–76
'Chorus, Conflict, Closure in Aeschylus' *Persians*', in R. Gagné and M. G. Hopman (eds.), *Choral Mediations in Greek Tragedy*, Cambridge (Cambridge University Press) 2013: 58–77
Hose, M., *Studien zum Chor bei Euripides*, 2 vols., Suttgart (Teubner) 1990
Hölscher, U., 'Wie soll ich noch tanzen? Über ein Wort des sophokleischen Chores', in E. Köhler (ed.), *Sprachen der Lyrik. Festschrift für Hugo Friedrich*, Frankfurt am Main (Klostermann) 1975: 376–93
Hurwit, J. M., *The Athenian Acropolis: History, Mythology, and Archaeology from the Neolithic Era to the Present*, Cambridge (Cambridge University Press) 1999
Impero, O., *Parabasi di Aristofane*, Acarnesi Cavalieri Vespe Uccelli, Bari (Adriatica) 2004

Bibliography 197

Irigoin, J., 'Construction métrique et jeux de sonorités dans la *parodos* des *Perses*', in P. Ghiron-Bistagne (et al.), *Les Perses d'Eschyle*, Montpellier (GITA) 1992/1993: 3–14

Jackson, L. C. M. M., *The Chorus of Drama in the Fourth Century BCE: Presence and Representation*, Oxford (Oxford University Press) 2020

Judet de La Combe, P., 'Entre philosophie et philologie. Définitions et refus du tragique', in C. Morenilla and B. Zimmermann (Eds.), *Das Tragische (Drama 9)*, Stuttgart and Weimar (Metzler) 2000: 97–107

Les tragédies grecques sont-elles tragiques? Théâtre et théorie, Paris (Bayard) 2010

Käppel, L., *Paian. Studien zur Geschichte einer Gattung*, Berlin and New York (de Gruyter) 1992

Kaimio, M., *The Chorus of Greek Drama within the Light of the Person and Number Used*, Helsinki (Societas scientiarum Fennica) 1970

Klimis, S., *Le statut du mythe dans la Poétique d'Aristote. Les fondements philosophiques de la tragédie*, Brussels (Ousia) 1997

Kolb, F., 'Polis und Theater', in G. A. Seeck (ed.), *Das griechische Drama*, Darmstadt (Wissenschaftliche Buchgesellschaft) 1979: 505–43

Kowalzig, B., *Singing for the Gods: Performance of Myth and Ritual in Archaic and Classical Greece*, Oxford (Oxford University Press) 2007a

'"And Now All the World Shall Dance!" (Eur. *Bacch.* 114): Dionysus' Choroi between Drama and Ritual', in E. Csapo and M. C. Miller (Eds.), *The Origins of Theater in Ancient Greece and Beyond. From Ritual to Drama*, Cambridge (Cambridge University Press) 2007b: 221–51

Kowalzig, B. and Wilson, P., 'Introduction: The World of Dithyramb', in B. Kowalzig, and P. Wilson (Eds.), *Dithyramb in Context*, Oxford (Oxford University Press) 2013: 1–27

Kranz, W., *Stasimon. Untersuchungen zu Form und Gehalt der griechischen Tragödie*, Berlin (Weidmann) 1933

Kühner, R. and Gerth, B., *Ausführliche Grammatik der griechischen Sprache II. Satzlehre I*, Hannover and Leipzig (Hahn) 1898

Laplanche, J. and Pontalis, J. B., *Vocabulaire de la psychanalyse*, Paris (Presses universitaires de France) 1982

Lavocat, F., *Fait et fiction. Pour une frontière*, Paris (Seuil) 2016

Lesky, A., *Die tragische Dichtung der Hellenen*, 3rd ed., Göttingen (Vandenhoeck & Ruprecht) 1972

Lesky, A., *Greek Tragic Poetry*, New Haven, CT (Yale University Press) 1983

Ley, G., *The Theatricality of Greek Tragedy: Playing Space and the Chorus*, Chicago, IL and London (University of Chicago Press) 2007

Lissarrague, F., *Un flot d'images: une esthétique du banquet grec*, Paris (Adam Biro) 1987

Lloyd-Jones, H., *The Justice of Zeus*, Berkeley, Los Angeles and London (University of California Press) 1971

Lobo, A. L., 'Freud face à l'Antiquité grecque: le cas du Complexe d'Œdipe', *Anabases* 8, 2008: 151–85

Longo, O., 'The Theater of the Polis', in J. J. Winkler and F. I. Zeitlin (eds.), *Nothing to Do with Dionysos? Athenian Drama in Its Social Context*, Princeton, NJ (Princeton University Press) 1990: 12–19

Loraux, N., *Façons tragiques de tuer une femme*, Paris (Hachette) 1985
  Les mères en deuil, Paris (Seuil) 1990
  Mothers in Mourning, Ithaca, NY (Cornell University Press) 1998
  La voix endeuillée. Essai sur la tragédie grecque, Paris (Gallimard) 1999

Loscalzo, D., *Il pubblico a teatro nella Grecia antica*, Roma (Bulzoni) 2008

Lucas, D. W., *Aristotle: Poetics*, Oxford (Clarendon Press) 1968

Maehler, H., *Die Lieder des Bacchylides II. Die Dithyramben und Fragmente*, Leiden, New York and Cologne (Brill) 1997

March, J., 'Euripides the Misogynist', in A. Powell (ed.), *Euripides, Women, and Sexuality*, London and New York (Routledge) 1990: 32–75

Marrou, H., *Histoire de l'éducation dans l'Antiquité I. Le monde grec*, 6th ed., Paris (Seuil) 1964

Marx, W., *Le tombeau d'Œdipe. Pour une tragédie sans tragique*, Paris (Minuit) 2012

Mastronarde, D. J., 'Il coro euripideo: autorità e integrazione', *Quaderni Urbinati di Cultura Classica* 89, 1998: 55–80

Matthey, A., 'De la *megíste mousiké* (*Phédon* 61a 3) à la *tragodía alethestáte* (*Lois* 817 b4-c2)', in M. Reig and X. Riu (eds.), *Drama, Philosophy, Politics in Ancient Greece. Contexts and Receptions*, Barcelona (University of Barcelona Press) 2014: 175–92

Medda, E., *Eschilo Agamennone. Edizione critica, traduzione e commento*, 2 vols., Roma (Bardi Edizioni) 2017
  'Ifigenia all'altare. Il sacrificio di Aulide fra testo et iconografia (Aesch. *Ag.* 231–242)', *Eikasmos* 23, 2012: 87–114

Most, G. W., 'Generating Genres: The Idea of the Tragic', in M. Depew and D. Obbink (eds.), *Matrices of Genre: Authors, Canons, and Society*, Cambridge, MA and London (Harvard University Press) 2000: 15–35

Müller, F., 'Vers armés et "perte de fiole": transactions tragi-comiques de mots et d'objets dans les *Grenouilles* d'Aristophane', in C. Calame (ed.), *Poétique d'Aristophane et langue d'Euripide en dialogue*, Lausanne (Études de Lettres) 2004: 27–57

Murnagham, S., 'Women in Groups: Aeschylus's *Suppliants* and the Female Choruses of Greek Tragedy', in V. Pedrick and S. M. Oberhelman (eds.), *The Soul of Tragedy: Essays on Athenian Drama*, Chicago, IL and London (University of Chicago Press) 2008: 183–98
  '*Choroi Achoroi*: The Athenian Politics of the Tragic Choral Identity', in D. M. Carter (ed.), *Why Athens? A Reappraisal of Tragic Politics*, Oxford (Oxford University Press) 2011: 245–67
  'The Euripidean Chorus', in L. K. McClure (ed.), *A Companion to Euripides*, Malden, MA, Oxford and Chichester (Wiley Blackwell) 2017: 412–27

Murray, P., *Plato on Poetry*, Cambridge (Cambridge University Press) 1996

Naerebout, F. G., 'Moving in Unison: The Greek Chorus in Performance', in L. Gianvittorio (ed.), *Choreutika: Performing and Theorising Dance in Ancient Greece*, Pisa and Rome (Fabrizio Serra) 2017: 39–66

Nagy, G., *Pindar's Homer: The Lyric Possession of an Epic Past*, Baltimore, MD and London (Johns Hopkins University Press) 1990
'Transformations of Choral Lyric Traditions in the Context of Athenian State Theater', *Arion* III 3, 1994/1995: 41–55
Homer the Preclassical, Berkeley, Los Angeles and London (University of California Press) 2010
Neschke, A., 'L'*Orestie* de Stésichore et la tradition littéraire du mythe dans les *Atrides* avant Eschyle', *Antiquité Classique* 55, 1986: 283–301
Nietzsche, F., *Die Geburt der Tragödie aus dem Geiste der Musik*, Leipzig (E. W. Fritzsch) 1872 (reprinted in Colli, G. and Montinari, M., *Sämtliche Werke. Kritische Studienausgabe*, Berlin (de Gruyter) 1980: I, 9–156)
Noel, A., 'L'arc, la lyre et le laurier d'Apollon: de l'attribut emblématique à l'objet théâtral', *Gaia* 17, 2014: 105–28
Nooter, S., *When Heroes Sing: Sophocles and the Shifting Soundscape of Tragedy*, Cambridge (Cambridge University Press) 2012
Osborne, R., 'Competitive Festivals and the Polis: A Context for Dramatic Festivals at Athens', in A. H. Sommerstein, S. Halliwell, J. Henderson and B. Zimmermann (eds.), *Tragedy, Comedy and the Polis*, Bari (Levante) 1993: 21–38
Owen, A. S., *Euripides: Ion*, Oxford (Oxford University Press) 1939
Padel, R., 'Making Space Speak', in J. J. Winkler and F. I. Zeitlin (eds.), *Nothing to Do with Dionysos? Athenian Drama in Its Social Context*, Princeton, NJ (Princeton University Press) 1990: 336–65
Panteli, T., 'Les chants de l'Hellade: les fêtes grecques dans les parties chorales d'Euripide', in I. Milliat-Pilot (ed.), *Texte du Monde – Monde du texte*, Grenoble (Jérôme Millon) 2010: 183–210
Parker, R., *Athenian Religion: A History*, Oxford (Clarendon Press) 1996
Polytheism and Society at Athens, Oxford (Oxford University Press) 2005
'Aeschylus' Gods: Drama, Cult, Theology', in *Eschyle à l'aube du théâtre occidental. Entretiens Hardt* 55, Vandœuvres and Geneva (Fondation Hardt) 2009: 127–64
Peponi, A., 'Dithyramb in Greek Thought: The Problem of Choral Mimesis', in B. Kowalzig and P. Wilson (eds.), *Dithyramb in Context*, Oxford (Oxford University Press) 2013: 353–67
Pickard-Cambridge, A. W., *Dithyramb, Tragedy and Comedy*, 2nd ed., revised by T. B. L. Webster, Oxford (Clarendon Press) 1962
The Dramatic Festivals of Athens, 2nd ed., revised by J. Gould and D. M. Lewis, Oxford (Clarendon Press) 1968
Pirenne-Delforge, V., 'Les Charites à Athènes et dans l'île de Cos', *Kernos* 9, 1996: 195–214
Pironti, G., *Entre ciel et guerre. Figures d'Aphrodite en Grèce ancienne*, Liège (CIERGA) 2007
Porter, J., *The Invention of Dionysus: An Essay on the Birth of Tragedy*, Stanford, CA (Stanford University Press) 2000
Power, T., *The Culture of Kitharôdia*, Washington, DC and Cambridge, MA (Center for Hellenic Studies, Harvard University Press) 2010

'*Kyklops* Kitharoidos: Dithyramb and Nomos in Play', in B. Kowalzig and P. Wilson (eds.), *Dithyramb in Context*, Oxford (Oxford University Press) 2013: 237–56

Prins, Y., 'The Power of the Speech Act: Aeschylus' Furies and Their Binding Song', *Arethusa* 24, 1991: 177–95

Pucci, L., 'Osservazioni critico-esegetiche su alcuni frammenti dell'*Orestea* di Stesicoro (Frr. 210, 211, 212 Davies/172, 173, 174 Davies-Finglass)', *Seminari Romani di Cultura Greca* 4, 2015: 15–40

Pucci, P., *Oedipus and the Fabrication of the Father: Oedipus Tyrannus in Modern Criticism and Philosophy*, Baltimore, MD and London (Johns Hopkins University Press) 1992

Euripide's Revolution under Cover: An Essay, Ithaca, NY and London (Cornell University Press) 2016

Rabinowitz, N. S., *Greek Tragedy*, Malden, MA, Oxford and Carlton (Blackwell) 2008

Rappaport, R. A., *Ritual and Religion in the Making of the Humanity*, Cambridge (Cambridge University Press) 1999

Rehm, R., *Understanding Greek Tragic Theatre*, London (Routledge) 1992

Ricœur, P., *Temps et récit. Tome I*, Paris (Seuil) 1983

Roberts, D. H., 'Parting Words: Final Lines in Sophocles and Euripides', *Classical Quarterly* 81, 1987: 51–64

Rodighiero, A., *Generi lirico-corali nella produzione drammatica di Sofocle*, Göttingen (Narr Verlag) 2012

La tragedia greca, Bologna (Il Mulino) 2013

'How Sophocles Begins: Reshaping Lyric Genres in Tragic Choruses', in R. Andújar, T. R. P. Coward and T. A. Hadjimichael (eds), *Paths of Songs: The Lyric Dimension of Greek Tragedy*, Berlin and Boston, MA (de Gruyter) 2018: 137–62

Rutherford, I., 'Apollo on Ivy: The Tragic Paean', *Arion III* 3, 1994/1995: 112–35

Saïd, S., *La faute tragique*, Paris (La Découverte) 1978

'Tragédie et renversement, l'exemple des *Perses*', *Mètis* 3, 1988: 321–41

'Tragedy and Politics', in D. Boedeker and K. A. Raaflaub (eds.), *Democracy, Empire and the Arts in Fith Century Athens*, Cambridge, MA and London (Harvard University Press) 1998: 275–95

'Entre l'artisan et le politique. Le statut social des poètes tragiques dans la démocratie athénienne', in M. Woronoff, S. Follet and J. Jouanna (eds.), *Dieux, héros et médecins grecs. Hommage à Fernand Robert*, Besançon (Presses universitaires Franc-Comtoises) 2001: 65–96

Sansone, D., 'The Third Stasimon of the Oedipus Tyrannos', *Classical Philolology* 70, 1975: 110–17

Scattolin, P., 'Aristotele e il coro tragico (*Poetica* 12, 18)', in A. Rodighiero and P. Scattolin (eds.), '... *un enorme individuo, dotato di polmono soprannaturali*' *Funzioni, interpretazioni e rinascite del coro drammatico greco*, Verona (Fiorini) 2011: 161–216

Bibliography 201

Schachter, A., *Cults of Boiotia 1: Acheloos to Hera*, Bulletin of the Institute of Classical Studies, Suppl. 38(1), 1981
Schechner, R., *Performance Studies: An Introduction*, 2nd ed., New York and London (Routledge) 2006
von Schelling, F. W. J., *Philosophie der Kunst. Sämtliche Werke I*, Abt., Bd. 5, Stuttgart (Cotta) 1859: 353–736 (trad. fr. par C. Sulzer and A. Pernet, *Philosophie de l'art*, Grenoble (Jérôme Million) 1999)
Schiller, F., 'Über die tragische Kunst', *Neue Thalia* 1, 1792: 176–228 (reprinted in *Sämtliche Werke in 5 Bänden, V, Philosophische Schriften, vermischte Schriften*, München (Winkler) 1968: 372–93)
Die Braut von Messina, in S. Seidel (ed.), *Schillers Werke. Nationalausgabe X*, Weimar (Publisher) 1980: 5–125 (original ed. 1803)
Schlegel, A. W., *Vorlesungen über dramatische Kunst und Literatur I*, in E. Böcking (ed.), *Sämtliche Werke V*, Leipzig (Weidmann) 1846 (original ed. 1809)
Scullion, S., 'Tradition and Invention in Euripidean Aetiology', in M. J. Cropp, K. Lee and D. Sansone (eds.), *Euripides and Tragic Theatre in the Late Fifth Century*, Urbana and Chicago, IL (*Illinois Classical Studies* 24/25) 1999/2000: 217–33
'"Nothing to Do with Dionysus": Tragedy Misconceived as Ritual', *Classical Quarterly* 52, 2002: 102–37
'Tragedy and Religion: The Problem of Origins', in J. Gregory (ed.), *A Companion to Greek Tragedy*, Oxford (Blackwell) 2005: 23–41
Seaford, R., 'The Tragic Wedding', *Journal of Hellenic Studies* 107, 1987: 106–30
Reciprocity and Ritual: Homer and Tragedy in the Developing City-State, Oxford (Clarendon Press) 1994
'Something to Do with Dionysos: Tragedy and the Dionysiac, Response to Friedrich', in M. S. Silk (ed.), *Tragedy and the Tragic: Greek Theatre and Beyond*, Oxford (Clarendon Press) 1996: 284–94
Segal, C. P., 'The Tragedy of *Hippolytos*: The Waters of Ocean and the Untouched Meadow', *Harvard Studies in Classical Philology* 70, 1965: 117–69
Tragedy and Civilization: An Interpretation of Sophocles, Cambridge, MA and London (Harvard University Press) 1981
'Theatre, Ritual, and Commemoration in Euripides' *Hippolytus*', *Ramus* 17, 1988: 52–74 ;(reprinted in *Euripides and the Poetics of Sorrow: Art, Gender, and Commemoration in Alcestis, Hippolytus, and Hecuba*, Durham, NC and London (Duke University Press) 1993: 110–35)
Sophocles' Tragic World: Divinity, Nature, Society, Cambridge, MA and London (Harvard University Press) 1995
'Catharsis, Audience, and Closure in Greek Tragedy', in M. S. Silk (ed.), *Tragedy and the Tragic: Greek Theatre and Beyond*, Oxford (Clarendon Press) 1996: 149–72
Sidwell, K., 'The Argument of the Second Stasimon of *Oedipus Tyrannus*', *Journal of Hellenic Studies* 112, 1992: 106–22
Silk, M. S., 'Style, Voice and Authority in the Choruses of Greek Drama', in P. Riemer and B. Zimmermannn (eds.), *Der Chor im antiken und modernen Drama (Drama 7)*, Stuttgart and Weimar (Metzler) 1998: 1–26

Silk, M. S. and Stern, J., *Nietzsche on Tragedy*, Cambridge (Cambridge University Press) 1981
Sommerstein, A. H., *Aeschylus: Eumenides*, Cambridge (Cambridge University Press) 1989
  Aeschylus: Oresteia, Cambridge, MA and London (Publisher) 2008
  'Notes on Euripides' Hippolytos', *Bulletin of the Institute of Classical Studies* 35, 1988: 23–41
Sourvinou-Inwood, C., *Tragedy and Athenian Religion*, Lanham, MD, Boulder, CO, New York and Oxford (Lexington Books) 2003
Spineto, N., *Dionisos a teatro. Il contesto festivo del dramna greco*, Rome ('L'Erma' di Bretschnieder) 2005
Steiner, D. T., *Choral Constructions in Greek Culture: The Idea of the Chorus in the Poetry, Art and Social Practices of the Archaic and Early Classical Period*, Cambridge and New York (Cambridge University Press) 2021
Stoessl, F., *Die Vorgeschichte des griechischen Theaters*, Darmstadt (Wissenschaftiliche Buchgesellschaft) 1987
Swift, L. A., *The Hidden Chorus: Echoes of Genre in Tragic Lyric*, Oxford and New York (Oxford University Press) 2010
  'Conflicting identities in the Euripidean Chorus', in R. Gagné and M. G. Hopman (eds.), *Choral Mediations in Greek Tragedy*, Cambridge (Cambridge University Press) 2013: 130–54
  'Stesichorus on Stage', in P. J. Finglass and A. Kelly (eds.), *Stesichorus in Context*, Cambridge (Cambridge University Press) 2015: 83–97
Szondi, P., *Versuch über das Tragische*, Frankfurt am Main (Insel-Verlag) 1961 (reprinted in *Schriften*, Frankfurt am Main (Suhrkamp) 1978: 149–260; trad. fr. par Jean-Louis Besson et al., Paris (Circé) 2003)
Taddei, A., 'Ifigenia e il Coro nella *Ifigenia tra i Tauri*. Destini rituali incrociati', *Lexis* 33, 2015: 150–67
  'Vergognarsi davanti al propio dio. Il coro nel terzo stasimo dello *Ione* di Euripide', *Quaderni Urbinati di Cultura Classica* 142, 2016: 47–64
Tambiah, S. J., 'A Performative Approach to Ritual', in *Culture, Thought and Social Action: An Anthropological Perspective*, Cambridge, MA and London (Harvard University Press) 1985: 123–66 (original ed. 1979)
Taplin, O., *The Stagecraft of Aeschylus: The Dramatic Use of Exits and Entrances in Greek Tragedy*, Oxford (Clarendon Press) 1977
Trieschnigg, C. P., *Dances with Girls: The Identity of the Chorus in Aeschylus'* Seven Against Thebes, Nijmegen (UB Nijmegen) 2009 (Ph.D.)
Turner, V., *From Ritual to Theatre: The Human Seriousness of Play*, New York (PAJ Publications) 1982
Vanden Broeck-Parant, J., 'Topographie sacrée et structure narrative chez Pausanias: du Dipylon à l'Académie', *Kernos* 28, 2015: 155–73
Vernant, J. and Vidal-Naquet, P., *Mythe et tragédie en Grèce ancienne*, Paris (Maspero) 1972 (reprinted in *Myth and Tragedy in Ancient Greece*, trans. J. Lloyd, New York (Publisher) 1988)

Myth and Tragedy in Ancient Greece, trans J. Lloyd, Hoboken, NJ (Prentice Hall) 1981
Mythe et tragédie en Grèce ancienne II, Paris (La Découverte) 1986 (reprinted in *Myth and Tragedy in Ancient Greece*, trans. J. Lloyd, New York (Publisher) 1988)
Vidal-Naquet, P., *Le miroir brisé. Tragédie athénienne et politique*, Paris (Les Belles Lettres) 2001
Visvardi, E., *Emotion in Action: Thucydides and the Tragic Chorus*, Leiden and Boston, MA (E. J. Brill) 2015
Voelke, P., *Un théâtre de la marge. Aspects figuratifs et configurationnels du drame satyrique dans l'Athènes classique*, Bari (Levante) 2001
Webster, T. B. L., *The Greek Chorus*, London (Methuen) 1970
Weiss, N., 'Noise, Music, Speech: The Representation of Lament in Greek Tragedy', *American Journal of Philology* 138(2), 2017: 243–66
 The Music of Tragedy: Performance and Imagination in Euripidean Theater, Berkeley (University of California Press) 2018a
 'Performing the Wedding Song in Euripides' *Iphigenia in Aulis*', in R. Andújar, T. R. P. Coward and T. A. Hadjimichael (eds), *Paths of Songs: The Lyric Dimension of Greek Tragedy*, Berlin and Boston, MA (de Gruyter) 2018b: 315–41
Wellenbach, M. C., 'Herodotus' Tragic Choruses', *Trends in Classics* 8, 2016: 17–32
West, M. L., 'Stesichorus', *Classical Quarterly* 65, 1971: 302–14
 'Epic, Lyric, and Lyric Epic', P. J. Finlass and A. Kelly (eds.), *Stesichorus in Context*, Cambridge (Cambridge University Press) 2015: 63–80
Wiles, D., *Tragedy in Athens: Performance Space and Theatrical Meaning*, Cambridge (Cambridge University Press) 1997
 Mask and Performances in Greek Tragedy: From Ancient Festival to Modern Experimentation, Cambridge (Cambridge University Press) 2007
Wilson, P. J., *The Athenian Institution of the Khoregia: The Chorus, the City and the Stage*, Cambridge (Cambridge University Press) 2000
Winnington-Ingram, R. P., 'Zeus in the *Persae*', *Journal of Hellenic Studies* 93, 1973: 210–19 (reprinted in *Studies in Aeschylus*, Cambridge (Cambridge University Press) 1983: 1–15)
Zeitlin, F. I., 'The Motif of the Corrupted Sacrifice in Aeschylus' *Oresteia*', *Transactions and Proceedings of the American Philological Association* 85, 1965: 463–508
 'The Power of Aphrodite: Eros and the Boundaries of the Self in the *Hippolytus*', in P. Burian (ed.), *Directions in Euripidean Criticism: A Collection of Essays*, Durham, NC (Duke University Press) 1985: 52–110 and 198–207 (reprinted in *Playing the Other: Gender and Society in Classical Greek Literature*, Chicago, IL and London (University of Chicago Press) 1996: 219–84)
 'Staging Dionysus between Thebes and Athens', in T. Carpenter and C. A. Faraone (Eds.), *Masks of Dionysus*, Ithaca, NY and London (Cornell University Press) 1993: 147–82
Zimmermann, B., *Die Griechische Tragödie*, Stuttgart (Kröner) 2018
Zografou, A., *Chemins d'Hécate. Portes, routes, carrefours et autres figures de l'entre-deux (Kernos Suppl. 24)* Liège (CIERGA) 2010

English Translations of Greek Texts and Other Modern Texts

Bury, R. G., *Plato: Laws, Volume II, Books 7–12*, Cambridge, MA (Harvard University Press) 1926
Campbell, D. A., *Greek Lyric, Volume II: Anacreon, Anacreontea, Choral Lyric from Olympus to Alcman*, Cambridge, MA (Harvard University Press) 1988
Campbell, D. A., *Greek Lyric, Volume IV: Bacchylides, Corinna, and Others*, Cambridge, MA (Harvard University Press) 1992
Davies, M. and Finglass, P. J., *Stesichorus: The Poems*, Cambridge (Cambridge University Press) 2014
Henderson, J. *Aristophanes: Clouds, Wasps, Peace*, Cambridge, MA (Harvard University Press) 1992
Kovacs, D., *Euripides: Children of Heracles, Hippolytus, Andromache, Hecuba*, Cambridge, MA (Harvard University Press) 1995
Lloyd-Jones, H., *Sophocles: Ajax. Electra. Oedipus Tyrannus*, Cambridge, MA (Harvard University Press) 1994
Race, W. H., *Pindar: Nemean Odes. Isthmian Odes. Fragments*, Cambridge, MA (Harvard University Press) 1997
Sommerstein, A. H., *Aeschylus: Oresteia: Agamemnon. Libation-bearers. Eumenides*, Cambridge, MA (Harvard University Press) 2009
Sommerstein, A. H., *Aeschylus: Persians, Seven Against Thebes, Suppliants, Prometheus Bound*, Cambridge, MA (Harvard University Press) 2008

Translations used in the English edition:
Benveniste, E., *Problems in General Linguistic*, trans. M. E. Meek, Miami (Miami University Press) 1971
Freud, S., Strachey, J. and Freud, A., *The Standard Edition of the Complete Psychological Works of Sigmund Freud*, London (Vintage) 2001
Hegel, G. W. F., *Aesthetics: Lectures on Fine Art*, trans. T. M. Knox, 2 vols., Oxford (Clarendon Press) 1975
Nietzsche, F., *The Birth of Tragedy and Other Writings*, ed. R. Geuss and R. Speirs, trans. R. Speirs, Cambridge (Cambridge University Press) 1999
Schelling, F. W. J., *The Philosophy of Art*, ed., trans. and intro. D. W. Scott, Minneapolis (University of Minnesota Press) 1989
Schiller, F., *Essays Æsthetical and Philosophical, including the Dissertation on the 'Spiritual Connexion between the Spiritual and the Animal in Man'*, London (George Bell and Sons) 1905
Szondi, P., *An Essay on the Tragic*, trans. P. Fleming, Stanford, CA (Stanford University Press) 2002

Index of Names

Acharnae, 10, 61
Achilles, 22, 43–4
Actaeon, 68
Adrastus, 17–18, 166, 168
Aegean, 139, 161
Aeschylus, xxi, xxvii, 9–11, 13–15, 24–5, 56, 58,
   67–8, 73, 84, 86, 93, 97, 110, 164, 168, 175,
   179, 182
   Agamemnon, 8, 41–3, 45–6, 83, 106,
     172, 175
   Choephoroi, 164
   Eumenides, 32, 83
   Oresteia, 41, 46
   Persians, xxviii, 67, 93–111, 167
   Proteus, 46
   Seven against Thebes, 11, 18, 73
   Suppliants, 68, 93, 97, 109, 126
Agamemnon, 8, 41–3, 45–6, 83, 106, 165,
   172, 175
Agathon, 16
Alcman, 12, 29, 70, 84
Amphion, 172
Anthesteria, 52–3, 63
Antigone, 32, 53, 141, 167–8
Aphrodite, Cypris, 38, 114–15, 117–24, 129
Apollo, xxv, 5, 11, 22, 33–5, 37–8, 51, 53, 62–3, 73,
   84, 107, 138–40, 143–5, 148, 150–2, 156, 159,
   164–7, 172, 174
   Delian, 58, 141, 161
   Ismenios, 73, 81
   Phoebus, 140
Archilochus, 57–8
Areopagus, 83, 89–90
Ares, 142, 173
Arion of Methymna, 15, 58–9, 172, 176
Aristophanes, 9–11, 14, 16, 19, 49, 59, 62, 90,
   174–5, 179, 182
   Acharnians, 9–10, 19, 51–2, 54, 61
   Clouds, 11
   Frogs, 10, 60, 175
   Peace, 16, 19, 165

Aristotle, xxvi–xxviii, 4, 6, 15, 18, 22–5, 27–9, 40,
   55, 58–9, 62, 65, 71, 75, 108, 112, 138, 146, 154–
   5, 159–60, 162–3, 175–6
   Poetics, xxvi–xxvii, 6, 18, 22–4, 27, 58–9, 62, 65,
     112, 136, 160, 163, 175
   Rhetoric, 176
Artemis
   Brauronia, 120
   Dictynna, 13, 127, 131
   Lochia, 120
   Saronis, 132
Athena
   Nike, 34
   Pallas, 35, 37
Atossa, 94, 99, 107
Austin, John L. 78–9
Azoulay, Vincent. xix

Bacchylides, 57–8, 160–3, 171
Bach, Johann Sebastian, 185–6
Bali. xxiii–xxv
Benveniste, Émile, 23, 78–80, 169
Briand, Michel. xxi
Brunel, Pierre, 7
Budelmann, Felix. xx–xxi
Bühler, Karl, 80, 89
Burkert, Walter, xi, 15, 173

Capponi, Matteo, xxi
Casato, Vanessa, 91
Charites, 101, 128–30, 165
Cithaeron, Mt, 150–2, 157, 172
Clisthenes of Sicyon, 17–18, 47
Clytemnestra, xii, xiv, 41–3, 45–6, 83, 165
Creon, xvi, 137–8, 140–1, 145–6, 157
Creusa, 32, 34–9
Cypris, 38, 114–15, 117–24, 129

Darius, 32, 94–7, 100, 104, 106–107, 110
Delian Apollo, 58, 141, 161
Delos, 11, 33, 38, 139, 141

Index of Names

Delphi, xvii, 17, 32–4, 39, 52, 137, 139–41, 143–6, 148, 150, 157
Demeter, 11, 15, 39, 52, 62–3
Demodocos, 172–3
Demosthenes, 16, 50, 53–4, 111
Dicaeopolis, 9–10, 51
Diogenes Laertius, 14, 48
Dionysos, xi–xii, xxiv, 5, 10–11, 13–14, 16–18, 25, 29, 39–41, 46–63, 65–7, 74, 77, 82, 85, 87, 89, 91–2, 109, 123, 133–4, 142–3, 149, 152, 159, 175, 177–83
   Baccheios, 143
   Eleuthereus, xxiv, 25, 49–50, 53–6, 63, 65, 67, 82, 91–2, 134, 143, 181, 183
   theatre of, xii, 47–8, 54, 85, 87, 89, 133, 178, 182
Dionysus of Halicarnassus, 171
Dioscorides, 48
Dupont, Florence, xxvii, xxix, 27–9, 177

Einodia, 39
Electra, 27, 83, 177
Eleuthereus, 49–50, 53–6, 63, 65, 67, 82, 91–2, 134, 181, 183
Ercoles, 164–5, 168, 170–1, 173–5
Erechtheus, 15, 32, 35–9, 132, 181
Erichthonios, 36, 39, 52
Erinyes, 83–91, 145, 167
Eteocles, 18, 166–8
Eumenides, 68, 83, 89–92
Euripides, xxvi, 9–13, 24–5, 28, 36–7, 39–40, 62, 67–70, 112, 117–18, 121, 130, 132, 162, 164, 167–8, 175, 181–2
   Bacchae, 58–9, 68
   Hippolytus, xxix, 40, 112–34, 167, 182
   Ion, xii, xvii, 32–6, 38, 40, 85, 141
   Iphigeneia at Aulis, 15, 41–5
   Medea, 67
   Phoenicians, 68–9, 73, 168

Foucault, Michel, 10
Freud, Sigmund, 135

Gianvittorio-Ungar, Laura, xix, xxi, 104
Girard, René, 45
Goethe, Johann Wolfgang, 1–2
Goldhill, Simon, xii–xiii, xv, 7, 47, 53–4, 70–2, 76, 155, 185
Graces, 128

Harrison, Jane E. 17
Hegel, Georg Wilhelm Friedrich, 2–4, 6, 159, 181
Henrichs, Albert, xxx, 36, 44, 62, 82, 85–6, 148–9, 151
Hephaistos, 172–3
Heracles, 15, 53, 123, 162, 165

Heraclides Ponticus, 172–3
Hermes, 32, 96, 152
Herodotus, 12, 16–18, 86, 95, 98, 107–108, 110, 139, 179
Hesiod, 11, 150, 157, 164, 166–7, 169
   Catalogue of Women, 157
   Works and Days, 150, 166
Hippolytus, xxix, 40, 112–34, 167, 182
Homer, 22, 62, 164, 169–72, 175
   Iliad, 18, 22, 136, 157, 165, 169, 172
   Odyssey, 167, 172–3
Homeric Hymn to Demeter, 15, 62
Homeric Hymns, 11, 15, 34, 62, 152, 169, 182

Icarios, 52–3
Iole, 123
Ion, xii, xvii, 32–6, 38, 40, 85, 141
Iphigeneia, 41–5
Ismard, Paulin, xix

Jocasta, 53, 137–8, 146–9, 151, 153–5, 166–9

Kranz, Walther, 76, 78, 98, 102, 162, 182

Labdacids, 167
Laius, 32, 137, 140, 143–4, 147–8, 150, 152–3
Leto, 33–4, 37–8, 53, 115–17, 127, 132
Louis, Annick, xxx

Maenads, 50, 61, 142
Melanippus of Thebes, 17–18
Murray, Gilbert, 17, 23, 163
Musaeus, 11

Nietzsche, Friedrich, x, xxiii, 4–5, 7, 21, 159, 184–5
Nike, Athena, 34

Odysseus, 167
Oedipus, 5–6, 28–9, 85, 90, 135–41, 143–7, 150–9, 166–8, 182
Oedipus at Colonus, 5, 136
Orestes, 12, 27, 83–4, 86–8, 164–5

Pallas Athena, 35, 37
Parian Marble, 48
Pausanias, 49–53, 167
Pegasos of Eleutherae, 52–3
Persians, xxviii, 11, 29, 32, 67–8, 93–111, 167, 182–3
Phaedra, 53, 112–13, 115, 117, 119–25, 127–8, 130, 132
Pherecydes of Athens, 167
Phillips, Tom, xx
Phoebus Apollo, 140
Phrynicus, 49, 57, 179
   Sack of Miletus, 12, 68, 110

Index of Names

Pindar, 12, 18, 29, 50, 57, 70, 73, 80–2, 84, 86, 101, 131, 138, 151, 161–2, 171, 174
Plataea, 95, 97
Plato, 14, 19, 22–3, 47–9, 62–3, 77, 160, 162–3, 169, 174, 176, 183
  Cratylus, 19
  Laws, 171, 183
  Minos, 49
  Republic, 23, 68
Polybus, 18, 136–7, 151
Polynices, 18, 166–8
Poseidon, 13, 50, 97, 113, 181

Ricœur, Paul, 23, 28

Sappho, 122–3, 171
Schaeffer, Jean-Marie, 177, 181
Schechner, Richard, 64
Schelling, Friedrich von, 6, 21
Schiller, Friedrich, 1
Schlapbach, Karin, xix
Schlegel, August Wilhelm, xv, 75–6
Segal, Charles, 74–5, 78, 109, 117, 119, 131, 133, 141, 144, 148–9, 151, 154, 182
Semele, 123
Socrates, 11, 14, 49, 62
Sophocles, xxvi, 5, 19, 24–5, 49, 62, 74–5, 90, 100, 112, 136, 138–9, 157, 159, 182
  Oedipus the King, xxix, 6, 67, 85, 107, 135
  Oedipus Tyrannus, 7, 32, 135–59, 167–8
  Women of Trachis, 68

Sourvinou-Inwood, Christiane, xi, 48, 50, 67–8, 71, 130
Steiner, Deborah, xix
Stesichorus, 163–76
  Geryoneis, 165, 171–2, 174
  Oresteia, 164–5, 170, 172, 174, 183
  Thebaid, 168, 170, 172
Suda, 48–9, 51, 53, 55, 57–9, 164, 171–6
Szondi, Peter, 5–7

Terpander, 172
Theseus, 19, 50, 58, 112–15, 118, 125, 132–3, 161–2
Turner, Victor, 64

Vernant, Jean-Pierre, xv, xxvi, 25–7, 42, 56, 66, 136, 157, 177
Vidal-Naquet, Pierre, xv, xxvi, 25–7, 42, 53, 56, 66–7, 136, 157, 177

Wagner, Richard, 4, 184–5
Weiss, Naomi, xii, xxi, 24, 36, 83
Wittgenstein, Ludwig, xxiv

Xenophanes, 60
Xerxes, 67, 93–108, 110
Xouthos, 34–7, 40

Zeus, 33–5, 38, 42, 53–4, 59, 81, 91, 95, 97–8, 105–108, 116, 123, 131, 138–45, 148–50, 154, 158–9, 172
  Olympian, 37

Subject Index

Introductory Note

References such as '178–9' indicate (not necessarily continuous) discussion of a topic across a range of pages. Wherever possible in the case of topics with many references, these have either been divided into sub-topics or only the most significant discussions of the topic are listed. Because the entire work is about 'choral tragedy', the use of this term (and certain others which occur constantly throughout the book) as an entry point has been restricted. Information will be found under the corresponding detailed topics.

Acropolis, 34, 36, 39, 47–50, 93, 120, 181
acts of song, xx, 40, 75
Aeolian metre/rhythm, 33–4, 39, 116, 122, 124, 153, 161–2
aesthetic jouissance, 185
aesthetics, xx, 2–3, 6, 26, 30, 76, 99, 186
  harmonious, 5
aetiological closure, 129–31
affective voice, 75, 88, 96, 109, 133, 150, 158, 178; *see also* emotive voice
agṓn, 11, 16, 61, 173
  mousikós, 11, 19, 49, 63, 65, 181
altars, 33–4, 42–4, 47–8, 50, 61, 66, 89, 97
ambiguity, 26, 92, 182
  sexual, xxix, 115–18, 127
anapaestic dimeters, 89, 165, 171
anapaests, 33–4, 36, 89, 94–6, 98–9, 115, 120, 133
Anthesteria, 52–3, 63
anthropological perspectives, xxviii–xxix, 21–30
anthropology, xxx, 25, 45, 168, 181
  historical, 26, 185
  social, xxv, 8, 22
anthropopoetics, 12
aoidḗ, 14–15
Aphrodite, xxix, 62, 113–24, 127–9, 132, 172–3
Argos, 17–18, 106, 129, 166, 168
Artemis, 34–6, 43–4, 53, 113, 115–20, 128–30, 132, 141–2
Asia, 93, 96–8, 100, 102, 107
Athena, 34–6, 39, 50, 83, 88–91, 131–2, 139–43

Attic tragedy, xxv–xxvii, 17, 19, 68–70, 74–6, 163–5, 181, 183–5
  choral definition, 16–20
  and cult of Dionysos, 40–57
  as ritual, 29–31
  ritual song in, 31–40
  towards, 175–6
audiences, 28–9, 65–6, 71–2, 74–5, 89–92, 133–4, 178–83, 185–6
  real-life, 88, 178, 182
  from second person to first, 177–9
  virtual, 88, 134, 150
authoritative voice, xvi, 72, 115
authority, mask of, 76, 79
authors
  ideal, 77, 158, 179–80
  implicit, 76, 86–8
  virtual, 76–7, 134, 179, 182

barong, xxiii
binding song, 83–92
blood sacrifices, 41–2, 44–5

catalogues, xix, 56, 97, 100–103, 170
children, 35, 47, 55, 60, 136, 140, 144, 153
choral conclusions, 98, 154–9
choral delegation, 82–3, 86, 174, 180
choral emotion, 2–5, 29
choral identification, 153–4, 178
choral identities, 66–72, 76, 104–107
  questioning, 93–111

208

Subject Index

choral performance, 16–17, 54, 77, 79, 169, 171, 173–4, 176
choral performativity, 78–80
choral polyphonies, 64–92, 177–81
  ending in, 133–4
choral projection, 36, 39, 85, 101, 106, 128
choral songs, 11–14, 83–6, 100–102, 117–19, 122–4, 130–2, 140–1, 147–8
  and hymns, 34–6
choral voice, xvi–xvii, 66–7, 73, 75, 77–8, 128–9, 134, 180–1
  and oracular voices, 144–7
  reasons for singing chorally, 147–50
chorality, xi, xv, xvii, xix, 6, 10, 63, 72
choregía, 20, 53
choregos/*choregós*, 20, 46, 104, 108, 110, 118, 120–1, 153
  role, 103–104
choreography, 14, 49, 63, 81, 185
choriambs, 99, 145, 153
chorus leaders, 20, 58–9, 82, 94, 121, 127
chorus masters, 10, 186
chorus of Hippolytus, 112–27
choruses, female, 67–70, 84, 126
citharodic nomoi, 18, 163–76
citharoidia, 175–6
civic community, xv, xxvi, 23, 27, 131, 179, 182, 186
civic identity, 55, 67, 126
collective entities, xix, 24, 120–1
comedy, 9–10, 14, 16, 18–19, 23–4, 55, 58–9, 163
community, civic, xv, xxvi, 23, 27, 131, 179, 182, 186
comparisons, xxiv, 23, 33, 44, 73, 92, 126, 184–5
competitions, musical, xxviii, 19, 46–7, 54, 60, 172, 178
conclusions, choral, 98, 154–9
contests, musical, 46–7, 49, 54, 60–1, 65, 110
contexts, xx–xxi, 8–9, 11, 16, 18, 35–6, 162–3, 165
Corinth, xiv, 67, 136–7, 157
coryphaeus, 36–7, 95, 103, 113–14, 120, 143–4, 146–7, 155–6
cretics, 43, 84, 99, 140, 147
cultic acts, 29, 40, 63, 84, 130, 149
cultic dramatizations, 61–3
cultic prayer, 114, 140–2
cults, 48, 50, 58–9, 61, 83, 90–1, 130–1, 143
cultural identity, 104–107
cultural memory, 30–1, 70, 72, 168, 183, 186

dactylic hexameter, 170–1, 176
dactylic metre, 83
dactylic tetrameter, 140
daímon, 51, 95, 97–8, 100, 103, 107–108
dances, xiv, xvii, xxiii, 11, 36, 49, 149, 151
daphnephoria, 81–2
deictic gestures, 83–7, 89, 101, 117

deictic *haíde*, 87
deixis, 64, 80, 89–90
  verbal, 37, 87–8, 103, 116, 132, 140, 142
delegation, choral, 82–3, 86, 174, 180
Delphic oracle, 52, 137, 140, 143, 146
destiny, 7, 91, 94, 105, 145, 147, 154–5, 157–9
didáskein, 10, 14, 19, 59, 179
diegesis, 169
  to mimesis, 160–3
diegetic mode, 22, 62, 160, 163
Dionysia
  Great, xiii, xxiv, xxviii, 9, 11, 19, 27–9, 46–51, 53–4, 60–1, 63, 70, 77, 87, 93, 131, 133, 160, 162, 181
  Rural, 51, 61
Dionysiac essentialism, against, 59–61
Dionysiac rituality, 54–7
discourse, 8, 19, 25, 32, 76–7, 79–80, 82, 87
  analysis, xxv, 8, 22, 76–7, 79
  direct, 166, 169
  indirect, 155
dithyramb, 18, 23, 47, 49, 57–9, 160–3, 174–6, 178
dochmiacs, 36, 96, 99, 121, 123, 125, 146, 156
double references, 79, 85–8, 150, 154
drâma, 14–15, 62
drama, xiii–xiv, xvi–xvii, 1–3, 21, 23–4, 32, 180, 182
dramatic action, 34–6, 38–40, 68–70, 85–8, 90–3, 128–32, 140–4, 178–83
dramatic form, x, xiv, 62, 165–9
dramatic identities, 66–8, 71, 99, 108–109, 111, 134
dramatic mode, 22–3, 62, 77, 160, 162
dramatizations, cultic, 61–3

elders, xiv, 98, 102, 106, 144
emic categories, xxv, 8–16, 20
emic designations, 59
emotions, xix–xx, 77–8, 103, 105, 107, 109–11, 123, 176–7
  strong, 36–7, 122, 146, 156
emotive voice, 77, 87, 103, 108, 121, 123, 146, 155–6; *see also* affective voice
enunciation, 23, 36, 73, 76–7, 79–82, 92, 104, 169
  linguistic, 177, 179
enunciations, gendered, 125–9
enunciative polyphonies, xxviii, 67, 72, 75–83, 86–8, 98–9, 111, 180–2
enunciative self-reference, 80–6
enunciative stances, 68, 75–7, 88
enunciative strategies, xxv, xxviii, 25, 76–7, 85, 88
epeisódia, 24
epic diction, xxv, 169–71
epic, poetry xxvi, 23, 163, 167
Eros, 114–15, 122–4
essentialism, xxvii
  Dionysiac, 59–61

ethnopoetics, xxv, xxvii, xxx, 185
excesses, 5–8
exodos, 28, 98–9, 102–104, 107, 113, 126, 131–4
extra-discursive references, xxv, 77, 133, 149–50, 154

fate, 94, 98, 107, 121–2, 126, 153–4, 157–8, 166–7
fathers, 123, 125, 129, 135–7, 145–6, 151–3, 156–7, 167
fear, xiv–xvi, 4, 22, 29, 94, 97, 121, 148
female choruses, 67–70, 84, 126
fiction, xxix, 27, 139
   dramatic, 158–9, 178
   referential, 181
   tragic, xxvi, 28, 56, 160–86
fictional identities, 69–72
fictional plane, 65, 71
fictional worlds, xx, xxv, 45, 67, 69
fictionality, 27, 177
first person, 78–82, 84–6, 88, 91–2, 146–7, 157–8, 177–80, 182
foreigners, 39, 47, 50, 69, 71
fortune, reversals of, 107, 109–10, 154
foundation myths, 26, 50–1, 53, 57, 62, 135, 185
functions, 23–4, 55–6, 63, 65, 71, 103, 113, 179–80
   cultic, 11, 32, 56, 141
   hermeneutic, 123, 153
   pragmatic, xxviii, 29, 31–2, 35–6, 79, 178
   of tragic song, 72–5

gamelan, xxiii
garlands, 38, 43–4, 53, 81, 117
gender, 67, 75, 106, 109, 112–34, 180
   identities, 69–72, 75, 128
gendered enunciations, 125–9
German Romanticism, xxvi–xxvii, 21–2, 25
gestures, ritual, xxiii, 32–3, 40, 43, 96, 103, 130–1
goats, 14–15, 46, 48
gold, 32, 38, 139, 166
Great Dionysia, 9, 11, 27–9, 46–51, 53–4, 60–1, 63, 131
Great Panathenaia, xiii, 32, 47, 51, 63, 85, 162
grief, 5–7, 95–6, 100, 102, 104–105, 107, 133, 155

here-and-now, xxv, 34–7, 71, 88, 90, 178, 180, 183
hermeneutic voice, 74–5, 77–8, 115–16, 118–19, 156, 158, 177–9, 182
heroes, 2–3, 5–8, 17–18, 22–3, 26–7, 61–2, 117–18, 136
   tragic, xxvi, 3, 5–6, 98–9, 105, 107, 158–9, 162
heroines, xii, 42–3, 53, 112, 120, 122, 124, 167
hexameters, xiii, 36, 165, 170–1
Homeric poetry, 23, 59, 68, 169, 172–3, 178
húbris, 97, 110, 118, 147
humanities, xvi, xxvi–xxvii, 8, 22, 25–9, 76

husbands, xii, 16, 38, 41, 137, 145, 153, 156
hymenaion, 40, 56, 74, 79
hymnic elements, 32, 36–7, 40, 84
hymnic parodos, 138–44
hymnic prayer, 38, 140–1
hymnic songs, 33, 37, 84–5, 115, 142
   in Euripides' *Ion*, 32–4
   and pragmatics, 38–40, 142–4
hymns, xii–xiii, 31–3, 37, 39–40, 83–4, 114–16, 143, 150–2
   and choral songs, 34–6
   cletic, 35, 123, 141–2

iambic dimeters, 43
iambic metre, 83–4, 96, 147
iambic trimeters, 10–11, 13, 36, 38, 94, 120, 122, 124–5
ideal author, 77, 158, 179–80
ideal narrator, 158
ideal spectator, xv–xvi, 75–6, 150, 157–8, 178
identification, choral, 153, 178
identities, 6, 66–7, 69–72, 92, 94, 107, 109, 151–2
   choral, 66–72, 76, 93, 104–105
   cultural, 104–7
   double, 67, 71, 83
   dramatic, 66–8, 71, 99, 108–9, 111, 134
   fictional, 69–72
   gender, 69–72, 75, 128
   political, 64, 66–8, 71
   polymorphic, 75
   ritual, 71, 109, 134
   true, 138, 145, 151–3
immortalization, 130
implicit author, 76, 86–8
imprecations, 39–40, 123, 143–4
incest, 135–6
insignificance, tragic, xxvii, 27, 29, 177
intra-discursive references, 82, 150, 154

justice, 4, 10, 13, 89–90, 144, 148, 168

kátharsis, 22, 108, 110, 155, 180–1
khorodidáskalos, xxv, 19
kommós/kommos, 24, 28, 36, 99–100, 102–103, 109, 146–7, 155–7
kômos, 51, 61, 116

lamentation, 94–6, 108, 110, 124, 130, 140, 142, 144
   and catalogue, 100–102
   ritual, xii, 17, 100–101, 108
   song of as choral ending, 98–104
laurel branches, 32–4
Lenaia, 19, 56
lexical field, 8–16, 20
'lyric' iambics, 89, 94

Subject Index

lyric I/we, 82
lyric poetry, xi, xx, 2, 6, 12

marginality, 67, 71, 77, 92, 109
 social, 69, 72
Mariandynoi, 101
marriage, 42–5, 53, 117, 127–9, 166
masks, 54–7, 61, 65, 94, 113, 118, 126, 144
 of authority, 76, 79
mediations, xxv, 65–6, 73, 99, 179
melic diction, xxvi, 29, 161, 163, 176
melic 'I'/'we', 78–80
melic lament, 37–8
melic poetry, xxv, xxviii–xxix, 73–5, 79–82, 85, 123, 162, 175–6
melic songs, 10, 12–14, 33, 36, 63, 73, 172, 175
melopoiós/melopoiía, xxvi, 13, 24, 28, 175
mélos, 10, 12, 14, 24, 29, 70, 84, 174–5
 in Euripides *Ion*, 32–4
memory
 cultural, 30–1, 70, 72, 168, 183, 186
 poetic, 63, 130
messengers, 44, 94–5, 132, 151, 155, 158
metre, 24, 36, 63, 99, 151, 155, 169–71, 175
 Aeolian metre/rhythm, 33–4, 39, 116, 122, 124, 153, 161–2
 anapaestic dimeters, 89, 165, 171
 anapaests, 33–4, 36, 89, 94–6, 98–9, 115, 120, 133
 choriambs, 99, 145, 153
 cretics, 43, 84, 99, 140, 147
 dactylic, 83
 dactylic hexameter, 170–1, 176
 dochmiacs, 36, 96, 99, 121, 123, 125, 146, 156
 iambic, 83–4, 96, 125, 147
 iambic dimeters, 43
 iambic trimeters, 10–11, 13, 36, 38, 94, 120, 122, 124–5
 'lyric' iambics, 89, 94
 paroemiacs, 36, 99
 prosodiac, 170
 trochaic, 24
 trochaic dimeters, 170
 trochaic rhythm, 43, 158
 trochaic tetrameters, 59, 94
metrical analysis, 36, 116, 140, 151, 155, 174
mimesis/*mímesis*, 22–3, 27–8, 175, 177
 diegesis to, 160–3
mimetic mode, 62, 86, 160–2, 166
moîra, 98, 105, 114, 126, 128, 147–8, 167
molpé/mélpein, 174
mothers, 105, 107, 129–30, 135–7, 142–6, 151–3, 155–7, 166–7
mourning, xii, xxvii, 100–102, 104–108, 125, 130
mousikòs agón, 11, 19, 49, 63, 65, 181

musical competitions, xxviii, 19, 46–7, 54, 60, 172, 178
musical contests, 46–7, 49, 54, 60–1, 65, 110
musical offerings, 60, 63, 182
musical performance, xix–xx, xxv, 28–30, 65–6, 84–5, 115–16, 181, 184–6
musical ritual, xi–xii, xvii, 87, 135
mùthos, xxvi–xxvii, 6, 19, 22–4, 28, 40, 62, 65
myths, xvi, 19, 28–9, 45, 83, 135–6, 152, 186
 founding/foundational, 26, 50–3, 57, 62, 135, 185

narrative action, 23, 80, 115, 158, 160, 167, 181
narrative development, 164–9
narrative modes, 62, 68, 161–2, 165–6, 169
narratives, xi, xiii, xvii, 27, 45, 58, 164–6; *see also* récit
narrators, 79, 150, 179–80
 ideal, 158
nómoi, 172, 174–5
numphagogía, 43
nurses, 120–2, 124, 151, 164

offerings, musical, 60, 63, 182
opera, 4, 38, 98
ópsis, xxvi, 28
oracular voices, 140, 144–7
oratorios, 28, 181, 184–6
orchestra/*orkhéstra*, 36, 43, 47–8, 65–6, 73–4, 82, 85–6, 88
oudèn pros tòn Diónuson, 57–9

paeans, 34, 38, 40, 43, 91, 139–40, 144, 161
palaiá, 65
Panathenaia, Great, xiii, 32, 47, 51, 63, 85, 162
parodies, xii, 9, 13, 175
parodos, 24, 28, 93–4, 101–102, 115–16, 138–9, 141–2, 145
 and consequences, 118–22
paroemiacs, 36, 99
parricide, 136
passions, 2–4, 111, 120–1, 124, 185–6
pémpso, 91, 101, 104
performance, x–xiii, xxiii–xxv, xxvii–xxix, 14–15, 64, 69, 71, 179–81
 choral, 16–17, 54, 77, 79, 169, 171, 173–4, 176
 dramatic, xxiii, 10, 36, 65, 162
 musical, xix–xx, xxv, 28–30, 65–6, 84–5, 115–16, 181, 184–6
 ritual/ritualized, 29–30, 32, 62–3, 81–2, 133–4, 143, 177–9, 181
performative dimension, 61, 104, 109, 139, 149, 154, 178, 182
performative future, 37, 81, 100
performative mode, 43, 73, 96, 118, 129, 134

performative self-reference, 80–4, 101, 104
performative utterances, 30, 78, 101
performative voice, 74–5, 77–8, 96, 115, 150, 152–3, 177–8, 182–3
performativity, choral, 78–80
Persian army, 94–5, 97, 99, 105, 110
phallic songs, 61, 163
pity, 1, 28–9, 140, 155
plots, xxvi–xxvii, 23, 28, 35–6, 68, 80, 137–8, 167–8
  malleable heroic, 136–8
poetic forms, 13, 29, 49, 56, 58, 175–6, 178, 183
poetic 'I', 12, 37, 75, 81, 101, 109, 169
poetic memory, 63, 130
poeticity, 28, 183
poetry, lyric, xi, xx, 2, 6, 12
poieîn/poíesis, 10–12, 14, 23, 59, 179
poietikḗ tékhnē, 22
political identities, 64, 66–8, 71
pollution, 84, 136–7, 140, 143, 148, 157
polymorphic identity, 75
polyphonies, x, xii, xvi–xvii, 3, 75, 133
  choral, 64–92, 133, 177
  double, 88, 134
  dramatic, 108
  enunciative, 67, 72, 77, 82–3, 86–8, 98–9, 111, 180–2
  of identity and emotions, 107–11
  semantic, 72–5, 77, 83, 86–8, 98–9, 108, 111, 180–2
pragmatic functions, xxviii, 29, 31–2, 35–6, 79, 178
pragmatic value, 34, 90
pragmatics, xxvii, xxix, 25, 75, 77, 177, 181, 185–6
  and hymnic songs, 38–40, 142–4
  and twofold reference, 88–92
prayer, xxiii, 11, 34–5, 39, 128, 138, 140–1, 148
  cultic, 114, 140–2
  hymnic, 38, 140–1
preludes, 11, 43, 84, 97, 99, 103, 105, 146
prenuptial rituals, 128, 130
priests, 44, 61, 139–40
processions, 31–2, 42–3, 50–1, 54, 60–1, 63, 73, 116
projection, choral, 36, 39, 85, 101, 106, 128
prosodiac metre, 170
purification, 22, 60, 111, 130

real-life audiences, 88, 178, 182
récit, 23, 76, 80, 162–3, 169; *see also* narratives
references, 8–9, 11–15, 82–3, 131–2, 135–6, 150–1, 154, 181–2; *see also* self-reference
  double, 79, 85–8, 150, 154
  extra-discursive, xxv, 77, 133, 149–50, 154
  intra-discursive, 82, 150, 154
referentiality, 183; *see also* self-referentiality
represented space, 131–2
reversals of fortune, 107, 109–10, 154

rhythm, 119, 122, 170, 172, 175–6, 181, 183, 186
  anapaestic, 10, 33, 100, 105, 133
  dactylic, 84, 96, 116, 140, 151
  metrical, 63, 69, 98, 170
ritual, Attic tragedy as, 29–31
ritual actions, 12, 15, 31, 36, 73, 85, 92, 182
ritual cries, 91, 96, 100, 139, 152
ritual gestures, xxiii, 32–3, 40, 43, 96, 103, 130–1
ritual identities, 71, 109, 134
ritual lamentation, xii, 17, 100–101, 108
ritual musical action, 157–9
ritual performance, 29–30, 32, 62–3, 81–2, 133–4, 143, 177–9, 181
ritual practices, xxviii, 12, 15, 40, 42, 45, 54, 118
ritual songs, 13, 28, 85, 91, 116, 119, 125, 130
  in Attic tragedy, 31–40
rituality, xxix, 45, 84, 159, 183
  Dionysiac, 54–7
  tragic, 57–61
rituals
  prenuptial, 128, 130
  sacrificial, 15, 40, 44–5
Romanticism, German, xxvi–xxvii, 21–2, 25
Rural Dionysia, 51, 61

sacrifices, xii–xiii, xxiv, 15, 17, 32, 41–6, 50–1, 60–1
  blood, 41–2, 44–5
  human, 15, 41, 43
sacrificial rituals, 15, 44–5
  and tragedy, 40–5
sacrificial victims, 41, 45, 84
Salamis, 49, 93, 95–7, 99, 101, 103, 106, 110
sanctuaries, xxiii–xxiv, 32–4, 49–51, 53, 57, 65, 81–2, 139–41
sanctuary-theatres, 66, 86, 143, 159, 182
satyrs, xxiv, 15, 46, 53, 55, 58–9, 61, 163
scapegoats, 26, 45, 157
scholia, 52, 116, 126, 131, 164, 175–6
scholiasts, 126, 131, 164, 176
second person, 37, 79–80, 157–8, 177, 180
self-reference, 8, 81–2, 85–6, 92
  double, 85–8
  enunciative, 80–6
  performative, 80–4, 101, 104
self-referentiality, 82, 104–105
semantic field, 8–16, 20
semantic polyphonies, 72–5, 77, 83, 86–8, 98–9, 108, 111, 180–2
semantics, xx, xxv, 8, 73, 75, 105, 128, 152
sexual ambiguity, xxix, 115–18, 127
slaves, 47, 69, 71, 94
songs, xix–xxi, 10–15, 28–31, 94–6, 99–101, 103–105, 113–16, 173–5
  binding, 83–92
  choral, *see* choral songs

Subject Index 213

hymnic, *see* hymnic songs
of lamentation, 98–9, 101, 103, 106, 121, 146
melic, 10, 12–14, 33, 36, 63, 73, 172, 175
phallic, 61, 163
ritual, *see* ritual songs
threnodic, xxix, 104–105, 107, 109
space, represented and space of the representation, 131–2
spectators, 83, 87–8, 111, 134, 149, 154–5, 179–80, 182
ideal, xv–xvi, 75–6, 150, 157–8, 178
sphragís, 86, 179
stance, 19, 26–7, 68, 70, 79–80, 82, 86, 123
stances, enunciative, 68, 75–7, 88
stasima/*stásima*, 24, 113–14, 125, 127, 129, 144–5, 148, 151–4
first, 83, 85, 95, 105–107, 122, 124, 144–5, 151
second, 96, 124, 147, 149–51
third, 39, 97, 100, 125, 128, 130–3, 150, 152–3
statistics, 58, 67–9
status, social, 3, 70, 113, 118, 124
strophic pairs, 84, 97, 101, 103–104, 140, 142, 145, 147
strophic structure, 99–100, 170
suicide, 39, 53, 113, 123
sunagonízesthai, 24, 40, 65, 112, 178
sung exchanges, 28, 42, 94, 100, 146, 156
suppliants, 35, 68, 93, 97, 109, 140
Susa, 93, 102, 105, 110
symbolic death, 42, 45
symbolism, xxiii, 18, 30–1, 42–5, 51, 53, 63–4, 186

tékhne, 13–14, 22
    poietiké, 22
    tragoidikè, 14
temples, xii, xxiii–xxiv, 34, 49–50, 53, 93, 97, 140–1
terminology, xiii, 14, 19–20, 45, 58, 170
terror, 6–7, 108, 139
Thargelia, 63, 162
Thebes, 17–18, 73, 80–1, 136–7, 139–44, 148–9, 157–8, 167–8
Thespis test, 15, 48–9, 53, 55, 176
third person, 23, 37, 80, 86, 105, 166, 169
threnodic songs, xxix, 104–105, 107, 109
thrēnos, 17–18, 24, 74, 79, 99–101, 104, 107, 109–10
tragedy, *see also* Introductory Note

Attic, *see* Attic tragedy
and comedy, 10, 23–4, 59, 163, 175
in cultic performance, 46–51
and sacrificial rituals, 40–5
Tragic, the, xxvii–xxviii, 1–20, 29
tragic composition and training, 10–12
tragic diction, 56, 160–86
tragic fiction, xxvi, 28, 56, 160–86
tragic heroes, 2–6, 8, 21–2, 25, 98–9, 105, 107, 158–9
tragic insignificance, xxvii, 27, 29, 177
tragic rituality, 57–61
tragikón, 16, 19
tragoidía/*tragoidoí*, 9–11, 14–16, 61
tragoidodidáskaloi, 16, 59, 163
tragoidopoiós, 16, 48
triads, 1, 165, 170–1, 174
trochaic dimeters, 170
trochaic metre, 24
trochaic rhythm, 43, 158
trochaic tetrameters, 59, 94
Troezen, 112–22, 126–7, 129–33

underworld, 13–14, 42, 104, 167

vengeance, 46, 90, 95, 129, 165
verbal deixis, 37, 87–8, 103, 116, 132, 140, 142
victims, 42, 44–5, 103, 105, 115, 117, 121, 123
    animal, 43
    sacrificial, 41, 45, 84
virtual audiences, 88, 134, 150
virtual author, 76–7, 134, 179, 182
voice
    affective, 75, 88, 96, 109, 133, 150, 158, 178
    authoritative, xvi, 72, 115
    choral, *see* choral voice
    emotive, 77, 87, 103, 108, 121, 123, 146, 155–6
    hermeneutic, 74–5, 77–8, 115–16, 118–19, 156, 158, 177–9, 182
    performative, 74–5, 77–8, 96, 115, 150, 152–3, 177–8, 182–3

war, xiv, 10–11, 15, 17, 44, 98, 109, 167
weddings, 45, 130, 165
wives, 108, 113, 116, 118, 128–9, 135–6, 142–6, 167–8

For EU product safety concerns, contact us at Calle de José Abascal, 56–1°,
28003 Madrid, Spain or eugpsr@cambridge.org.

www.ingramcontent.com/pod-product-compliance
Ingram Content Group UK Ltd.
Pitfield, Milton Keynes, MK11 3LW, UK
UKHW020700060925
462614UK00020B/407